Complete American Presidents Sourcebook

Complete American Presidents Sourcebook

Volume 4
Woodrow Wilson through Dwight D. Eisenhower
1913-1961

Roger Matuz

Lawrence W. Baker, Editor

AN IMPRINT OF THE GALE GROUP

DETROIT · NEW YORK · SAN FRANCISCO
LONDON · BOSTON · WOODBRIDGE, CT

Complete American Presidents Sourcebook

Roger Matuz

Staff

Lawrence W. Baker, *U•X•L Senior Editor*
Gerda-Ann Raffaelle, *U•X•L Contributing Editor*
Carol DeKane Nagel, *U•X•L Managing Editor*
Thomas L. Romig, *U•X•L Publisher*

Rita Wimberley, *Senior Buyer*
Dorothy Maki, *Manufacturing Manager*
Evi Seoud, *Assistant Manager, Composition Purchasing and Electronic Prepress*
Mary Beth Trimper, *Manager, Composition Purchasing and Electronic Prepress*

Cynthia Baldwin, *Senior Art Director*
Michelle DiMercurio, *Senior Art Director*
Kenn Zorn, *Product Design Manager*

Shalice Shah-Caldwell, *Permissions Associate (text and pictures)*
Maria L. Franklin, *Permissions Manager*
Kelly A. Quin, *Editor, Imaging and Multimedia Content*
Pamela A. Reed, *Imaging Coordinator*
Leitha Etheridge-Sims, *Image Cataloger*
Mary Grimes, *Image Cataloger*
Robert Duncan, *Imaging Specialist*
Dan Newell, *Imaging Specialist*
Randy A. Bassett, *Image Supervisor*
Barbara J. Yarrow, *Imaging and Multimedia Content Manager*

Marco Di Vita, Graphix Group, *Typesetting*

Library of Congress Cataloging-in-Publication Data

Matuz, Roger.
    Complete American presidents sourcebook / Roger Matuz ; Lawrence W. Baker, editor.
        p. cm.
    Includes bibliographical references and indexes.
    ISBN 0-7876-4837-X (set) — ISBN 0-7876-4838-8 (v. 1) — ISBN 0-7876-4839-6 (v. 2) — ISBN 0-7876-4840-X (v. 3) — ISBN 0-7876-4841-8 (v. 4) — ISBN 0-7876-4842-6 (v. 5)
        1. Presidents—United States—Biography—Juvenile literature. 2. Presidents' spouses—United States—Biography—Juvenile literature. 3. United States—Politics and government—Sources—Juvenile literature. I. Baker, Lawrence W. II. Title.

E176.1 .M387 2001
973'.09'9—dc21
[B]
                                                                    00-056794

Cover illustration of Abraham Lincoln is reproduced courtesy of the Library of Congress; Franklin and Eleanor Roosevelt, reproduced by permission of the Corbis Corporation; George W. Bush, reproduced by permission of Archive Photos; Thomas Jefferson, reproduced by permission of the National Portrait Gallery, Smithsonian Institution; Washington Monument, reproduced by permission of PhotoDisc, Inc.; Clintons, Bushes, Reagans, Carters, and Fords, reproduced by permission of Archive Photos; Theodore Roosevelt, reproduced by permission of Archive Photos.

Printed in the United States of America

10 9 8 7 6 5 4 3 2 1

Contents

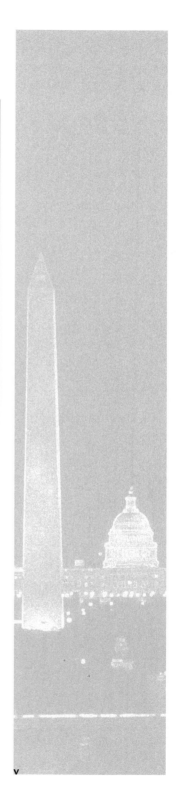

Reader's Guide xxi

Timeline of the American Presidents xxix

Words to Know lxi

Research and Activity Ideas lxxxiii

Volume 1

George Washington (1789–1797) 1

   George Washington 3

      Fast Facts about George Washington (box) 4

      George Washington Timeline (box) 5

      Words to Know (box) 6

      Washington and the American Revolution
      Timeline (box) 12

      Benjamin Franklin (box) 17

      Election Results (box) 19

      George Washington Administration (box) 20

      Washington Slept Here (box) 21

      Constitutional Flexibility (box) 23

      Alexander Hamilton (box) 24

John Jay (box). 27
Barbary Pirates (box) 29
A Selection of Washington Landmarks (box). 30
Martha Washington. 31
Articles of Confederation 37
Washington's Farewell Address of 1796 45

John Adams (1797–1801). **53**
John Adams **55**
Fast Facts about John Adams (box) 56
John Adams Timeline (box). 57
Words to Know (box) 58
Election Results (box) 61
John Adams Administration (box) 62
John Marshall (box) 64
The Alien and Sedition Acts (box). 68
A Selection of Adams Landmarks (box) 72
Abigail Adams. **75**
Adams's "Thoughts on Government". **81**

Thomas Jefferson (1801–1809) **91**
Thomas Jefferson. **93**
Fast Facts about Thomas Jefferson (box). 94
Thomas Jefferson Timeline (box) 95
Words to Know (box) 96
Patrick Henry (box) 99
Richard Henry Lee (box) 100
John Locke (box) 102
Sally Hemings (box) 104
Election Results (box) 109
District of Columbia (box). 110
Thomas Jefferson Administration (box) 111
Lewis and Clark Expedition (box) 114
Aaron Burr (box) 116
A Selection of Jefferson Landmarks (box) 120
Martha Jefferson **121**
The Declaration of Independence **125**
Jefferson's Opinion on the Constitutionality
of a National Bank. **135**

James Madison (1809–1817) **143**

  James Madison **145**

    Fast Facts about James Madison (box) 146

    James Madison Timeline (box) 147

    Words to Know (box) 148

    George Mason (box) 151

    Election Results (box) 155

    James Madison Administration (box) 156

    Francis Scott Key (box) 158

    A Selection of Madison Landmarks (box) 161

  Dolley Madison **163**

  Madison's Bill of Rights Proposal **169**

    Bill of Rights (box) 177

James Monroe (1817–1825) **179**

  James Monroe **181**

    Fast Facts about James Monroe (box) 182

    James Monroe Timeline (box) 183

    Words to Know (box) 184

    Major General Lafayette (box) 186

    Thomas Paine (box) 190

    Election Results (box) 193

    Napoleon I (box) 194

    James Monroe Administration (box) 196

    The Missouri Compromise (box) 198

    A Selection of Monroe Landmarks (box) 202

  Elizabeth Monroe **205**

  The Monroe Doctrine **209**

John Quincy Adams (1825–1829) **217**

  John Quincy Adams **219**

    Fast Facts about John Quincy Adams (box) 220

    John Quincy Adams Timeline (box) 221

    Words to Know (box) 222

    Election Results (box) 227

    Henry Clay (box) 228

    John Quincy Adams Administration (box) 230

    A Selection of Adams Landmarks (box) 236

  Louisa Adams **239**

  Adams's Closing Argument in the
  Amistad **Case** **245**

Andrew Jackson (1829–1837) **255**
   Andrew Jackson 257
      Fast Facts about Andrew Jackson (box) 258
      Andrew Jackson Timeline (box) 259
      Words to Know (box) 260
      Election Results (box) 267
      Andrew Jackson Administration (box) 268
      John C. Calhoun (box) 270
      A Selection of Jackson Landmarks (box) 277
   Rachel Jackson 279
   Jackson's Veto Message Regarding the Bank
   of the United States 285

Martin Van Buren (1837–1841) **291**
   Martin Van Buren 293
      Fast Facts about Martin Van Buren (box) 294
      Martin Van Buren Timeline (box) 295
      Words to Know (box) 296
      Election Results (box) 301
      Martin Van Buren Administration (box) 302
      Winfield Scott (box) 304
      A Selection of Van Buren Landmarks (box) 310
   Hannah Van Buren 311
   Van Buren's Inaugural Address 315

Where to Learn More . . . . **lxxxix**
Index . . . . **xciii**

Volume 2

William Henry Harrison (1841) **323**
   William Henry Harrison 325
      Fast Facts about William Henry Harrison (box) . . 326
      William Henry Harrison Timeline (box) 327
      Words to Know (box) 329
      Tecumseh (box) 332
      Tippecanoe and Cider, Too! (box) 335
      Election Results (box) 336
      William Henry Harrison Administration (box) . . . 337
      A Selection of Harrison Landmarks (box) 338
   Anna Harrison 341
   Harrison's Inaugural Address 347

John Tyler (1841–1845) 355

  John Tyler 357

    Fast Facts about John Tyler (box) 358

    John Tyler Timeline (box) 359

    Words to Know (box) 360

    Edmund Jennings Randolph (box) 362

    Tyler Becomes President (box) 364

    Presidential Succession (box) 366

    John Tyler Administration (box) 368

    Daniel Webster (box) 370

    A Selection of Tyler Landmarks (box) 373

  Letitia Tyler 375

    Charles Dickens Meets John Tyler (box) 377

  Julia Tyler 379

    "Hail to the Chief" (box) 381

  Tyler's Final Annual Address to Congress 385

James K. Polk (1845–1849) 393

  James K. Polk 395

    Fast Facts about James K. Polk (box) 396

    James K. Polk Timeline (box) 397

    Words to Know (box) 398

    Election Results (box) 401

    James K. Polk Administration (box) 403

    John C. Frémont (box) 408

    A Selection of Polk Landmarks (box) 412

  Sarah Polk 415

  Polk's Inaugural Address 419

Zachary Taylor (1849–1850) 427

  Zachary Taylor 429

    Fast Facts about Zachary Taylor (box) 430

    Zachary Taylor Timeline (box) 431

    Words to Know (box) 432

    Black Hawk (box) 434

    Election Results (box) 439

    Lewis Cass (box) 440

    Zachary Taylor Administration (box) 443

    A Taylor Landmark (box) 445

  Margaret Taylor 447

  Taylor's Only Annual Address to Congress 451

Millard Fillmore (1850–1853) 457
   Millard Fillmore 459
      Fast Facts about Millard Fillmore (box) 460
      Millard Fillmore Timeline (box) 461
      Words to Know (box) 462
      Fillmore Becomes President (box) 465
      Millard Fillmore Administration (box) 466
      Harriet Beecher Stowe (box) 470
      A Selection of Fillmore Landmarks (box) 473
   Abigail Fillmore 475
   Fillmore's First Annual Address to Congress 479

Franklin Pierce (1853–1857) 485
   Franklin Pierce 487
      Fast Facts about Franklin Pierce (box) 488
      Franklin Pierce Timeline (box) 489
      Words to Know (box) 490
      Election Results (box) 495
      Franklin Pierce Administration (box) 497
      Matthew C. Perry (box) 498
      A Selection of Pierce Landmarks (box) 502
   Jane Pierce 505
   Pierce's Inaugural Address 509

James Buchanan (1857–1861) 515
   James Buchanan 517
      Fast Facts about James Buchanan (box) 518
      James Buchanan Timeline (box) 519
      Words to Know (box) 520
      Election Results (box) 523
      James Buchanan Administration (box) 525
      John Brown (box) 528
      A Selection of Buchanan Landmarks (box) 532
   Harriet Lane 535
   Buchanan's Final Annual Address to Congress . . . 539

Abraham Lincoln (1861–1865) 549
   Abraham Lincoln 551
      Fast Facts about Abraham Lincoln (box) 552
      Abraham Lincoln Timeline (box) 553
      Words to Know (box) 554
      Lincoln-Douglas Debates (box) 560

Election Results (box) 562
Abraham Lincoln Administration (box) 563
Jefferson Davis (box). 564
A Selection of Lincoln Landmarks (box) 572
Mary Lincoln 575
Lincoln's Emancipation Proclamation 581
Lincoln's Gettysburg Address 587
Lincoln's Second Inaugural Address. 593

Andrew Johnson (1865–1869). 599
Andrew Johnson 601
Fast Facts about Andrew Johnson (box) 602
Andrew Johnson Timeline (box) 603
Words to Know (box) 604
Johnson Becomes President (box) 607
Thaddeus Stevens (box). 608
Andrew Johnson Administration (box). 610
Thirteenth Amendment (box) 611
William H. Seward (box) 612
Fourteenth Amendment (box) 615
The Impeachment of Andrew Johnson (box). . . . 616
A Selection of Johnson Landmarks (box) 620
Eliza Johnson 623
Johnson's Final Annual Address to Congress 629

Where to Learn More lxxxix
Index xciii

Volume 3

Ulysses S. Grant (1869–1877) 637
Ulysses S. Grant 639
Fast Facts about Ulysses S. Grant (box) 640
Ulysses S. Grant Timeline (box) 641
Words to Know (box) 642
Ulysses S. Grant Civil War Timeline (box). 644
Robert E. Lee (box) 648
Election Results (box) 651
Ulysses S. Grant Administration (box) 653
Hamilton Fish (box) 654
A Selection of Grant Landmarks (box) 662

Julia Grant 665
Grant's Recollection of the Confederate Surrender . . 671
    Official Terms of Confederate Surrender (box) . . . 674

Rutherford B. Hayes (1877–1881) 679
  Rutherford B. Hayes 681
    Fast Facts about Rutherford B. Hayes (box) 682
    Rutherford B. Hayes Timeline (box) 683
    Words to Know (box) 684
    Fifteenth Amendment (box) 687
    Samuel J. Tilden (box) 690
    Election Results (box) 693
    Rutherford B. Hayes Administration (box) 695
    A Hayes Landmark (box) 698
  Lucy Hayes 699
  Hayes's Speech on the End of Reconstruction 705

James A. Garfield (1881) 711
  James A. Garfield 713
    Fast Facts about James A. Garfield (box) 714
    James A. Garfield Timeline (box) 715
    Words to Know (box) 716
    Election Results (box) 718
    James A. Garfield Administration (box) 719
    Alexander Graham Bell (box) 724
    A Selection of Garfield Landmarks (box) 726
  Lucretia Garfield 729
  **Garfield's "Revolution Against the
  Constitution" Speech** 735

Chester A. Arthur (1881–1885) 745
  Chester A. Arthur 747
    Fast Facts about Chester A. Arthur (box) 748
    Chester A. Arthur Timeline (box) 749
    Words to Know (box) 750
    Roscoe Conkling (box) 752
    James G. Blaine (box) 756
    Arthur Becomes President (box) 758
    Chester A. Arthur Administration (box) 760
    A Selection of Arthur Landmarks (box) 762
  Ellen Arthur 765
  Arthur's First Annual Address to Congress 769

Grover Cleveland (1885–1889, 1893–1897) **775**

Grover Cleveland **777**

Fast Facts about Grover Cleveland (box) 778

Grover Cleveland Timeline (box) 779

Words to Know (box) 780

Election Results (box) 782

Grover Cleveland Administrations (box) 785

Susan B. Anthony (box) 786

J. P. Morgan (box) 792

A Selection of Cleveland Landmarks (box) 794

Frances Cleveland **797**

**Cleveland's Message to Congress Opposing the
Annexation of Hawaii** **803**

Benjamin Harrison (1889–1893) **809**

Benjamin Harrison **811**

Fast Facts about Benjamin Harrison (box) 812

Benjamin Harrison Timeline (box) 813

Words to Know (box) 814

Election Results (box) 819

Benjamin Harrison Administration (box) 821

What's in a Nickname? (box) 822

The Emergence of Populism (box) 823

James B. Weaver (box) 824

A Selection of Harrison Landmarks (box) 826

Caroline Harrison **827**

**Harrison's Message to the Senate Supporting the
Annexation of Hawaii** **831**

William McKinley (1897–1901) **837**

William McKinley **839**

Fast Facts about William McKinley (box) 840

William McKinley Timeline (box) 841

Words to Know (box) 842

Election Results (box) 848

William McKinley Administration (box) 850

Joseph Pulitzer (box) 852

William Randolph Hearst (box) 854

William Jennings Bryan (box) 856

A Selection of McKinley Landmarks (box) 862

Ida McKinley **863**

McKinley's First Inaugural Address **869**

Theodore Roosevelt (1901–1909) 877
  Theodore Roosevelt 879
    Fast Facts about Theodore Roosevelt (box) 880
    Theodore Roosevelt Timeline (box) 881
    Words to Know (box) 882
    Roosevelt Becomes President (box) 890
    Oliver Wendell Holmes Jr. (box) 892
    Election Results (box) 895
    Upton Sinclair and the Muckrakers (box) 896
    Theodore Roosevelt Administration (box). 897
    A Selection of Roosevelt Landmarks (box). 902
  Edith Roosevelt 905
  Roosevelt's First Annual Address to Congress 909
  Roosevelt's "The Man with the Muck Rake"
  Speech 917

William Howard Taft (1909–1913) 925
  William Howard Taft 927
    Fast Facts about William Howard Taft (box) 928
    William Howard Taft Timeline (box) 929
    Words to Know (box) 930
    Election Results (box) 933
    William Howard Taft Administration (box). 934
    Taft and Sports (box). 935
    Robert A. Taft and the Taft Family (box) 938
    A Selection of Taft Landmarks (box) 940
  Helen Taft 943
  Taft's Final Annual Address to Congress 949

Where to Learn More lxxxix

Index xciii

Volume 4

Woodrow Wilson (1913–1921) 957
  Woodrow Wilson 959
    Fast Facts about Woodrow Wilson (box) 960
    Woodrow Wilson Timeline (box) 961
    Words to Know (box) 962
    Election Results (box) 966
    Woodrow Wilson Administration (box) 967
    John J. "Black Jack" Pershing (box) 970

    The League of Nations (box). 977

    Henry Cabot Lodge (box) 980

    A Selection of Wilson Landmarks (box) 982

Ellen Wilson 987

Edith Wilson 991

Wilson's War Message to Congress 997

Wilson's Fourteen Points 1005

Warren G. Harding (1921–1923) **1013**

  Warren G. Harding **1015**

    Fast Facts about Warren G. Harding (box) 1016

    Warren G. Harding Timeline (box) 1017

    Words to Know (box) 1018

    Election Results (box) 1021

    Andrew W. Mellon (box) 1022

    Warren G. Harding Administration (box) 1024

    Charles Evans Hughes (box) 1026

    A Selection of Harding Landmarks (box) 1031

  Florence Harding **1033**

  Harding's Speech to a Special Session of Congress . . **1039**

Calvin Coolidge (1923–1929) **1047**

  Calvin Coolidge **1049**

    Fast Facts about Calvin Coolidge (box) 1051

    Calvin Coolidge Timeline (box) 1052

    Words to Know (box) 1053

    Coolidge Becomes President (box) 1056

    Calvin Coolidge Administration (box) 1058

    Election Results (box) 1060

    Frank B. Kellogg (box) 1062

    Charles A. Lindbergh (box). 1064

    A Selection of Coolidge Landmarks (box) 1068

  Grace Coolidge **1071**

  Coolidge's Speech on Government and Business . . **1077**

Herbert Hoover (1929–1933) **1085**

  Herbert Hoover **1087**

    Fast Facts about Herbert Hoover (box) 1088

    Herbert Hoover Timeline (box) 1089

    Words to Know (box) 1090

    Alfred E. Smith (box). 1094

    Election Results (box) 1096

Herbert Hoover Administration (box) 1097
Henry L. Stimson (box) 1100
A Selection of Hoover Landmarks (box) 1106
Lou Hoover **1109**
Hoover's "Rugged Individualism" Campaign
Speech **1115**

Franklin D. Roosevelt (1933–1945) **1123**
   Franklin D. Roosevelt **1125**
      Fast Facts about Franklin D. Roosevelt (box) . . . 1126
      Franklin D. Roosevelt Timeline (box) 1127
      Words to Know (box) 1128
      Physically Challenged Presidents (box) 1132
      Election Results (box) 1134
      Franklin D. Roosevelt Administration (box) 1136
      Major Acts of the New Deal (box) 1138
      Frances Perkins (box) 1142
      Inauguration Day Calendar Change (box) 1145
      Winston Churchill (box) 1148
      A Selection of Roosevelt Landmarks (box) 1155
   Eleanor Roosevelt **1159**
   Roosevelt's First Inaugural Address **1167**
   Roosevelt's First Fireside Chat **1175**
   Roosevelt's War Message to the American People . . **1181**

Harry S. Truman (1945–1953) **1187**
   Harry S. Truman **1189**
      Fast Facts about Harry S. Truman (box) 1190
      Harry S. Truman Timeline (box) 1191
      Words to Know (box) 1192
      Truman Becomes President (box) 1196
      Harry S. Truman Administration (box) 1197
      George C. Marshall (box) 1200
      Election Results (box) 1205
      Douglas MacArthur (box) 1208
      A Selection of Truman Landmarks (box) 1211
   Bess Truman **1215**
   Truman's Address to the Nation About the
   Bombing of Japan **1221**
   Truman's Executive Order Banning Segregation
   in the Military **1229**

Dwight D. Eisenhower (1953–1961) **1233**

  Dwight D. Eisenhower **1235**

    Fast Facts about Dwight D. Eisenhower (box) . . . 1236

    Dwight D. Eisenhower Timeline (box) 1237

    Words to Know (box) 1238

    Election Results (box) 1244

    Adlai E. Stevenson (box) 1246

    Dwight D. Eisenhower Administration (box) . . . 1250

    Nikita Khrushchev (box) 1252

    The Iron Curtain (box) 1254

    A Selection of Eisenhower Landmarks (box) . . . 1255

  Mamie Eisenhower **1257**

  Eisenhower's Farewell Address to the Nation **1263**

Where to Learn More . . . . **lxxxix**

Index . . . . **xciii**

Volume 5

John F. Kennedy (1961–1963) **1271**

  John F. Kennedy **1273**

    Fast Facts about John F. Kennedy (box) 1274

    John F. Kennedy Timeline (box) 1275

    Words to Know (box) 1276

    JFK and PT-109 (box) 1277

    The Lodge Connection (box) 1279

    Election Results (box) 1282

    John F. Kennedy Administration (box) 1283

    Robert F. Kennedy (box) 1288

    Martin Luther King Jr. (box) 1292

    A Selection of Kennedy Landmarks (box) 1296

  Jacqueline Kennedy **1299**

  Kennedy's Inaugural Address **1307**

Lyndon B. Johnson (1963–1969) **1315**

  Lyndon B. Johnson **1317**

    Fast Facts about Lyndon B. Johnson (box) 1318

    Lyndon B. Johnson Timeline (box) 1319

    Words to Know (box) 1320

    Johnson Becomes President (box) 1323

    Election Results (box) 1326

    Lyndon B. Johnson Administration (box) 1327

Gulf of Tonkin Incident (box). 1330
Thurgood Marshall (box) 1332
Hubert Humphrey (box) 1336
A Selection of Johnson Landmarks (box). 1339
Lady Bird Johnson 1341
Johnson's "Great Society" Speech. 1349

Richard Nixon (1969–1974) 1357
Richard Nixon. 1359
Fast Facts about Richard Nixon (box) 1360
Richard Nixon Timeline (box). 1361
Words to Know (box) 1362
Election Results (box) 1366
Richard Nixon Administration (box) 1368
Henry Kissinger (box) 1370
Nixon and Foreign Relations (box) 1372
The Watergate Hearings (box). 1376
A Selection of Nixon Landmarks (box) 1382
Pat Nixon 1385
Nixon's "Silent Majority" Speech 1391

Gerald R. Ford (1974–1977) 1399
Gerald R. Ford 1401
Fast Facts about Gerald R. Ford (box) 1403
Gerald R. Ford Timeline (box). 1404
Words to Know (box) 1405
Ford Becomes President (box) 1408
Gerald R. Ford Administration (box) 1410
Nelson Rockefeller (box) 1412
A Selection of Ford Landmarks (box) 1418
Betty Ford 1421
Ford's Pardon of Richard Nixon. 1427

Jimmy Carter (1977–1981) 1433
Jimmy Carter. 1435
Fast Facts about Jimmy Carter (box). 1436
Jimmy Carter Timeline (box) 1437
Words to Know (box) 1438
Election Results (box) 1442
Jimmy Carter Administration (box) 1443
Camp David Principals: Anwar Sadat and
Menachem Begin (box) 1446

The Iran Hostage Crisis (box) 1450
A Selection of Carter Landmarks (box) 1454
Rosalynn Carter 1457
Carter's "Human Rights and Foreign Policy"
Speech 1461

Ronald Reagan (1981–1989) **1469**
Ronald Reagan **1471**
Fast Facts about Ronald Reagan (box) 1472
Ronald Reagan Timeline (box) 1474
Words to Know (box) 1475
Election Results (box) 1477
Ronald Reagan Administration (box) 1480
Mikhail Gorbachev (box) 1484
Sandra Day O'Connor (box) 1486
A Selection of Reagan Landmarks (box) 1491
Nancy Reagan **1493**
Reagan's First Inaugural Address **1501**

George Bush (1989–1993) **1509**
George Bush **1511**
Fast Facts about George Bush (box) 1512
George Bush Timeline (box) 1513
Words to Know (box) 1514
Election Results (box) 1519
George Bush Administration (box) 1520
H. Ross Perot (box) 1526
A Selection of Bush Landmarks (box) 1529
Barbara Bush **1531**
Bush's Address to Congress on the Crisis
in Kuwait **1537**

Bill Clinton (1993–2001) **1545**
Bill Clinton **1547**
Fast Facts about Bill Clinton (box) 1548
Bill Clinton Timeline (box) 1549
Words to Know (box) 1550
Election Results (box) 1555
Al Gore (box) 1556
Bill Clinton Administration (box) 1559
Madeleine Albright (box) 1562
Alan Greenspan (box) 1566

Janet Reno (box). 1570
"High Crimes and Misdemeanors" (box). 1572
The Impeachment of Bill Clinton (box) 1574
A Selection of Clinton Landmarks (box) 1578
Hillary Rodham Clinton 1581
Clinton's Final State of the Union Address 1587

George W. Bush (2001–) 1595
  George W. Bush 1597
Fast Facts about George W. Bush (box) 1598
George W. Bush Timeline (box). 1599
Words to Know (box) 1600
Dick Cheney (box) 1606
Election Results (box) 1609
How the Electoral College Works (box). 1610
The Electoral College Through the Years (box). . 1612
Closest Election Results in Presidential
History (box) 1615
  Laura Bush 1621
  Bush's Presidential Nomination Acceptance
  Speech 1625

Where to Learn More lxxxix
Index xciii

Reader's Guide

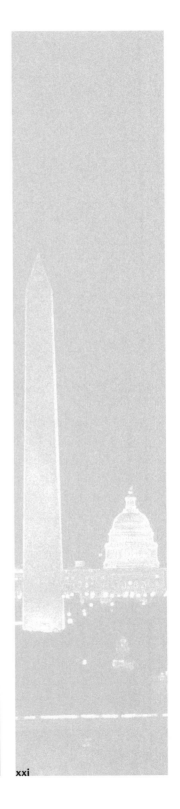

An "embarrassed pause" fell on the gathering of delegates at the Constitutional Convention of 1787 when James Wilson of Pennsylvania suggested the idea of a chief executive. Wanting "no semblance of a monarch," as Edmund Randolph of Virginia put it, delegates moved on to other matters.

So went the first real "discussion" about the office of president, according to Virginia delegate James Madison. Madison, later nicknamed "the Father of the Constitution," took lengthy notes on the proceedings. They were published in 1840 in a book, *Journal of the Federal Convention.*

The Convention was called to address the weakness of the American government formed under the Articles of Confederation that was approved in 1781. By the end of the Convention of 1787, delegates had cautiously agreed on a new system. They had debated ideas of government ranging in history from ancient Greece and Rome to the "Age of Enlightenment" (eighteenth century) in Europe; they considered the workings of the Iroquois confederacy of Native American tribes as well as the state governments in America; and they held to their ideals of liberty and their dislike of monarchy, a system in which one person rules a country for life. The delegates eventually returned to Wilson's suggestion and debated it. The new system of government they cautiously agreed to in the end did indeed include an elected chief executive—the president.

"President" was a title used for the position of governor in three states—Delaware, Pennsylvania, and New Hampshire. They were among the first nine states to ratify the Constitution, helping provide the majority (nine of thirteen states) needed for the Constitution to become legally binding.

The process of ratification was not easy. In Virginia, for example, which finally approved the Constitution in 1788 by a slim majority (89-79), there were significant concerns about the powers of the president. Former Continental congressman and former Virginia governor Patrick Henry called it "a squint toward monarchy."

The delegates of Virginia, however, had an example of the kind of leader envisioned when the office of president was created. George Washington had presided over the Constitutional Convention. He introduced no ideas and seldom participated in debates, but he kept delegates focused on the cause of improving the system of government. Washington was known for his honesty and for not being overly ambitious. Americans had turned to him to lead their military struggle in the Revolutionary War (1775–81). After the Constitution was ratified (approved), delegates turned to him to lead the new nation as its first president.

Washington's example as president reveals the realities of political leadership. He was voted unanimously into office, and left office in the same high regard, but he had faced resistance in between. Some viewed his version of the federal government as being too powerful: he had called on state militias to put down a rebellion in Pennsylvania against taxes; and for economic reasons, he sided in foreign relations with Great Britain—still a hated enemy to some Americans—over France, the nation that had assisted Americans in winning independence.

Washington was among those presidents who made firm decisions, then awaited the consequences. Some had viewed the presidency as being more impartial. Such are the perils of the presidency. John Adams, the second president, followed the more forceful actions of members of his party and became so unpopular that he had no real hope for reelection. Thomas Jefferson, whose ideals shaped the Declaration of Independence, lost much popularity by the time he left office as the third president. Jefferson had ordered foreign trade restrictions to assert America's strength and to demand respect from Great Britain and France, but the action ended up hurting the American economy.

Like the Constitution, the office of the president was never intended to be perfect. The Constitution is flexible, meant to be used and adapted to form "a more perfect union." The presidency has ranged at times from being a near monarchy to having little real strength. President Andrew Jackson was dubbed "King Andrew" by his opponents, who felt he overstepped his power in several instances. Franklin D. Roosevelt was given tremendous powers and support, first in 1933 to combat the effects of the Great Depression (1929–41), and later to direct the nation's economy during World War II (1939–45). But when Roosevelt tried to change the Supreme Court, he was met with swift criticism. Roosevelt was the only president elected to office four times, the last time being 1944. (In 1945, he died only three months into his fourth term.) By 1951, a constitutional amendment was passed to limit presidents to two terms in office.

Other presidents were far less powerful or effective. Prior to the Civil War, two presidents from the North (Franklin Pierce and James Buchanan) supported the rights for states to decide whether to permit slavery. Abraham Lincoln was elected to challenge that notion, and the Civil War (1861–65) followed. Lincoln took a more aggressive approach than his two predecessors, and he emerged in history as among the greatest presidents.

After Lincoln's assassination in 1865, the presidency was dominated by Congress. In 1885, future president Woodrow Wilson criticized that situation in a book he wrote, *Congressional Government,* while he was a graduate student at Johns Hopkins University. By the time Wilson was elected president in 1912, a series of strong presidents—Grover Cleveland, William McKinley, and Theodore Roosevelt—had reasserted the president's power to lead.

The presidency, then, has passed through various stages of effectiveness. The dynamics of change, growth, and frustration make it fascinating to study. Different ideas of leadership, power, and the role of government have been pursued by presidents. Chief executives have come from various backgrounds: some were born in poverty, like Andrew Johnson and Abraham Lincoln, and others had the advantages of wealth, like the Roosevelts and Bushes; some were war heroes, like Ulysses S. Grant and Dwight D. Eisenhower, others were more studious, like Thomas Jefferson and Woodrow Wilson. Some came to the presidency by accident, like John Tyler and Gerald R. Ford, others campaigned long and hard for the position, like Martin Van Buren and Richard Nixon.

There are various ways to present information on the presidency. In 2000, a Public Broadcasting System (PBS) television series called *The American President* divided presidents into ten categories (such as presidents related to each other, those who were prominent military men, and chief executives who became compromise choices of their parties). The same year, a group of presidential scholars also used ten categories (such as crisis leadership, administrative skills, and relations with Congress) to rank presidents in order of effectiveness

Complete American Presidents Sourcebook uses a chronological approach, beginning with George Washington in 1789, and ending with George W. Bush in 2001. Each president's section contains three types of entries.

Biography of the president

Each of the forty-two men who have served in the nation's top political office is featured in *Complete American Presidents Sourcebook*.

- Each entry begins with a general overview of the president's term(s) in office, then follows his life from birth, through his service as president, to his post-presidency (if applicable).

- Outstanding events and issues during each presidential administration are described, as are the president's responses in his role as the nation's highest elected official.

- Sidebar boxes provide instant facts on the president's personal life; a timeline of key events in his life; a "Words to

Know" box that defines key terms related to the president; results of the president's winning election(s); a list of Cabinet members for each administration; and a selection of homes, museums, and other presidential landmarks.

- A final summary describes the president's legacy—how his actions and the events during his administration influenced the historical period and the future.

Biography of the first lady

Forty-four first ladies are featured in *Complete American Presidents Sourcebook*. Though some of the women died before their husbands became president, all had an important influence on the men who would serve as president. The profiles provide biographical information and insight into the ways in which the women lived their lives and defined their public roles. Like the presidents, first ladies have responded in different ways to their highly public position.

Primary source entry

Another important feature of interest to students is a selection of forty-eight primary source documents—speeches, writings, executive orders, and proclamations of the presidents. At least one primary source is featured with each president.

In the presidents' own words, the documents outline the visions and plans of newly elected presidents, the reasons for certain actions, and the responses to major world events. Students can learn more about key documents (such as the Declaration of Independence and the Monroe Doctrine); famous speeches (such as George Washington's Farewell Address and Abraham Lincoln's Gettysburg Address); presidential orders (the Emancipation Proclamation issued by Abraham Lincoln in 1863 and Harry S. Truman's executive order on military desegregation in 1946); responses to ongoing issues, from tariffs (William McKinley) to relations between the government and Native Americans (Chester A. Arthur); different views on the role of the federal government (from extensive programs advocated by Franklin D. Roosevelt and Lyndon B. Johnson, to reducing the influence of government by Warren G. Harding and Ronald Reagan); and many inaugural addresses, including the memorable speeches of Abraham Lincoln and John F. Kennedy.

Each document (or excerpt) presented in *Complete American Presidents Sourcebook* includes the following additional material:

- **Introduction** places the document and its author in a historical context.

- **Things to remember** offers readers important background information and directs them to central ideas in the text.

- **What happened next** provides an account of subsequent events, both during the presidential administration and in future years.

- **Did you know** provides significant and interesting facts about the excerpted document, the president, or the subjects discussed in the excerpt.

- **For further reading** lists sources for more information on the president, the document, or the subject of the excerpt.

Complete American Presidents Sourcebook also features sidebars containing interesting facts and short biographies of people who were in some way connected with the president or his era. Within each entry, boldfaced cross-references direct readers to other presidents, first ladies, primary sources, and sidebar boxes in the five-volume set. Finally, each volume includes approximately 70 photographs and illustrations (for a total of 350), a "Timeline of the American Presidents" that lists significant dates and events related to presidential administrations, a general "Words to Know" section, research and activity ideas, sources for further reading, and a cumulative index.

This wealth of material presents the student with a variety of well-researched information. It is intended to reflect the dynamic situation of serving as the leader of a nation founded on high ideals, ever struggling to realize those ideals.

Acknowledgments from the author

Many individuals, many institutions, and many sources were consulted in preparing *Complete American Presidents Sourcebook*. A good portion of them are represented in bibliographies and illustration and textual credits sprinkled throughout the five volumes. The many excellent sources and the ability to access them ensured a dynamic process that made the project lively and thought-provoking, qualities reflected in the presentation.

Compilation efforts were organized through Manitou Wordworks, Inc., headed by Roger Matuz with contributions from Carol Brennan, Anne-Jeanette Johnson, Allison Jones, Mel Koler, and Gary Peters. On the Gale/U•X•L side, special recognition goes to U•X•L publisher Tom Romig for his conceptualization of the project. Thanks, too, to Gerda-Ann Raffaelle for filling in some editorial holes; Pam Reed, Kelly A. Quin, and the rest of the folks on the Imaging team for their efficient work; and Cindy Baldwin for another dynamite cover.

The author benefited greatly through his association and friendship with editor Larry Baker and his personal library, tremendous patience, and great enthusiasm for and knowledge of the subject matter.

Finally, with love to Mary Claire for her support, interest (I'll miss having you ask me the question, "So what new thing did you learn about a president today?"), and understanding from the beginning of the project around the time we were married through my frequent checking of the latest news before and after the election of 2000.

Acknowledgments from the editor

The editor wishes to thank Roger Matuz for a year and a half of presidential puns, for putting up with endless Calvin Coolidge tidbits, and—above all—for producing a tremendously solid body of work. You've got my vote when Josiah Bartlet's time in office is up. Thank you, Mr. Author.

Thanks also to typesetter Marco Di Vita of The Graphix Group who always turns in top-quality work and is just a lot of fun to work with; Terry Murray, who, in spite of her excellent-as-usual copyediting and indexing, still couldn't resist suggesting a sidebar for Zachary Taylor's horse, Old Whitey (um, no . . . maybe if we do *Complete American Presidents' Pets Sourcebook);* and proofer Amy Marcaccio Keyzer, whose sharp eye kept the manuscript clean and whose election e-mails kept me laughing.

In addition, the editor would be remiss if he didn't acknowledge his first family. Decades of thanks go to Mom & Dad, for starting it all by first taking me to the McKinley Memorial in Canton, Ohio, all those years ago. Love and appreciation go to editorial first lady Beth Baker, for putting up with all of the presidential homes and museums and grave markers and books, but who admits that touring FDR's Campobello during a nor'easter storm is pretty cool. And to Charlie & Dane—please don't fight over who gets to be president first!

Finally, a nod to Al Gore and George W. Bush for adding some real-life drama to the never-ending completion of this book . . . and who *did* fight over who got to be president first!

Comments and suggestions

We welcome your comments on the *Complete American Presidents Sourcebook* and suggestions for other topics in history to consider. Please write: Editors, *Complete American Presidents Sourcebook,* U•X•L, 27500 Drake Rd., Farmington Hills, Michigan 48331-3535; call toll-free: 800-877-4253; fax to 248-414-5043; or send e-mail via http://www.galegroup.com.

Timeline of the American Presidents

1776 The Declaration of Independence is written, approved, and officially issued.

1781 The Articles of Confederation are approved, basing American government on cooperation between the states. Congress is empowered to negotiate treaties, but has few other responsibilities.

1787 A national convention called to strengthen the Articles of Confederation develops the U.S. Constitution instead, defining a new system of American government. The powers of Congress are broadened. Congress forms the legislative branch of the new government, and the Supreme Court forms the judicial

1773
Boston Tea Party
takes place.

1783
Beethoven's
first works are
published.

1787
The first
hydrogen balloon
is launched.

| 1770 | 1775 | 1785 | 1787 |

branch. An executive branch is introduced and will be led by an elected official, the president. The president and vice president are to be inaugurated on March 4 of the year following their election (a date that remains in practice until 1933, when the Twentieth Amendment is ratified, changing inauguration day to January 20).

1787   Three of the original thirteen colonies—Delaware, Pennsylvania, and New Jersey—ratify the Constitution, thereby becoming the first three states of the Union.

1788   Eight of the original thirteen colonies—Georgia, Connecticut, Massachusetts, Maryland, South Carolina, New Hampshire, Virginia, and New York—ratify the Constitution, thereby becoming the fourth through eleventh states of the Union. The Constitution becomes law when New Hampshire is the ninth state to ratify it (two-thirds majority of the thirteen states had to approve the Constitution for it to become legally binding).

1789   One of the original thirteen colonies—North Carolina—ratifies the Constitution, thereby becoming the twelfth state of the Union.

1789   The first presidential election is held. Voting is done by electors appointed by each state, and the number of electors are based on the state's population. Each elector votes for two candidates. Whomever finishes with the most votes becomes president, and whomever finishes second becomes vice president.

1789   Revolutionary War hero George Washington is elected president, receiving votes from each elector.

1789   The French Revolution begins.

1787
Dollar currency is introduced in the United States.

1788
New York City becomes the temporary U.S. capital.

1789
U.S. Army is established.

1787   1788   1789

1789   George Washington is inaugurated in New York City. A site for the national capital is selected along the Potomac River in Washington, D.C., and the federal government will be situated in Philadelphia, Pennsylvania, until the new capital is completed.

1789   One of the original thirteen colonies—Rhode Island—ratifies the Constitution, thereby becoming the thirteenth state of the Union.

1789   Political factions solidify. Federalists, who support a strong federal government, are led by Secretary of the Treasury Alexander Hamilton, and Anti-Federalists, who support limited federal power and strong states' rights, are led by Secretary of State Thomas Jefferson.

1791   Vermont becomes the fourteenth state of the Union.

1792   President George Washington is reelected unanimously.

1792   Kentucky becomes the fifteenth state of the Union.

1794   American forces defeat a confederacy of Native American tribes at the Battle of Fallen Timbers in Ohio, opening up the midwest for settlement.

1796   When Vice President John Adams finishes first and former Secretary of State Thomas Jefferson finishes second in the presidential election, two men with conflicting political views and affiliations serve as president and vice president. Political parties—the Federalists and the Democratic-Republicans—become established.

1796   Tennessee becomes the sixteenth state of the Union.

1798   The United States engages in an undeclared naval war with France.

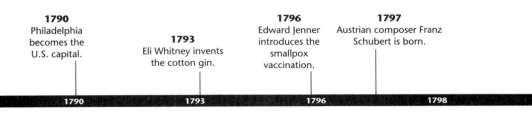

1790
Philadelphia
becomes the
U.S. capital.

1793
Eli Whitney invents
the cotton gin.

1796
Edward Jenner
introduces the
smallpox
vaccination.

1797
Austrian composer Franz
Schubert is born.

1790   1793   1796   1798

1798 Federalists in Congress pass and President John Adams signs into law the Alien and Sedition Acts. The laws, which expand the powers of the federal government, prove unpopular and bolster the prospects of anti-Federalists.

1800 The seat of government moves from Philadelphia, Pennsylvania, to Washington, D.C.; President John Adams and first lady Abigail Adams move into the White House (officially called The Executive Mansion until 1900).

1800 In the presidential election, Vice President Thomas Jefferson and former New York senator Aaron Burr (both of the Democratic-Republican Party) finish tied with the most electoral votes. The election is decided in the House of Representatives, where Jefferson prevails after thirty-six rounds of voting.

1803 The historic *Marbury v. Madison* decision strengthens the role of the U.S. Supreme Court to decide constitutional issues.

1803 The Louisiana Purchase more than doubles the size of the United States.

1803 Ohio becomes the seventeenth state of the Union.

1804 The Twelfth Amendment to the Constitution mandates that electors must distinguish between whom they vote for president and vice president (to avoid repeating the problem of the 1800 election, where most voters selected both Jefferson and Burr with their two votes).

1804 President Thomas Jefferson wins reelection. He selects a new running mate, New York governor George Clinton, to replace Vice President Aaron Burr.

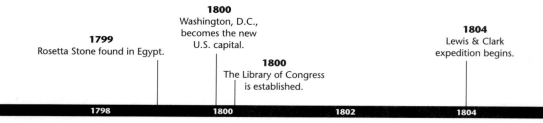

1799
Rosetta Stone found in Egypt.

1800
Washington, D.C., becomes the new U.S. capital.

1800
The Library of Congress is established.

1804
Lewis & Clark expedition begins.

1798   1800   1802   1804

Complete American Presidents Sourcebook

1804 After losing an election for governor of New York, outgoing vice president Aaron Burr kills former U.S. secretary of the treasury Alexander Hamilton in a duel. Hamilton had influenced voters against Burr in the presidential campaign of 1800 and during Burr's campaign to be governor of New York in 1804.

1806 The Lewis and Clark expedition, commissioned by President Thomas Jefferson, is completed when explorers Meriwether Lewis and William Clark return to St. Louis, Missouri, after having traveled northwest to the Pacific Ocean.

1807 President Thomas Jefferson institutes an embargo on shipping to England and France, attempting to pressure the nations to respect American rights at sea. The embargo is unsuccessful and unpopular.

1807 Former vice president Aaron Burr is tried and acquitted on charges of treason.

1808 Secretary of State James Madison, the "Father of the Constitution," is elected president. Vice President George Clinton campaigns and places third as a member of the Independent Republican Party after having accepted Madison's offer to continue in his role as vice president.

1811 At the Battle of Tippecanoe, American forces (led by future president William Henry Harrison) overwhelm a Native American confederacy led by Shawnee chief Tecumseh.

1811 Vice President George Clinton casts the tie-breaking vote in the U.S. Senate (a responsibility of the vice president under the U.S. Constitution) against rechartering the National Bank, and against President James Madison's wishes.

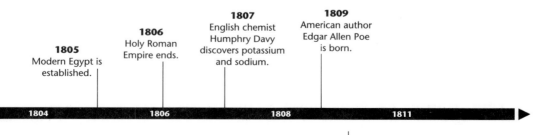

1805
Modern Egypt is established.

1806
Holy Roman Empire ends.

1807
English chemist Humphry Davy discovers potassium and sodium.

1809
American author Edgar Allen Poe is born.

1804   1806   1808   1811

1812	War of 1812 (1812–15) begins.
1812	President James Madison is reelected.
1812	Louisiana becomes the eighteenth state of the Union.
1813	After having suffered military defeats in Canada, U.S. naval forces win control of the Great Lakes.
1814	British military forces burn the White House and the Capitol during the War of 1812.
1815	The Battle of New Orleans, where American forces (led by future president Andrew Jackson) rout a superior British force, occurs after an armistice was agreed on, but news had not yet reached Louisiana. The War of 1812 officially ends a month later.
1816	Secretary of State James Monroe is elected president. The "Era of Good Feelings" begins: the war is over, America is expanding, and Monroe is a popular president.
1816	Indiana becomes the nineteenth state of the Union.
1817	President James Monroe moves into an incompletely reconstructed White House.
1816	Mississippi becomes the twentieth state of the Union.
1818	Illinois becomes the twenty-first state of the Union.
1819	Alabama becomes the twenty-second state of the Union.
1819	Bank Panic slows economic growth.
1820	President James Monroe is reelected by winning every state. One elector casts a vote for John Quincy Adams as a symbolic gesture to ensure that George Washington remains the only president to win all electoral votes in an election.

1812
The Brothers Grimm publish their book of fairy tales.

1814
Francis Scott Key writes the "Star Spangled Banner."

1818
Mary Shelley writes *Frankenstein.*

1818
Congress adopts a U.S. flag.

1812   1815   1818   1820

1820 The Missouri Compromise sets a boundary (the southern border of present-day Missouri): slavery is not permitted north of that boundary for any prospective territory hoping to enter the Union.

1820 Maine, formerly part of Massachusetts, becomes the twenty-third state of the Union.

1821 Missouri becomes the twenty-fourth state of the Union.

1823 In his annual message to Congress, President James Monroe introduces what will become known as the Monroe Doctrine. Although not very significant at the time, the Doctrine, which warns European nations against expansionist activities in the Americas, sets a foreign policy precedent several later presidents will invoke.

1824 Electoral votes are based on the popular vote for the first time. Tennessee senator Andrew Jackson bests Secretary of State John Quincy Adams with over 45,000 more popular votes and a 99-84 Electoral College lead, but does not win a majority of electoral votes, split among four candidates. The election is decided in Adams's favor by the House of Representatives. The support of powerful Speaker of the House Henry Clay, who finished fourth in the election, helps sway the House in favor of Adams. When Adams names Clay his secretary of state, Jackson supporters claim a "corrupt bargain" had been forged between Adams and Clay.

1824 John Quincy Adams is the fourth straight and last president from the Democratic-Republican Party, which held the White House from 1800 to 1829. The party splits into factions around Adams and his elec-

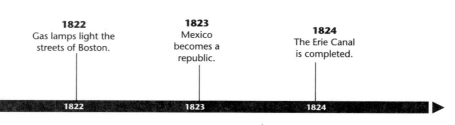

1822
Gas lamps light the streets of Boston.

1823
Mexico becomes a republic.

1824
The Erie Canal is completed.

1820   1822   1823   1824

tion opponent, Andrew Jackson (called Jacksonian Democrats), respectively.

1826   Former presidents John Adams and Thomas Jefferson die on the same day, July 4—fifty years to the day after the Declaration of Independence was officially issued.

1828   Former Tennessee senator Andrew Jackson defeats President John Quincy Adams. Modern-day political parties are established: Jackson leads the Democratic Party, and Adams leads the National Republican Party. The National Republicans are also represented in the 1832 presidential election, but most party members are joined by anti-Jackson Democrats to form the Whig Party in 1834.

1832   President Andrew Jackson is reelected. Candidates from the Nullifier Party (based on the proposition that states have the right to nullify federal laws) and the Anti-Masonic Party receive electoral votes. Future president Millard Fillmore was elected to the U.S. House of Representatives in 1831 as a member of the Anti-Masonic Party (a pro-labor group against social clubs and secret societies).

1832   The Black Hawk War leads to the taking of Native American land west to the Mississippi River. Future president Abraham Lincoln is among those fighting.

1832   President Andrew Jackson vetoes the charter for the Second National Bank (the federal banking system), creating great controversy between Democrats (favoring states' rights) and proponents for a strong federal government, who gradually unite to form the Whig Party in 1834.

1833   Running water is installed in the White House.

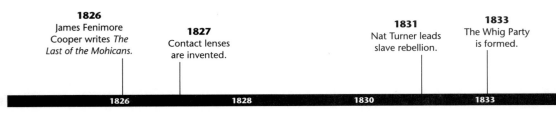

1826
James Fenimore Cooper writes *The Last of the Mohicans.*

1827
Contact lenses are invented.

1831
Nat Turner leads slave rebellion.

1833
The Whig Party is formed.

1826   1828   1830   1833

1834   Congress censures (publicly rebukes) President Andrew Jackson for having taken funds from the federal bank and depositing them in various state banks.

1836   Vice President Martin Van Buren is elected president after defeating three Whig candidates. Whigs hoped that their three regional candidates would win enough electoral votes to deny Van Buren a majority and throw the election to the House of Representatives, where Whigs held the majority.

1836   The last surviving founding father, James Madison, dies the same year the first president born after the American Revolution (Martin Van Buren) is elected.

1836   Arkansas becomes the twenty-fifth state of the Union.

1837   The Panic of 1837 initiates a period of economic hard times that lasts throughout President Martin Van Buren's administration.

1837   Michigan becomes the twenty-sixth state of the Union.

1840   Military hero and Ohio politician William Henry Harrision (known as "Old Tippecanoe") defeats President Martin Van Buren.

1841   President William Henry Harrison dies thirty-one days after being inaugurated president. A constitutional issue arises because the document is unclear as to whether Vice President John Tyler should complete Harrison's term or serve as an interim president until Congress selects a new president. Tyler has himself sworn in as president. Controversy follows, but Tyler sets a precedent on presidential succession.

1841   The President's Cabinet, except for Secretary of State Daniel Webster, resigns, and some congressmen con-

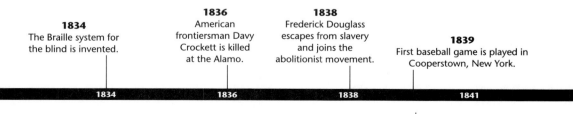

1834
The Braille system for the blind is invented.

1836
American frontiersman Davy Crockett is killed at the Alamo.

1838
Frederick Douglass escapes from slavery and joins the abolitionist movement.

1839
First baseball game is played in Cooperstown, New York.

1834   1836   1838   1841

sider impeachment proceedings against President John Tyler (but the impeachment fails to materialize). Though a member of the Whig Party, Tyler opposes the Whig program for expanding federal powers. He is kicked out of the Whig Party.

1842 The Webster-Ashburton Treaty settles a border dispute between Maine and Quebec, Canada, and averts war between the United States and Great Britain.

1844 Congress approves a resolution annexing Texas.

1844 Tennessee politician James K. Polk, strongly associated with former president Andrew Jackson, is elected president. The years beginning with Jackson's presidency in 1829 and ending with Polk's in March 1849 are often referred to historically as The Age of Jackson.

1845 Congress passes and President James K. Polk signs legislation to have presidential elections held simultaneously throughout the country on the Tuesday following the first Monday in November.

1845 Florida becomes the twenty-seventh and Texas the twenty-eighth states of the Union.

1845 The U.S. Naval Academy opens.

1846 The Mexican War begins.

1846 Iowa and Wisconsin expand the Union to thirty states.

1848 Gas lamps are installed in the White House to replace candles and oil lamps.

1848 The Mexican War ends. The United States takes possession of the southwest area from Texas to California.

1848 General Zachary Taylor, a Mexican War hero, is elected president in a close race. He had joined the Whig

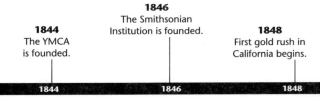

1844
The YMCA
is founded.

1846
The Smithsonian
Institution is founded.

1848
First gold rush in
California begins.

| 1842 | 1844 | 1846 | 1848 |

Party but promised to remain above partisan causes and announced that he was against the expansion of slavery into new territories. Ex-president Martin Van Buren finishes a distant third as a candidate for the Free-Soil Party that also opposes the expansion of slavery into new territories. Van Buren likely drew enough votes from the Democratic candidate, former Michigan senator Lewis Cass, to tip the election to Taylor.

1849 The California Gold Rush brings thousands of people into the new American territory.

1850 President Zachary Taylor dies in office, and Vice President Millard Fillmore becomes president.

1850 President Millard Fillmore supports and signs into law the series of bills called the Compromise of 1850 that the late president Zachary Taylor had opposed. The Fugitive Slave Act, which forces northern states to return runaway slaves, becomes law.

1850 California becomes the thirty-first state of the Union.

1850 The Pony Express begins operation, providing mail service to the far west.

1852 Former New Hampshire senator Franklin Pierce is elected president.

1852 *Uncle Tom's Cabin,* by Harriet Beecher Stowe, is published and further fuels growing support in the North for complete abolition of slavery.

1853 The Gadsden Purchase adds southern areas of present-day New Mexico and Arizona as American territory.

1854 The Republican Party is formed by those against the expansion of slavery and by abolitionists wanting to outlaw the institution, drawing from the Whig Party

1851
The New York Times begins publication.

1853
Steinway pianos begin manufacturing.

1854
The Kansas-Nebraska Act returns slavery decisions to states.

1849　　　1850　　　1852　　　1854

(which becomes defunct) and Democrats opposed to slavery.

1854 Diplomatic and trade relations begin between the United States and Japan.

1856 Civil war breaks out in Kansas Territory between pro- and anti-slavery proponents.

1856 Former secretary of state James Buchanan, a states' rights advocate, is elected president. Former California senator John Frémont finishes second as the Republican Party's first presidential candidate. Former president Millard Fillmore finishes third with about twenty percent of the popular vote and eight electoral votes, as the nominee of the American Party (also nicknamed the Know-Nothing Party).

1857 The *Dred Scott* decision by the U.S. Supreme Court limits the power of Congress to decide on slavery issues in American territories petitioning to become states.

1858 The Lincoln-Douglas debates in Illinois, between U.S. Senate candidates Abraham Lincoln and incumbent Stephen Douglas, receive national press coverage.

1858 Minnesota becomes the thirty-second state of the Union.

1859 Abolitionist John Brown leads a raid on a federal arsenal in Harper's Ferry, Virginia (now West Virginia), hoping to spark and arm a slave rebellion.

1859 Oregon becomes the thirty-third state of the Union.

1860 Former Illinois congressman Abraham Lincoln is elected president despite winning less than forty percent of the popular vote. Democratic votes are split among three candidates. One of the party's candidates, Illi-

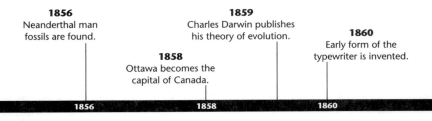

1856
Neanderthal man fossils are found.

1859
Charles Darwin publishes his theory of evolution.

1860
Early form of the typewriter is invented.

1858
Ottawa becomes the capital of Canada.

1854　　　1856　　　1858　　　1860

nois senator Stephen Douglas, finishes second in the popular vote but places fourth in electoral votes.

1860   South Carolina secedes from the Union.

1861   Confederate States of America formed; Civil War begins.

1861   Kansas becomes the thirty-fourth state of the Union.

1863   President Abraham Lincoln, sitting in what is now called the Lincoln Bedroom in the White House, signs the Emancipation Proclamation, freeing slaves in the states in rebellion.

1863   West Virginia becomes the thirty-fifth state of the Union.

1863   President Abraham Lincoln proposes a policy for admitting seceded states back into the Union on moderate terms.

1864   Pro-Union Republicans and Democrats unite as the National Union Party under President Abraham Lincoln (Republican) and Tennessee senator Andrew Johnson, who had remained in Congress after his southern colleagues walked out. The Lincoln-Johnson ticket wins 212 of 233 electoral votes.

1864   Nevada becomes the thirty-sixth state of the Union.

1865   The Civil War ends.

1865   President Abraham Lincoln is assassinated, and Vice President Andrew Johnson succeeds him as president.

1865   The Thirteenth Amendment to the Constitution, outlawing slavery, is ratified.

1867   Over objections and vetoes by President Andrew Johnson, Congress passes harsher Reconstruction

1862
Victor Hugo publishes
Les Misérables.

1864
"In God We Trust" is
imprinted on U.S. coins.

1865
Ku Klux Klan
is founded.

1861   1863   1865   1867

policies (terms under which former Confederate states can operate) than the Johnson (and Lincoln) plans.

1867   Nebraska becomes the thirty-seventh state of the Union.

1867   The United States purchases Alaska (a deal called "Seward's Folly" after Secretary of State William H. Seward, who negotiated the acquisition) from Russia.

1868   President Andrew Johnson becomes the first president to be impeached by the House of Representatives. He is acquitted by one vote in a trial in the U.S. Senate.

1868   Civil War hero Ulysses S. Grant is elected president.

1869   The Transcontinental railroad is completed.

1869   President Ulysses S. Grant fails in attempts to annex the Dominican Republic.

1872   President Ulysses S. Grant is reelected. His opponent, newspaper publisher Horace Greeley, dies shortly after the election, and his electoral votes are dispersed among several other Democrats.

1873   The Crédit Mobilier scandal reflects widespread corruption among some officials in the Ulysses S. Grant administration and some congressmen.

1876   Colorado becomes the thirty-eighth state of the Union.

1876   In the hotly contested presidential election, the Democratic candidate, New York governor Samuel J. Tilden, outpolls the Republican nominee, Ohio governor Rutherford B. Hayes, by over two hundred thousand votes, but falls one electoral vote short of a majority when twenty electoral votes (from the states of Florida, South Carolina, Louisiana, and Oregon) are contested with claims of fraud. The House of Representatives fails to resolve the issue.

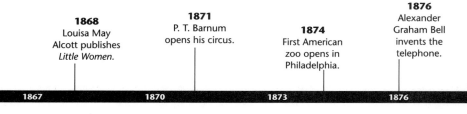

1868
Louisa May Alcott publishes *Little Women.*

1871
P. T. Barnum opens his circus.

1874
First American zoo opens in Philadelphia.

1876
Alexander Graham Bell invents the telephone.

1867   1870   1873   1876

1877   A special Electoral Commission is established to re-
       solve the 1876 presidential election controversy. Days
       before the scheduled inauguration of the new presi-
       dent in March, the Commission awards the 20 disput-
       ed votes to Republican Rutherford B. Hayes, who
       edges Democrat Samuel J. Tilden, 185-184, in the Elec-
       toral College. Some historians refer to the decision as
       the Compromise of 1877, believing that Republicans
       and southern Democrats struck a deal: Hayes would be
       president, and Reconstruction (federal supervision of
       former Confederate states) would end.

1877   Federal troops are withdrawn from South Carolina
       and Louisiana, where troops had been stationed since
       the end of the Civil War to enforce national laws. Re-
       construction ends, and southern states regain the
       same rights as all other states.

1878   Attempting to reform the civil service (where jobs
       were often provided by the party in power to party
       members), President Rutherford B. Hayes suspends
       fellow Republican Chester A. Arthur (a future U.S.
       president) as the powerful head of the New York Cus-
       tom's House (which collects import taxes).

1879   The first telephone is installed in the White House.
       The phone number: 1.

1879   Thomas Edison invents the incandescent light bulb.

1880   Ohio congressman James A. Garfield is elected presi-
       dent.

1881   President James A. Garfield is assassinated by an ex-
       tremist who lost his job under civil service reform.
       Chester A. Arthur becomes the fourth vice president
       to assume the presidency upon the death of the chief
       executive. Like the previous three (John Tyler, Millard

1877
The first Wimbledon
tennis championship
is played.

1879
British Zulu War
takes place.

1880
Gilbert and
Sullivan compose
"The Pirates of
Penzance."

1877   1878   1880   1881

Fillmore, and Andrew Johnson), Arthur is not selected by his party to run for the presidency after completing the elected president's term.

1883 The Pendleton Act, mandating major civil service reform, is signed into law by President Chester A. Arthur.

1884 New York governor Grover Cleveland is elected as the first Democrat to win the presidency since 1856. Tariffs (taxes on imported goods) and tariff reform become major issues during his presidency and the following three elections.

1885 The Statue of Liberty is dedicated.

1886 President Grover Cleveland marries Frances Folsom, becoming the only president to marry at the White House.

1888 Former Indiana senator Benjamin Harrison is elected president despite receiving 90,000 fewer popular votes than President Grover Cleveland. Harrison wins most of the more populated states for a 233-168 Electoral College advantage.

1889 North Dakota, South Dakota, Montana, and Washington enter the Union, expanding the United States to forty-two states.

1890 Idaho and Wyoming become the forty-third and forty-fourth states of the Union.

1891 Electric wiring is installed in the White House.

1892 Former president Grover Cleveland becomes the first person to win non-consecutive presidential terms by defeating incumbent president Benjamin Harrison (in the popular vote *and* the Electoral College). Iowa politician James B. Weaver of the People's Party (also

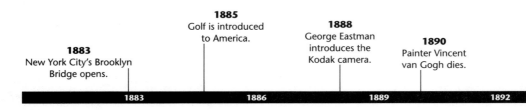

1883
New York City's Brooklyn
Bridge opens.

1885
Golf is introduced
to America.

1888
George Eastman
introduces the
Kodak camera.

1890
Painter Vincent
van Gogh dies.

1883   1886   1889   1892

known as the Populists) finishes a distant third in the popular vote but garners twenty-two electoral votes.

1893 Lame duck (an official completing an elected term after having failed to be reelected) President Benjamin Harrison presents a treaty to annex Hawaii to the U.S. Congress.

1893 President Grover Cleveland rescinds former president Benjamin Harrison's treaty for the annexation of Hawaii and calls for an investigation of the American-led rebellion that overthrew the Hawaiian native monarchy.

1894 An economic downturn and numerous strikes paralyze the American economy.

1895 With gold reserves (used to back the value of currency) running low, President Grover Cleveland arranges a gold purchase through financier J. P. Morgan.

1896 Ohio governor William McKinley, the Republican Party nominee, is elected president over the Democratic candidate, former Nebraska congressman William Jennings Bryan.

1896 Utah becomes the forty-fifth state of the Union.

1898 The Spanish-American War takes place. The United States wins quickly and takes possession of overseas territories (the former Spanish colonies of Cuba, Puerto Rico, and the Philippines).

1898 President William McKinley reintroduces the Hawaii annexation issue and Congress approves it.

1899 President William McKinley expands U.S. trade with China and other nations through his Open Door Policy.

1900 President William McKinley is reelected by defeating William Jennings Bryan a second time.

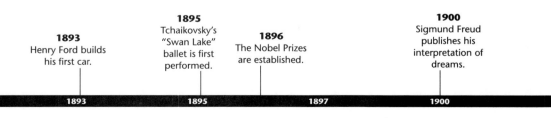

1893
Henry Ford builds his first car.

1895
Tchaikovsky's "Swan Lake" ballet is first performed.

1896
The Nobel Prizes are established.

1900
Sigmund Freud publishes his interpretation of dreams.

1893　1895　1897　1900

1900 Chinese nationalists take arms against growing foreign influences in their country, an uprising called the Boxer Rebellion. American military forces join those of other foreign nations to put down the uprising. American military forces are also stationed in the Philippines to combat revolts.

1901 President William McKinley is assassinated; Vice President Theodore Roosevelt assumes the presidency and, at age 42, becomes the youngest man to become president.

1902 To combat the growing influence of trusts (business combinations intended to stifle competition), President Theodore Roosevelt orders vigorous enforcement of antitrust laws, and an era of business and social reform gains momentum.

1903 The United States quickly recognizes and supports a rebellion in the nation of Colombia through which Panama becomes an independent nation. Through the Panama Canal treaty, which provides a strip of land to be developed by the United States, President Theodore Roosevelt spearheads plans to build a canal across Panama, linking the Atlantic and Pacific oceans.

1904 Theodore Roosevelt becomes the first president who assumed office upon the death of the elected president to win election for a full term.

1905 President Theodore Roosevelt serves as mediator during the Russo-Japanese War. His success at helping end the conflict earns him a Nobel Peace Prize.

1907 Oklahoma becomes the forty-sixth state.

1908 William Howard Taft, who served in the William McKinley and Theodore Roosevelt administrations, is

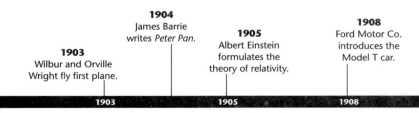

1904
James Barrie writes *Peter Pan.*

1905
Albert Einstein formulates the theory of relativity.

1908
Ford Motor Co. introduces the Model T car.

1903
Wilbur and Orville Wright fly first plane.

1901   1903   1905   1908

elected president. William Jennings Bryan loses in his third presidential bid.

1909   In a sign of the times, President William Howard Taft purchases official automobiles and has the White House stable converted into a garage.

1909   The North Pole is reached.

1912   New Jersey governor Woodrow Wilson is elected president. Former president Theodore Roosevelt, running as the Progressive Party candidate (nicknamed "the Bull Moose Party"), finishes second. Roosevelt outpolls his successor, President William Howard Taft, by about seven hundred thousand popular votes and wins eighty more electoral votes.

1912   New Mexico and Arizona enter the Union, expanding the United States to forty-eight states.

1912   The Sixteenth Amendment, authorizing the collection of income taxes, is ratified.

1912   The Federal Reserve, which regulates the nation's money supply and financial institutions, is established.

1913   The Seventeenth Amendment changes the system for electing U.S. senators. The popular vote replaces the system where most senators were elected by state legislatures.

1914   World War I begins.

1914   U.S. military forces begin having skirmishes with Mexican rebels in a series of incidents that last until 1916.

1914   The Panama Canal is opened.

1916   President Woodrow Wilson is reelected by a slim Electoral College margin, 277-254. He defeats the Repub-

1910
First Father's Day is celebrated.

1912
The *Titanic* hits an iceberg and sinks.

1913
The first Charlie Chaplin silent movie is released.

1915
The U.S. Coast Guard is established.

1910   1912   1914   1916

lican candidate, former U.S. Supreme Court justice Charles Evans Hughes.

1916 President Woodrow Wilson acts as mediator for the nations in conflict in World War I.

1917 Citing acts of German aggression, President Woodrow Wilson asks Congress to declare war. The United States enters World War I. The Selective Service (a system through which young men are called on for military duty) is established.

1918 World War I ends.

1919 Congress rejects the Treaty of Versailles negotiated by President Woodrow Wilson and other leaders representing the nations involved in World War I. Congress also rejects American participation in the League of Nations that Wilson had envisioned.

1919 Attempting to rally support of the Treaty of Versailles and the League of Nations during a long speaking tour, President Woodrow Wilson collapses with a debilitating stroke. The public is not made aware of the severity of the affliction that leaves Wilson bedridden.

1919 The Eighteenth Amendment, outlawing the manufacture and sale of alcohol, is ratified.

1920 Women are able to participate in national elections for the first time.

1920 Ohio senator Warren G. Harding is elected president.

1922 Illegal deals are made by some officials of the Warren G. Harding administration. Two years later, they are implicated in the Teapot Dome scandal.

1923 President Warren G. Harding dies in San Francisco, California; Vice President Calvin Coolidge assumes the presidency.

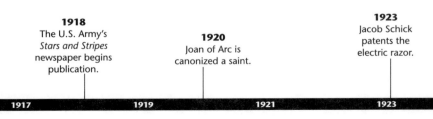

1918
The U.S. Army's *Stars and Stripes* newspaper begins publication.

1920
Joan of Arc is canonized a saint.

1923
Jacob Schick patents the electric razor.

1917   1919   1921   1923

1924   Calvin Coolidge is elected president in a landslide, defeating West Virginia politician John W. Davis, the Democratic candidate. Progressive Party candidate Robert M. LaFollette, a future Wisconsin senator, garners over thirteen percent of the popular vote and wins thirteen electoral votes.

1925   The Scopes Trial is held in Dayton, Tennessee, after a public school teacher instructs his class on the theory of evolution in defiance of a state law.

1927   Charles Lindbergh becomes the first pilot to fly solo across the Atlantic Ocean.

1928   Former secretary of commerce Herbert Hoover, who also supervised international relief efforts during World War I, wins his first election attempt in a landslide (by over six million popular votes and a 444-87 Electoral College triumph).

1929   The stock market crashes.

1930   President Herbert Hoover assures the nation that "the economy is on the mend," but continued crises become the Great Depression that lasts the entire decade.

1932   The Bonus March, in which World War I veterans gather in Washington, D.C., to demand benefits promised to them, ends in disaster and death when military officials forcibly remove them and destroy their campsites.

1932   New York governor Franklin D. Roosevelt defeats President Herbert Hoover by over seven million popular votes and a 472-59 margin in the Electoral College.

1933   President Franklin D. Roosevelt calls a special session of Congress to enact major pieces of legislation to combat the Great Depression. Over a span called The

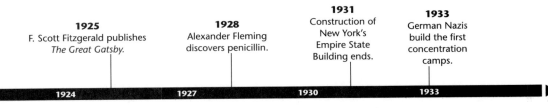

1925
F. Scott Fitzgerald publishes *The Great Gatsby.*

1928
Alexander Fleming discovers penicillin.

1931
Construction of New York's Empire State Building ends.

1933
German Nazis build the first concentration camps.

1924   1927   1930   1933

Hundred Days, much of Roosevelt's New Deal program of social and economic relief, recovery, and reform is approved.

1933 As part of the Twentieth Amendment to the Constitution, the inauguration date of the president is changed to January 20 of the year following the election.

1933 The Twenty-first Amendment repeals prohibition.

1936 President Franklin D. Roosevelt is reelected by a popular vote margin of eleven million and wins the Electoral College vote, 523-8.

1937 Frustrated when the U.S. Supreme Court declares several New Deal programs unconstitutional, President Franklin D. Roosevelt initiates legislation to add more justices to the court and to set term limits. His attempt to "stack the court" receives little support.

1939 World War II begins.

1939 Physicist Albert Einstein informs President Franklin D. Roosevelt about the possibility for creating nuclear weapons and warns him that Nazi scientists are already pursuing experiments to unleash atomic power.

1940 President Franklin D. Roosevelt wins an unprecedented third term by slightly less than five million popular votes and a 449-82 win in the Electoral College.

1941 Pearl Harbor, Hawaii, is attacked; the United States enters World War II.

1942 The success of the first nuclear chain reaction is communicated to President Franklin D. Roosevelt through the code words, "The eagle has landed." A secret program for manufacturing and testing atomic bombs begins.

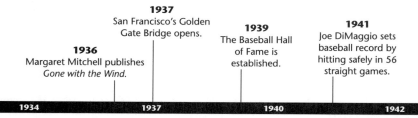

1937
San Francisco's Golden Gate Bridge opens.

1936
Margaret Mitchell publishes *Gone with the Wind.*

1939
The Baseball Hall of Fame is established.

1941
Joe DiMaggio sets baseball record by hitting safely in 56 straight games.

1934   1937   1940   1942

1944 President Franklin D. Roosevelt is elected to a fourth term by over five million popular votes and a 432-99 Electoral College triumph.

1945 President Franklin D. Roosevelt attends the Yalta Conference and meets with British prime minister Winston Churchill and Soviet leader Joseph Stalin to discuss war issues and the postwar world.

1945 President Franklin D. Roosevelt dies; Vice President Harry S. Truman becomes president. It is only then that Truman learns about development and successful testing of the atomic bomb.

1945 World War II ends in Europe.

1945 The United States drops atomic bombs on Japan. Japan surrenders, and World War II ends.

1946 The U.S. government seizes coal mines and railroads to avoid labor strikes and business practices that might contribute to inflation.

1947 An economic aid package called the Marshall Plan, named after its architect, Secretary of State George C. Marshall, helps revive war-torn Europe.

1947 The Cold War, a period of strained relations and the threat of nuclear war between the United States and the Soviet Union, and their respective allies, settles in and continues for more than forty years.

1948 Renovation of the White House begins. Four years later, the project has completely reconstructed the interior and added two underground levels.

1948 Despite the *Chicago Daily Tribune* headline "DEWEY DEFEATS TRUMAN" on the morning after election day, President Harry S. Truman wins the presidency,

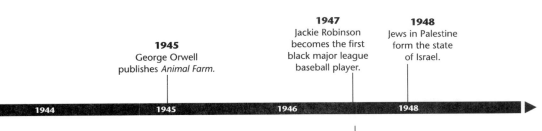

1945
George Orwell
publishes *Animal Farm*.

1947
Jackie Robinson
becomes the first
black major league
baseball player.

1948
Jews in Palestine
form the state
of Israel.

1944   1945   1946   1948

taking over two million more popular votes and winning 303-189 in the Electoral College. The State's Rights Party candidate, South Carolina governor J. Strom Thurmond, places third, slightly outpolling the Progressive Party candidate, former vice president Henry Wallace, and winning thirty-nine electoral votes. Thurmond led a contingent of Southern politicians away from the Democratic Party in protest of Truman's support for civil rights legislation.

1949 The North Atlantic Treaty Organization (NATO) is formed by the United States and its European allies to monitor and check acts of aggression in Europe.

1950 The United States becomes involved in a police action to protect South Korea from invasion by communist North Korea. The police action intensifies into the Korean War.

1951 The Twenty-second Amendment to the Constitution is ratified, limiting presidents to two elected terms and no more than two years of a term to which someone else was elected.

1952 Dwight D. "Ike" Eisenhower, famous as the Supreme Commander of Allied Forces during World War II, is elected president.

1953 An armistice is signed in Korea.

1954 The Army-McCarthy hearings are held. Wisconsin senator Joseph McCarthy presents accusations that the U.S. military and Department of State are deeply infiltrated by communists. McCarthy is eventually disgraced when most of his accusations prove groundless.

1954 In *Brown v. Board of Education,* the U.S. Supreme Court rules that racially segregated public schools are un-

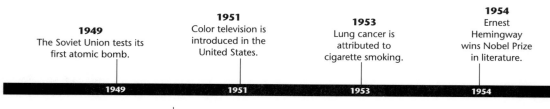

1949
The Soviet Union tests its first atomic bomb.

1951
Color television is introduced in the United States.

1953
Lung cancer is attributed to cigarette smoking.

1954
Ernest Hemingway wins Nobel Prize in literature.

1949   1951   1953   1954

constitutional. In 1957, President Dwight D. Eisenhower sends troops to Little Rock, Arkansas, to enforce desegregation of schools.

1956 An uprising in Hungary against Soviet domination is quickly crushed.

1956 President Dwight D. Eisenhower wins reelection, his second straight triumph over his Democratic challenger, former Illinois governor Adlai Stevenson.

1957 The Soviet Union launches the first space satellite, *Sputnik I.*

1958 The United States launches its first space satellite, *Explorer I,* and the National Aeronautics and Space Agency (NASA) is created.

1959 Alaska and Hawaii enter the Union as the forty-ninth and fiftieth states.

1960 The Cold War deepens over the *U2* incident, where a U.S. spy plane is shot down inside the Soviet Union.

1960 Massachusetts senator John F. Kennedy outpolls Vice President Richard Nixon by slightly more than 100,000 votes while winning 303-219 in the Electoral College. Kennedy, at age 43, is the youngest elected president. A dispute over nine thousand votes in Illinois, that might have resulted in Nixon winning that state instead of Kennedy, is stopped by Nixon. A change of electoral votes in Illinois would not have affected the overall electoral majority won by Kennedy.

1961 The District of Columbia is allowed three electoral votes.

1961 An invasion of Cuba by American-supported rebels at the Bay of Pigs fails when an internal rebellion does

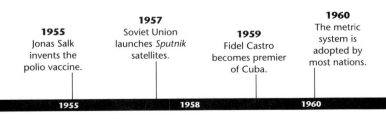

1955
Jonas Salk invents the polio vaccine.

1957
Soviet Union launches *Sputnik* satellites.

1959
Fidel Castro becomes premier of Cuba.

1960
The metric system is adopted by most nations.

1955   1958   1960   1961

not materialize and President John F. Kennedy refuses to provide military backing.

1962   The Cuban Missile Crisis puts the United States and the Soviet Union on the brink of nuclear war after the Soviets are discovered building missile launch sites in Cuba. After a tense, ten-day standoff, the missiles are removed.

1963   A military coup overthrows the political leader of South Vietnam, where American military advisors are assisting South Vietnamese to repel a communist takeover.

1963   A large civil rights march on Washington, D.C., culminates with the famous "I Have a Dream" speech by Rev. Martin Luther King Jr.

1963   President John F. Kennedy is assassinated; Vice President Lyndon B. Johnson assumes the presidency.

1964   President Lyndon B. Johnson steers major civil rights legislation through Congress in memory of the late president John F. Kennedy. The Twenty-fourth Amendment to the Constitution is ratified and ensures the right of citizens of the United States to vote shall not be denied "by reason of failure to pay any poll tax or other tax."

1964   President Lyndon B. Johnson is elected in a landslide, winning almost sixteen million more popular votes than Arizona senator Barry Goldwater.

1965   The Vietnam conflict escalates. President Lyndon B. Johnson is given emergency powers by Congress. Massive bombing missions begin, and U.S. military troops begin engaging in combat, although the U.S. Congress never officially declares war.

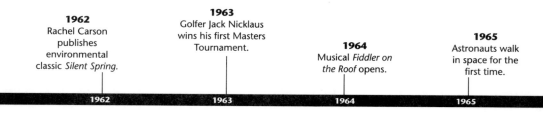

1962
Rachel Carson publishes environmental classic *Silent Spring*.

1963
Golfer Jack Nicklaus wins his first Masters Tournament.

1964
Musical *Fiddler on the Roof* opens.

1965
Astronauts walk in space for the first time.

1962   1963   1964   1965

1966 An unmanned American spacecraft lands on the moon.

1967 Protests, including a march on Washington, D.C., escalate against American involvement in the Vietnam War.

1967 Thurgood Marshall becomes the first African American Supreme Court justice.

1967 The Twenty-fifth Amendment to the Constitution is ratified and provides clear lines of succession to the presidency: "Section 1. In case of the removal of the President from office or of his death or resignation, the Vice President shall become President. Section 2. Whenever there is a vacancy in the office of the Vice President, the President shall nominate a Vice President who shall take office upon confirmation by a majority vote of both Houses of Congress."

1968 Civil rights leader Rev. Martin Luther King Jr. is assassinated in April, and leading Democratic presidential candidate Robert F. Kennedy is assassinated in June.

1968 Former vice president Richard Nixon is elected president, winning with 500,000 more popular votes than incumbent vice president Hubert H. Humphrey and a 301-191 Electoral College edge. Former Alabama governor George C. Wallace of the American Independent Party (for state's rights and against racial desegregation) nets over nine million popular votes and wins forty-six electoral votes.

1969 American troop withdrawals from South Vietnam begin.

1969 U.S. astronaut Neil Armstrong becomes the first man to walk on the moon.

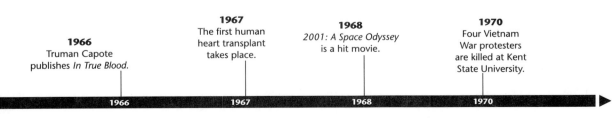

1966
Truman Capote publishes *In True Blood.*

1967
The first human heart transplant takes place.

1968
2001: A Space Odyssey is a hit movie.

1970
Four Vietnam War protesters are killed at Kent State University.

1966   1967   1968   1970

1972 President Richard Nixon reestablishes U.S. relations with the People's Republic of China that were ended after a communist takeover in China in 1949. He visits China and the Soviet Union, where he initiates a policy of détente (a relaxing of tensions between rival nations).

1972 An investigation of a burglary of Democratic National Headquarters at the Watergate Hotel and Office Complex in Washington, D.C., begins and leads to connections with officials in the Richard Nixon administration.

1972 President Richard Nixon is reelected in a landslide.

1973 The Paris Peace Agreement, between the United States and North Vietnam, ends American military involvement in the Vietnam War.

1973 Vice President Spiro T. Agnew resigns over income tax evasion; he is replaced by Michigan congressman Gerald R. Ford.

1974 Nationally televised U.S. Senate hearings on the Watergate scandal confirm connections between the 1972 burglary and officials of the Richard Nixon administration as well as abuses of power.

1974 The House Judiciary Committee begins impeachment hearings and plans to recommend to the House the impeachment of President Richard Nixon.

1974 President Richard Nixon resigns from office over the Watergate scandal. Vice President Gerald R. Ford assumes office.

1974 President Gerald R. Ford issues a pardon, protecting former president Richard Nixon from prosecution in an attempt to end "our national nightmare."

1972
Longtime FBI director J. Edgar Hoover dies.

1973
Skylab space missions take place.

1974
Hank Aaron passes Babe Ruth as baseball's all-time home run hitter.

1972　　　　1973　　　　1974　　　　1975

1976 In a close election, former Georgia governor Jimmy Carter defeats President Gerald R. Ford.

1977 Beset by rising fuel costs and a continued sluggish economy, President Jimmy Carter calls an energy shortage "the moral equivalent of war" and attempts to rally conservation efforts.

1979 The Camp David Accords, the result of negotiations spearheaded by President Jimmy Carter, is signed by the leaders of Egyptian president Anwar Sadat and Israeli prime minister Menachem Begin in Washington, D.C.

1979 Fifty-two Americans are taken hostage in Iran following a religious revolution in that nation in which the American-supported leader was overthrown. The hostage crisis lasts 444 days, with the hostages released on the day President Jimmy Carter leaves office.

1980 Former California governor Ronald Reagan wins a landslide (489-49 in the Electoral College) over President Jimmy Carter. Independent candidate John Anderson, a longtime Republican congressman from Illinois, polls over five million votes. Reagan becomes the oldest president.

1981 Sandra Day O'Connor becomes the first female U.S. Supreme Court justice.

1982 Economic growth begins after a decade of sluggish performance.

1984 President Ronald Reagan is reelected in another landslide, drawing the most popular votes ever (54,455,075) and romping in the Electoral College, 525-13.

1987 A sudden stock market crash and growing federal deficits threaten economic growth.

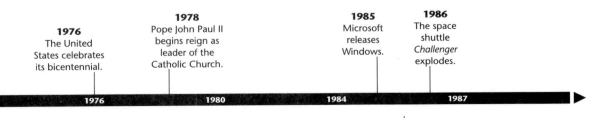

1976
The United States celebrates its bicentennial.

1978
Pope John Paul II begins reign as leader of the Catholic Church.

1985
Microsoft releases Windows.

1986
The space shuttle *Challenger* explodes.

1976   1980   1984   1987

1988   George Bush becomes the first sitting vice president since Martin Van Buren in 1836 to be elected president.

1989   Several East European nations become independent from domination by the U.S.S.R. Reforms in the U.S.S.R. eventually lead to the breakup of the Soviet Union; the former Soviet states become independent nations in 1991, and the Cold War ends.

1991   After the Iraqi government fails to comply with a United Nations resolution to abandon Kuwait, which its military invaded in August of 1990, the Gulf War begins. Within a month, Kuwait is liberated by an international military force. President George Bush's popularity soars over his leadership in rallying U.N. members to stop Iraqi aggression.

1992   An economic downturn and a huge budget deficit erode President George Bush's popularity. Arkansas governor Bill Clinton defeats Bush for the presidency. The Reform Party candidate, Texas businessman H. Ross Perot, draws 19,221,433 votes, the most ever for a third-party candidate, but wins no electoral votes. Clinton and running mate Al Gore are the youngest president–vice president tandem in history.

1994   An upturn in the economy begins the longest sustained growth period in American history.

1996   President Bill Clinton is reelected.

1998   President Bill Clinton is implicated in perjury (false testimony under oath in a court case) and an extramarital affair. The House Judiciary Committee votes, strictly on party lines, to recommend impeachment of the president, and the House impeaches the president for perjury and abuse of power.

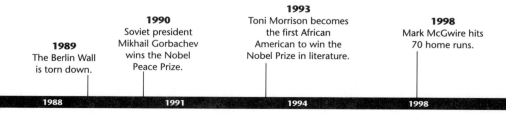

1993
Toni Morrison becomes
the first African
American to win the
Nobel Prize in literature.

1990
Soviet president
Mikhail Gorbachev
wins the Nobel
Peace Prize.

1989
The Berlin Wall
is torn down.

1998
Mark McGwire hits
70 home runs.

1988   1991   1994   1998

    Complete American Presidents Sourcebook

1999 President Bill Clinton remains in office after being acquitted in a Senate trial.

2000 In the closest and most hotly contested election since 1876, Texas governor George W. Bush narrowly defeats Vice President Al Gore in the Electoral College, 271-266. Gore wins the popular vote by some three hundred thousand votes. The final victor cannot be declared until after a recount in Florida (with its twenty-five electoral votes at stake) takes place. Five weeks of legal battles ensue and Gore officially contests the results before Bush is able to claim victory in the state and, therefore, in the national election.

2000 Hillary Rodham Clinton becomes the first first lady to be elected to public office when she is elected U.S. senator from New York.

2000 In one of his last functions as president, Bill Clinton attends an international economic summit in Asia and visits Vietnam, twenty-five years after the end of the conflict that deeply divided Americans.

2001 George W. Bush is inaugurated the nation's forty-third president and becomes the second son of a president to become president himself.

1999
The euro is accepted as legal tender in Europe.

2000
Lavish worldwide celebrations usher in the new year.

2001
The Federal Reserve lowers its lending rate by one-half point.

1999　　　　2000　　　　2001

Words to Know

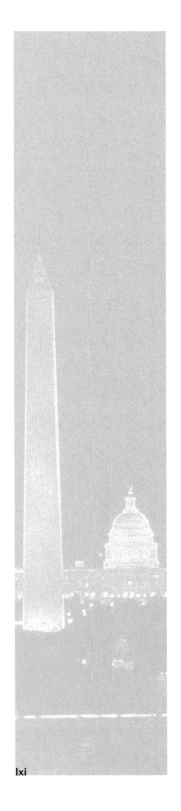

A

Abolitionists: People who worked to end slavery.

Agrarian: One who believes in and supports issues beneficial to agriculture.

Alien and Sedition Acts: Four bills—the Naturalization Act, Alien Act, Alien Enemies Act, and Sedition Act—passed by Congress in 1798 and signed into law by President John Adams. The Naturalization Act extended from five to fourteen years the waiting period before citizenship—and with it, the right to vote—could be obtained by new immigrants. The two Alien acts gave the president the right to deport or jail foreign citizens he deemed a threat to the nation's stability, especially during wartime. The Sedition Act criminalized criticism of the government. To write or publish views that disparaged the administration was punishable by harsh fines and jail terms.

Allied forces (allies): Alliances of countries in military opposition to another group of nations. Twenty-eight nations made up the Allied and Associated powers in World War I. In World War II, the Allied powers included Great Britain, the United States, and the Soviet Union.

Anarchist: One against any form of government.

Annexing: Adding a new state or possession to the existing United States of America.

Annual Message to Congress: A speech the president delivers before Congress each year. Originally called the Annual Message to Congress and delivered each November, the speech became known as the State of the Union Address and is delivered each January.

Anti-Federalists: A group who wanted a limited federal government and more power for individual states.

Antitrust: Government action against businesses that dominate a certain industry or market and that are alleged to have stifled competing businesses.

Appropriations: Funds authorized for a particular project.

Armistice: An agreement to cease fire while warring parties negotiate a peace settlement.

Articles of Confederation: From March 1, 1781, to June 21, 1788, the Articles served as the equivalent of the Constitution (1787). The Constitution replaced the Articles, which had failed to produce a strong central government, and the present-day United States was formed.

Axis: The countries that fought together against the Allies in World War II. Germany, Italy, and Japan formed the first coalition; eventually, they were joined by Hungary, Romania, Slovakia, Finland, and Bulgaria.

B

Bar: A term that encompasses all certified lawyers—those who have passed all official requirements (the bar exam) to be certified as lawyers.

Bar exam: A test that lawyers must pass in order to become legally certified to practice law.

Battle of the Bulge: Battles surrounding the last German offensive (1944–45) during World War II. Allied forces moving toward Germany from France following the D-Day invasion were stalled by bad weather along the German border. Germans launched a counteroffensive to divide American and British forces. Germans created a "bulge" in the Allied lines, but they were halted and then withdrew.

Bay of Pigs invasion: Failed U.S.-backed invasion of Cuba at the Bay of Pigs by fifteen hundred Cuban exiles opposed to Fidel Castro, on April 17, 1961.

"Big stick" foreign policy: Theodore Roosevelt's theory that in diplomatic efforts, it was wise to "speak softly and carry a big stick," meaning that one should attempt peaceful solutions while at the same time being prepared to back up the talk with action when necessary.

Bill of Rights: The first ten amendments to the American Constitution of rights and privileges guaranteed to the people of the United States.

Black Codes: Laws and provisions that limited civil rights and placed economic restrictions on African Americans.

"Bleeding Kansas": The conflict in Kansas in 1854 between slavery advocates and abolitionists—in the form of both residents and transients, and two different governments—that led to bloodshed. It was the first indication that the issue of slavery would not be settled diplomatically.

Bloc: A unified group able to wield power through its size and numbers.

Boston Tea Party: An event in 1773 in which colonists spilled shipments of tea into Boston harbor to protest taxes imposed on various products.

Bull market: A stock market term that describes a period of aggressive buying and selling of stock that proves profitable for most investors; in contrast, "bear market" is used to describe a more sluggish trading period.

Bureaucracy: A government or big business set up to be run by bureaus, or departments, that strictly follow rules and regulations and a chain of authority.

C

Camp David Accords: An agreement of peace following negotiations led by President Jimmy Carter and signed by Israeli prime minister Menachem Begin and Egyptian president Anwar Sadat on March 26, 1979.

Capitol Hill: A nickname for Congress, since the Capitol building where Congress holds sessions is located on a small hill.

Carpetbaggers: A term of contempt used by Southerners about agents, humanitarians, politicians, and businessmen who came to the South to assist or to exploit Reconstruction policies. The term suggests that Northerners could stuff everything they owned into a bag made from carpet.

Caucus: An organized vote by registered and designated members of a political party to determine the amount of support within a state for the party's presidential candidates.

Censure: To publicly condemn an individual; in Congress, the act of censure expresses Congress's condemnation of an individual's actions and is entered into the *Congressional Record.*

Central Intelligence Agency (CIA): A U.S. government agency charged with accumulating information on foreign countries.

Checks and balances: The system in which the three branches of the U.S. government can review and dismiss acts passed by one of the other branches.

Civil service: Positions under the authority of the federal government.

Civil War: Conflict that took place from 1861 to 1865 between the Northern states (Union) and the Southern seceded states (Confederacy); also known in the South as the War between the States and in the North as the War of the Rebellion.

Coalitions: Groups of people supporting a political issue or cause.

Cold War: A term that describes a period from 1945 to the late 1980s characterized by tense conflicts and failed diplomacy between the Soviet Union and the United States and their respective allies.

Communism: A system in which the government controls the distribution of goods and services and limits individual freedom.

Compromise of 1850: Legislation passed by Congress and signed into law by President Millard Fillmore consisting of five bills: (1) California was admitted as a free state; (2) Texas was compensated for the loss of territory in a boundary dispute with New Mexico; (3) New Mexico was granted territorial status; (4) the slave trade—but not slavery itself—was abolished in Washington, D.C; (5) and most controversially, the Fugitive Slave Law was enacted, allowing slaveowners to pursue fleeing slaves and recapture them in free states.

Confederate States of America (Confederacy): The eleven Southern states that seceded (separated) from the United States during the 1860s and fought the Union during the American Civil War.

Congressional Record: A document that records all speeches and votes made in Congress.

Conservative: A political philosophy of limited government influence and support for conventional social values.

Constitutional Convention: The 1787 convention attended by delegates to strengthen the Articles of Confederation. Instead, delegates adopted the American Constitution that formed the United States.

Constructionist: One who bases decisions on literal readings of the Constitution.

Consul: A diplomat stationed in a foreign country who advises people from his or her own country on legal matters.

Continental Army: The American army during the Revolutionary War against Great Britain.

Continental Congress: The group of representatives who met to establish the United States.

Coup: A sudden overthrow of a government, often by the country's military.

Covert operations: Secret, undercover acts used to help influence the outcome of events.

Cuban missile crisis: A showdown in October 1962 that brought the Soviet Union and the United States close to war over the existence of Soviet nuclear missiles in Cuba.

D

D-Day: A military term that describes the day when an event can be scheduled. D-Day in World War II was June 6, 1944, when Allied forces landed in Normandy, France.

Dark horse: A little-known candidate with modest chances for success who might emerge surprisingly strong.

Delegate: A member of a party or organization who has a vote that represents a larger group and helps determine the leader of that party or organization.

Democratic Party: One of the oldest political parties in the United States, developed out of the Democratic-Republican Party of the late eighteenth century. Andrew Jackson was one of its first leaders. In the years before the Civil War (1861–65), Democrats became increasingly associated with the South and slavery. Following the war, the party gradually transformed and became associated with urban voters and liberal policies. In the twentieth and twenty-first centuries, Democrats have generally favored freer trade, more international commitments, greater government regulations, and social programs.

Democratic-Republican Party: One of the first political parties in the United States, led by Thomas Jefferson and James Madison in the 1790s to oppose the Federalist Party and close ties with Great Britain. It was also called the Republican Party and the Jeffersonian Republican Party at the time, but the term Democratic-Republican helps distinguish that early political group from the Democratic and Republican parties that were formed later. The Democratic-Republican Party dissolved in the 1820s. Many former members began supporting the formation of the Democratic Party led by Andrew Jackson, who was elected president in 1828 and 1832. The modern-day Republican Party was formed in 1854.

Depression: *See* **Great Depression.**

Deregulation: Removal of guidelines and laws governing a business or financial institution.

Détente: A relaxing of tensions between rival nations, marked by increased diplomatic, commercial, and cultural contact.

Draft cards: From the mid-1960s through the mid-1970s, all males had to register for the draft upon turning eighteen. After registering, an individual received a draft card that contained a draft number. A lottery system was used to determine which available males would be "drafted"—required to serve in the military.

E

Election board: A group authorized to operate elections and count votes.

Electoral College: A body officially responsible for electing the president of the United States. In presidential elections, the candidate who receives the most popular votes in a particular state wins all of that state's electoral votes. Votes are distributed among states in ratios based on population. A candidate must win a majority of electoral votes (over fifty percent) in order to win the presidency.

Electoral votes: The votes a presidential candidate receives for having won a majority of the popular vote in a state. In presidential elections, the candidate who receives the most popular votes in a particular state wins all of that states' electoral votes. Votes are distributed among states in ratios based on population. A candidate must win a majority of electoral votes (over fifty percent) in order to win the presidency.

Emancipation: The act of freeing people from slavery.

Enfranchisement: Voting rights.

Expansionism: The policy of a nation that plans to enlarge its size or gain possession of other lands.

Exploratory committee: A group established by a potential political candidate to examine whether enough party, public, and financial support exists for the potential candidate to officially announce that he or she is running for an elected position.

F

Federal budget: The list of all planned expenditures the federal government expects to make over a year.

Federal budget deficit: When government spending exceeds income (from taxes and other revenue).

Federal Reserve System: The central banking system of the United States, which serves as the banker to the financial sector and the government, issues the national currency, and supervises banking practices.

Federalist: A proponent for a strong national (federal) government.

Federalist Party: An American political party of the late eighteenth century that began losing influence around 1820. Federalists supported a strong national government. Growing sentiments for states' rights and rural regions led to the demise of the party. Many Federalists became Democratic-Republicans until that party was split into factions in the mid-1820s. Those favoring states' rights became Jackson Democrats and formed the Democratic Party in 1832.

First Continental Congress: A group of representatives from the thirteen colonies who met in Philadelphia in 1774 to list grievances (complaints) against England.

Fiscal: Relating to financial matters.

Fourteen Points: Famous speech given by Woodrow Wilson that includes reasons for American involvement in war, terms for peace, and his vision of a League of Nations.

Freedmen's Bureau: An agency that provided federal help for freed slaves.

Fugitive Slave Law: The provision in the Compromise of 1850 that allowed Southern slaveowners to pursue and capture runaway slaves into Northern states.

G

General assembly: A state congressional system made up only of representatives from districts within that particular state.

Gerrymandering: A practice whereby the political party in power changes boundaries in a voting area to include more people likely to support the party in power. This can occur when Congressional districts are rezoned (marked off into different sections) following the national census that occurs every ten years.

Gold standard: The economic practice whereby all of the money printed and minted in a nation is based on the amount of gold the nation has stored. (Paper money is printed; coins are minted, or stamped.)

GOP: Short for "Grand Old Party," a nickname of the Republican Party.

Grand jury: A group empowered to decide whether a government investigation can provide enough evidence to make criminal charges against a citizen.

Grass roots: A term that describes political activity that begins with small groups of people acting without the influence of large and powerful groups.

Great Depression: The worst financial crisis in American history. Usually dated from 1929, when many investors lost money during a stock market crash, to 1941, when the last Depression-related relief effort to help impoverished and unemployed people was passed by the government. When America entered World War II (1939–45) in 1941, many more employment opportunities became available in war-related industries.

Great Society: A set of social programs proposed by President Lyndon B. Johnson designed to end segregation and reduce poverty in the United States.

Gross national product (GNP): An economic measurement of a nation's total value of goods and services produced over a certain period (usually a year); the GNP became an official economic statistic in 1947.

H

House of Burgesses: A representative body made up of Virginia colonists but under the authority of British rule.

Human rights: Principles based on the belief that human beings are born free and equal; governments must respect those rights or they can be accused of human rights violations.

I

Immunity: Protection from prosecution; usually extended to someone who can help the prosecution win its case.

Impeachment: A legislative proceeding charging a public official with misconduct. Impeachment consists of the formal accusation of such an official and the trial that follows. It does not refer to removal from office of the accused.

Imperialism: The process of expanding the authority of one government over other nations and groups of people.

Incumbent: The person currently holding an elected office during an election period.

Independent counsel: A federal position established during the 1970s to investigate federal officials accused of crimes. The Independent Counsel Act, intended to perform in a nonpartisan manner in rare occasions, was not renewed in 1999.

Indictment: An official charge of having committed a crime.

Industrialization: The use of machinery for manufacturing goods.

Inflation: An economic term that describes a situation in which money loses some of its value, usually because the cost of goods is more expensive.

Infrastructure: The system of public works—the physical resources constructed for public use, such as bridges and roads—of a state or country.

Injunction: A legal maneuver that suspends a certain practice until a legal decision can be reached.

Insurrections: Armed rebellions against a recognized authority.

Integration: The bringing together of people of all races and ethnic backgrounds without restrictions; desegregation.

Interest rates: The percentage of a loan that a person agrees to pay for borrowing money.

Internationalism: Interest and participation in events involving other countries.

Iran-Contra scandal: A scandal during the Ronald Reagan administration during which government officials made illegal sales of weapons to Iran. Money made from those sales were diverted to secret funds provided to the Contras in the civil war in El Salvador. This was illegal, since Congress must authorize foreign aid.

Iran hostage crisis: A 444-day period from November 4, 1979, to Inauguration Day 1981 when Iran held 52 American embassy officials hostage following the toppling of the American-backed Shah of Iran.

Iron Curtain: A term describing Eastern European nations dominated by the Soviet Union.

Isolationism: A national policy of avoiding pacts, treaties, and other official agreements with other nations in order to remain neutral.

K

Kansas-Nebraska Act: A U.S. law authorizing the creation of the states of Kansas and Nebraska and specifying that the inhabitants of the territories should decide whether or not to allow slaveholding.

Keynote address: The most important speech during opening ceremonies of an organized meeting.

Korean War: A war from 1950 to 1953 fought between communist North Korea and non-communist South Korea; China backed North Korea and the United Nations backed South Korea.

L

Laissez faire: A French term (roughly translated as "allow to do") commonly used to describe noninterference by government in the affairs of business and the economy.

Lame duck: An official who has lost an election and is filling out the remainder of his or her term.

League of Nations: An organization of nations, as proposed by President Woodrow Wilson, that would exert moral leadership and help nations avoid future wars.

Legal tender: Bills or coin that have designated value.

Lobbyist: A person hired to represent the interests of a particular group to elected officials.

Louisiana Purchase: A vast region in North America purchased by the United States from France in 1803 for $15 million.

Loyalists: Americans who remained loyal to Great Britain during the Revolutionary War (1775–83).

M

Manifest Destiny: The belief that American expansionism is inevitable and divinely ordained.

Marshall Plan: A post–World War II program led by Secretary of State George C. Marshall that helped rebuild European economies (also benefiting U.S. trade) and strengthened democratic governments.

Martial law: A state of emergency during which a military group becomes the sole authority in an area and civil laws are set aside.

Medicare: A government program that provides financial assistance to poor people to help cover medical costs.

Mercenaries: Soldiers hired to serve a foreign country.

Merchant marine: Professional sailors and boat workers involved with commercial marine trade and maintenance (as opposed to branches of the military such as the navy and the coast guard).

Midterm elections: Congressional elections that occur halfway through a presidential term. These elections can affect the president's dealings with Congress. A president is elected every four years; representatives (members of the House of Representatives), every two years; and senators, every six years.

Military dictatorships: States in which military leaders have absolute power.

Military draft: A mandatory program that requires that all males register for possible military service. Those who pass a medical test receive a draft number. A lottery system is used to determine which available males must serve in the military. Those whose numbers are drawn are "drafted" into military service.

Military governments: Governments supervised or run by a military force.

Military tribunal: A court presided over by military officials to try cases in an area under a state of war.

Militia: A small military group, not affiliated with the federal government, organized for emergency service.

Missing in action: A term that describes military personnel unaccounted for. They might have been captured by the enemy, in which case they become prisoners of war; they might be hiding out and attempting to return to safety; or they might have been killed.

Missouri Compromise: Legislation passed in 1820 that designated which areas could enter the Union as free states and which could enter as slave states. It was repealed in 1854.

Monarchy: A form of government in which a single person (usually a king or queen) has absolute power.

Monroe Doctrine: A policy statement issued during the presidency of James Monroe (1817–25) that explained the position of the United States on the activities of European powers in the western hemisphere; of major significance was the stand of the United States against European intervention in the affairs of the Americas.

Muckrakers: A circle of investigative reporters during Theodore Roosevelt's term in office who exposed the seamier (unwholesome) side of American life. These reporters thoroughly researched their stories and based their reports on provable facts.

N

National Security Council: A group of military advisors assisting the president.

Nationalism: Loyalty to a nation that exalts that quality above all other nations.

Nazi: The abbreviated name for the National Socialist German Workers' Party, the political party led by Adolf Hitler, who became dictator of Germany. Hitler's Nazi Party controlled Germany from 1933 to 1945. The Nazis promoted racist and anti-Semitic (anti-Jewish) ideas and enforced complete obedience to Hitler and the party.

Neutrality: A position in which a nation is not engaged with others and does not take sides in disputes.

New Deal: A series of programs initiated by the administration of President Franklin D. Roosevelt to create jobs and stimulate the economy during the Great Depression (1929–41).

North Atlantic Treaty Organization (NATO): An alliance for collective security created by the North Atlantic Treaty in 1949 and originally involving Belgium, Canada, Denmark, France, Great Britain, Iceland, Italy, Luxembourg, the Netherlands, Norway, Portugal, and the United States.

Nuclear test ban treaty: An agreement to stop testing nuclear weapons.

Nullification: Negatation; the Theory of Nullification was proposed by John C. Calhoun, a South Carolina congressman who later served as vice president to Andrew Jackson. In Calhoun's theory, a state has the right to nullify federal laws that it deems harmful to the state's interests.

O

Open Door Policy: A program introduced by President William McKinley to extend trade and relations with China, opening up a vast new market.

Oppression: Abuse of power by one party against another.

P

Pacifist: A person opposed to conflict.

Panic of 1837: An economic slump that hit the United States in 1837.

Pardon: A power that allows the president to free an individual or a group from prosecution for a crime.

Parliamentary government: A system of government in which executive power resides with Cabinet-level officials responsible to the nation's legislature. The highest-ranking member of the political party with a majority in such a system of government is usually made the nation's chief executive.

Partisan: Placing the concerns of one's group or political party above all other considerations.

Patronage system: Also called spoils system; a system in which elected officials appoint their supporters to civil service (government) jobs.

Peace Corps: A government-sponsored program that trains volunteers for social and humanitarian service in underdeveloped areas of the world.

Peacekeeping force: A military force sponsored by the United Nations that polices areas that have been attacked by another group clearly defined as aggressors.

Pearl Harbor: An American naval station in Hawaii attacked without warning by Japanese forces in December 1941.

Pendleton Civil Service Reform Act: A congressional act signed into law by President Chester A. Arthur that established the Civil Service Commission, an organization that oversees federal appointments and ensures that appointees do not actively participate in party politics while holding a federal job.

Perjury: The voluntary violation of an oath or a vow; answering falsely while under oath (having previously sworn to tell the truth).

Platform: A declaration of policies that a candidate or political party intends to follow if the party's candidate is elected.

Political boss: A politically powerful person who can direct a group of voters to support a particular candidate.

Political dynasty: A succession of government leaders from the same political party.

Political machine: An organized political group whose members are generally under the control of the leader of the group.

Populism: An agricultural movement of rural areas between the Mississippi River and the Rocky Mountains of the late nineteenth century that united the interests of farmers and laborers. In 1891, the movement formed a national political party, the People's Party, whose members were called Populists. Populist ideals remained popular even when the party faded early in the twentieth century.

Presidential primaries: Elections held in states to help determine the nominees of political parties for the general election. Each party disperses a certain number of delegates to each state. A candidate must win support of a majority of those delegates to win the party's presidential nomination. In states that hold primary elections, delegates are generally awarded to candidates based on the percentage of votes they accumulate; in some states, the leading vote-getter wins all of those state's delegates.

Presidential veto: When a president declines to sign into law a bill passed by Congress.

Primaries: *See* **Presidential primaries.**

Progressive "Bull Moose" Party: Party in which Theodore Roosevelt ran as a third-party candidate in 1912. He came in second to incumbent president William Howard Taft, but lost to New Jersey governor Woodrow Wilson.

Progressivism: A movement that began late in the nineteenth century whose followers pursued social, economic, and government reform. Generally located in urban areas, Progressivists ranged from individuals seeking to improve local living conditions to radicals who pursued sweeping changes in the American political and economic system.

Prohibition: The constitutional ban on the manufacture and sale of alcohol and alcoholic beverages from 1920 to 1933.

Prosecuting attorney: The attorney who represents the government in a law case.

Protectorate: A relationship in which an independent nation comes under the protection and power of another nation.

Proviso: A clause in a document making a qualification, condition, or restriction.

R

Racial desegregation: A policy meant to ensure that people of all racial origins are treated equal.

Rapprochement: Reestablishment of relations with a country after it has undergone a dramatic change in government.

Ratification: A vote of acceptance. A majority of the representatives from each of the thirteen colonies had to vote for the U.S. Constitution (1787) in order for the document to become legally binding.

Recession: A situation of increasing unemployment and decreasing value of money.

Recharter: To renew a law or an act.

Reciprocal trade agreements: When participating nations promise to trade in a way that will benefit each nation equally.

Reconstruction: A federal policy from 1865 to 1877 through which the national government took an active part in assisting and policing the former Confederate states.

Reconstruction Act of 1867: An act that placed military governments (governments supervised by a military force) in command of states of the South until the Fourteenth Amendment was ratified in 1868.

Regulation: Monitoring business with an established set of guidelines.

Reparations: Payments for damage caused by acts of hostility.

Republican government: A form of government in which supreme power resides with citizens who elect their leaders and have the power to change their leaders.

Republican Party: Founded in 1854 by a coalition (an alliance) of former members of the Whig, Free-Soil, and Know-Nothing parties and of northern Democrats dissatisfied with their party's proslavery stands. The party quickly rose to become one of the most important parties in the United States, and the major opposition to the Democratic Party. Republicans are generally associated with conservative fiscal and social policies. The Republican Party is not related to the older Democratic-Republican Party, although that party was often called the Republicans before the 1830s.

Riders: Measures added on to legislation. Riders are usually items that might not pass through Congress or will be vetoed by the president if presented alone. Congressmen attempt to attach such items to popular bills, hoping they will "ride" along with the more popular legislation.

S

Sanctions: Punishment against a nation involved in activities considered illegal under international law; such punishment usually denies trade, supplies, or access to other forms of international assistance to the nation.

Satellite nations: Countries politically and economically dominated by a larger, more powerful nation.

Secession: Formal withdrawal from an existing organization. In 1860–61, eleven Southern states seceded from the Union to form the Confederate States of America.

Second Continental Congress: A group of representatives from the thirteen colonies who began meeting in Philadelphia in 1775 and effectively served as the American government until the Constitution was adopted in 1787.

Sectionalism: The emphasis that people place on policies that would directly benefit their area of the country.

Segregation: The policy of keeping groups of people from different races, religions, or ethnic backgrounds separated.

Social Security: A government program that provides pensions (a regular sum of money) to American workers after they reach age sixty-five.

Social welfare: A term that encompasses government programs that provide assistance, training, and jobs to people.

Solicitor: An attorney who represents a government agency.

Solicitor general: An attorney appointed by the president to argue legal matters on behalf of the government.

South East Asia Treaty Organization: An alliance of nations founded in 1954 to prevent the spread of communism in Asian and Pacific island nations. Original members included Australia, France, Great Britain, New Zealand, Pakistan, the Philippines, Thailand, and the United States. The alliance disbanded in 1977.

Speaker of the House: The person in charge of supervising activity in the House of Representatives. The Speaker is elected by colleagues of the party with a majority in Congress.

Spin doctoring: A late twentieth-century term that describes the practice of having political aides offer the best possible interpretation of a political statement or the effects of an event on their political boss.

State militia: An organized military unit maintained by states in case of emergency; often called the National Guard.

Stock market crash: A sudden decline in the value of stocks that severely affects investors.

Strategic Arms Limitation Treaty (SALT): Missile reduction program between the United States and the Soviet Union.

Strategic Defense Initiative (SDI): A proposed—but never approved—technological system (nicknamed "Star Wars," after the popular movie) that combined several advanced technology systems that could, in theory, detect and intercept missiles fired by enemies of the United States.

Subpoena: A formal legal document that commands a certain action or requires a person to appear in court.

T

Taft-Hartley Act: Act that outlawed union-only workplaces, prohibited certain union activities, forbade unions to contribute to political campaigns, established loyalty oaths for union leaders, and allowed court orders to halt strikes that could affect national health or safety.

Tariff: A protective tax placed on imported goods to raise their price and make them less attractive than goods produced by the nation importing them.

Teapot Dome scandal: Incident that became public following the death of President Warren G. Harding that revealed that Navy secretary Edwin Denby transfered control of oil reserves in Teapot Dome, Wyoming, and Elk Hill, California, to the Department of the Interior, whose secretary, Albert Fall, secretly leased the reserve to two private oil operators, who paid Fall $400,000.

Tenure of Office Act: A law passed by Congress to limit the powers of the presidency.

Terrorist: A person who uses acts of violence in an attempt to coerce by terror.

Theater: A large area where military operations are occurring.

Thirteenth Amendment: An amendment to the U.S. Constitution that outlawed slavery.

Tonkin Gulf Resolution: Passed by Congress after U.S. Navy ships supposedly came under attack in the Gulf of Tonkin, this resolution gave President Lyndon B. Johnson the authority to wage war against North Vietnam.

Tribunal: A court of law.

Truman Doctrine: A Cold War–era program designed by President Harry S. Truman that sent aid to anticommunist forces in Turkey and Greece. The Union of Soviet Socialist Republics (U.S.S.R.) had naval stations in Turkey, and nearby Greece was fighting a civil war with communist-dominated rebels.

U

Underground railroad: A term that describes a series of routes through which escaped slaves could pass through free Northern states and into Canada. The escaped slaves were assisted by abolitionists and free African Americans in the North.

Union: Northern states that remained loyal to the United States during the Civil War.

V

Veto: The power of one branch of government—for example, the executive—to reject a bill passed by a legislative body and thus prevent it from becoming law.

Vietcong: Vietnamese communists engaged in warfare against the government and people of South Vietnam.

W

War of 1812: A war fought from 1812 to 1815 between the United States and Great Britain. The United States wanted to protect its maritime rights as a neutral nation during a conflict between Great Britain and France.

Warren Commission: A commission chaired by Earl Warren, chief justice of the Supreme Court, that investigated President John F. Kennedy's assassination. The commission concluded that the assassination was the act of one gunman, not part of a larger conspiracy. That conclusion remains debated.

Watergate scandal: A scandal that began on June 17, 1972, when five men were caught burglarizing the offices of the Democratic National Committee in the Watergate complex in Washington, D.C. This led to a cover-up, political convictions, and, eventually, the resignation of President Richard Nixon.

Welfare: Government assistance to impoverished people.

Whig Party: A political party that existed roughly from 1836 to 1852, composed of different factions of the former Democratic-Republican Party. These factions refused to join the group that formed the Democratic Party led by President Andrew Jackson.

Y

Yalta Conference: A 1944 meeting between Allied leaders Joseph Stalin, Winston Churchill, and Franklin D. Roosevelt in anticipation of an Allied victory in Europe over the Nazis. The leaders discussed how to manage lands conquered by Germany, and Roosevelt and Churchill urged Stalin to enter the Soviet Union in the war against Japan.

Research and Activity Ideas

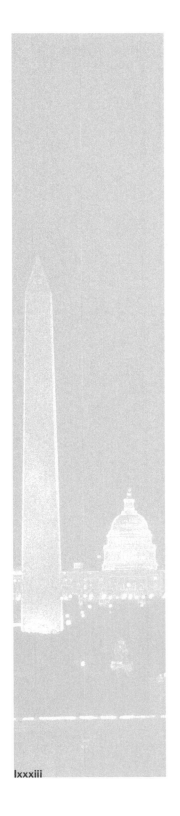

The following research and activity ideas are intended to offer suggestions for complementing social studies and history curricula, to trigger additional ideas for enhancing learning, and to suggest cross-disciplinary projects for library and classroom use.

- The aftermath of the 2000 race between George W. Bush and Al Gore renewed debate over whether the Electoral College system should be abandoned in favor of the popular vote. Research the reasons why the Founding Fathers instituted the Electoral College. Write a paper on arguments for and against the Electoral College, or take one side and have a partner take the other side.

- Several Web sites on presidents are listed in the "Where to Learn More" section. Additional Web sites, linked to presidential libraries and historical sites, are listed at the end of many individual president entries. Using a president of particular interest to you, compare the descriptions of his life and his presidency on the various Web sites. The comparison will show how presidents are appraised by different sources. Pretend you are a media critic. Write a review of the various sites, comparing their different features, the ways they treat the president, and what you find interesting and not useful in each site.

• Plan a debate or a series of debates on important issues in American history. One issue could be the powers of the federal government in relation to the states. That issue can be explored and debated by contrasting the views of a president who took a different view of federal power from the president who preceded him. Such contrasting pairs include John Adams and Thomas Jefferson; James Buchanan and Abraham Lincoln; Herbert Hoover and Franklin D. Roosevelt; and George Bush and Bill Clinton.

• In contemporary times, when a president makes his State of the Union address each year, television networks provide equal time for a member of the opposing party to present his or her party's views. After reading and making notes on one of the speeches in the primary documents section, prepare a response—a speech that takes an opposite view on issues presented by the president.

• Create a timeline of a fifty-year period to parallel the "Timeline of the American Presidents," found on pages xxix–lix. Your timeline might list important inventions, world events, or developments in science and technology. Placing the timelines side by side, consider ways in which the events on your timeline might be connected with events in the presidential timeline.

• Using the resources of your local library, find magazines and newspapers that were published near the time you were born, or pick a date earlier in time. What were some of the big national news stories back then? How did the press view the performance of the president concerning those issues?

• Pretend you are a reporter preparing to interview one of the presidents. Just before your interview is to begin, the president is informed about a major event (select one from the president's entry). You are allowed to follow the president as he plans a course of action. Write an article providing an "insider's view" of the president in action.

• The Congressional cable network C-Span commissioned presidential scholars to rate presidents in ten categories (see http://www.americanpresidents.org/survey/historians/overall.asp). Compare that ranking with other sources that rank presidents in terms of effectiveness. How are the rankings similar and different? What criteria do they use for judging presidents? Consider whether or not you feel the rankings are fair, and write an essay supporting your view.

- Visit a historical site or Web sites devoted to a particular president. Listings for both can often be found in each president's entry. Using biographical information about the president's childhood, his schooling, and his career as president, write a short play in which the president is surrounded by loved ones and aides at a crucial moment during his presidency.

- There were many different kinds of first ladies. Some were politically active (such as Sarah Polk and Eleanor Roosevelt), others believed they should not participate in politics because they were not the one elected to office (such as Bess Truman and Pat Nixon). Compare and contrast those different approaches by profiling several first ladies.

- Research more about a leading opponent of a particular president, perhaps someone he faced in an election. Imagine that the opponent was able to convince voters that he or she should be elected. Write about how history would have been different if the opponent had become president. The focus could be on an election that was very close (such as Rutherford B. Hayes over Samuel Tilden in 1876 or George W. Bush over Al Gore in 2000) or one in which the victor won by a large margin (such as Franklin D. Roosevelt over Alfred Landon in 1936 or Ronald Reagan over Walter Mondale in 1984).

Complete American Presidents Sourcebook

Woodrow Wilson

Twenty-eighth president (1913–1921)

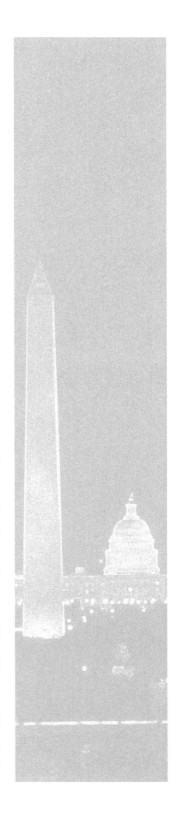

Woodrow Wilson . . . 959

    Fast Facts about Woodrow Wilson (box) . . . 960

    Woodrow Wilson Timeline (box) . . . 961

    Words to Know (box) . . . 962

    Election Results (box) . . . 966

    Woodrow Wilson Administration (box) . . . 967

    John J. "Black Jack" Pershing (box) . . . 970

    The League of Nations (box) . . . 977

    Henry Cabot Lodge (box) . . . 980

    A Selection of Wilson Landmarks (box) . . . 982

Ellen Wilson . . . 987

Edith Wilson . . . 991

Primary source: Wilson's War Message to Congress
President Wilson asks Congress to declare war on Germany, beginning American military participation in World War I . . . **997**

Primary source: Wilson's Fourteen Points
President Wilson defines America's goals for fighting in World War I and proposes the League of Nations, an international body that can address future conflicts . . . **1005**

Woodrow Wilson

Born December 28, 1856
Staunton, Virginia
Died February 3, 1924
Washington, D.C.

**Twenty-eighth president of the United States
(1913–1921)**

**Guided the United States
through World War I**

Woodrow Wilson was widely admired as a writer, a scholar, and an educator more than two decades before he became president. His first book, *Congressional Government* (1885), criticized the influence of Congress and argued that the president—as the highest elected official of the land—had the authority to set the political agenda of the nation.

Wilson immediately acted on this belief when he was elected president in 1912. He called a special joint session of Congress to spell out his agenda, the New Freedom. He began by concentrating on reducing tariff rates (taxes on imports). When legislation on tariff reform began to slow down in Congress, Wilson called what can be considered the first modern presidential press conference; his suggestion to reporters that big business interests were unduly influencing congressmen against tariff reduction was reported in newspapers and helped rally support for his program from voters. A flood of mail from congressmen's constituents (citizens in their districts) and numerous pro-Wilson editorials led to swift passage of the Underwood Tariff Act and a major victory for the new administration.

"It is not men that interest or disturb me primarily; it is ideas. Ideas live; men die."

Woodrow Wilson

Woodrow Wilson.
Courtesy of the Library of Congress.

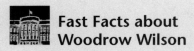

Fast Facts about Woodrow Wilson

Full name: Thomas Woodrow Wilson

Born: December 28, 1856

Died: February 3, 1924

Burial site: National Cathedral, Washington, D.C.

Parents: Joseph and Jessie Woodrow Wilson

Spouse: Ellen Louise Axson (1860–1914; m. 1885); Edith Bolling Galt (1872–1961; m. 1915)

Children: Margaret Woodrow (1886–1944); Jessie Woodrow (1887–1933); Eleanor Randolph (1889–1967)

Religion: Presbyterian

Education: Princeton University (B.A., 1879; M.A., 1882); University of Virginia Law School (LL.B., 1881); Johns Hopkins University (Ph.D., 1886)

Occupations: Lawyer; Princeton University president; professor

Government positions: New Jersey governor

Political party: Democratic

Dates as president: March 4, 1913–March 4, 1917 (first term); March 4, 1917–March 4, 1921 (second term)

Age upon taking office: 56

Wilson's programs were quickly enacted, helped by a Democratic majority in Congress elected with the president. But this rousing early success was reduced by foreign conflicts, beginning with a series of failures Wilson endured in relations with Mexico and followed by war in Europe. Wilson's domestic agenda gradually lost momentum, but his skillful leadership during World War I (1914–18) and, especially, his efforts to win and maintain peace, make him generally considered one of the most successful of American presidents.

Slowly finding his way

Thomas Woodrow Wilson was born in Staunton, Virginia, on December 28, 1856. His father, Joseph, was a Presbyterian minister who shaped Wilson's lifelong values in faith and education. There is evidence that during his childhood Wilson suffered from dyslexia—a condition in which letters and words appear in reverse order to a reader—but he eventually overcame that problem. Health problems, though, recurred throughout his life. He would grow up to be tall and dignified looking, but Wilson had continual problems with breathing and blood flow. Twice he left college for extended periods to recuperate from illnesses, and he suffered a stroke that weakened him during the last year of his presidency. (A stroke is a sudden loss of consciousness and motion caused by an interruption of blood flow to the brain.)

When Woodrow was still an infant, Joseph Wilson accepted a ministry in Augusta, Geor-

Woodrow Wilson Timeline

1856: Born in Virginia; family moves to Georgia the following year

1882: Opens law office in Atlanta, Georgia

1883: Enrolls at Johns Hopkins University to prepare for a career as an academician

1885: Publishes first book, *Congressional Government*; begins teaching at Bryn Mawr College

1888–89: Teaches at Wesleyan College; publishes second book, *The State*

1890: Takes academic position at Princeton University

1893: Publishes book about the Civil War, *Division and Reunion*

1902–10: Serves as president of Princeton

1911–13: Serves as governor of New Jersey

1912: Defeats incumbent president William Howard Taft and former president Theodore Roosevelt in three-party presidential race

1913–21: Serves as twenty-eighth U.S. president

1914: Archduke Franz Ferdinand of Austria is assassinated, beginning a series of events that results in World War I; first lady Ellen Wilson dies

1915: United States remains neutral in the war despite the loss of one hundred Americans in the German torpedoing of British ocean liner *Lusitania;* Wilson marries Edith Bolling Galt

1916: Troops are sent to Mexico; Wilson wins close election to second term

1917: United States settles with Mexico; diplomatic relations with Germany are broken; United States enters World War I

1918: Wilson gives famous Fourteen Points speech, which includes reasons for American involvement in war, terms for peace, and his vision of a League of Nations; armistice signed in November

1919: Wilson helps negotiate Treaty of Versailles in Paris and undertakes grueling tour to win popular support for treaty; suffers a stroke

1921: Retires; stays in Washington, D.C.

1924: Wilson dies in Washington, D.C.

gia, and the family settled there. One of Woodrow's earliest recollections, he would say later in life, occurred when he was four and he overheard someone say that **Abraham Lincoln** (1809–1865; see entry in volume 2) was elected president and there would be war. The Civil War (1861–65) did indeed break out soon after. Young Wilson witnessed some of the hardships and damage of armed conflict.

Words to Know

Antitrust: Government action against businesses that dominate a certain industry or market and that are alleged to have stifled competing businesses.

Armistice: An agreement to cease fire while warring parties negotiate a peace settlement.

Bar exam: A test that lawyers must pass in order to become legally certified to practice law.

Electoral votes: The votes a presidential candidate receives for having won a majority of the popular vote in a state. In presidential elections, the candidate who receives the most popular votes in a particular state wins all of that states' electoral votes. Votes are distributed among states in ratios based on population. A candidate must win a majority of electoral votes (over fifty percent) in order to win the presidency.

Federal Reserve System: The central banking system of the United States, which serves as the banker to the financial sector and the government, issues the national currency, and supervises banking practices.

Fourteen Points: Famous speech given by Woodrow Wilson that includes reasons for American involvement in war, terms for peace, and his vision of a League of Nations.

Imperialists: Persons who favor expanding the authority of their government over other nations and groups of people.

Incumbent: The person currently holding an elected office during an election period.

League of Nations: An organization of nations, as proposed by Woodrow Wilson, that would exert moral leadership and help nations avoid future wars.

Lobbyists: People paid to represent the business and political interests of a particular group.

Mobilized: When a nation's army is called into a state of preparedness.

Neutrality: A position in which a nation is not engaged with others and does not take sides in disputes.

New Freedom: The name of Woodrow Wilson's platform during his first campaign for president. Wilson promised to strengthen antitrust laws, reorganize banking and credit systems, and reduce tariffs.

Nobel Peace Prize: An annual award given to an individual or a group that promotes the cause of peace.

Serbians: An ethnic group that speaks the Serbo-Croatian language and inhabits an area between Albania and Hungary.

Tariffs: Taxes placed on imported goods to raise their price and make them less attractive than goods produced by the nation importing them.

Wilson's father served the Confederacy as a chaplain. After the war, the Wilson family moved to Columbia, South Carolina, where Wilson's father became a professor at Columbia Theological Seminary. The ruins of the war were still evident there over five years after the conflict had ended.

Wilson entered Davidson College in North Carolina in 1873, but illness forced him to leave school the following year. He recovered at the home of his parents, who now lived in Wilmington, North Carolina. He continued his studies on his own. The family's large library and Joseph's excellent teaching skills had always provided Woodrow with home learning to enrich his public education.

In 1875, Wilson entered Princeton University (then called the College of New Jersey), the same school from which his father had graduated. Wilson graduated in 1879. He focused his studies on literature and history and participated in several political debates. That summer, his essay, "Cabinet Government in the United States," was published in the journal *International Review*. The essay addressed what Wilson viewed as the extreme influence that congressional committees had on creating and passing legislation.

Wilson moved on to law school at the University of Virginia, but he suffered a physical breakdown the following year and returned home. After studying law on his own, he passed the Georgia bar exam (the test that lawyers must pass in order to become legally certified to practice law) and opened up a law office in Atlanta in 1882. But Wilson did not prosper as a lawyer and was unhappy with his work. He returned to school—Johns Hopkins University—in 1883 to prepare to teach history and political science.

The mid-1880s were good years for Wilson. In 1885, he published his first book, *Congressional Government,* an expanded version of his earlier essay on congressional committees. In this book, he extended his exploration of American politics to argue that ultimate political authority rested with the president. During this period, Congress had become the most forceful branch of the federal government. That same year, Wilson married Ellen Louise Axson (1860–1914; see entry on **Ellen Wilson** in volume 4). Wilson and "Miss Ellie Lou," as she was called, first met when they were children and met again in 1883 when Wilson was a young lawyer in

In addition to teaching at Wesleyan College in 1888 and 1889, Wilson coached the school's football team.

Atlanta. A professional visit to the Axson's home in Rome, Georgia, turned into romance for Wilson and Miss Ellie Lou. Wilson landed a teaching position at Bryn Mawr College in 1885; all the while, he continued to work on his doctorate (the highest academic degree given by a college or university), which he completed in 1886.

Wilson moved to Wesleyan College in 1888. He taught and he published his second book, *The State*. After turning down several offers from other colleges, Wilson returned to Princeton in 1890, this time as a professor and an administrator. He was already popularly known as an academic, a speaker, and a writer. In addition to addressing political themes, as he had in his first two books, Wilson wrote essays on literature (collected in *Mere Literature and Other Essays*, 1896) and history (*A History of the American People*, 1902).

University president and New Jersey governor

Wilson became president of Princeton University in 1902 and soon demonstrated strong and effective leadership. He hired many young scholars to help form discussion groups, creating a more dynamic interaction between professors and students. He changed the university curriculum (a school's courses). Wilson emphasized certain basic courses that all students had to take while still allowing individuals to choose their remaining courses. Those changes and others brought noticeable improvement to Princeton's academic standards within four years.

Wilson was president of Princeton for about the same amount of time—roughly eight years—that he would later serve as president of the United States. His progress in both positions was somewhat similar. He demonstrated firm leadership and won early success and solid support. However, the endings of both terms were soured when his most ambitious plans were stalled by forceful opponents and by his own unwillingness to compromise.

Wilson's most ambitious plan for Princeton was to do away with a kind of class system present at the school, where students from wealthier families enjoyed exclusive living arrangements. He proposed a series of buildings that would form four quadrangles, or "quads." The quad, a square space enclosed by four buildings, is now a common feature on college campuses. Each building in Princeton's quad featured similar housing, dining, and study facilities. Wilson wanted to centralize all university activities, but a wealthy donor to Princeton had provided a large sum of money for a graduate school to be constructed away from the main campus. Wilson fought for his centralized plan for the final two years of his time at Princeton without success.

In 1910, Wilson was approached by New Jersey's Democratic Party through Colonel George Harvey (1864–1928), editor of *Harper's Weekly* magazine and part of a powerful Democratic coalition (alliance of groups within a party). He offered to support Wilson as a candidate for governor. Exhausted and disappointed with his efforts at Princeton, Wilson accepted Harvey's support. He won the nomination, owing at least in part to support of political "bosses"—powerful figures who dominate local politics and deliver votes in exchange for influence.

Woodrow Wilson's success as New Jersey governor made him a popular candidate for the Democratic nomination for president in 1912. In this cartoon, the academic robes recall the time he spent as president of Princeton University.
Reproduced by permission of the Corbis Corporation.

After winning the nomination, Wilson abruptly announced a progressive platform that, among other things, challenged the influence of bosses and other forms of political and economic influence. He was elected in a landslide. His ideas moved quickly into law: Public utilities came under state regulation; the state school system was reorganized and improved; and antitrust legislation—legislation against businesses that dominate a certain industry or market and that are alleged to have purposely overwhelmed competing businesses—was enacted.

Wilson's resounding success made him a popular candidate for the Democratic nomination for president just two years later in 1912. At the Democratic national convention that summer in Baltimore, he made a strong showing against Speaker of the House James B. "Champ" Clark (1850–1921),

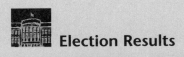

Election Results

1912

Presidential / Vice presidential candidates	Popular votes	Presidential electoral votes
Woodrow Wilson / Thomas R. Marshall (Democratic)	6,293,454	435
Theodore Roosevelt / Hiram W. Johnson (Progressive)	4,119,538	88
William Howard Taft / James S. Sherman (Republican)	3,484,980	8

Former president Roosevelt lost the Republican nomination to incumbent president Taft, so he ran as a third-party candidate. Wilson gained the Democratic nomination after defeating Speaker of the House James B. "Champ" Clark on the forty-sixth ballot.

1916

Presidential / Vice presidential candidates	Popular votes	Presidential electoral votes
Woodrow Wilson / Thomas R. Marshall (Democratic)	9,129,606	277
Charles Evans Hughes / Charles W. Fairbanks (Republican)	8,538,221	254

Former president Roosevelt was again nominated as the Progressive Party candidate, but he declined. Hughes was then nominated, but the party dissolved before the election. Republican vice presidential nominee Fairbanks was a second-time candidate; he had been vice president under Roosevelt.

who held a small lead but did not have the number of delegates needed to win the nomination. By the tenth ballot—the tenth time delegates voted to determine whether a candidate had enough votes to win the nomination—Clark pulled further ahead through the support of New York City political bosses, but he still did not have enough votes to win. Wilson gained momentum when three-time presidential nominee William Jennings Bryan (1860–1925; see box in **William McKinley** entry in volume 3) announced his support for Wilson just before the sixteenth ballot. It took thirty more rounds of voting before Wilson won the position as the party's presidential candidate.

The election of 1912 was closely contested between Wilson, incumbent president **William Howard Taft** (1857–1930; see entry in volume 3), and third-party candidate **Theodore Roosevelt** (1858–1919; see entry in volume 3), who had been president before Taft. (The incumbent is the person

Woodrow Wilson Administration

Administration Dates
March 4, 1913–March 4, 1917
March 4, 1917–March 4, 1921

Vice President
Thomas Riley Marshall (1913–21)

Cabinet

Secretary of State
William Jennings Bryan (1913–15)
Robert Lansing (1915–20)
Bainbridge Colby (1920–21)

Secretary of the Treasury
William G. McAdoo (1913–18)
Carter Glass (1918–20)
David F. Houston (1920–21)

Secretary of War
Lindley M. Garrison (1913–16)
Newton D. Baker (1916–21)

Attorney General
James C. McReynolds (1913–14)

Thomas W. Gregory (1914–19)
Alexander M. Palmer (1919–21)

Secretary of the Navy
Josephus Daniels (1913–21)

Postmaster General
Albert S. Burleson (1913–21)

Secretary of the Interior
Franklin K. Lane (1913–20)
John B. Payne (1920–21)

Secretary of Agriculture
David F. Houston (1913–20)
Edwin Thomas Meredith (1920–21)

Secretary of Labor
William B. Wilson (1913–21)

Secretary of Commerce
William C. Redfield (1913–19)
Joshua W. Alexander (1919–21)

currently holding an elected office during an election period.) Taft was overshadowed by Roosevelt, who removed his supporters from the Republican national convention when Taft was nominated to run for a second term. As the Progressive (Bull Moose) Party candidate, Roosevelt ran a vigorous campaign in which he called for a New Nationalism that would fight economic domination by big business through federal regulation. Wilson campaigned on a platform called the New Freedom, which promised to strengthen antitrust laws, reorganize banking and credit systems, and reduce tariffs. Although the popular vote was close—Wilson led with only forty-two percent—Wilson was easily elected by getting 435 of the possible 531 electoral votes. Electoral votes are the votes a presidential candidate receives for having won a majority of the popular vote in a state. Electoral votes are distributed among states in ratios based on population. A candidate must win a majority of electoral votes (over fifty percent) in order to win the presidency.

Triumphant beginning

Wilson's first year in office was successful from the beginning. He was determined to assert his leadership in accordance with his view of the role of president, as he had spelled out in *Congressional Government* and other writings. Wilson began his term by immediately calling a special session of Congress and making his first speech before them. Though Wilson had a broad domestic agenda for progressive reform, he focused on winning one battle at a time.

The first area of success for the New Freedom was tariff reform: Wilson wanted to reduce government-imposed taxes on imported goods. The special session and Wilson's speech were widely reported in newspapers and enthusiastically applauded by citizens. When legislation on tariff reform began to slow down in Congress, Wilson called a spontaneous (unplanned) news conference—the first time a president used that set-up in such a way—to make his appeal to the people via the media. Wilson claimed that special interests were pressuring congressmen to vote against lowering tariffs. The special interests—in this case, big business—sent lobbyists, people paid to represent the business and political interests of a particular group, to visit congressmen. The news conference produced its intended response: It sparked a huge amount of mail to congressmen from voters in their districts. This response influenced Congress to vote into law the Underwood Tariff Act. The act drastically reduced tariffs to levels of seventy years earlier.

During his first year of office, Wilson also introduced or supported several other measures that would be enacted during his first term. Among them was the creation of the Federal Reserve System, which improved and regulated banking by establishing twelve banking centers spread throughout the United States. Wilson introduced the graduated income tax, which bases taxes on income level. His vigorous support for antitrust legislation led to the creation of the Federal Trade

Commission, empowered to investigate and prosecute "unfair" trade practices. Other acts he pushed through Congress included a maximum forty-hour week for railroad workers, a law making child labor illegal, a bill that provided funding for vocational and agricultural training outside of colleges, and the establishment of the federal highway system.

Rarely has a president been able to accomplish so much so quickly. Wilson was able to count on support from a Democratic majority in Congress that was elected with him in 1912. He also effectively used the press to publicize and explain his positions and goals. He had a persuasive speaking style, which combined a firm voice, use of colorful language, and progressive ideas.

Even as he enjoyed a series of successes on the domestic front, Wilson's attention was taken away from his New Freedom platform halfway through the second year of his first term. The United States had been experiencing tensions with Mexico. At about the same time, Ellen Wilson's health began to deteriorate. War broke out in Europe—Germany invaded France on August 1. The conflict would eventually embroil thirty-two countries and would become known in history as World War I.

Failure with Mexico

A series of revolutions in Mexico left the country unstable and ruled by a military dictator, Victoriano Huerta (1854–1916). Wilson supported Huerta's rivals, a group called the Constitutionalists. Tensions escalated in April 1914 when American sailors were briefly arrested in Mexico. At about the same time, German ships were approaching Mexico, reportedly carrying munitions (guns and ammunition). Those two circumstances prompted Wilson to order a naval blockade to stop ships from entering into or leaving Mexico. When American troops subsequently occupied the city of Veracruz, a battle erupted in which over five hundred Mexicans and Americans were either killed or wounded.

Tensions were eased when the nations of Colombia and Argentina offered to mediate the dispute, but conflict eventually returned. Wilson had supported Huerta's rival, Venustiamo Carranza (1859–1920), who became Mexico's new

John J. "Black Jack" Pershing

John J. Pershing was born on September 13, 1860, in Laclede, Missouri. He grew up to become a teacher in Laclede's school for blacks. Pershing enrolled in the Missouri State Normal School and won a competition for entrance into the Military Academy at West Point. He graduated in 1886 as a senior cadet captain and developed a reputation as a leader. After graduation, he asked to be posted to the Sixth Cavalry Regiment, then nearing the end of operations against the Apaches in the Southwest. With the capture of their leaders, the last independent Apaches were brought to the reservations by late 1886.

In late 1890, Pershing and the Sixth Cavalry were called to the Dakotas to help in operations against the Sioux. Arriving after the massacre of the Sioux at Wounded Knee on December 29, the Sixth remained in the Dakotas until mid-1891. From late 1891 to 1898, Pershing served mostly as a military instructor, first at the University of Nebraska and then at West Point. In 1895 and 1896 he commanded a black cavalry unit, the Tenth Regiment, in Montana. In 1896, at West Point, he resumed teaching. Pershing's harsh personality made him unpopular; his students nicknamed him Black Jack because of his association with the Montana command.

In 1898, the United States went to war with Spain over Cuba. Pershing, still in command of the Tenth Cavalry Regiment, struggled to organize his unprepared troops, their supplies, and their departure. Still, the Tenth fought bravely, taking many casualties. Pershing and his men helped Colonel Theodore Roosevelt and the Rough Riders in the famous battle for San Juan Hill. Pershing's courage resulted in his promotion to major. His next assignment was in the Philippine Islands, which had been part of the Spanish empire and were taken over by the United States after Spain's defeat. Islanders had fought hard against the Spanish and were now unwilling to accept American authority. In 1902, Pershing was promoted to captain and given command of a small outpost in an area inhabited by the Moro tribe. Though Pershing battled the Moros in war, he aided those struck by disease. His fairness led them to vote him as an honorary chief.

In 1905, Pershing married Frances Warren, the daughter of a Wyoming senator. The two spent their honeymoon in Tokyo, where Pershing was assigned to the American embassy. For the next two years he acted as an official observer of Japan's war against Russia, which resulted in Russia's defeat. In 1906, President Theodore Roosevelt promoted him to general.

The new general was given command of Fort William McKinley at the Philippine capital of Manila. For the next four years, he fought several tough military campaigns against dissatisfied Moro groups,

John J. "Black Jack" Pershing.
Courtesy of the Library of Congress.

whose traditional love of independence inspired them to resist American rule. Assigned in 1914 to command the Eighth Brigade, stationed in San Francisco, California, Pershing was soon ordered to take the Eighth to Texas. While in Texas, a fire at his San Francisco house killed his wife and three of his four children. Promoted again in 1916, to major general, a sad Pershing said, "All the promotion in the world would make no difference now."

In March 1916, Mexican rebel leader Francisco Pancho Villa, angered by U.S. support for his enemies, killed eighteen Americans during a raid on Columbus, New Mexico. Immediately, President Woodrow Wilson ordered Pershing into Mexico. For almost a year, Pershing chased Villa deep into the Mexican desert. Unable to capture Villa, Pershing did succeed in breaking up Villa's guerrilla army.

America entered World War I on April 6, 1917, shortly after Pershing's return from Mexico. At fifty-seven, Pershing was young and energetic enough to take the stress of commanding American military forces. He met with British and French leaders to plot strategy. Pershing refused to put his American soldiers under their command. The American Expeditionary Force stood at about two hundred thousand men, insignificant compared to the Allied and German forces. Pershing decided he needed one million men in France by the middle of 1918, with more to follow.

By the summer of 1918, Pershing had persuaded the Allies to give the Americans a section of the front. By late August, Pershing's army crushed a German offensive in only two days, taking sixteen thousand prisoners. Within two weeks, Pershing moved six hundred thousand of his men to their new position at the Argonne Forest for the Allied offensive. It proved to be one of several key victories for Allied forces that brought Germany to surrender later that year.

Following the end of the war, Pershing was named general of the armies. He served as army chief of staff until 1924, then retired. He died on July 15, 1948, and is buried at Arlington National Cemetery.

leader, but Carranza rejected the peacemaking efforts. Wilson turned his support to rebel leader and peasant favorite Francisco "Pancho" Villa (1878–1923). (The word "peasant" usually refers to a small farmer or a person of low social status.) However, Villa was encouraged by Carranza to make bandit forays across the border into the United States. When Pancho Villa sacked the town of Columbus, New Mexico, on March 9, 1916, Wilson took stronger action. He dispatched General John J. "Black Jack" Pershing (1860–1948; see box) to undertake an expedition to Mexico to capture and punish Pancho Villa. The expedition was largely a failure. Villa lured Pershing and his forces deep into Villa's territory, and American forces were unable to capture him. When mediation was finally acceptable to both nations, Pershing was recalled in January 1917.

From the beginning of his administration, Wilson and his secretary of state, William Jennings Bryan, had undertaken an aggressive approach to improving American foreign relations. They met with representatives from dozens of different countries and signed thirty treaties of cooperation. Unfortunately, such treaties led the United States to send in troops to troubled areas, including Haiti, Nicaragua, and the Dominican Republic, in 1915 and 1916.

World War I

Meanwhile, tensions had been building throughout Europe for over a decade. Political boundaries were in dispute, nationalism was running high, nations were building up their military arsenals (stockpiles of weapons), and conflicts over international expansionism, especially in Africa, were increasingly unfriendly. The more powerful nations generally divided into two factions, with England and France on one side, and Germany, Turkey, and Austria-Hungary on the other. Russia leaned to the side of England and France because of tense relations with Germany. Italy shared Germany's imperialist aims in Africa. (Imperialists favor expanding the authority of their government over other nations and groups of people.)

These larger nations dominated smaller countries and ethnic groups: For example, Austria-Hungary held political power over Serbians. (Serbians are an ethnic group that speaks the Serbo-Croatian language and inhabits an area between Albania and Hungary.) The Serbians wanted to be independent. A Serbian nationalist assassinated (murdered) the archduke of Austria-Hungary, sparking a chain of events that led to what would become known as World War I.

Archduke Franz Ferdinand (1863–1914), who would have been a future leader of Austria-Hungary, was assassinated on July 28, 1914. Austria-Hungary declared war on Serbia. Russia immediately moved to defend Serbia by declaring war on Austria-Hungary. On August 1, Germany declared war on Russia. The following day, a mobilized German force (a force prepared for war) also began marching westward, intending to cross through neutral Belgium and invade France. France declared war on Germany. When German forces crossed into Belgium, England declared war on Germany. All these events occurred during the same week that Ellen Wilson became gravely ill; she died on August 6 of a kidney ailment.

The grieving Wilson buried himself in work and confided in his few close friends. His grief lightened early the following year, when he met Edith Bolling Galt (1872–1961; see entry on **Edith Wilson** in volume 4). The couple married in December 1915.

America maintained a position of neutrality (in which a nation is not engaged with others and does not take sides in disputes) as the war quickly intensified. Wilson stated the position of the United States: to remain neutral; to protect American trade and Americans abroad; to increase the preparedness of U.S. forces in case the United States should become involved in war; and to serve as mediator. Although America was officially neutral, many policies favored the Allied countries (Great Britain, France, and Russia) over the Axis powers (Germany, Austria-Hungary, Italy, and Turkey). For example, President Wilson did not protest a British blockade (closing off) of German ports, even though the blockade damaged U.S. trade in a large and vital market.

Germany established military superiority on land, but Great Britain ruled the seas. Germany relied on submarines, called U-boats, to steal through the blockade and into open seas where they could attack British vessels. As the British blockade continued, Germany began attacking nonmilitary sea vessels that could carry supplies or arms to their enemies.

American popular sentiment fell clearly on the side of the Allies when a U-boat torpedoed the British ocean liner

Woodrow Wilson toured the country in 1915 to convince Americans that the nation was prepared for war, in case the country should enter the war in Europe that would become known as World War I. Sensing the public's desire to avoid war, however, his campaign managers promoted him for the election of 1916 with the slogan, "He kept us out of war." Within four months of his second term, however, Wilson asked Congress to declare war on Germany.

Lusitania, killing over 1,000 passengers, including 128 Americans. Following international pressure over the *Lusitania* incident and others involving merchant ships, Germany agreed to attack only military vessels. Meanwhile, Wilson and his envoys (diplomatic agents) continued to mediate the conflict; they asked each of the nations involved to state their respective terms for peace as a means for beginning negotiations.

Wilson's domestic triumphs were overshadowed by foreign conflicts. Additionally, his New Freedom program—meant to reform business and banking and provide more safeguards for the working class—were opposed by big business and the wealthy. At the Democratic convention in 1916, there was no doubt that Wilson would be nominated as the party's candidate, but there were concerns about his fading popularity. When Wilson accepted the nomination, he addressed the concerns of many Americans about the war in Europe by stressing how well his administration had put the country into a state of preparedness. The enthusiastic reception that this part of his speech received produced a campaign theme that would prove to be ironic: his campaign slogan became "He kept us out of war." Early in his second term, Wilson would ask Congress to declare war on Germany.

Americans were angered when a German U-boat torpedoed the British ocean liner *Lusitania,* killing over one thousand passengers. This cartoon likens Germany to a pirate with no respect for other countries; the sinking *Lusitania* is in the background.
Drawing by John Scott Clubb. Courtesy of the Library of Congress.

Wilson was reelected by a slim margin—so thin, in fact, that if fifteen hundred votes in California had gone to his opponent, Charles Evans Hughes (1862–1948; see box in **Warren G. Harding** entry in volume 4), instead of to Wilson, Hughes would have won enough electoral votes to become president.

A world safe for democracy

Shortly into his second term, Wilson's hopes for peace ended. Germany renewed its aggression at sea early in 1917,

The "Big Three" Allied heads of state: (Left to right) British prime minister David Lloyd George, French prime minister Georges Clemenceau, and U.S. president Woodrow Wilson, at a peace conference in Paris, France, in 1919. *Reproduced by permission of Archive Photos.*

attempting to move to an ultimate triumph and feeling that the United States was already involved with German enemies. Diplomatic relations between the United States and Germany were broken off in February 1917. The president who had "kept us out of war" addressed Congress in April and asked it for a declaration of war. As usual, Wilson's eloquence (clear, well-formed speaking) helped provide a clear understanding of goals. He spoke of the need for "disciplined might"—military

On the home front, President Wilson mobilized the country for war: Railroads fell under government control when their service was needed; Henry Ford's new automobile factory was converted to produce submarine-chasing boats; and even the White House lawn served the country—a flock of sheep grazed there, and their wool was sold to raise money for the Red Cross.

power that would "make the world safe for democracy," while he continued to pursue diplomatic solutions to conflict.

Wilson proceeded vigorously in his role as commander in chief. The American military expanded from 225,000 men (compared with 11 million Germans pressed into service) to over 4 million. When some railroad authorities were slow to respond to government demands for service at the sake of their business interests, Wilson led the government in assuming control of all industries needed to further the war effort. In addition, Wilson appointed a professional soldier— General Pershing—to command American forces in Europe.

Wilson believed that World War I could be—as some optimists termed it—"the war to end all wars." This idealism was clearly spelled out in Wilson's famous Fourteen Points speech (see **Woodrow Wilson** primary source entry in volume 4). As the war dragged on through 1917 into 1918, Wilson released a document to Congress on January 4, 1918, to clearly spell out his mission, which he presented as fourteen points. Along with diplomatic means for securing peace, the speech called for the establishment of a League of Nations (see box) that could exert moral leadership and help nations avoid future wars. Wilson's pursuit of peace based on his Fourteen Points made him an internationally respected statesman of a stature no previous American president had attained. His mediation efforts contributed greatly to the armistice that was reached in November 1918. (An armistice is an agreement to cease fire while warring parties negotiate a peace settlement.) The following year, Wilson was awarded the Nobel Peace Prize, an annual award given to an individual or a group that promotes the cause of peace.

Loses the battle at home

While he had won international admiration, Wilson's fortunes at home were less solid. He actively campaigned for Democrats during the November 1918 congressional elections, but American voters elected Republican majorities to both the Senate and the House for the first time during Wilson's presidency. The next month Wilson traveled to Paris to personally attend peace talks—the first time a sitting American president had left the country for an extended period. For

The League of Nations

The League of Nations was proposed by Woodrow Wilson in Article XIV of his Fourteen Points, forming the basis of the Covenant of the League of Nations that was part of the Treaty of Versailles. However, the treaty was never ratified by the U.S. Senate. Among the concerns of senators was Article X of the treaty, which required all members to preserve the territorial independence of all other members. Violations could be met with joint action among nations against aggressors. A strong group of politicians and citizens objected to the U.S. military participating with those of other nations, preferring that the United States maintain independence and free decision-making in employing military forces.

Without treaty ratification, the United States never became an official member of the League, which existed from 1920 to 1946. American diplomats assisted in League activities and attended meetings, but lack of official American participation lessened the effectiveness of the League. For example, the League rarely had the resources to support its innovative concept that defined "criminal" threats of war against which the collective security of the League's nations could be marshalled. The League was successful in supervising and eventually granting independence to territories that had been colonies of Germany and Turkey before World War I, restricting international drug traffic, and aiding refugees of World War I. Some other effec-

President Woodrow Wilson on a train tour in 1919 to promote the League of Nations. He suffered a stroke shortly thereafter.
Reproduced by permission of the Corbis Corporation.

tive League activities, such as monitoring and improving international health and labor conditions, were continued through the United Nations (UN).

In 1946, the League of Nations voted to dissolve, and much of its organization was subsumed by the United Nations. The UN had more active participation from major powers, including the United States, making it a more effective peacekeeping organization while continuing the social work. The UN benefitted from the successes and failures of the League to effect a stronger international alliance.

Woodrow Wilson is viewed as having been an excellent wartime president, effectively using his power as commander in chief while also seeking diplomatic solutions to end the war. His diplomacy made him an international hero, and he was awarded the Nobel Peace Prize in 1919.

his delegation, Wilson picked almost all Democrats, further offending Republicans.

At the talks that eventually led to the Treaty of Versailles (vair-SIGH), Wilson argued successfully for fairness on many issues, but he had to compromise on two vital points: France and England insisted on huge war reparations against Germany; and Japan, which had joined the Allies late in the war, was allowed to keep control of a province of China it had invaded. Wilson deeply opposed both resolutions, but he compromised to keep alive his vision for the League of Nations.

Wilson had arrived in Europe triumphant in his role as peacemaker, but he returned to an uninterested public in the United States that was tired of war and foreign entanglements. The U.S. Senate, which must ratify all treaties by a two-thirds majority, began debating various aspects of the Treaty of Versailles and proposed amendments. Wilson misjudged the country's political and popular sentiments. He insisted to the Senate that no modifications to the treaty were acceptable, and he fought hard for the establishment of a League of Nations against lukewarm interest. When he met stern opposition on the treaty from Republicans, Wilson tried to take his case to the American people, as he had done successfully on domestic issues at the beginning of his presidency.

Starting in Columbus, Ohio, on September 4, 1919, Wilson went on an exhausting cross-country tour in which he often made several speeches a day. Everywhere he went, he was greeted with enthusiastic crowds wanting to cheer the president who had led the nation through war, but he was unable to collect enough support to pressure Congress to pass the treaty. He pressed on to the West Coast, and then turned back east, but the strain of the effort overcame him. Wilson collapsed after making a speech in Pueblo, Colorado, on September 25. He returned to Washington, D.C., to recover, but he suffered a severe stroke on October 2.

Meanwhile, debate on the treaty raged on in the Senate. Wilson was ill, unable to lobby senators. Republicans, led by U.S. senator Henry Cabot Lodge (1850–1924; see box) of Massachusetts, had many doubts, including America's participation in the League of Nations. Wilson continued to insist on the entire treaty as it stood and instructed Democrats to vote against any modifications. Twice the treaty was voted on and both times—in November 1919 and March 1920—it failed to pass. Wilson responded to the second failed vote by announcing that the 1920 presidential election would serve as a referendum on the treaty and his vision of the League of Nations. (A referendum is the submission of a piece of legislation to a direct popular vote.)

Battle fatigue

Wilson's all-or-nothing approach on the Treaty and his inability to inspire the people to rally for its ratification cost him and his supporters. If the 1920 election was indeed a referendum, then it showed how clearly the people were tired of war issues and progressive domestic policies. Republican **Warren G. Harding** (1865–1923; see entry in volume 4) won in a landslide over Democrat James M. Cox (1870–1957). The United States soon made a separate peace with Germany, and Harding vowed that the United States would never enter the League of Nations. Harding conducted a pro-business administration in perfect timing with a postwar economic boom that ushered in a period of prosperity called the "Roaring Twenties."

Wilson remained debilitated (ill and disabled) from the stroke he suffered in 1919. The public was never fully informed about the severity of the stroke and his incapacitation (inability to function normally). Wilson retired quietly to a large home in Washington, D.C., and lived there for the remainder of his life with his wife, Edith. She had been his closest companion during his final year as president, making decisions about which issues he would address and which advisors he would see. Wilson died on February 3, 1924.

Edith Wilson continued to live in the house until her death in 1961. She left the house to the National Trust for Historic Preservation. The house has served since as the Woodrow Wilson House Museum.

Legacy

Woodrow Wilson's lasting influence on the nation is as strong as that of any president. Many of the early reforms of his New Freedom program, including the Federal Reserve

When Woodrow Wilson appointed Anne Abbott Adams to be assistant attorney general in 1920, it marked the highest level of the executive branch—a subcabinet post—that a woman had attained.

Henry Cabot Lodge

Henry Cabot Lodge was the man who led the successful fight against President Woodrow Wilson's plan for American involvement in the League of Nations. Lodge was born May 12, 1850, in Boston, Massachusetts. His father, John Ellerton Lodge, was a prosperous merchant who added to his fortune when U.S. trade with China was expanded. Lodge's mother, Anna Cabot, was granddaughter of George Cabot (1752–1823), a leading Federalist (proponent for a strong federal government) during the early years of the nation. Lodge graduated with a bachelor's degree from Harvard University, then married his cousin, Anna Cabot Davis, daughter of Rear Admiral Charles H. Davis (1807–1877).

From 1873 to 1876, Lodge was assistant editor of the *North American Review,* which published his doctoral thesis (a scholarly paper), "The Anglo-Saxon Land Law." Graduated from Harvard Law School in 1874, Lodge was admitted to the Boston bar (certified to practice law) in 1875. Meanwhile, he completed his work for the first doctorate in political science ever obtained at Harvard. He also wrote several books, including three biographies in the American Statesman Series, *Alexander Hamilton* (1882), *Daniel Webster* (1882), and *George Washington* (1888).

In 1879, Lodge was elected to the Massachusetts House of Representatives and was reelected to a second term, but he failed in a bid for state Senate and in an attempt to secure the Republican nomination for Congress. After managing the successful Massachusetts gubernatorial campaign of George D. Robinson (1834-1896), Lodge was a delegate to the Republican National Convention in 1884. In 1886, he was elected to Congress by a narrow margin. In January 1893, the Massachusetts state legislature voted him to the U.S. Senate (in those days, U.S. senators were elected by state legislators). In all, Lodge served as a U.S. congressman for six years and a senator for thirty years.

As a congressman, Lodge was a consistent supporter of civil service reform and the protective tariff during the administrations of **Benjamin Harrison** (1833–1901; see entry in volume 3), **Grover Cleveland** (1837–1908; see entry in volume 3), and William McKinley. Like his friend, President Theodore Roosevelt, Lodge supported several measures where the government regulated industry, including the Pure Food and Drug Act (1906) and the Hepburn Act (1906), where he wrote a provision that put private oil lines under the supervision of the Interstate Commerce Commission. With McKinley and Roosevelt, Lodge believed that American expansion was necessary for economic progress; thus, he supported a strong navy,

Henry Cabot Lodge.
Courtesy of the Library of Congress.

territorial acquisition, and power diplomacy—and called for the annexation of Hawaii during the controversy over that issue in the 1890s. He was a leading advocate of war in 1898 with Spain; urged annexation of the Philippines after the United States won control of that territory following victory in the Spanish-American War (1889); and supported the aggressive Caribbean policy of Theodore Roosevelt.

Lodge had several disagreements with President Woodrow Wilson. He did not believe Wilson was sufficiently aggressive toward Mexico during conflicts between the two nations from 1913 to 1917. He challenged Wilson's neutrality policies and reluctance to arm the nation during World War I. Most significantly, his leadership of the fight against the ratification of the Treaty of Versailles and the Covenant of the League of Nations made him a national figure. Lodge favored heavy reparations (payment for damages) against Germany and was opposed to coupling the Versailles Treaty and the League of Nations. As chairman of the Senate's Foreign Relations Committee, Lodge presented reservations against the treaty and the covenant. The two documents (with the reservations added) were rejected, chiefly by the votes of Democratic senators following the advice of President Wilson, who insisted on no reservations or revisions. Neither side compromised; Wilson lost when the treaty and U.S. participation in the League of Nations was twice rejected by the Senate.

The presidential election of 1920, where the issue of the entry of the United States into the League of Nations was an outstanding issue, was won by Republican Warren G. Harding. Lodge was one who had been chiefly responsible for the nomination of Harding; with Harding's election, Lodge's influence in the field of foreign relations became even greater. Lodge's triumphs at this time were overshadowed by his failing health. He underwent two surgeries and never recovered. He died on November 9, 1924, at the age of 74.

A Selection of Wilson Landmarks

Boyhood Home of President Woodrow Wilson. 419 Seventh St., Augusta, GA 30903. (706) 724-0436. Home of the future president from 1857 to 1870.

Washington National Cathedral. Final resting place of Woodrow Wilson. See http://www.cathedral.org/cathedral/ (accessed on August 17, 2000).

Woodrow Wilson Birthplace. 18-24 Coalter St., Staunton, VA 24402-0024. (540) 885-9897. Large twelve-room house and nearby museum are filled with Wilson artifacts. See http://www.woodrowwilson.org/index2.html (accessed on August 17, 2000).

Woodrow Wilson Boyhood Home. 1705 Hampton St., Columbia, SC 29201. (803) 252-3964. Victorian-style home of the Wilson family from 1870 to 1874. See http://www.columbiasc.net/city/homes.htm#woodrow (accessed on August 17, 2000).

Woodrow Wilson House. 2340 S St., N.W., Washington, DC 20008. (202) 387-4062. Woodrow and Edith Wilson retired to this home following the end of his presidency in 1921. The former president died here in 1924 and the former first lady lived here until her death in 1961. See http://www.woodrowwilsonhouse.org/ (accessed on August 17, 2000).

System, the graduated income tax, and the Federal Trade Commission, were still intact at the end of the twentieth century. Other measures significantly reformed labor laws and banking practices.

His lasting importance is at least as strong internationally. The League of Nations failed, in general, but its successor, the United Nations, continued the positive work of the League and became a more effective body through greater international cooperation, including the active participation of the United States.

Wilson's conduct as a president during wartime remains highly respected. He kept the nation from entering the conflict and then ensured that the United States was prepared with the necessary resources to win once the country did enter the war. Many of the same methods of preparedness on the home front (civilian activities during wartime) were used by President **Franklin D. Roosevelt** (1882–1945; see entry in volume 4) during World War II (1939-45); Roosevelt had

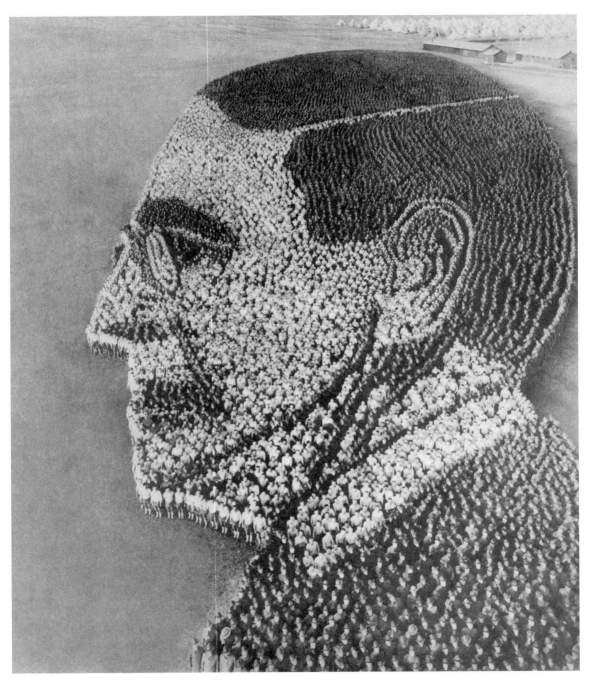

U.S. Army soldiers honor Woodrow Wilson by forming a profile of the president on the parade grounds of Camp Sherman in January 1918.

Photograph by Arthur Mole. Reproduced by permission of the Corbis Corporation.

served in the Wilson administration as assistant secretary of the navy.

Wilson's policies with Mexico and Latin America were not as fruitful. Additionally, his domestic program, the New Freedom, began to lose momentum in the latter part of his first term, perhaps reflected best in the slim margin of victory with which he was elected to a second term.

Many of Wilson's failures, particularly the League of Nations, were noble causes. Had the Treaty of Versailles been more to his expectations, many argue, war reparations against Germany would not have been so severe. The severe compensations demanded of Germany plunged that country into a decade of economic hardship and a turn to fascism in the 1930s that led to World War II.

Wilson increased the United States' participation in world affairs more than any previous president, setting America on its course of becoming a world power. Many of his progressive domestic ideas not fully realized during his term were revived and reformed by Roosevelt, contributing to the New Deal policies of the 1930s. The New Deal helped the country survive the Great Depression (1929–41).

Where to Learn More

Bailey, Thomas A. *Woodrow Wilson and the Lost Peace.* New York: Macmillan, 1944.

Baker, Ray Stannard. *Woodrow Wilson, Life and Letters.* Garden City, NY: Doubleday, Page, 1927. Reprint, New York: Greenwood Press, 1968.

Blum, John M. *Woodrow Wilson and the Politics of Morality.* Boston: Little, Brown, 1956.

Bragdon, Henry Wilkinson. *Woodrow Wilson: The Academic Years.* Cambridge, MA: Harvard University Press, 1967.

Clements, Kendrick A. *The Presidency of Woodrow Wilson.* Lawrence: University Press of Kansas, 1992.

Ferrell, Robert H. *Woodrow Wilson and World War I: 1917–1921.* New York: Harper, 1986.

Knock, Thomas J. *To End All Wars: Woodrow Wilson and the Quest for a New World Order.* New York: Oxford University Press, 1992.

Levin, Norman Gordon, Jr. *Woodrow Wilson and World Politics: America's Response to War and Revolution.* New York: Oxford University Press, 1968.

Link, Arthur S. *Wilson.* 5 vols. Princeton, NJ: Princeton University Press, 1947.

Miller, William J. *Henry Cabot Lodge: A Biography.* New York: Heineman, 1967.

Pershing, John J. *My Experiences in the First World War.* New York: Da Capo Press, 1995.

Seymour, Charles. *Woodrow Wilson in Perspective.* Stamford, CT: Overbrook Press, 1956.

Smith, Gene A. *Until the Last Trumpet Sounds: The Life of General of the Armies John J. Pershing.* New York: Wiley, 1998.

Wilson, Woodrow. *Congressional Government: A Study in American Politics.* Boston: Houghton Mifflin, 1885. Reprint, Baltimore: Johns Hopkins University Press, 1981.

Wilson, Woodrow. *Division and Reunion, 1829–1889.* New York: Longmans, Green, 1893. Reprint, 1926.

Wilson, Woodrow. *George Washington.* New York: Harper, 1897. Reprint, New York: Schocken Books, 1969.

Wilson, Woodrow. *A History of the American People.* New York: Harper, 1902. Reprint, 1918.

Wilson, Woodrow. *Mere Literature, and Other Essays.* Boston: Houghton Mifflin, 1896. Reprint, Freeport, NY: Books for Libraries Press, 1971.

Wilson, Woodrow. *An Old Master, and Other Political Essays.* New York: C. Scribner's, 1893. Reprint, Freeport, NY: Books for Libraries Press, 1973.

Wilson, Woodrow. *The Papers of Woodrow Wilson.* Edited by Arthur S. Link. 69 volumes. Princeton, NJ: Princeton University Press, 1966–94.

Wilson, Woodrow. *The State: Elements of Historical and Practical Politics: A Sketch of Institutional History and Administration.* Boston: D.C. Heath, 1889. Reprint, Farmingdale, NY: Dabor Social Science Publications, 1978.

Ellen Wilson

Born May 15, 1860
Savannah, Georgia
Died August 6, 1914
Washington, D.C.

Brief first lady was dedicated to humanitarian causes

Ellen Wilson was modest and artistic. She preferred private, small dinners at the White House instead of large-scale parties and balls. She had a studio room with a skylight built in the White House, where she could practice her painting. She did not have much time to pursue the craft, however, since she helped arrange White House weddings for two daughters and served as hostess for many private dinners. Her time for painting was also cut short when she was stricken by Bright's disease, a kidney ailment. Ellen Wilson died on August 6, 1914, just a year and a half into her husband's presidency.

With her love of art and her gentle nature, Ellen was a good companion for **Woodrow Wilson** (1856–1924; see entry in volume 4), who was studious and enjoyed literature, along with history, law, and political science. She would have been an especially valuable companion to him during the period when she died, as a crisis in Europe occurred that quickly grew into World War I (1914–18).

Ellen Louise Axson was born in Rome, Georgia, on May 15, 1860. Like Woodrow Wilson's father, her father was a Presbyterian minister. Shortly after Ellen was born, the two

"I am naturally the most unambitious of women and life in the White House has no attractions for me."

Ellen Wilson

Ellen Wilson.
Courtesy of the Library of Congress.

ministers had a meeting. Joseph Wilson brought along his son, Woodrow, who was four, and that was the first time that Woodrow and Ellen met. The next time was over twenty years later, in 1883, when they soon fell in love. "Miss Elly Lou," as she was called, was caring for her father, who was in despair over the death of Ellen's mother.

Ellen had graduated from Rome Female College in Georgia, showing talent as an artist and a teacher. Lack of funds stopped her from moving forward with those pursuits, and she returned home. Woodrow Wilson journeyed to Rome, Georgia, in April 1883 to attend to Axson family legal matters. At the time, Woodrow was a lawyer with a practice in Atlanta, Georgia. He was unhappy with his occupation and returned to college that fall, studying at Johns Hopkins University in Baltimore to become a teacher. During the summer of 1883, Wilson courted Miss Elly Lou and proposed to her in August before leaving for school.

While Wilson completed his education in Baltimore, Ellen continued to care for her father and her younger brother. Her father committed suicide in 1884. Ellen and her brother moved to New York, where she enrolled in New York's Art Students League. She and Woodrow were married in 1885, the same year he graduated from Johns Hopkins and accepted a teaching position at Bryn Mawr College in Pennsylvania. Wilson's career as an academic began to prosper when he took a position at Wesleyan College in Middletown, Connecticut, in 1887. He also became a popular author during the 1880s and 1890s for works on American government, essays on literature, and a biography of **George Washington** (1732–1799; see entry in volume 1). Ellen, who shared his passion for literature, helped review his writings.

Both Ellen and Woodrow were proud of their southern roots. They lived in the North, but when time neared for Ellen to deliver each of the couple's first two daughters, Ellen traveled back home to Rome. The couple's first two daughters—Margaret and Jessie—were born southerners. A third daughter—Eleanor—was born in Connecticut.

After Wilson turned down several offers for teaching and administrative positions, he became a professor at Princeton University in 1890. While Ellen was raising her daughters during the 1890s, she was also able to pursue her interest in painting. Already accomplished in doing crayon portraits, she practiced and became an expert landscape painter. She also took an interest in the American impressionist style while attending an artist colony in Old Lyme, Connecticut. Her painting was so accomplished that Ellen Wilson began entering them in juried competitions under pseudonyms (other names). Her landscape paintings won awards in New York and Chicago art shows, and she sold several paintings to help raise funds for an art school in her native Rome, Georgia. After Wilson became president of Princeton in 1902, Ellen redesigned the presidential grounds. She was also active in helping to improve student living conditions, including modernizing the college's infirmary (medical center).

Ellen was not outwardly active politically. She preferred quiet, private dinners as opposed to public parties. Her influence on the president, then, was more subtle and behind-the-scenes. For example, during Wilson's campaign to become the Democratic Party nominee for president in 1912, she convinced her husband to renew acquaintances with William Jennings Bryan (1860–1925; see box in **William McKinley** entry in volume 3). The relationship between the two men had been strained after Wilson criticized Bryan's policies when Bryan was a presidential candidate several years earlier. They settled their differences at Ellen's urging. Bryan later proved essential to Wilson's successful Democratic nomination as president.

Another behind-the-scenes triumph for Mrs. Wilson occurred early in Wilson's presidency. Ellen arranged a small dinner with several congressmen who were wary of Wilson's plan to reduce tariffs (taxes on imports). At the dinner, Wilson was able to convince the congressmen about the importance of tariff reform, which helped lead to the first significant legislation to pass during Wilson's presidency.

Ellen Wilson's time in the White House was short—a year and a half—but quite eventful. Daughters Jessie and Eleanor had White House weddings, and Ellen Wilson also presided over the first national celebration of Mother's Day, in May 1913. Shortly after her husband's election, she became active in promoting better living conditions for federal employees and for residents in the nation's capital. Astonished at slums and alleyways of Washington, D.C., Ellen Wilson led a delegation of congressmen to tour those areas in hopes of convincing them to enact legislation.

In 1914, Ellen Wilson was slowed by Bright's disease—the most common form of nephritis, a general term that describes inflammatory diseases of the kidney. Following her death in August 1914, Congress enacted legislation in her honor for funding to improve living conditions among the economically disadvantaged of Washington, D.C.

Where to Learn More

McAdoo, Eleanor Wilson, ed. *The Priceless Gift: The Love Letters of Woodrow Wilson and Ellen Axson Wilson.* New York: McGraw-Hill, 1962. Reprint, Westport, CT: Greenwood Press, 1975.

Saunders, Frances Wright. *Ellen Axson Wilson: First Lady Between Two Worlds.* Chapel Hill: University of North Carolina Press, 1985.

Edith Wilson

Born October 15, 1872
Wytheville, Virginia
Died December 28, 1961
Washington, D.C.

Stood personal guard over her husband President Wilson after he suffered a stroke and was accused by some of directing policy during that time

Edith Wilson grew up from being a girl who did not leave her hometown until she was twelve to become a world traveler, successful businesswoman, and influential first lady. According to some sources, she virtually ran the country during the last year of her husband's administration, when **Woodrow Wilson** (1856–1924; see entry in volume 4) had become disabled by a stroke. It is more likely that during this period she simply expanded the role of confidante and advisor that she had always enjoyed with the president.

Mrs. Wilson was born Edith Bolling in Wytheville, Virginia, on October 15, 1872. She was the seventh of eleven children and fourth of five daughters in the family of Judge William Holcombe Bolling and his wife, Sallie. Edith's mother, born Sallie White, could trace her ancestry back seven generations to an original Virginia colonist, John Rolfe (1585–1622). He was the white man who married Native American princess Pocahontas (c.1595–1617).

During the Civil War (1861–65), the Bolling family lost their property, including the family plantation and the slaves they owned. The large family lived in "genteel pover-

> "Woodrow Wilson was first my beloved husband who I was trying to save, after that he was president of the United States."
>
> *Edith Wilson*

Edith Wilson.
Courtesy of the Library of Congress.

ty," a term that describes people who do not have much money but who have social status and do not face desperate conditions. As the family gradually regained financial standing, they lived simply: Edith did not leave town until she was twelve years old, but at fifteen she was able to attend Martha Washington College, where she studied music. She received a fine education at home while growing up and helped raise her four younger siblings.

In 1893, while visiting her sister in Washington, D.C., Edith met businessman Norman Galt. He was a senior partner in his family's jewelry business and a cousin to her sister's husband. After a courtship of several years, Edith and Norman Galt were married in 1896. By that time, Norman Galt had assumed control of the family business, which included a jewelry store that was popular among the elite of Washington, D.C. The coupled traveled often. They had a child born in 1903, but the baby died in infancy.

Norman Galt, who was quite a few years older than Edith, died in 1908. Edith took control of her husband's business and promoted one of the firm's assistants, longtime employee Henry Christian Bergheimer, to manage the firm with her. Together they ran the business successfully for many years. Edith continued to travel, making frequent trips to Europe and Asia. She became the first woman in Washington to own and drive an electric car. She lived comfortably, and although she was well known in Washington, she rarely dabbled in political activities and was not active in such issues as women's suffrage.

In 1915, Edith became acquainted with Cary T. Grayson, President Woodrow Wilson's personal physician. Grayson introduced her to Wilson's cousin, Helen Woodrow Bones. Mrs. Bones was serving in many of the social capacities of first lady since the death in August 1914 of the president's wife, **Ellen Wilson** (1860–1914; see entry in volume 4). Edith and Helen became friends.

One day during mid-March 1915, Edith and Helen went for a walk on the White House grounds. Upon their return to the White House, they encountered the president and Grayson, who had just returned from playing a round of golf. Wilson, who had been in gloomy mourning since the death of his wife, was enchanted with Edith. He began writing notes and letters to Edith, then began courting her. They became engaged, but some of Wilson's advisors suggested that their relationship should remain private, fearing the public would not accept a president marrying so soon after the death of his wife.

Nevertheless, the engagement was announced in October, and Edith and Woodrow were married in a private ceremony in December 1915. There was no public backlash over the events. The White House staff noticed that the saddened president perked up and the White House again became festive.

As he had with Ellen, Wilson depended on his new wife for companionship. He read his speeches to Edith and used her suggestions. They discussed policy matters and she decoded messages from diplomat Edward House (1858–1938), who was trying to secure peace between Great Britain and Germany to end World War I (1914–18). Edith accompanied Wilson on major presidential trips, including the Paris peace talks that followed the 1918 armistice, which ended the fighting during World War I. She later accompanied him on tour across the United States when the president tried to rally the people to urge Congress to ratify the peace accord—the Treaty of Versailles (vair-SIGH)—without modifications. Significantly, Edith tried to convince the president to compromise on a few points in order for the treaty to pass the Senate and save his vision for a League of Nations (see box in **Woodrow Wilson** entry in volume 4). The president, however, resisted any modifications, and the treaty was never ratified by the Senate.

Wilson's health had been fragile throughout his lifetime. Edith Wilson saw that he maintained a healthy exercise routine, and she often golfed with the president. In mid-September 1919, during the speaking tour when Wilson tried to inspire public support for the Treaty of Versailles, the president collapsed in Colorado. While recovering back in Washington, D.C., he suffered a stroke on October 2. The public was not made aware of the severity of the stroke, which left Wilson bedridden, weak, and able to work only sparingly.

Edith Wilson took over routine duties, functioning as a sort of chief of staff. She decided which issues were most pressing for the president's attention, and she determined which staff members and officials the president would meet. While the presidency continued to operate successfully, this

Edith Wilson (far right), representing the Freedom from Hunger Campaign, meets with (left to right) singer Marian Anderson; George McGovern, director of the Food for Peace Program; President John F. Kennedy; and German chancellor Konrad Adenauer on November 22, 1961, about a month before she died.

Reproduced by permission of the Corbis Corporation.

"stewardship" on the part of the first lady proved controversial; some claim that Edith Wilson actually ran the country during the last year of the Wilson presidency. Most historians condemn this claim and agree with Edith Wilson's description of her role, which she later spelled out in her book, *My Memoir* (1938). She had always been a political confidante with the president, more so than any other previous first lady. Following his stroke and on the advice of the president's doctors, she managed his reduced schedule, which allowed the president to operate most effectively in short periods of activity to maintain his health. She did not initiate or make policy decisions and did not control the administration.

Edith and Woodrow Wilson retired to a large private home in Washington, D.C., in 1921. She nursed Wilson until his death in 1924. Edith Wilson remained active in Democratic politics and continued to operate her jewelry business. She sold the business to employees in 1934. She was active in foundations bearing the president's name and helped establish the Woodrow Wilson School of Public and International Affairs at Princeton University. At eighty-eight years of age, she took part in the inaugural (the swearing-in ceremony) of President **John F. Kennedy** (1917–1963; see entry in volume 5). She died later that year, on December 28, 1961—the anniversary of the date on which her second husband was born 105 years earlier.

Where to Learn More

Flanagan, Alice K. *Edith Bolling Galt Wilson*. New York: Children's Press, 1998.

Ross, Ishbel. *Power with Grace: The Life Story of Mrs. Woodrow Wilson*. New York: Putnam, 1975.

Shachtman, Tom. *Edith & Woodrow: A Presidential Romance*. New York: Putnam, 1981.

Smith, Gene. *When the Cheering Stopped: The Last Years of Woodrow Wilson*. New York: Morrow, 1964. Reprint, Alexandria, VA: Time-Life Books, 1982.

Wilson's War Message to Congress

Delivered on April 2, 1917; excerpted from
The World War I Document Archive **(Web site)**

*President Wilson asks Congress to declare war on Germany,
beginning American military participation in World War I*

Outlining the powers of the presidency, Article II of the Constitution states, "The President shall be Commander in Chief of the Army and Navy of the United States, and of the Militia of the several States, when called into the actual Service of the United States." The president, then, is the nation's chief commander during time of war. But the act of declaring war resides with Congress, as spelled out in the Constitution in Article I, Section 8. Therefore, the United States is never officially at war with another nation unless declared so by Congress. The powers to declare and lead in war are subject to the same checks and balances as other powers of the federal government. A president cannot pursue war without the permission of Congress.

In 1916, President **Woodrow Wilson** (1856–1924; see entry in volume 4) pursued negotiations between nations involved in World War I (1914–18). In December of that year, the German government informed the United States that it was prepared to participate in peace negotiations, but Great Britain refused because Germany had not announced any peace terms and its military alliance (called the Central Pow-

"[World War I] was a war determined upon as wars used to be determined upon in the old, unhappy days when peoples were nowhere consulted by their rulers and wars were provoked and waged in the interest of dynasties or of little groups of ambitious men who were accustomed to use their fellowmen as pawns and tools."

Woodrow Wilson

ers) had just conquered Romania and was in a favorable negotiating position. Wilson continued his efforts, but in January 1917 Germany announced that it would engage in full submarine warfare to stop shipping by or to Great Britain beginning on February 1; Germany hoped to defeat Great Britain in six months.

The United States had already expressed the view that unrestricted submarine warfare violated its rights as a neutral nation. When Germany proceeded to renew unrestricted submarine warfare, the United States on February 3 broke diplomatic relations with Germany for the first time, as did several Latin American nations. After several submarine attacks on American vessels, President Wilson asked Congress to declare war on Germany.

Things to remember while reading an excerpt from President Wilson's war message to Congress:

- The opening remarks by President Wilson reflected on a sequence of events culminating with Germany's unrestricted submarine warfare beginning in February 1917. Previously, German submarine warfare was restricted to its enemies' warships or ships suspected of carrying war-related cargoes. Wilson called the unrestricted submarine warfare being engaged by Germany since February 1 "warfare against mankind." Wilson was expressing outrage while being careful to place Germany's actions as a threat to all other nations.

- After stating alternatives to declarations of war, including "armed neutrality" (where a nation is prepared to engage in battle only after being attacked), Wilson declared that an officially declared war would be best. He was careful then to describe what would result (in the paragraph beginning "What this will involve is clear"). Many Americans did not want the United States to enter the war. Wilson was careful to try and persuade them with reasons why America should be involved.

- In the final paragraph, Wilson made it clear that America would be at war with the German government, not the German people. There were incidents of intimidation against German Americans in the United States since World War I began in 1914. Wilson concluded by calling the war an unjust action by the German government, begun by overly ambitious men without consulting the German people. That action contrasted with the more orderly and official process through which the United States was entering the war.

Excerpt from President Wilson's war message to Congress

I have called the Congress into extraordinary session because there are serious, very serious, choices of policy to be made, and made immediately, which it was neither right nor constitutionally permissible that I should assume the responsibility of making.

On the 3rd of February last, I officially laid before you the extraordinary announcement of the Imperial German government that on and after the 1st day of February it was its purpose to put aside all restraints of law or of humanity and use its submarines to sink every vessel that sought to approach either the ports of Great Britain and Ireland or the western coasts of Europe or any of the ports controlled by the enemies of Germany within the Mediterranean.

*That had seemed to be the object of the German submarine warfare earlier in the war, but since April of last year the Imperial government had somewhat restrained the commanders of its undersea craft in conformity with its promise then given to us that passenger boats should not be sunk and that due warning would be given to all other vessels which its submarines might seek to destroy, when no resistance was offered or escape attempted, and care taken that their crews were given at least a fair chance to save their lives in their open boats. The precautions taken were meager and **haphazard** enough, as was proved in distressing instance after instance in the progress of the cruel and unmanly business, but a certain degree of restraint was observed.*

The new policy has swept every restriction aside. Vessels of every kind, whatever their flag, their character, their cargo, their destination, their errand, have been ruthlessly sent to the bottom without

Haphazard: Disorderly or random.

*warning and without thought of help or mercy for those on board, the vessels of friendly neutrals along with those of **belligerents**. Even hospital ships and ships carrying relief to the sorely bereaved and stricken people of Belgium, though the latter were provided with safe conduct through the proscribed areas by the German government itself and were distinguished by unmistakable marks of identity, have been sunk with the same reckless lack of compassion or of principle.*

*I was for a little while unable to believe that such things would in fact be done by any government that had hitherto subscribed to the humane practices of civilized nations. International law had its origin in the attempt to set up some law which would be respected and observed upon the seas, where no nation had right of **dominion** and where lay the free highways of the world. By painful stage after stage has that law been built up, with meager enough results, indeed, after all was accomplished that could be accomplished, but always with a clear view, at least, of what the heart and conscience of mankind demanded. . . .*

The present German submarine warfare against commerce is a warfare against mankind. It is a war against all nations. American ships have been sunk, American lives taken in ways which it has stirred us very deeply to learn of; but the ships and people of other neutral and friendly nations have been sunk and overwhelmed in the waters in the same way. There has been no discrimination. The challenge is to all mankind.

*Each nation must decide for itself how it will meet it. The choice we make for ourselves must be made with a moderation of counsel and a **temperateness** of judgment befitting our character and our motives as a nation. We must put excited feeling away. Our motive will not be revenge or the victorious assertion of the physical might of the nation, but only the vindication of right, of human right, of which we are only a single champion.*

*When I addressed the Congress on the 26th of February last, I thought that it would suffice to assert our neutral rights with arms, our right to use the seas against unlawful interference, our right to keep our people safe against unlawful violence. But armed neutrality, it now appears, is impracticable. Because submarines are in effect outlaws when used as the German submarines have been used against merchant shipping, it is impossible to defend ships against their attacks as the law of nations has assumed that merchantmen would defend themselves against **privateers** or cruisers, visible craft giving chase upon the open sea. . . .*

Belligerents: Those who instigate a conflict.

Dominion: Power over an area.

Temperateness: Even temper.

Privateers: Non-military merchants who are paid and prepared to fight for a nation.

Complete American Presidents Sourcebook

Armed neutrality is ineffectual enough at best; in such circumstances and in the face of such pretensions it is worse than ineffectual: it is likely only to produce what it was meant to prevent; it is practically certain to draw us into the war without either the rights or the effectiveness of belligerents. There is one choice we cannot make, we are incapable of making: we will not choose the path of submission and suffer the most sacred rights of our nation and our people to be ignored or violated. The wrongs against which we now array ourselves are no common wrongs; they cut to the very roots of human life.

With a profound sense of the solemn and even tragical character of the step I am taking and of the grave responsibilities which it involves, but in unhesitating obedience to what I deem my constitutional duty, I advise that the Congress declare the recent course of the Imperial German government to be in fact nothing less than war against the government and people of the United States; that it formally accept the status of belligerent which has thus been thrust upon it; and that it take immediate steps, not only to put the country in a more thorough state of defense but also to exert all its power and employ all its resources to bring the government of the German Empire to terms and end the war.

What this will involve is clear. It will involve the utmost practicable cooperation in counsel and action with the governments now at war with Germany and, as incident to that, the extension to those governments of the most liberal financial credits, in order that our resources may so far as possible be added to theirs. It will involve the organization and mobilization of all the material resources of the country to supply the materials of war and serve the incidental needs of the nation in the most abundant and yet the most economical and efficient way possible. It will involve the immediate full equipment of the Navy in all respects but particularly in supplying it with the best means of dealing with the enemy's submarines. It will involve the immediate addition to the armed forces of the United States already provided for by law in case of war at least 500,000 men, who should, in my opinion, be chosen upon the principle of universal liability to service, and also the authorization of subsequent additional increments of equal force so soon as they may be needed and can be handled in training.

It will involve also, of course, the granting of adequate credits to the government, sustained, I hope, so far as they can equitably be sustained by the present generation, by well-conceived taxation. I *say sustained so far as may be equitable by taxation because it seems to me that it would be most unwise to base the credits which will now be necessary entirely on money borrowed. It is our duty, I most respectfully urge, to protect our people so far as we may against the very serious hardships and evils which would be likely to arise out of the **inflation** which would be produced by vast loans.*

In carrying out the measures by which these things are to be accomplished, we should keep constantly in mind the wisdom of interfering as little as possible in our own preparation and in the equipment of our own military forces with the duty—for it will be a very practical duty—of supplying the nations already at war with Germany with the materials which they can obtain only from us or by our assistance. They are in the field and we should help them in every way to be effective there.

I shall take the liberty of suggesting, through the several executive departments of the government, for the consideration of your committees, measures for the accomplishment of the several objects I have mentioned. I hope that it will be your pleasure to deal with them as having been framed after very careful thought by the branch of the government upon which the responsibility of conducting the war and safeguarding the nation will most directly fall. . . .

We have no quarrel with the German people. We have no feeling toward them but one of sympathy and friendship. It was not upon their impulse that their government acted in entering this war. It was not with their previous knowledge or approval. It was a war determined upon as wars used to be determined upon in the old, unhappy days when peoples were nowhere consulted by their rulers and wars were provoked and waged in the interest of dynasties or of little groups of ambitious men who were accustomed to use their fellowmen as pawns and tools. (The World War I Document Archive [Web site])

Inflation: An economic term that describes a situation where the costs of goods rise.

What happened next . . .

Congress declared war, and nearly two hundred thousand American troops were training in France within two months. By November 1918, the American Expeditionary

Force (AEF), as the U.S. military fighting in World War I was called, numbered nearly two million troops. By spring of 1918, U.S. troops were playing a major role as momentum in the war shifted to the side of the Allies—those nations, including the United States and Great Britain, at war with the Central Powers, led by Germany.

By November 1918, the German army was defeated, and national and local governments in Germany were replaced by a democratic government, the Republic of Germany. That government signed an armistice (a cease fire agreement) with the Allied nations. In the armistice, the German government acknowledged its acceptance of President Wilson's Fourteen Points (see **Woodrow Wilson** primary source entry in volume 4), an outline of peace terms and post-war activities. Negotiations for a peace treaty were held at the Palace of Versailles near Paris, France, beginning in 1919.

During the negotiations, the Allied Nations except for the United States sought revenge against the Central Powers—including payment for the cost of the war and control over lands Germany occupied during the war. Wilson opposed such stern measures, but he eventually relented in exchange for support for his proposed League of Nations (see box in **Woodrow Wilson** entry in volume 4). The League was to be an international alliance of nations through which conflicts could be addressed. The Treaty of Versailles was completed with harsh surrender terms against Germany. Some historians believe that the Treaty sowed the seeds for World War II, which began in 1939. The German nation suffered greatly during the 1920s, a circumstance preyed upon by Adolf Hitler (1889–1945), who became Germany's leader in the 1930s. Hitler soon had his army involved in armed aggression against neighboring nations of Germany.

The Treaty of Versailles was never ratified in the United States, where the executive branch negotiates treaties but the U.S. Senate has the power to accept or reject them (a two-thirds majority of senators must vote to accept a treaty for it to be ratified). Rejection of the treaty was a stunning blow to Wilson's presidency. His Democratic Party lost the presidential election of 1920. The United States made a separate peace pact with Germany and never joined the League of Nations. The League existed as a weak international body for more than two decades before being replaced by the much stronger United Nations in 1946, in which the United States participates.

Did you know . . .

- The Central Powers consisted of Germany, Austria-Hungary, and Turkey. Nations that declared war on one or all three of those nations included Brazil, China, Costa Rica, Cuba, France, Great Britain, Greece, Guatemala, Haiti, Honduras, Italy, Japan, Liberia, Montenegro, Nicaraugua, Panama, Romania, Russia, Serbia, and the United States.

Where to Learn More

Bailey, Thomas Andrew. *Wilson and the Peacemakers.* 2 vols. New York: Macmillan Co., 1947.

Clements, Kendrick A. *Woodrow Wilson, World Statesman.* Boston: Twayne, 1987. Reprint, Chicago: I. R. Dee, 1999.

Ferrell, Robert H. *Woodrow Wilson and World War I, 1917–1921.* New York: Harper & Row, 1986.

Great War Primary Documents Archive, Inc. "2 April, 1917: President Woodrow Wilson's War Message." *The World War I Document Archive.* [Online] http://www.lib.byu.edu/~rdh/wwi/1917/wilswarm.html (accessed on August 17, 2000).

Wilson's Fourteen Points

**Delivered to Congress on January 8, 1918;
excerpted from *InfoUSA* (Web site)**

*President Wilson defines America's goals for fighting in World
War I and proposes the League of Nations, an international body
that can address future conflicts*

The United States entered World War I (1914–18) in April 1917. A massive build-up of American troops occurred, swelling the military ranks from around five hundred thousand combat-ready soldiers in 1917 to around two million in 1918. Vital industries at home were geared to the war effort, building the boats, vehicles, and supplies needed for the war.

In January 1918, as American troops were being prepared for a more massive involvement, President **Woodrow Wilson** (1856–1924; see entry in volume 4) presented his Fourteen Points to Congress. The Fourteen Points summarize the aims of the Allied Powers—those nations united in the war against the Central Powers of Germany, Austria-Hungary, and Turkey. Later in 1918, the Fourteen Points became the list of demands the Central Powers had to meet in order to secure an armistice (cease fire) and begin serious peace negotiations.

Throughout the war, Wilson pursued various means to spur peace negotiations. Several key victories by Allied forces helped turn the momentum of the war against the Central Powers in 1918. With defeat imminent, the government of Germany was replaced and the nation was renamed

"What we demand in this war . . . is nothing peculiar to ourselves. It is that the world be made fit and safe to live in; and particularly that it be made safe for every peace-loving nation which, like our own, wishes to live its own life, determine its own institutions, be assured of justice and fair dealing by the other peoples of the world as against force and selfish aggression. "

Woodrow Wilson

the Republic of Germany. That government met the terms outlined in the Fourteen Points and an armistice was called in the fall of 1918. Peace negotiations and an official end to the war followed in 1919.

Things to remember while reading President Wilson's Fourteen Points:

- The opening statements presented legal reasons for America's involvement in World War I. Acts of aggression had threatened Americans ("violations of right had occurred"). President Wilson was careful to note that Americans were not engaged in war for gain, but simply to defend their rights. The passage ended by stating that peace was the ultimate goal (or "programme," as Wilson called it), and the terms of peace were then presented as fourteen points.

- The opening statements called for a free and open peace process, where negotiations were publicized. During the events that led to World War I, several nations had been engaged in secret negotiations against other nations. Those secret negotiations continued during the war. In early 1917, for example, before the United States entered World War I in April, a telegram from Germany's minister of foreign affairs, Alfred Zimmerman, to the German ambassador in Mexico was intercepted. The telegram was decoded and then released for publication. Known as the Zimmerman Note, the telegram revealed that Germany was prepared to offer an alliance to Mexico if the United States entered war against Germany. The German government would offer assistance to Mexico to regain territory in present-day Texas, Arizona, and New Mexico that Mexico lost in the Mexican War (1846–48). The Mexican government was also encouraged to try and convince Japan to join in an attack on the United States.

- Points I–V reiterated the demand for open negotiations and stated general international laws that should be respected by all nations. Points VI–XIII cited specific acts of aggression by the Central Powers and demanded that the illegal domination of nations and peoples that resulted from that aggression should be ended.

• Point XIV expressed Wilson's desire for a league of nations that would meet regularly to address potential conflicts of the future. Protection of political independence and respect for national boundaries would be the purpose of such an international alliance.

The Fourteen Points

It will be our wish and purpose that the processes of peace, when they are begun, shall be absolutely open and that they shall involve and permit henceforth no secret understandings of any kind.

*The day of conquest and **aggrandizement** is gone by; so is also the day of secret **covenants** entered into in the interest of particular governments and likely at some unlooked-for moment to upset the peace of the world. It is this happy fact, now clear to the view of every public man whose thoughts do not still linger in an age that is dead and gone, which makes it possible for every nation whose purposes are consistent with justice and the peace of the world to avow nor or at any other time the objects it has in view.*

*We entered this war because violations of right had occurred which touched us to the quick and made the life of our own people impossible unless they were corrected and the world secure once for all against their recurrence. What we demand in this war, therefore, is nothing peculiar to ourselves. It is that the world be made fit and safe to live in; and particularly that it be made safe for every peace-loving nation which, like our own, wishes to live its own life, determine its own institutions, be assured of justice and fair dealing by the other peoples of the world as against force and selfish aggression. All the peoples of the world are in effect partners in this interest, and for our own part we see very clearly that unless justice be done to others it will not be done to us. The **programme** of the world's peace, therefore, is our programme; and that programme, the only possible programme, as we see it, is this:*

I. Open covenants of peace, openly arrived at, after which there shall be no private international understandings of any kind but diplomacy shall proceed always frankly and in the public view.

Aggrandizement: Greatness.

Covenants: Agreements.

Programme: An older style of spelling "program," still used in Great Britain.

II. Absolute freedom of navigation upon the seas, outside territorial waters, alike in peace and in war, except as the seas may be closed in whole or in part by international action for the enforcement of international covenants.

III. The removal, so far as possible, of all economic barriers and the establishment of an equality of trade conditions among all the nations consenting to the peace and associating themselves for its maintenance.

IV. Adequate guarantees given and taken that national armaments will be reduced to the lowest point consistent with domestic safety.

*V. A free, open-minded, and absolutely impartial adjustment of all **colonial claims**, based upon a strict observance of the principle that in determining all such questions of sovereignty the interests of the populations concerned must have equal weight with the equitable claims of the government whose title is to be determined.*

VI. The evacuation of all Russian territory and such a settlement of all questions affecting Russia as will secure the best and freest cooperation of the other nations of the world in obtaining for her an unhampered and unembarrassed opportunity for the independent determination of her own political development and national policy and assure her of a sincere welcome into the society of free nations under institutions of her own choosing; and, more than a welcome, assistance also of every kind that she may need and may herself desire. The treatment accorded Russia by her sister nations in the months to come will be the acid test of their good will, of their comprehension of her needs as distinguished from their own interests, and of their intelligent and unselfish sympathy.

VII. Belgium, the whole world will agree, must be evacuated and restored, without any attempt to limit the sovereignty which she enjoys in common with all other free nations. No other single act will serve as this will serve to restore confidence among the nations in the laws which they have themselves set and determined for the government of their relations with one another. Without this healing act the whole structure and validity of international law is forever impaired.

*VIII. All French territory should be freed and the invaded portions restored, and the wrong done to France by **Prussia** in 1871 in the matter of **Alsace-Lorraine**, which has unsettled the peace of the world for nearly fifty years, should be righted, in order that peace may once more be made secure in the interest of all.*

Colonial claims: Part of the hostilities among European nations that led to World War I involved conflicts over their colonies in Africa.

Prussia: A kingdom and later a state of Germany. Prussia was the most powerful German state in the mid-nineteenth century after winning a series of wars against it neighbors.

Alsace-Lorraine: A region between Belgium, France, Germany, and Switzerland that had been controlled by France until Germany won it in 1871 after the Franco-Prussian War. The region went back to France following the Treaty of Versailles in 1919.

IX. A readjustment of the frontiers of Italy should be effected along clearly recognizable lines of nationality.

X. The peoples of Austria-Hungary, whose place among the nations we wish to see safeguarded and assured, should be accorded the freest opportunity to autonomous development.

XI. Rumania, Serbia, and Montenegro should be evacuated; occupied territories restored; Serbia accorded free and secure access to the sea; and the relations of the several **Balkan states** *to one another determined by friendly counsel along historically established lines of allegiance and nationality; and international guarantees of the political and economic independence and territorial integrity of the several Balkan states should be entered into.*

XII. The Turkish portion of the present **Ottoman Empire** *should be assured a secure sovereignty, but the other nationalities which are now under Turkish rule should be assured an undoubted security of life and an absolutely unmolested opportunity of autonomous development, and the* **Dardanelles** *should be permanently opened as a free passage to the ships and commerce of all nations under international guarantees.*

XIII. An independent Polish state should be erected which should include the territories inhabited by indisputably Polish populations, which should be assured a free and secure access to the sea, and whose political and economic independence and territorial integrity should be guaranteed by international covenant.

XIV. A general association of nations must be formed under specific covenants for the purpose of affording mutual guarantees of political independence and territorial integrity to great and small states alike.

In regard to these essential **rectifications** *of wrong and assertions of right we feel ourselves to be intimate partners of all the governments and peoples associated together against the* **Imperialists.** *We cannot be separated in interest or divided in purpose. We stand together until the end.*

For such arrangements and covenants we are willing to fight and to continue to fight until they are achieved; but only because we wish the right to prevail and desire a just and stable peace such as can be secured only by removing the chief provocations to war, which this programme does remove. We have no jealousy of German greatness, and there is nothing in this programme that impairs it.

Balkan states: Nations situated near the Balkan Peninsula in the Adriatic Sea. At that time, this included Serbia, which was taken over by Austria-Hungary, one of the Central Powers.

Ottoman Empire: A Turkish state that dominated the eastern Mediterranean area from the sixteenth through the nineteenth century. Following World War I, present-day Turkey was formed from the former Ottoman Empire.

Dardanelles: Narrow strait between the Gallipoli Peninsula in Europe and Turkey in Asia; site of World War I battles.

Rectifications: Actions taken to set things right.

Imperialists: Nations that seek to expand their area of land and the people under its command.

We grudge her no achievement or distinction of learning or of pacific enterprise such as have made her record very bright and very enviable. We do not wish to injure her or to block in any way her legitimate influence or power. We do not wish to fight her either with arms or with hostile arrangements of trade if she is willing to associate herself with us and the other peace-loving nations of the world in covenants of justice and law and fair dealing. We wish her only to accept a place of equality among the peoples of the world—the new world in which we now live—instead of a place of mastery. (InfoUSA [Web site])

What happened next . . .

The Fourteen Points was important for clarifying the goals of the United States and the Allied Powers in World War I. As the momentum of the war shifted to the Allies in 1918, the Points became the demands the Central Powers had to satisfy in order to begin peace negotiations. In the fall of 1918, a new German government accepted the terms of the Fourteen Points and an armistice was declared. Peace talks began in 1919.

Peace negotiations resulted in the Treaty of Versailles, named for the French palace outside of Paris where the negotiations were held. President Wilson represented the United States during the Treaty negotiations. He was dismayed at the hard line against Germany demanded by other Allied nations. Wilson's vision for an alliance of nations was only agreed to after he accepted the harsh surrender terms the other Allied nations imposed on Germany.

The League of Nations was established during the 1920s but proved mostly ineffective during the next two decades. The United States never joined the League, nor approved of the Treaty of Versailles. Despite the heroic stature as an international statesman that Wilson had attained—above that of any previous president—he could not rally Congress or the American people to favor the Treaty of Versailles and enter the League of Nations. It was a crushing defeat that left Wilson exhausted and his administration weak after nearly two full terms of triumphs. Tired of war and foreign entanglements, Americans voted Republican **Warren G. Harding** (1865–1923; see entry in volume 4) president in 1920 over Democrat James M. Cox (1870–1957), who had pledged to continue President Wilson's policies, including pushing for American involvement in the League of Nations.

Did you know . . .

- The leaders of the nations that won World War I were far less allied during the peace talks that led to the Treaty of Versailles than their nations' armies had been during the war. English prime minister David Lloyd George (1863–1945) and French premier Georges Clemenceau (1841–1929) nearly came to blows. Italian prime minister Vittorio Orlando (1860–1952) left the conference after U.S. president Wilson made a plea to the Italian people when Orlando disagreed with him on one issue. Clemenceau stated on one occasion that "Mr. Wilson bores me with his Fourteen Points; why, God Almighty has only ten!" (Clemenceau was referring to the ten commandments). In the end, the leaders of France, Germany, and Italy succeeded in their goal of "making Germany pay" (for war damages), while Wilson won acceptance of his plan for the League of Nations. However, Wilson faced more resistance at home.

Where to Learn More

Fleming, Denna Frank. *The United States and the League of Nations, 1918–1920.* New York: G. P. Putnam, 1932. Reprint, New York: Russell & Russell, 1968.

Jacobs, David. *An American Conscience: Woodrow Wilson's Search for World Peace.* New York: Harper & Row, 1973.

Smith, Gaddis. *Woodrow Wilson's Fourteen Points after 75 Years.* New York: Carnegie Council on Ethics and International Affairs, 1993.

Stone, Ralph A., ed. *Wilson and the League of Nations: Why America's Rejection?* New York: Holt, Rinehart and Winston, 1967. Reprint, Huntington, NY: R. E. Krieger, 1978.

U.S. Department of State. "Fourteen points speech (1918): Woodrow Wilson." *InfoUSA.* [Online] http://usinfo.state.gov/usa/infousa/facts/democrac/51.htm (accessed on August 17, 2000).

Warren G. Harding

Twenty-ninth president (1921–1923)

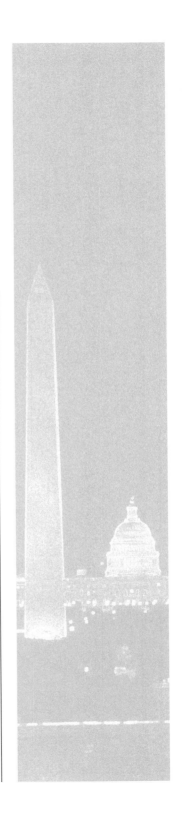

Warren G. Harding . . . 1015

    Fast Facts about Warren G. Harding (box) . . . 1016

    Warren G. Harding Timeline (box) . . . 1017

    Words to Know (box) . . . 1018

    Election Results (box) . . . 1021

    Andrew W. Mellon (box) . . . 1022

    Warren G. Harding Administration (box) . . . 1024

    Charles Evans Hughes (box) . . . 1026

    A Selection of Harding Landmarks (box) . . . 1031

Florence Harding . . . 1033

Primary source: Harding's Speech to a Special Session of Congress
President Harding announces what would become known as his "return to normalcy" plan for America following years of war and business regulation . . . **1039**

Warren G. Harding

Born November 2, 1865
Blooming Grove, Ohio
Died August 2, 1923
San Francisco, California

Twenty-ninth president of the United States
(1921–1923)

Unknowingly appointed to his administration
people who were corrupt and used their offices
for financial gain

When Warren G. Harding died about halfway through his term as president of the United States, he was unaware that several scandals would become the most remarkable events of his administration. Shortly after his death, the public learned that some of his appointees had defrauded (cheated) the government of millions, taken illegal kickbacks (secret payments) from private industry, and sold federal oil leases without proper approval.

A career politician, Harding rewarded his strongest supporters with important government posts when he was elected president. Those friends took advantage of Harding's trusting nature. But Harding had personal scandals as well. Although his wife, **Florence Harding** (1860–1924; see entry in volume 4), was the model of a modern, independent woman and an ambitious supporter for many of his plans, Harding indulged in extramarital affairs with at least two other women. One of them, Nan Britton (1896–1991), published a "tell-all" autobiography *(The President's Daughter)* in 1927. She claimed in the book that Harding was the father of her child.

"I can take care of my enemies all right. But my friends . . . they're the ones that keep me walking the floor nights!"

Warren Harding

Warren G. Harding.
Courtesy of the Library of Congress.

1015

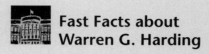

Fast Facts about Warren G. Harding

Full name: Warren Gamaliel Harding

Born: November 2, 1865

Died: August 2, 1923

Burial site: Marion Cemetery, reinterred in Harding Memorial Tomb, Marion, Ohio

Parents: George Tryon and Phoebe Elizabeth Dickerson Harding

Spouse: Florence Mabel Kling (1860–1924; m. 1891)

Children: None legitimate; one or two rumored illegitimate

Religion: Baptist

Education: Attended Iberia College (later Ohio Central College)

Occupations: Teacher; insurance salesman; editor; publisher

Government positions: Ohio state senator and lieutenant governor; U.S. senator from Ohio

Political party: Republican

Dates as president: March 4, 1921–August 2, 1923

Age upon taking office: 55

The news of scandal, both personal and political, served to make the president's achievements seem less important. But Harding was successful in bringing to America what he called a "return to normalcy." World War I (1914–18) was over: People wanted to return to their normal lives and many wanted the United States to be free of involvement in the affairs of foreign countries. During Harding's administration, business began booming, and the exciting period of prosperity known as "the Roaring '20s" came alive.

Ohio farmer's son

Warren G. Harding's family roots stretched back to an English Puritan, Richard Harding, who arrived in Massachusetts in 1623. The Puritans were a Protestant religious sect persecuted during the 1600s in England; many Puritans migrated to America in search of religious freedom. As settlement expanded from the original thirteen colonies, various Harding descendants moved westward, first to the Wyoming Valley of Pennsylvania, and then later to Ohio. Warren Harding, the first president born after the Civil War (1861–65), entered the world on November 2, 1865, in a farmhouse near Blooming Grove, Ohio. He was the oldest of eight children.

Harding's father, George (1844–1928), had various interests. He was a farmer who turned his attention to the study of medicine and became a physician. Then he bought a local newspaper. Young Warren, not yet ten, worked with the paper's printer as an errand boy. By the time he reached his teens, Harding had learned how to complete simple printing jobs and run a small printing press.

Meanwhile, his early education came in one-room schools. In his later teens, he attended Ohio Central College and graduated in 1882. He was trained as a teacher for rural schools.

While Harding was finishing his studies, his parents moved to Marion, Ohio, a busy, rapidly growing county seat (a town where all official business of a county is conducted). After deciding against a career as a teacher, Harding joined his parents and looked for a more suitable line of work. He sold insurance and earned enough money that he was able—with the help of two partners—to buy the struggling *Marion Star* newspaper for $300. Within a short time Harding had the newspaper on its feet. Subscriptions and advertising poured in, and he was able to buy out his partners. His publication became so popular, it put two rival newspapers out of business.

The success of the *Marion Star* helped to mold Harding's political philosophy. He beat his rivals by providing a newspaper that matched the strongly Republican views of the area. Harding's newspaper was careful not to offend Democratic readers. Whenever Republicans disagreed on issues and split into factions, Harding's newspaper urged compromise and party unity.

Still in his early twenties, Harding was publishing a newspaper with growing political influence. At about that time he met Florence Kling, an independent woman whose father was a merchant and the wealthiest man in Marion County. She had helped manage her father's business, but the relationship between Florence and her father had become strained after she became a single mother. In 1891, Harding and Florence were married. In Florence, who was five years older than her husband, Harding found a spouse who supported his political and professional ambitions and exerted herself tirelessly to advance his career.

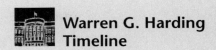

Warren G. Harding Timeline

1865: Born in Ohio

1884: Buys the *Marion Star* newspaper with the help of two partners

1891: Marries Florence Kling

1889–1903: Serves in Ohio state senate

1904–6: Serves as lieutenant governor of Ohio

1912: Makes speech for the renomination of President William Howard Taft at the 1912 Republican Party convention

1915–21: Serves in U.S. Senate

1921–23: Serves as twenty-ninth U.S. president

1923: Dies in California

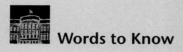 **Words to Know**

Federal budget: The list of all planned expenditures the federal government expects to make over a year.

GOP: Short for "Grand Old Party," a nickname of the Republican Party.

Immunity: Protection from prosecution; usually extended to someone who can help the prosecution win its case.

Keynote address: The most important speech during opening ceremonies of an organized meeting.

Kickbacks: Secret payments made to a group or business for having arranged a work or supply contract with another business. The other business makes a secret payment to influence the awarding of the contract.

Lieutenant governor: Similar to vice-president; an official who serves under an elected governor and succeeds to office if the governor is unable to perform his or her duties.

Lobbyist: A person hired to represent the interests of a particular group to elected officials.

Midterm elections: Congressional elections that occur halfway through a president's term. Midterm elections often determine which party will have House and Senate majorities during the final two years of a president's term.

Prohibition: The constitutional ban on the manufacture and sale of alcohol and alcoholic beverages from 1920 to 1933.

Spin doctoring: A late twentieth-century term that describes the practice of having political aides offer the best possible interpretation of a political statement or the effects of an event on their political boss.

Tariffs: Taxes placed on imported goods to raise their price and make them less attractive than goods produced by the nation importing them.

Teapot Dome scandal: Incident that became public following the death of Warren G. Harding that revealed that Navy secretary Edwin Denby transfered control of oil reserves in Teapot Dome, Wyoming, and Elk Hill, California, to the Department of the Interior, whose secretary, Albert Fall, secretly leased the reserve to two private oil operators, who paid Fall $400,000.

From Ohio to Washington, D.C.

Florence Harding began running the day-to-day operations of the *Marion Star* while Warren Harding expanded his political work. He had attended the Ohio State Republican Party convention in 1887 and was becoming quite well

known for his efforts—both in print and in person—on behalf of the GOP—the "Grand Old Party," as the Republican
Party is nicknamed. Handsome and well spoken, he projected
a good political image, that of a small-town, self-made man—
a man who has won success through hard work without the
financial help of others. After twelve years of stumping (campaigning; traveling around making speeches) for Republicans
and working for party unity, Harding won election to the
Ohio state senate in 1900.

Harding spent two terms in the Ohio senate. He was
loyal to Republican causes, continued his role as a peacemaker,
and gained a number of influential friends. Among them was
Harry M. Daugherty (1860–1941), a business lobbyist with political ambitions. (A lobbyist is a person hired to represent the
interests of a particular group to elected officials.) Daugherty
helped to further Harding's influence in the hotbed of Ohio
politics. In 1903, Harding was elected lieutenant governor (one
step below governor) of Ohio. He served one term in that post
and then returned to Marion and his newspaper work.

Although he spent the next few years out of political
office, Harding remained a prominent member of the Republican Party. In 1910, he ran for the position of governor of
Ohio. He lost the race but he gained national exposure. Just
two years later, President **William Howard Taft** (1857–1930;
see entry in volume 3)—an Ohio-born president—selected
Harding to nominate him again as Republican presidential
candidate at the party's national convention. Harding's political fortunes soared, and in 1914 he was elected to the U.S.
Senate by a margin of one hundred thousand votes.

Harding spent six undistinguished years in the U.S.
Senate. He missed forty percent of the roll-call votes during
that time, and he did not introduce any important legislation. Unlike a majority of Americans, he supported steps that
prepared the United States to fight in World War I, and he
was openly critical of the attempts of President **Woodrow
Wilson** (1856–1924; see entry in volume 4) to stay out of the
conflict. Otherwise, Harding voted in favor with Republicans
on matters that supported business. In 1916, Harding delivered the keynote address at the Republican National Convention. (A keynote address is the most important speech during
opening ceremonies of an organized meeting.)

When the United States entered World War I in 1917, Democrats and Republicans set aside their differences and acted in concert to win the conflict. Prohibition (a period of time after a constitutional amendment made the production and sale of alcohol a crime) and women's suffrage (women's right to vote) were two issues that Harding supported more for their political value than out of personal belief. As a social drinker, Harding did not practice the law of Prohibition; however, he could see that most of his constituents (the citizens he represented) supported the amendment. The same was true of giving women the right to vote. Harding cast his vote in favor of universal suffrage, even though he was privately opposed to it.

An issue that arose in 1919 concerning America's entrance into the League of Nations (see box in **Woodrow Wilson** entry in volume 4) was much more of a problem. In helping negotiate the Treaty of Versailles (1919) that ended World War I, President Woodrow Wilson pledged American involvement in the League of Nations—an organization made up of various nations that could address international disputes and avoid another massive war.

Some Americans, particularly a majority of Republicans, were against a provision that called for the American government to provide military support for any other League member facing an aggressor (another nation on the attack). Republicans objected that this provision would lead to U.S. involvement in any European conflict, no matter how minor. Republicans wanted to change the treaty, but President Wilson insisted that the treaty, which had to be ratified (passed) by the U.S. Senate, must be approved as it was presented. Debate over the League of Nations quickly turned hostile and was defined by outgoing president Wilson as the major issue of the 1920 presidential election.

The "smoke-filled room"

Harding's old friend Harry Daugherty convinced him to try for the presidential nomination in 1920. Harding was a longshot: Republicans boasted two popular frontrunners for the nomination—Frank O. Lowden (1861–1943) and General Leonard Wood (1860–1927), both of whom enjoyed wide

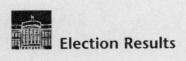

Election Results

1920

Presidential / Vice presidential candidates	Popular votes	Presidential electoral votes
Warren G. Harding / Calvin Coolidge (Republican)	16,152,200	404
James M. Cox / Franklin D. Roosevelt (Democratic)	9,147,353	127

Cox won the Democratic nomination on the forty-fourth ballot; one of the early leaders was former U.S. secretary of the treasury William G. McAdoo, who was also the son-in-law of the outgoing president, Woodrow Wilson.

popular support. Nevertheless, Harding allowed his name to be put into the field at the Republican National Convention.

To win the nomination, Harding needed 493 votes. Harding received sixty-five votes on the first ballot, while the two frontrunners split the rest of the vote so evenly that a tie appeared possible. Subsequent rounds of voting did little to alter matters, although Harding picked up a few additional votes in each round.

While supporters for the candidates debated with each other on the convention floor and tried to win more votes for their respective candidates, a private meeting occurred in a hotel room. Several influential Republicans discussed other possible presidential candidates, alternatives to Wood and Lowden. Harding's name came up repeatedly. Although a consensus (general agreement) was not reached in that "smoke-filled room," the influence of the men meeting in that room was quite evident the next morning. Harding gained steadily in several rounds of balloting and won the nomination on the tenth ballot.

Harding did not campaign actively: Daugherty and other advisors—in an early display of spin doctoring—ensured that Harding campaigned without having to answer on-the-spot questions, for fear that he might reveal his lack of understanding on major issues. ("Spin doctoring" is a late twentieth-century term that describes the practice of having political aides offer the best possible interpretation of a political statement or the effects of an event on their political

Andrew W. Mellon

Andrew W. Mellon was influential in American financial practices for nearly six decades. Mellon was born on March 24, 1855, in Pittsburgh, Pennsylvania, the fourth son and sixth of eight children of Thomas and Sarah Jane (Negley) Mellon. When Andrew was four, his father was elected judge of Allegheny County, a post he held for the next ten years. In 1869, Thomas Mellon turned to finance, establishing the T. Mellon & Sons banking firm. Andrew studied in college for four years, but he left three months before graduating to start a lumber and building business. He was so financially astute in this venture and others that in 1882 he became the owner and manager of T. Mellon & Sons.

At that time, Pittsburgh was a significant part of the industrial boom in America, and Mellon helped establish the important role of banks in supplying capital for expanding industries. One such investment helped fund development of the manufacture of aluminum, resulting in the formation of the Aluminum Company of America (Alcoa), with the Mellons as principal holders. Andrew began to invest in the oil industry in the 1890s and helped organize the Gulf Oil Corporation in 1901. Mellon invested in other industrial firms and became a director of many of them. He helped establish the Union Steel Company and a construction firm that built the Panama Canal locks. In 1902, the family's private banking house was converted into a commercial bank, the Mellon National Bank of Pittsburgh, and he was designated president. By then he was one of the richest men in America.

In 1898, Mellon met the Alexander P. McMullen family, who had a brewing empire, on a transatlantic ocean liner and fell in love with Nora Mary McMullen, a beautiful, high-spirited twenty-year-old. Andrew followed her to England and courted her. They were married in September 1900, but it was not a happy union. Mrs. Mellon did not like life in industrial Pittsburgh and resented her husband's devotion to business. In 1910, he filed for divorce.

Mellon became increasingly involved in Republican politics in Pennsylvania. He was close friends with Philander C. Knox (1853–1921), who served as attorney general from 1905 to 1909 for President **Theodore Roosevelt** (1858–1919; see entry in volume 3) and as secretary of state for President William Howard Taft, who succeeded Roosevelt. Opposed to President Woodrow Wilson, Mellon donated money to Wilson's opponents in the election of 1916 and contributed $10,000 to a campaign against Wilson's plan for the League of Nations. In 1920, Mellon backed Knox for the presidential nomination. Warren G. Harding was nominated and elected president in 1920 and he accepted Knox's advice for selecting Mellon to be secretary of the Treasury. Partly because of his talent

Andrew W. Mellon.
Photograph by Harris & Ewing. Courtesy of the
Library of Congress.

and the significance of economic matters during the 1920s, Mellon became the most influential member of the Cabinet under Harding and his successor, Calvin Coolidge. Mellon was called the "greatest secretary of the Treasury since Alexander Hamilton."

Mellon faced several difficult problems during these administrations that began after the end of World War I: reduction of the national debt, readjustment of taxation, and financial settlements with many nations were immediate issues. His tax reform proposal, the "Mellon Plan," caused controversy because it sharply cut taxes on the wealthy. Nevertheless, the economy began booming. Prosperity and peace helped him to steadily lower the na-

tional debt. He was credited for budget, debt, and tax reduction, and remained supportive of large business interests. When the Great Depression (1929–41) began, Mellon's policies were less successful. Serving under his third president, Herbert Hoover, Mellon believed that the economic downturn was inevitable and saw no real problems. As conditions continued to worsen, Mellon came under criticism and Hoover turned to other advisers. In February 1932, Mellon was asked to accept a new position, ambassador to Great Britain.

Mellon died in 1937. His last five years of life were marked by legal troubles and his great success in making public his substantial art collection. Returning to Pittsburgh in 1933, he resumed activities at his position in the Mellon National Bank. He faced charges of underpaying taxes on large business deals, but insufficient evidence led to decisions in his favor. He was especially involved in the founding in Washington, D.C., of what became the National Gallery of Art. In 1937, Mellon donated his $35 million art collection to the federal government together with securities to erect a building costing about $15 million and to establish a $5 million endowment (continuous income). Construction of the National Gallery began before Mellon's death. Living in the capital to direct work for the National Gallery, Mellon suffered a lung ailment and died soon after in Long Island, New York.

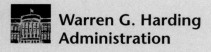

Warren G. Harding Administration

Administration Dates
March 4, 1921–August 2, 1923

Vice President
Calvin Coolidge (1921–23)

Cabinet

Secretary of State
Charles Evans Hughes (1921–23)

Secretary of the Treasury
Andrew W. Mellon (1921–23)

Secretary of War
John W. Weeks (1921–23)

Attorney General
Harry M. Daugherty (1921–23)

Secretary of the Navy
Edwin Denby (1921–23)

Postmaster General
William H. Hays (1921–22)
Hubert Work (1922–23)
Harry S. New (1923)

Secretary of the Interior
Albert B. Fall (1921–23)
Hubert Work (1923)

Secretary of Agriculture
Henry C. Wallace (1921–23)

Secretary of Labor
James J. Davis (1921–23)

Secretary of Commerce
Herbert C. Hoover (1921–23)

boss.) Harding delivered carefully written statements from the front porch of his home in Marion. Meanwhile, his opponent, Ohio governor James M. Cox (1870–1957), toured the country in an aggressive attempt to win votes.

From his front porch, Harding offered Americans what he called a "return to normalcy" after eight years of Democratic rule, a world war, and an economic downturn. He hit the right note with that promise, and he won by a stunning sixty percent of the popular vote—a landslide victory.

Betrayed by friends

For his Cabinet (presidential advisors) and other political appointments, Harding picked some men based on their merits—their skills, education, and experience—and some men on the basis of friendship. The Cabinet members that he chose based on merit proved quite capable: Charles Evans Hughes (1862–1948; see box) as secretary of state, **Herbert Hoover** (1874–1964; see entry in volume 4) as secretary of commerce, and Andrew W. Mellon (1855–1937; see box) as secretary of the treasury. Among the friendship-inspired appointments were Harry Daugherty as attorney general, Albert Fall (1861–1944) as secretary of the interior, and Charles Forbes (1866–1933) as director of the Veterans' Bureau. Those three friends would betray the chief executive.

When he took office in 1921 with his own Republican Party in the majority in both houses, Harding expected to have a smooth early presidency. However, members of both parties debated his proposals. He was able to push through some measures of the "America First" agenda that he campaigned on: tariffs (taxes) on imported goods were raised, immigration was restricted, and the Budget and Accounting Act was passed in 1921. This bill placed stricter accounting practices to develop the annual federal budget—the list of all planned expenditures the federal government expects to make over a year—and led to huge savings.

After having pledged not to support the Treaty of Versailles (vair-SIGH), Harding was able to conclude peace treaties with Germany and Austria, finally putting a formal end to World War I without the United States having to join the League of Nations. Harding then sent Charles Evans Hughes to an international conference that resulted in significant reductions to the navies of the United States, Japan, France, England, and Italy. The agreement ended an expensive arms race (a race to have the best weapons) among those nations.

Those accomplishments did not impress common Americans who wanted more attention paid to their concerns. Harding refused to support legislation that would give World War I soldiers a federal bonus, believing it would prove too costly to a nation paying off war debts. Harding supported measures aimed at helping distressed farmers, but most farmers themselves considered his actions insufficient. When Harding proved ineffective and antiunion (against unions) during a railroad workers' strike in the summer of 1922, his popularity fell to such an extent that Democrats picked up numerous seats in midterm elections, Congressional elections that occur halfway through a president's term. Midterm elections determine the party that will have House and Senate majorities during the final two years of a president's term.

By the fall of 1922, Harding was visibly tired and clearly overwhelmed by his duties. Late in the autumn, Mrs. Harding became ill and nearly died, adding to his burden. "It seems as though I have been president for twenty years," he admitted sadly. During this period, rumors of scandal began to reach him.

Behind the scenes, Harry Daugherty, through his position with the Justice Department, took bribes to provide immunity (protection) from prosecution to certain liquor dealers and sellers. He also provided paroles (early release) to

Harry Daugherty, Warren Harding's corrupt attorney general. After Harding died, new president Calvin Coolidge asked for and received Daugherty's resignation.
Courtesy of the Library of Congress.

Charles Evans Hughes

During his distinguished career of governmental service, Charles Evans Hughes served as secretary of state and two different terms as a justice on the Supreme Court. He also lost a close presidential election in 1916 to Woodrow Wilson. Hughes was born in Glens Falls, New York, on April 14, 1862. He entered Madison University (now Colgate) at the age of fourteen, transferring later to Brown University. Hughes taught school for a year at Delaware Academy in Delhi, New York, and read law in his spare time. In 1882, he entered Cornell Law School, and he graduated in 1884. For the next twenty years, he practiced law, briefly interrupting his work to teach law at Cornell.

At the age of forty-three, Hughes was chosen by a legislative committee to investigate the gas and electric industry in New York. His success in exposing fraud led to other high profile investigations, and in 1906 he was nominated as the state's Republican candidate for governor. He won in a bitter campaign against newspaper publisher William Randolph Hearst (1863–1951; see box in **William McKinley** entry in volume 3). The active governor won battles to regulate public utilities and to curtail racetrack gambling. He was also interested in conservation and in an employment compensation law. After a second term as governor, Hughes was appointed an associate justice of the Supreme Court by President William Howard Taft.

As a justice, Hughes supported national railroad rate regulation and wrote one of the most important decisions in this field. In a 1914 decision, he asserted in his majority opinion the supreme power of Congress over interstate commerce. In an era of government reform of business, Hughes defined the regulatory power of states and cities. In 1916, Hughes resigned from the Court to accept the Republican presidential nomination. He was narrowly beaten by Woodrow Wilson. Hughes had demanded bolder policies than Wilson against both Germany and Mexico and sterner measures of preparation for World War I. He could not challenge Wilson on business reform and ended up projecting a pro-business image that obscured his own reform credentials.

After returning to New York to practice law, Hughes reemerged as a critic of Wilson's plans for the League of Nations. During the presidential campaign of 1920, he joined thirty other distinguished Republicans in an appeal for Republican victory to ensure that American involvement in the League would not include making the U.S. military available to help in foreign conflicts. Republican Warren Harding was elected president and named Hughes to the post of secretary of state. Overturning Wilson's work on the Treaty of Versailles that ended World War I, Hughes negotiated a separate peace with Germany.

Hughes favored cooperation on matters of international law. He was successful in arranging for American participa-

Charles Evans Hughes.
Courtesy of the Library of Congress.

tion, without congressional interference, in the work of the League's Reparations Commission (payment for war damages). In 1923, his suggestion that the commission invite American experts to help untangle Germany's postwar fiscal problems led to the adoption of the Dawes Plan, which—backed by Wall Street loans solicited by Hughes—brought momentary relief to the German economy.

At the Washington Conference (1921–22) on the worldwide buildup of naval forces, Hughes was able to win international cooperation to halt the naval arms race for a decade. In Latin America, Hughes moved American policy gradually away from the more aggressive stances of presidents Wilson and Theodore Roosevelt. Hughes's achievements won praise, but

they did not last: reparations agreements collapsed, as did the Washington Conference treaties. Hughes left office in 1925 to return to law practice, but returned to the Supreme Court in 1930 when President Herbert Hoover named him chief justice.

The early 1930s marked the worst economic crisis in American history. Hughes was prepared to adapt the language of the Constitution flexibly to the needs of the Great Depression. He differed more often than not with the Court's conservative justices appointed during twelve years of Republican presidential leadership. Nevertheless, he agreed when the Court found unconstitutional the National Industrial Recovery Act of **Franklin D. Roosevelt** (1882–1945; see entry in volume 4). Hughes clashed with Roosevelt over the president's court-packing plan in February 1937, when the president wanted to appoint more justices (in order to have more supporters on the court). On the other hand, Hughes helped inspire a momentous change of judicial attitude that proved favorable to Roosevelt. Believing that the Constitution was responsive to needs of a particular time, he helped expand government intervention in the economy. Throughout the 1930s, his decisions supported civil liberties and civil rights.

After his retirement from the Court in 1941, Hughes continued to live in Washington, D.C., where he died of heart failure at the age of eighty-six in 1948.

Artist's conception of the Teapot Dome scandal. *Reproduced by permission of the Corbis Corporation.*

wealthy federal prisoners. At the same time, the Justice Department was in confusion, and many Congressional leaders began calling for Daugherty's resignation.

Meanwhile, it was discovered that Veterans' Bureau chief Charles Forbes was illegally selling government medical supplies to private interests and taking kickbacks on contracts for new hospital buildings and site selections. When Harding confronted his old friend about the possibility of these activities, Forbes quickly resigned and sailed for Europe. Later, when he returned to America, Forbes was subjected to a thorough Senate investigation, convicted of defrauding the government, and sentenced to two years in jail.

The worst of the scandals involved Secretary of the Interior Albert B. Fall and became known as the Teapot Dome conspiracy. (A conspiracy is an agreement between two or more people to commit a crime.) The full extent of the scandal would not become known until after Harding's death.

On a tour to repair his declining reputation, Warren G. Harding became the first president to visit the Alaska Territory. Pictured (left to right): President Harding, Alaska Territory governor Scott C. Bone, and first lady Florence Harding.
Courtesy of the Library of Congress.

Harding was the first president to set foot in Alaska.

Fall illegally leased federal oil deposits in Elk Hill, California, and Teapot Dome, Wyoming, to two oil-company chiefs. The act violated an order by former President Wilson, who had the oil deposits set aside for use by the navy. For his "services," Fall received an estimated $400,000 from the two oil barons. Evidence of this scandal had begun to show by the early months of 1923. Eventually, Fall was convicted of bribery and conspiracy to defraud the government. He spent a year in jail and was forced to pay a $100,000 fine.

As newspapers began to investigate the scandals, Harding and his wife set off on a national speaking tour. The trip took them all the way to Alaska, marking Harding as the first chief executive ever to visit that territory. (Alaska became a state in 1959.) On the way home from Alaska, Harding became ill suddenly in Seattle, Washington. His personal physician diagnosed food poisoning and refused to let other doctors examine him—even turning away army surgeons who were sure the president had suffered a heart attack. The stricken president continued the journey. Harding died on August 2, 1923, in San Francisco, California.

As his flag-draped coffin traveled back across the country for the official ceremonies in Washington, hundreds of thousands of mourners gathered to watch the train pass. The entourage was then greeted in Washington, D.C., by Harding's successor, **Calvin Coolidge** (1872–1933; see entry in volume 4).

Legacy

When Calvin Coolidge succeeded Warren G. Harding, he faced two main tasks: to sustain the prosperity Americans were enjoying in the years after World War I and to restore faith in government. Coolidge, a much less active personality than Harding, succeeded on both counts.

Harding was successful in stopping two key aims of his predecessor, Woodrow Wilson. He reversed Wilson policies that had the federal government monitoring business practices, and he slowed American participation in international affairs by withdrawing the Treaty of Versailles. Wilson had won a Nobel Peace Prize in 1919 for his efforts in negotiating the treaty and conceptualizing the League of Nations, but

A Selection of Harding Landmarks

Harding Home and Museum. 380 Mount Vernon Ave., Marion, OH 43302. (740) 387-9630. Home of Warren and Florence Harding before he became president. From his porch, the campaigning candidate spoke to crowds that gathered on his front lawn. The press house near the house used during his presidential campaign serves as a small Harding museum. See http://www.ohiohistory.org/places/harding/ (accessed on August 30, 2000).

Harding Tomb. Vernon Heights Blvd., Marion, OH 43302. (740) 387-9630. The final resting place of Warren and Florence Harding is a couple miles from the Harding home. See http://www.ohiohistory.org/places/hardtomb/ (accessed on August 30, 2000).

Harding pursued different policies. Meanwhile, the American economy prospered. Harding enjoyed the popularity a president usually enjoys when the economy is doing well, and he was undoubtedly one of America's most beloved presidents during the first two years of his term. But although he was not directly linked to corruption, Harding's reputation sank steadily beginning near the time of his death as the depth of scandal within his administration was gradually revealed.

Where to Learn More

Canadeo, Anne. *Warren G. Harding: 29th President of the United States.* Ada, OK: Garrett Educational Corp., 1990.

Denton, Frank R. *The Mellons of Pittsburgh.* New York: Newcomen Society of England, American Branch, 1948.

Downes, Randolph Chandler. *The Rise of Warren Gamaliel Harding, 1865–1920.* Columbus: Ohio State University Press, 1970.

Ferrell, Robert H. *The Strange Deaths of President Harding.* Columbia: University of Missouri Press, 1996.

Kurland, Gerald. *Warren Harding: A President Betrayed by Friends.* Charlotteville, NY: SamHar Press, 1971.

Mee, Charles L. *The Ohio Gang: The World of Warren G. Harding.* New York: M. Evans, 1981.

Murray, Robert K. *The Harding Era: Warren G. Harding and His Administration.* Minneapolis: University of Minnesota Press, 1969.

Pusey, Merlo J. *Charles Evans Hughes.* New York: Macmillan, 1951. Reprint, New York: Garland, 1979.

Russell, Francis. *The Shadow of Blooming Grove: Warren G. Harding in His Times*. New York: McGraw-Hill, 1968.

Sinclair, Andrew. *Available Man: The Life Behind the Masks of Warren Gamaliel Harding*. New York: Macmillan, 1965.

Trani, Eugene P, and David L. Wilson. *The Presidency of Warren G. Harding*. Lawrence: Regents Press of Kansas, 1977.

Florence Harding

Born August 15, 1860
Marion, Ohio
Died November 21, 1924
Marion, Ohio

Began a new style of first lady leadership

A new era for American women began in 1920. That was the first year women were allowed to vote in a presidential election. In the 1920s, more females were holding professional jobs and living independently. Florence Harding fit perfectly into that era. A strong-willed, ambitious woman, Mrs. Harding was prominent in her husband's administration. She created a whole new image for the first lady by holding her own press conferences, at which she expressed her own opinions. She helped humanize a president who was quickly losing popularity, and when her husband's administration became tainted with scandal, Mrs. Harding did all she could to protect his name.

"If the career is the husband's, the wife can merge her own with it. . . ."

Florence Harding

Early independence

Born in Marion, Ohio, in 1860, Florence Kling grew up in a wealthy household. Her father, Amos Kling, was a merchant and the richest man in Marion. While growing up, Florence developed confidence and independence. She worked with her father, learning how to manage his business

Florence Harding.
Courtesy of the Library of Congress.

and how to communicate effectively with men and women, employees and customers.

The relationship between father and daughter became strained when, as a teen, Florence became pregnant. She left town with Henry De Wolfe, the baby's father. No legal records have ever turned up to show that De Wolfe and Florence married. De Wolfe proved to be a chronic alcoholic who could not earn a living. Florence was able to get a divorce. (After unmarried couples live together for a period of time, their relationship can be considered a "common law marriage," subject to the same laws as married couples.)

As a single mother who needed to earn a living, Florence Kling gave piano lessons. She was able to repair the relationship with her family back in Marion.

Florence met **Warren G. Harding** (1865–1923; see entry in volume 4) after he became the owner of the *Marion Star* newspaper in the late 1880s. Harding made the newspaper popular and attracted a substantial political following. Handsome and respected in the community, Harding was considered the most eligible bachelor in Marion. Florence married Harding in 1891 and moved into a large house Harding had built for himself in Marion.

Because Florence was five years older than her husband and an heiress to a fortune, there were some who viewed their relationship as a marriage of convenience—a business and political partnership. That view gained further support when evidence of Warren Harding's extramarital affairs was made public. Still, a wealth of stories and memoirs from those close to the couple shows that Florence Harding was deeply in love with her husband when she married him and deeply hurt when she discovered his unfaithfulness.

Soon after they married, Harding became more active in politics. Florence took over the day-to-day operations of the *Marion Star,* supervising circulation (the number of copies distributed to the public) and bookkeeping (the keeping of the business's accounts). The newspaper flourished, and Harding became an important political figure in the state of Ohio. As Harding advanced through Ohio politics and on to the U.S. Senate in 1914, Florence was always hard at work by his side. She expressed her opinion on issues and helped him address negative press. She was so effective in keeping private

A strong-willed, ambitious woman, Florence Harding (right) was prominent in her husband's administration. Warren Harding (left) called her "the Duchess."
Courtesy of the Library of Congress.

his extramarital affairs that most people did not know he was unfaithful until after his death. Meanwhile, she began suffering from chronic kidney problems.

Active first lady

When Harding was nominated for president in 1920, Mrs. Harding courted the press and all different types of media (means of communication), including news highlights that were shown with motion pictures, which were beginning to grow in popularity. She endeared herself to female voters by speaking out on women's rights.

Both the White House and its grounds had been closed while President **Woodrow Wilson** (1856–1924; see entry in volume 4) was ill during the last year of his term. After Harding was elected, Florence again held garden parties on the White House lawn. Many of the parties were for veterans of World War I. The festivities were well covered by the media, and newspapers printed her remarks in favor of women competing in sports and running their own businesses. Behind the scenes she encouraged her husband to speak more forcefully on racial equality and religious tolerance.

Mrs. Harding encouraged the appointment of female federal employees, contributed her views to some of Harding's most important domestic and foreign accomplishments, and occasionally even gave speeches when her husband was ill or delayed. Editorial cartoons called her "Chief Executive" and made much of her new style of leadership as first lady, but she was flattered by the attention. She correctly perceived that the role of first lady was becoming more important as the twentieth century provided an expanded set of opportunities for women.

Some of Mrs. Harding's contributions to her husband's presidency were not quite so praiseworthy. She mixed and served alcoholic beverages to White House guests, even though Prohibition, by constitutional amendment, had made alcohol illegal in the United States. She also recommended the Hardings' friend Charles Forbes (1866–1933) to head the newly created Veterans' Bureau. Forbes was later convicted and imprisoned for defrauding the bureau of millions of dollars. Mrs. Harding insisted that her husband's health be supervised by a personal physician of her choice. When President Harding collapsed during a national tour, that personal physician would not allow any other doctors to examine the president, calling his illness a case of food poisoning. Harding in fact was suffering from heart problems, and he died slightly halfway through his presidency on August 2, 1923.

By that time, Mrs. Harding was aware that several massive scandals were about to undermine her husband's presidency. No one would have known that she was burdened by this information as she accompanied Harding's body back to Washington, D.C., on a train greeted by many thousands of mourners. In his biography of Mrs. Harding, *Florence Harding: The First Lady, the Jazz Age, and the Death of America's Most Scandalous President,* Carl Sferrazza Anthony asserts that the first lady quickly burned many personal papers belonging to her husband that might have involved him in the scandals.

Harding died before his administration became disgraced by numerous scandals that were uncovered from 1923 through 1925. Florence Harding's health suffered, and she died on November 21, 1924, barely a year after her husband passed away. She was buried in the magnificent Harding burial plot in Marion, Ohio.

Where to Learn More

Anthony, Carl Sferrazza. *Florence Harding: The First Lady, the Jazz Age, and the Death of America's Most Scandalous President*. New York: W. Morrow & Co., 1998.

Harding's Speech to a Special Session of Congress

Delivered on April 12, 1921; excerpted from *Annals of America*

President Harding announces what would become known as his "return to normalcy" plan for America following years of war and business regulation

Following the end of World War I (1914–18), Americans were eager to return to normal life. The war had disrupted families, created shortages of many basic necessities, and filled the daily newspapers with stories from foreign locales. Nearly every aspect of life seemed geared to the war effort. **Warren G. Harding** (1865–1923; see entry in volume 4) rode the sentiment for normalcy to victory in the presidential election of 1920.

Harding campaigned against the views of outgoing president **Woodrow Wilson** (1856–1924; see entry in volume 4) and the Democratic Party candidate James M. Cox (1870–1957). They wanted the United States to ratify the Treaty of Versailles, the pact that ended the war. However, Harding and many others were against ratification of the treaty because it called for U.S. involvement in the League of Nations (see box in **Woodrow Wilson** entry in volume 4). As a League member, the United States would be required to deploy military support for any other League member facing an aggressor. Republicans objected that this article would lead to U.S. involvement in all future European conflicts, no matter how petty.

> "First in mind must be the solution of our problems at home. . . . The surest procedure in every government is to put its own house in order."
>
> *Warren G. Harding*

Another area of disagreement between Harding and his Democratic counterparts concerned the relationship between government and business. President Wilson had supported regulations to ensure that business practices were fair. Harding planned to free business from government controls.

Before a special session of Congress shortly after taking office in 1921, Harding spelled out the agenda for his administration. With support from a Republican majority in Congress, Harding wanted America to "put its own house in order"—to be concerned with problems at home instead of international affairs.

Things to remember while reading an excerpt from President Harding's speech to a special session of Congress:

- Harding was elected based on his promise to find solutions to problems at home. Appropriately, he began his first address to Congress as president by stressing that the "surest procedure in every government" was to "put its own house in order." He quickly listed spending less and taxing less as priorities for his administration. Continuing with economic themes, he proposed paying off the country's debt that occurred because of the war effort; raising tariff rates to protect American business; and creating a national budget system that closely planned and monitored government spending.

- Harding differed from his predecessor, Woodrow Wilson, in his approach to business. Wilson had introduced several kinds of regulations that brought much-needed reform to business practices. Harding, as reflected in the middle portion of this excerpt, believed that freeing business from government regulations would result in general economic improvement.

- Some of the technological developments and social issues of the times were addressed by Harding in his speech. For example, he strongly supported development of communication technology—particularly radio, which was just coming into wide use. On social issues, Harding expressed his support for the formation of a Department of Public Welfare that would oversee national efforts in such areas as education and health. The president also expressed support for the development of a commission to study ways to improve race relations.

- Harding concluded his speech by reemphasizing his opposition to America entering the League of Nations.

Excerpt from Harding's speech to a special session of Congress

Under our political system the people of the United States have charged the new Congress and the new administration with the solution—the readjustments, reconstruction, and restoration which must follow in the wake of war. . . .

*First in mind must be the solution of our problems at home, even though some phases of them are inseparably linked with our foreign relations. The surest procedure in every government is to put its own house in order. I know of no more pressing problem at home than to restrict our national expenditures within the limits of our national income and at the same time measurably lift the burdens of **war taxation** from the shoulders of the American people. . . .*

*The staggering load of war debt must be cared for in orderly funding and gradual **liquidation**. We shall hasten the solution and aid effectively in lifting the tax burdens if we strike resolutely at **expenditure**. It is far more easily said than done. In the fever of war our expenditures were so little questioned, the emergency was so impelling, appropriation was so unimpeded that we little noted millions and counted the Treasury inexhaustible. It will strengthen our resolution if we ever keep in mind that a continuation of such a course means inevitable disaster. . . .*

*The most substantial relief from the tax burden must come for the present from the readjustment of internal taxes, and the revision or repeal of those taxes which have become unproductive and are so artificial and burdensome as to defeat their own purpose. A prompt and thoroughgoing revision of the **internal tax laws**, made with due regard to the protection of the revenues, is, in my judgment, a requisite to the revival of business activity in this country. It is earnestly hoped, therefore, that the Congress will be able to enact without*

War taxation: Taxes introduced to help a government raise more money to help fight a war.

Liquidation: The selling off of items at a lower price in order to obtain money to pay off debt.

Expenditure: Spending.

Internal tax laws: The complete set of taxes a government levies on its people.

*delay a revision of the revenue laws and such emergency **tariff** measures as are necessary to protect American trade and industry.*

*It is of less concern whether internal taxation or tariff revision shall come first than has been popularly imagined because we must do both, but the practical course for earliest accomplishment will readily suggest itself to the Congress. We are committed to the repeal of the **excess-profits tax** and the abolition of inequities and unjustifiable **exasperations** in the present system.*

The country does not expect and will not approve a shifting of burdens. It is more interested in wiping out the necessity for imposing them and eliminating confusion and cost in the collection.

The urgency for an instant tariff enactment, emergency in character and understood by our people that it is for emergency only, cannot be too much emphasized. I believe in the protection of American industry, and it is our purpose to prosper America first. The privileges of the American market to the foreign producer are offered too cheaply today, and the effect on much of our own productivity is the destruction of our self-reliance, which is the foundation of the independence and good fortune of our people. Moreover, imports should pay their fair share of our cost of government. . . .

*It is proper to invite your attention to the importance of the question of radio communication and cables. To meet strategic, commercial, and political needs, active encouragement should be given to the extension of American-owned and operated cable and radio services. Between the United States and its possessions there should be ample communication facilities providing direct services at reasonable rates. Between the United States and other countries, not only should there be adequate facilities but these should be, so far as practicable, direct and free from foreign intermediation. Friendly cooperation should be extended to international efforts aimed at encouraging improvement of international communication facilities and designed to further the exchange of messages. Private **monopolies** tending to prevent the development of needed facilities should be prohibited. Government-owned facilities, wherever possible without unduly interfering with private enterprise or government needs, should be made available for general uses.*

Particularly desirable is the provision of ample cable and radio services at reasonable rates for the transmission of press matter, so that the American reader may receive a wide range of news and the foreign reader receive full accounts of American activities. The daily

Tariff: A tax that a government places on imported goods to make them more expensive; tariffs are used to protect domestic industries against foreign competition.

Excess-profits tax: A kind of tax that goes into effect when a business makes huge profits during an uncommon or emergency situation.

Exasperations: Annoyances.

Monopolies: Exclusive domination of entire industries by one company.

press of all countries may well be put in position to contribute to international understandings by the publication of interesting foreign news. . . .

*During the recent political **canvass** the proposal was made that a Department of Public Welfare should be created. It was endorsed and commended so strongly that I venture to call it to your attention and to suggest favorable legislative consideration.*

Government's obligation affirmatively to encourage development of the highest and most efficient type of citizenship is modernly accepted, almost universally. Government rests upon the body of citizenship; it cannot maintain itself on a level that keeps it out of touch and understanding with the community it serves. Enlightened governments everywhere recognize this and are giving their recognition effect in policies and programs. Certainly no government is more desirous than our own to reflect the human attitude, the purpose of making better citizens—physically, intellectually, spiritually. To this end I am convinced that such a department in the government would be of real value. It could be made to crystallize much of rather vague generalization about social justice into solid accomplishment. Events of recent years have profoundly impressed thinking people with the need to recognize new social forces and evolutions, to equip our citizens for dealing rightly with problems of life and social order.

In the realms of education, public health, sanitation, conditions of workers in industry, child welfare, proper amusement and recreation, the elimination of social vice, and many other subjects, the government has already undertaken a considerable range of activities. . . .

*Somewhat related to the foregoing human problems is the race question. Congress ought to wipe the stain of barbaric **lynching** from the banners of a free and orderly, representative democracy. We face the fact that many millions of people of African descent are numbered among our population, and that in a number of states they constitute a very large proportion of the total population. It is unnecessary to recount the difficulties incident to this condition, nor to emphasize the fact that it is a condition which cannot be removed. There has been suggestion, however, that some of its difficulties might be **ameliorated** by a humane and enlightened consideration of it, a study of its many aspects, and an effort to formulate, if not a policy, at least a national attitude of mind calculated to bring about the most satisfaction possible adjustment of relations between the races, and of each race to the national life. One propos-*

Canvass: A survey of public opinion, such as an election.

Lynching: Public hanging by a mob without any legal authority.

Ameliorated: Improved.

al is the creation of a commission embracing representatives of both races, to study and report on the entire subject. The proposal has real merit. I am convinced that in mutual tolerance, understanding, charity, recognition of the interdependence of the races, and the maintenance of the rights of citizenship lies the road to righteous adjustment. . . .

Nearly two and a half years ago the World War came to an end, and yet we find ourselves today in the technical state of war, though actually at peace, while Europe is at technical peace, far from tranquillity and little progressed toward the hoped-for restoration. It ill becomes us to express impatience that the European **belligerents** are not yet in full agreement, when we ourselves have been unable to bring **constituted authority** into accord in our own relations to the formally proclaimed peace.

Little avails in reciting the causes of delay in Europe or our own failure to agree. But there is no longer excuse for uncertainties respecting some phases of our foreign relationship. In the existing League of Nations, world-governing with its superpowers, this republic will have no part. There can be no misinterpretation, and there will be no betrayal of the deliberate expression of the American people in the recent election; and, settled in our decision for ourselves, it is only fair to say to the world in general, and to our associates in war in particular, that the League Covenant can have no sanction by us. The aim to associate nations to prevent war, preserve peace, and promote civilization our people most cordially applauded. We yearned for this new instrument of justice, but we can have no part in a committal to an agency of force in unknown **contingencies**; we can recognize no super-authority.

Manifestly, the highest purpose of the League of Nations was defeated in linking it with the treaty of peace and making it the enforcing agency of the victors of the war. International association for permanent peace must be conceived solely as an instrumentality of justice, unassociated with the passions of yesterday, and not so constituted as to attempt the dual functions of a political instrument of the conquerors and of an agency of peace. There can be no prosperity for the fundamental purposes sought to be achieved by any such association so long as it is an organ of any particular treaty or committed to the attainment of the special aims of any nation or group of nations.

The American aspiration, indeed, the world aspiration, was an association of nations, based upon the application of justice and right, binding us in conference and cooperation for the prevention of

Belligerents: Those involved in war.

Constituted authority: Power granted by the U.S. Constitution.

Contingencies: Emergencies.

Manifestly: Obviously.

war and pointing the way to a higher civilization and international
fraternity in which all the world might share. In rejecting the League
Covenant and uttering that rejection to our own people and to the
world, we make no surrender of our hope and aim for an association
to promote peace in which we would most heartily join. We wish it to
be conceived in peace and dedicated to peace, and will relinquish no
effort to bring the nations of the world into such fellowship, not in the
surrender of national sovereignty but rejoicing in a nobler exercise of
it in the advancement of human activities, amid the compensations
of peaceful achievement. . . . (Annals of America, pp. 292–7)

What happened next . . .

Harding's economic policies were enacted and helped
fuel a post–World War I boom called "the Roaring '20s." After
Harding died in office in 1923, his successor, **Calvin
Coolidge** (1872–1933; see entry in volume 4), continued the
policy of low taxation and minimal government interference
in business. Economic prosperity continued through 1929,
when a financial crisis led to the Great Depression that lasted
through the 1930s and into the early 1940s.

There were some areas where government became
more involved in monitoring business. The federal government took an active role in regulating development of
promising new technologies to ensure that one company did
not dominate an entire industry. Radio and commercial aviation are the two most noteworthy industries that made great
strides during the 1920s with the assistance and supervision
of the federal government.

Harding's proposed Department of Welfare and the
commission on race relations proved insignificant. Only in
1939 did an executive level agency arise that fulfilled the
goals noted by Harding. And while there were slight advances
in relations between whites and African Americans, segregation was still widespread. It was during the 1920s, for example, that baseball became "America's pastime," but it was two
decades later when the first African American played in a
major league baseball game.

The United States never entered the League of Nations or ratified the Treaty of Versailles. The United States, unlike other Allied Nations that fought the Axis Powers (Germany and Austria) in World War I, made separate peace pacts with the defeated nations. The United States never became an official member of the League, which existed from 1920 to 1946. American diplomats assisted League activities and attended meetings, but lack of official American participation lessened the effectiveness of the League. In 1946, the League of Nations voted to dissolve. Much of its organization was assumed by the United Nations (UN). The UN had more active participation from major powers, including the United States, making it a more effective peacekeeping organization while continuing the social work of the League to effect a stronger international alliance.

Did you know . . .

- Though Harding, as president, led the United States to refuse to join the League of Nations, his administration achieved one of the most successful international peace agreements of the twentieth century. Nine treaties were signed at a conference on naval disarmament in Washington, D.C., in 1923. The treaties stopped naval military build-ups among Japan, England, France, Italy, Russia, and the United States that could lead to future battles and large-scale war.

Where to Learn More

Annals of America. New York: H. H. Wilson, 1988.

Gross, Edwin K. *Vindication for Mr. Normalcy.* Buffalo: American Society for the Faithful Recording of History, 1965.

Murray, Robert K. *The Politics of Normalcy: Governmental Theory and Practice in the Harding-Coolidge Era.* New York: Norton, 1973.

Trani, Eugene P, and David L. Wilson. *The Presidency of Warren G. Harding.* Lawrence: Regents Press of Kansas, 1977.

Calvin Coolidge

Thirtieth president (1923–1929)

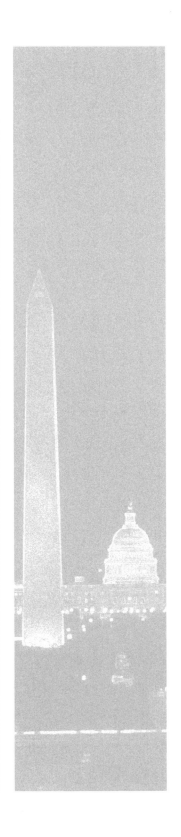

Calvin Coolidge . . . 1049

   Fast Facts about Calvin Coolidge (box) . . . 1051

   Calvin Coolidge Timeline (box) . . . 1052

   Words to Know (box) . . . 1053

   Coolidge Becomes President (box) . . . 1056

   Calvin Coolidge Administration (box) . . . 1058

   Election Results (box) . . . 1060

   Frank B. Kellogg (box) . . . 1062

   Charles A. Lindbergh (box) . . . 1064

   A Selection of Coolidge Landmarks (box) . . . 1068

Grace Coolidge . . . 1071

Primary source: Coolidge's Speech on Government and Business
*"Silent Cal" elaborates on his theme, "the chief business of the American
   people is business." . . .* **1077**

Calvin Coolidge

Born July 4, 1872
Plymouth, Vermont
Died January 5, 1933
Northampton, Massachusetts

Thirtieth president of the United States
(1923–1929)

Reserved and uncharismatic, "Silent Cal"'s personality was the direct opposite of the spirit of "the Roaring '20s," "the Jazz Age," and "the Era of Good Feeling"

"The Roaring '20s." That term is used to describe the 1920s, when American cities were expanding outward and upward, toward the skies. Automobiles ruled the streets. A lively bull market—a profitable period of aggressive buying and selling of stock—was creating new wealth by the hour. Babe Ruth (1895–1948) popularized baseball and smacked sixty home runs in 1927. That same year, Charles Lindbergh (1902–1974; see box) flew an airplane solo across the Atlantic Ocean. Even the 1919 constitutional amendment banning the manufacture or sale of alcohol did not slow revelers in "the Jazz Age," another colorful description of the era.

Calvin Coolidge, the man who led the nation during much of the decade, was the very opposite of the Roaring '20s image. A sober, reserved New England Republican with a distinct lack of charisma (personal charm), "Silent Cal" simply went about his business—working and spending time with his family—while the country was enjoying a period of economic growth that it had never seen before.

Coolidge's low-key image worked to his advantage as a politician. He was a reassuring figure to many Americans

". . .the chief business of the American people is business. They are profoundly concerned with producing, buying, selling, investing, and prospering in the world."

Calvin Coolidge

Calvin Coolidge.
Courtesy of the Library of Congress.

Although a shy man, Calvin Coolidge did not mind being photographed, regardless of the setting. Here, the president, clad in a hat and bib overalls, uses a scythe to tend to the fields on the family farm in Plymouth Notch, Vermont. *Courtesy of the Library of Congress.*

with his famously brief and to-the-point public statements—like, "the chief business of America is business." Such terse remarks highlighted his ideas about being president. He believed that his role was to cut costs and interfere as little as possible with the inner workings of the country.

That approach has led some historians and political analysts to view Coolidge as a "do-nothing" chief executive who happily delegated (gave responsibility to his staff) many decisions, was merely a tool of powerful American business interests, and left behind no truly noteworthy legislation or legacy.

Yet, Coolidge was, by all accounts, a strictly honest politician, a candidate who won nearly every election he ever entered, and a family man, whose White House years were saddened by the death of his teenage son. The tax cuts Coolidge championed during his term furthered economic growth, and he recognized that the times did not call for forceful leadership. Having emerged from the horrors of World War I (1914–18), people were ready to get back to work and to enjoy themselves as well. Coolidge was the last president to write nearly all of his own speeches, and he was the first to successfully use the new medium (method of passing information) of radio to deliver his speeches to a national audience.

Newspapers of the time usually portrayed Coolidge quite well. Good-naturedly, he even allowed himself to be photographed in non-presidential situations (such as donning Native American garb or working on his Vermont farm). Although he was drawn in political cartoons as dour (stern or gloomy), Coolidge actually smiled often for the cameras and was known in private for his sharp wit.

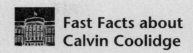

Fast Facts about Calvin Coolidge

Full name: John Calvin Coolidge

Born: July 4, 1872

Died: January 5, 1933

Burial site: Plymouth Notch Cemetery, Plymouth, Vermont

Parents: John and Victoria Moor Coolidge

Spouse: Grace Anna Goodhue (1879–1957; m. 1905)

Children: John (1906–2000); Calvin Jr. (1908–1924)

Religion: Congregational

Education: Amherst College (B.A., 1895)

Occupations: Attorney

Government positions: Northampton, Massachusetts, councilman and mayor; Massachusetts state congressman, senator, lieutenant governor, and governor; vice president under Warren G. Harding

Political party: Republican

Dates as president: August 3, 1923–March 4, 1925 (first term); March 4, 1925–March 4, 1929 (second term)

Age upon taking office: 51

Early years

John Calvin Coolidge was born on the fourth of July, 1872, and named after his father. Father John Calvin Coolidge (1845–1926), an entrepreneur (a person who invests time and money in new business ventures), held various public offices at

Calvin Coolidge Timeline

1872: Born in Vermont

1895 Graduates from Amherst College

1897: Admitted to the Massachusetts bar; attorney in private practice in Northampton, Massachusetts, after 1898

1899–1901: Holds two elected positions in Northampton, Massachusetts

1907–8: Serves in Massachusetts state house

1910–11: Serves as mayor of Northampton, Massachusetts

1912–15: Serves in Massachusetts state senate

1916–18: Serves as Massachusetts lieutenant governor

1919–20: Serves as Massachusetts governor; gains national attention for firing striking police officers in Boston and using the state militia as temporary replacements

1921–23: Serves as U.S. vice president under Warren G. Harding

1923: Teapot Dome scandal rocks Harding administration

1923–29: Serves as thirtieth U.S. president, following death of Harding; fires all administration officials implicated in the Teapot Dome scandal

1929: After having declined to seek reelection, Coolidge retires to Northampton, Massachussetts; stock market crashes in October, beginning the Great Depression

1933: Dies in Massachusetts

the local and state level. Coolidge grew up in Plymouth Notch, an isolated, rural Vermont town. The nearest railroad stop was about ten miles away in Ludlow, where his mother, Victoria Moor Coolidge (1846–1885), had attended a private academy. She was an avid reader who passed on this trait to her children, Calvin and his sister Abigail (1875–1890). Victoria Coolidge was unfortunately beset by poor health even as a young woman. She died when her son was just twelve. The loss affected him deeply: He would carry her portrait with him for the rest of his life, and it was in his breast pocket on the day that he died.

As a youth, Coolidge was a loner—a shy, frail boy who suffered from asthma. Six years after his mother died, tragedy visited the household again. When he was eighteen, his sister Abbie died at the age of fifteen from acute appen-

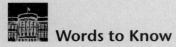

Words to Know

Bar: An exam lawyers must pass in order to become legally certified to practice law.

Bull market: A stock market term that describes a period of aggressive buying and selling of stock that proves profitable for most investors; in contrast, "bear market" is used to describe a more sluggish trading period.

Dow Jones Industrial Average: A means for measuring the health of the stock market by charting the progress of a select group of representative businesses.

Entrepreneur: A person who invests time and money in new business ventures.

Gross national product (GNP): An economic measurement of a nation's total value of goods and services produced over a certain period (usually a year); the GNP became an official economic statistic in 1947.

Lieutenant governor: Second in command behind the governor of a state; similar to the role of vice president.

Merchant marine: Professional sailors and boat workers involved with commercial marine trade and maintenance (as opposed to branches of the military such as the navy and the coast guard).

Middle class: Generally used to describe working people who earn enough money to own property and live comfortably.

Prohibition: The constitutional ban on the manufacture and sale of alcohol and alcoholic beverages from 1920 to 1933.

Solicitor: An attorney who represents a government agency.

State militia: An organized military unit maintained by states in case of emergency; often called the National Guard.

dicitis (swelling of the appendix). Both Calvin and his sister had been students at the same school in nearby Ludlow, Black River Academy, that their mother had once attended.

After he graduated from the academy, Coolidge enrolled in 1891 at Amherst College in Northampton, Massachusetts. His four years there were recalled later as altogether unremarkable by his classmates; none of them ever imagined he would be destined for the White House or even a career in politics, since he was not very sociable. He was studious, if nothing else.

Coolidge remained in Northampton after graduation from Amherst in 1895, studying law while working as a clerk

Vice President Coolidge learned of President Harding's death while vacationing at his father's home in Vermont. The news came in the middle of the night, via messenger, since Coolidge's father did not have a telephone. Coolidge was sworn into office by his father, a justice of the peace, just before 3 A.M. In Coolidge's characteristically undisturbable style, he then went back to bed.

in the offices of a private firm. Since the firm's partners were involved in local politics, Coolidge began to help with their campaigns. He was still shy and had few friends, but he made an effort to be more social. Still, he never dated. In 1897, at the age of twenty-five, Coolidge passed the Massachusetts bar (the exam to enter the legal profession). In early 1898, he opened his own law practice in Northampton.

Coolidge won his first election in 1898 when he ran for a seat on the Northampton city council. Over the next decade, he made a name for himself as a dependable Republican and local favorite of the state party bosses. After serving as city solicitor (an attorney who represents a government agency) for Northampton, he was appointed court clerk for Hampshire County and earned a good salary. At that time, he met Grace Goodhue (1879–1957; see **Grace Coolidge** entry in volume 4), a young woman from Burlington, Vermont. Grace had recently joined the staff of a school for the deaf in Northampton after graduating from the University of Vermont. She and Calvin were married in October 1905, and the first of their two sons, John Coolidge (1906–2000), was born a year later.

After working in the general court, or lower house, of the Massachusetts state legislature, Coolidge served two terms as mayor of Northampton. In 1912, he successfully ran for a seat in the upper chamber in Boston, the state senate. He later served as lieutenant governor (second in command to the governor) and was elected governor of Massachusetts in 1918.

Coolidge won national recognition in 1919 for his decisive handling of a police strike in Boston. He called in the state militia to maintain order and fired all of the striking police officers. (An organized military unit maintained by states in case of emergency, the state militia is often called the National Guard.) While Coolidge was being hailed in conservative newspapers across the country as a hero of law and order, the nation's most famous labor figure, American Federation of Labor president Samuel Gompers (1850–1924), tried to intervene on behalf of the fired officers. Coolidge replied to Gompers in a telegram with a short summary of his stance on labor unrest. Widely reprinted in newspapers across America, the statement read, "There is no right to strike against the public safety by anybody, anywhere, any time."

As a result of this new fame, Republican foes of organized labor began declaring their support for the nomination of Coolidge as their candidate for president in 1920. However, Ohioan **Warren G. Harding** (1865–1923; see entry in volume 4) emerged as the surprise Republican frontrunner, and Coolidge was nominated to be vice president. Harding won the election, beginning what would become twelve years of Republican administrations.

Coolidge and the president were drastically opposite in personality. Coolidge was modest and kept a low profile, while Harding was outgoing and always shaking hands. But Harding showed a disastrous shortcoming in his inability to judge character: He made several unwise choices in selecting his Cabinet (his presidential advisors) and White House staff, favoring men who had helped build his political career. Those men led the Harding administration into a political scandal that headlined the news stories of the early 1920s.

After Massachusetts governor Calvin Coolidge fired striking policemen in 1919 and American Federation of Labor president Samuel Gompers (above) tried to defend them, Coolidge told Gompers, "There is no right to strike against the public safety by anybody, anywhere, any time." *Courtesy of the Library of Congress.*

It was learned that some of Harding's Cabinet officials profited from secret deals involving leases for land that contained oil reserves used by U.S. Navy ships. The Teapot Dome scandal, as it came to be known after the name of one of the tracts in Wyoming, would result in a jail term for Harding's secretary of the interior, Albert Fall (1861–1944). Some believed that the strain of the Senate investigation and public outcry concerning the Teapot Dome scandal were too much for Harding, who already suffered from heart trouble. During a cross-country train lecture tour—optimistically called "the Voyage of Understanding" and designed to restore confidence in his administration—the president died on August 2, 1923, in San Francisco, California.

Coolidge and his family were vacationing at his father's home in Vermont at the time. The vice president

Coolidge Becomes President

Calvin Coolidge became president of the United States following the death of Warren G. Harding. (See Harding entry for election results from the Harding/Coolidge campaign.) This marked the sixth time in U.S. history that a vice president became president following the death of his predecessor. Coolidge's victory in 1924 marked the second time that a former vice president finishing his predecessor's term was elected as president on his own in the next election.

learned of Harding's death from a messenger who arrived in the middle of the night. Coolidge's father's home did not have a telephone. Coolidge was sworn into office by his father, a notary public, just before 3 A.M. In Coolidge's characteristically calm style, he then went back to bed. When he returned to Washington, however, the new president acted swiftly to restore faith in the Republican administration as the full story of the Teapot Dome deals were revealed. Coolidge immediately replaced Harding appointees associated with scandal and named a special counsel (legal counselor) to investigate the misconduct on the part of government officials.

Campaign of 1924

After less than a year in office—a successful period during which Coolidge did much to renew public confidence—the president secured all the votes in the Republican nomination for the presidential election of 1924. His running mate was banker and financier Charles Dawes (1865–1951). The reelection slogan played on the sober, serene Coolidge style: "Keep Cool with Coolidge."

Tragedy struck the Coolidge family not long after the Republican convention. Following a few tennis matches with his brother, sixteen-year-old Calvin Jr. developed a blister on one of his toes. The blister became infected and he soon developed blood poisoning. He did not tell anyone about his injury until it was too late. Despite the best medical treatment available, Calvin Coolidge Jr. died a few days later on July 7, 1924.

Overwhelmed by the loss, Coolidge was grief-stricken and never the same. He barely participated in his own reelection campaign, leaving much of the actual campaigning to Dawes. Still, Coolidge easily beat his opponents, Progressive Party candidate Robert La Follette (1855–1925) and West Virginia Democrat John W. Davis (1873–1955), by a landslide. The low voter turnout for the election showed the national

political mood of those years of progress and prosperity. A new middle class in America was rapidly multiplying, the result of steady economic growth since the end of World War I. (The middle class consists of working-class people who earn enough money to own property and live comfortably.)

Coolidge maintained a pro-business atmosphere: Corporate taxes were low and government regulation almost nonexistent. The stock market was surging, and labor unions were struggling. Many of the comforts of modern life—electricity, telephones, cars, radios, refrigerators, and even the ability to buy a home on credit—were becoming within the reach of the average worker. The wages of the average worker were increasing, while the Revenue Acts of 1924 and 1926, signed by Coolidge, lessened the tax burden for that income bracket.

"The chief business of the American people is business"

In a January 17, 1925, speech before the American Society of Newspaper Editors, Coolidge spoke about the need

President Calvin Coolidge in the Oval Office shortly after succeeding Warren G. Harding to the presidency. *Courtesy of the Library of Congress.*

Calvin Coolidge Administration

Administration Dates
August 3, 1923–March 4, 1925
March 4, 1925–March 4, 1929

Vice President
None (1923–1925)
Charles G. Dawes (1925–29)

Cabinet

Secretary of State
Charles Evans Hughes (1923–25)
Frank B. Kellogg (1925–29)

Secretary of the Treasury
Andrew W. Mellon (1923–29)

Secretary of War
John W. Weeks (1923–25)
Dwight F. Davis (1925–29)

Attorney General
Harry M. Daugherty (1923–24)
Harlan F. Stone (1924–25)
John G. Sargent (1925–29)

Secretary of the Navy
Edwin Denby (1923–24)
Curtis D. Wilbur (1924–29)

Postmaster General
Harry S. New (1923–29)

Secretary of the Interior
Hubert Work (1923–28)
Roy O. West (1928–29)

Secretary of Agriculture
Henry C. Wallace (1923–24)
Howard M. Gore (1924–25)
William M. Jardine (1925–29)

Secretary of Labor
James J. Davis (1923–29)

Secretary of Commerce
Herbert C. Hoover (1923–28)
William F. Whiting (1928–29)

for the American press to serve as a trustworthy source of information concerning business and finance matters. "It is probable that a press which maintains an intimate touch with the business currents of the nation, is likely to be more reliable than it would be if it were a stranger to these influences," Coolidge declared. "After all, the chief business of the American people is business. They are profoundly concerned with producing, buying, selling, investing, and prospering in the world."

Meanwhile, Prohibition had widespread effects on the American public during Coolidge's years. Prohibition was the constitutional ban on the manufacture and sale of alcohol

and alcoholic beverages from 1920 to 1933. Few Americans actually gave up the habit of drinking alcoholic beverages—bootleg liquor was relatively easy to purchase, and speakeasies, places that served liquor illegally, were easy to find. (Bootleg liquor was illegally produced liquor; the term comes from the practice of smugglers of carrying bottles of liquor in the sides of their tall boots.) Even President Harding was known to keep a private supply at the White House. Though Coolidge rarely

President and Mrs. Coolidge with their sons Calvin Jr. (far left) and John (far right) and their pet dog on June 30, 1924. Calvin Jr. died tragically of blood poisoning one week later. *Courtesy, Library of Congress.*

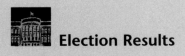

Election Results

1924

Presidential / Vice presidential candidates	Popular votes	Presidential electoral votes
Calvin Coolidge / Charles G. Dawes (Republican)	15,725,016	382
John W. Davis / Charles W. Bryan (Democratic)	8,386,503	136
Robert M. La Follette / Burton K. Wheeler (Progressive)	4,822,856	13

West Virginia politician Davis, a former ambassador to Great Britain, won the Democratic nomination on the 103rd ballot; former treasury secretary William G. McAdoo and New York governor Alfred E. Smith were early ballot leaders.

drank alcohol, he was privately opposed to Prohibition. He viewed the ban as an example of government interfering in people's lives, but he was compelled to publicly support it as the law of the land. He did utter one telling statement on the matter in 1924: "Any law that inspires disrespect for other laws—the good laws—is a bad law."

Most Americans at the time enjoyed their prosperity, but some unfortunate incidents occurred as well. The great Mississippi River flood of 1927 left large areas in the South devastated, as damage reached hundreds of millions of dollars. Coolidge opposed a congressional relief bill, arguing that the federal government should not favor one section of the country at the expense of another. But the legislation passed with a provision that gave the Army Corps of Engineers the task of future preventative measures. This act signaled expansion of government responsibilities and obligations in an era when both the people and the politicians wanted individual states to bear the responsibility for the health and welfare of its citizens.

Foreign policy

Coolidge's foreign policy mirrored his domestic (meaning pertaining to his own country's) administrative style: He favored nonintervention and the protection of American financial interests. Coolidge supported legislation that funded an expanded merchant marine fleet, believing that the fleet would provide America with greater opportunities to prosper in international commerce. (The merchant marine consists of nonmilitary professional sailors and boat workers involved with commercial marine trade and maintenance.) He called for a joint venture with Canada for construction on the St. Lawrence Seaway to open the Great Lakes region to European trade.

Conflicts erupted with Mexico in the mid-1920s when lands under lease to American oil companies were seized by the Mexican government. The conflict was later resolved through negotiation, but some Americans called for invasion. Coolidge authorized marines to land in Nicaragua in 1926 to put down a guerrilla war (unconventional warfare fought by rebellious military forces) supported with Mexican arms, but again diplomats to the region resolved the situation. The only time in his life that Coolidge set foot outside American borders came when he attended the Sixth International Conference of American States in Havana, Cuba, in 1928.

The most notable foreign-policy event of the Coolidge years was the Kellogg-Briand Pact. His secretary of state, Frank Kellogg (1856–1937; see box), was awarded the Nobel Peace Prize for engineering what was viewed as an international law against war. Also named for Kellogg's French counterpart, Aristide Briand (1862–1932), the pact was proclaimed at the time as a groundbreaking achievement in international relations. A response to the recent horrors of World War I, the nations signing the formal declaration agreed not to use force to solve disputes. The pact was signed by Coolidge on January 17, 1929. Sixty-one other countries also agreed to the terms.

Unparalleled prosperity

The 1920s are often described as a "golden era" in America for the prosperity and optimism that pervaded the times. In 1921, the country's gross national product (GNP; measurement of a nation's total value of goods and services produced over a certain period) was $69.9 billion. Three years later, that figure had soared to $93.1 billion. Unemployment fell rapidly, declining from 11.7 percent in 1921 to just 5 per-

Frank B. Kellogg

President Calvin Coolidge was generally inclined to let the country run by itself, and his secretary of state, Frank B. Kellogg, pursued a similar course in international affairs. Yet Kellogg was instrumental in negotiating the Kellogg-Briand Pact, a stunning agreement intended to achieve international peace. The pact was eventually compromised, but it was a major achievement for an administration often accused of doing nothing to lead the country and of being disinterested in foreign affairs.

Frank Billings Kellogg was born in Potsdam, New York, on December 22, 1856. In 1867, the family joined many other Americans moving westward following the Civil War (1861–65). The Kelloggs settled in Minnesota. Frank Kellogg worked on the family farm and had a very general education before moving to Rochester, Minnesota, to study law. He was admitted to the bar in 1877. Over the next ten years, he established a modest practice, and he married Clara M. Cook of Rochester in 1886. They did not have children. The following year, Minnesota's most prominent lawyer, former governor Cushman K. Davis

(1838–1900), was so impressed with Kellogg that he invited him into his firm.

Kellogg's career took a sudden twist in the early 1900s as he became involved in suits against large companies. During the administration of **Theodore Roosevelt** (1858–1919; see entry in volume 3), who governed from 1901 to 1909, Kellogg became involved in government antitrust suits (prosecution of companies for illegal activities). He was successful as the federal prosecutor in the government's case against General Paper Company, a monopolistic combination of newsprint manufacturers. That case ended in 1906, the same year he served as counsel to the Interstate Commerce Commission in its investigation of the activities of a railroad financier. At the same time, he was involved in the government's antitrust suit against Standard Oil. Kellogg pursued the case for several years, winning a favorable verdict in 1909 and in the appeal to the Supreme Court that resulted in a breakup of the trust. His success led to election as president of the American Bar Association in 1912.

In 1916, Kellogg was elected to the U.S. Senate but was defeated for re-

cent in the year of Coolidge's election. In 1927, the Dow Jones Industrial Average—a method of charting the progress of a select group of representative businesses to show the health of the stock market—closed at an unheard of measurement at that time of 200 points. (By comparison, the number reached 11,000 points in 1999).

Frank B. Kellogg.
Courtesy of the Library of Congress.

election in 1922. He served as ambassador to Great Britain from 1923 to 1925. In this post, he participated in the London and Paris conferences where the Dawes Plan for payment of German reparations (payment for damages during World War I) was negotiated, and he brought French and German leaders together.

In 1925, Kellogg was appointed secretary of state by President Calvin Coolidge. Kellogg regarded his negotiation of the Kellogg-Briand Pact for the maintenance of world peace as his most important State Department work. Taking advantage of a proposal by French foreign minister Aristide Briand for a pact binding France and the United States to refrain from war with each other, Kellogg proposed a much more ambitious policy—a general international agreement for the preservation of peace. Signed in August 1928 and ratified by most of the nations of the world, this pact bound the nations not "to resort to war as an instrument of national policy" and to settle all disputes by peaceful means. For his work on the pact, Kellogg received the Nobel Peace Prize in 1929 and was appointed a member of the Permanent Court of International Justice at The Hague, a post he held from 1930 to 1935. However, the pact proved ineffectual in preventing war because it did not address actions to be taken against an aggressor nation. For example, the pact had no effect when Nazi Germany invaded Czechoslovakia and Poland in 1939, actions that sparked World War II (1939–45).

Kellogg died in 1937 in St. Paul, Minnesota, and was buried in the National Cathedral in Washington, D.C.

That same year of 1927, the fourth year of the Coolidge administration, New York Yankee slugger Babe Ruth set a new home-run record. The first major motion picture to use sound, *The Jazz Singer,* opened and ushered in Hollywood's Golden Age. The first-ever solo airplane flight across the Atlantic was achieved by a young, handsome pilot named

Charles A. Lindbergh

Born in Detroit, Michigan, on February 4, 1902, Charles A. Lindbergh spent his childhood in Little Falls, Minnesota. He also lived in Washington, D.C., while his father served in the U.S. Congress. From 1920 to 1922, Lindbergh attended the University of Wisconsin, but he dropped out to go to an aviation school in Lincoln, Nebraska. After fewer than eight hours of instruction, he began flying with a stunt aviator and made his first parachute jump in June 1922. Lindbergh bought his first plane for $500 and made his first solo flight in April 1923. The following year he went through flight training in San Antonio, Texas, and in 1925 he was commissioned in the U.S. Air Service Reserve. He began flying air mail service flights between Chicago and St. Louis on April 15, 1926.

Lindbergh soon learned of a $25,000 prize being offered to the first person to fly nonstop from New York to Paris. Thinking a successful flight would help promote St. Louis as a future site of aviation, some St. Louis businessmen agreed to fund Lindbergh's attempt. He traveled to San Diego, California, to oversee the construction of his airplane, which he named the *Spirit of St. Louis*. On May 10, 1927, he flew from San Diego to St. Louis and on to Long Island, New York, in 21 hours and 20 minutes, a new record.

Lindbergh began his New York to Paris flight at 7:52 A.M. on May 20, 1927. His flight plan took him up the coast of New England and Nova Scotia and then over the Gulf of St. Lawrence and the island of Newfoundland. He flew across the North Atlantic Ocean, eating only sandwiches. He dozed off several times and once awoke to find his plane skimming the ocean waves. Since his plane was without a radio, no one could track his flight. He also had to make all of his own navigational calculations with the chance that any error could push him off course. Lindbergh knew he was safe when he flew over the southern coast of Ireland in daylight on May 21, 1927. When Lindbergh reached the coast of Normandy, France, it was approaching nightfall. He found his way to Paris by following the Seine River upstream. Unknown to him, his progress was reported by telephone and radio by watchers who passed the news to Paris. As he approached the city, Parisians began heading for Le Bourget Field, where Lindbergh was to land. The first flight across the North Atlantic from New York to Paris covered 3,610 miles. Lindbergh completed it in 33 hours, 29 minutes, and 30 seconds.

Lindbergh instantly became a world hero. He was received by royalty, President Coolidge, and other heads of state. After arriving in New York City, Lindbergh was treated to a parade that was the largest ever to date in the United States. Afterward, Lindbergh traveled to Washington, D.C., where Coolidge gave a medal—the Distinguished Flying Cross—to Lindbergh,

Charles A. Lindbergh.
Courtesy of the Library of Congress.

and the pilot dined at the White House. He made an air tour of the United States, traveling to seventy-five cities. At a reception at the American Embassy, he met Anne Morrow, the daughter of Dwight Morrow, U.S. ambassador to Mexico. Lindbergh married Morrow on May 27, 1929; she became his copilot and navigator as they flew together to foreign countries.

Lindbergh was an intensely private person. After his marriage, he took a job as technical adviser to Transcontinental Air Transport and Pan American Airways, flying many of their new routes. The Lindberghs lived in a quiet estate in New Jersey. Their peace was shattered in 1932 when twenty-month-old Charles Augustus, the Lindbergh's only child, was kidnapped. The kidnapping soon became the world's biggest media event, labeled as the crime of the century. After several months, the boy's body was found, and an unemployed German immigrant, Bruno Richard Hauptmann (1899–1936), was found guilty of the crime and executed. The Lindberghs soon moved to England.

In 1938 and 1939, Lindbergh traveled to Germany, was decorated by the Nazi government, and commented favorably on the state of the German Luftwaffe. When Lindbergh returned to the United States, he spoke out forcefully in favor of American neutrality when World War II (1939–45) began. These actions were unpopular with the public. Lindbergh was forced to resign his Air Corps Reserve commission.

Industrialist Henry Ford, who had several government war contracts, hired Lindbergh in 1943 to plan aircraft operations in the South Pacific during World War II. After the war, it was revealed that Lindbergh had worked as an unpaid consultant to the air force on secret projects from 1943 to 1945. This news helped regain some of Lindbergh's popularity. Lindbergh's book *The Spirit of St. Louis* won a Pulitzer Prize in 1953 and was made into a movie. President **Dwight D. Eisenhower** (1890–1969; see entry in volume 4) appointed Lindbergh a brigadier general in the air force in 1954. Lindbergh died on August 26, 1974.

President Calvin Coolidge tips a hat that was a special headpiece of the Smoki Indians of Prescott, Arizona. He was inducted into the tribe on October 22, 1924, after signing a bill nearly five months earlier that granted Native Americans full U.S. citizenship. *Courtesy of the Library of Congress.*

Charles Lindbergh. The arrival of his plane, the *Spirit of St. Louis*, in Paris, France, received massive international press coverage. On Coolidge's orders, Lindbergh was returned to America on board a large Navy cruiser. "I was informed that while it wasn't an order to come back home," Lindbergh remarked about Coolidge's gesture, "there'd be a battleship waiting for me. . . ."

Other domestic issues

Though generally a popular president, Coolidge was labeled by many segments of rural America as an enemy of the farmer. American farmers went deeper into debt, a situation that worsened each year. Coolidge twice vetoed (rejected) the McNary-Haugen Bill, first introduced in 1926, which had been designed to protect farmers from fluctuations (ups and downs) in crop prices by allowing the federal government to purchase crop surpluses (excess product) at a fixed price in order to sell them abroad—sometimes at a loss. Coolidge opposed the bill on the principal of a free-market economy, believing that such legislation would compel farmers to simply continue to produce more and more surpluses.

On the other hand, contemporary commercial aviation (the business of flying goods and passengers) owes much to Coolidge's foresight. He recognized that federal regulation could assist American success in the new industry. The Air Commerce Act of 1926 brought government regulation to commercial aviation and approval of the first two commercial airline routes.

Coolidge declined to seek reelection in 1928, though there was great public support for his candidacy. Characteristically, he refused to discuss his reasons for declining to seek another term. When his term ended, Calvin and Grace departed Washington at Union Station on a train bound for Northampton. Before boarding, the ex-president made a typically succinct statement to the assembled press: "Good-bye. I have had a very enjoyable time in Washington."

Coolidge left office at the peak of American optimism and prosperity, but that era ended dramatically in October 1929 when stock prices on Wall Street fell hard. With the slide came an economic crisis, bank failures, and the loss of millions of jobs. Some Americans, longing for the Coolidge-era prosperity and optimism during the worst days of the Great Depression (1929–41), suggested his name as the 1932 Republican nominee, but Coolidge had made clear he had retired from politics forever. He died at the age of sixty on January 5, 1933, after a heart attack at his home. Congress adjourned the next day, and his Republican successor, President **Herbert Hoover** (1874–1964; see entry in volume 4), declared thirty days of national mourning.

Legacy

Two of the major achievements of the Coolidge era were later obscured by events of the 1930s. Some have blamed Calvin Coolidge's lack of government regulation of business for contributing to events that sparked the Great Depression. A more balanced view recognizes that no single leader could have engineered the American prosperity of the

When his term ended, Calvin and Grace Coolidge departed Washington at Union Station on a train bound for Northampton, Massachusetts. Before boarding, the ex-president made a typically short-but-sweet statement to the assembled press: "Good-bye. I have had a very enjoyable time in Washington."

A Selection of Coolidge Landmarks

Black River Academy Museum. 14 High St., Ludlow, VT 05149. (802) 228-5050. A special Coolidge section of this local historical museum is devoted to its most famous graduate.

Calvin Coolidge Memorial Room. Forbes Library, 20 West St., Northampton, MA 01060. (413) 587-1014. Coolidge artifacts, as well as his personal and presidential papers, are housed in this public library, in the town he lived in before and after he was president. See http://www.gazettenet.com/forbeslibrary/coolidge.html (accessed on August 31, 2000).

Plymouth Notch Historic District. Vermont Route 100A, Box 79, Plymouth, VT 05056. (802) 672-3773. This majestic site includes the birthplace of Calvin Coolidge, the home in which he took the presidential oath from his father, the church he attended, the town store (whose upstairs was converted into a temporary White House when the president would visit), a museum, and the cemetery in which the president, his family, and his ancestors are buried. See http://www.cit.state.vt.us/dca/historic/Coolidg.htm (accessed on August 31, 2000).

1920s nor effectively foreseen the economic disaster that followed. The failure of the McNary-Haugen Bill continued the poor economic situation of many American farmers during the 1920s, which worsened with the Great Depression. Also, in light of the events of the 1930s, as fascist governments (which place a nation or a particular race of people above individual rights) in Europe bullied their way to power, the celebrated Coolidge-era Kellogg-Briand Pact has been viewed as an unrealistic and unenforceable agreement.

Noted newspaper editor and author H. L. Mencken (1880–1956) once said of Coolidge that as a president, "he will be ranked among the vacuums." However, when writing an obituary of the president in 1933, Mencken softened his view and said that Coolidge was perhaps a more complex man and politician than first thought. "We suffer most when the White House bursts with ideas," noted Mencken with his characteristic dry sense of humor. "His failings are forgotten; the country remembers only the grateful fact that he let it alone." He further contemplated, "Should the day ever dawn when . . . we reduce government to its simplest terms, it may very well happen that Calvin's bones now resting inconspicuously in the Vermont granite will come to be revered as those of a man who really did the nation some service."

Where to Learn More

Berg, A. Scott. *Lindbergh.* New York: Putnam, 1998.

Bryn-Jones, David. *Frank B. Kellogg: A Biography.* New York: G. P. Putnam's Sons, 1937.

"Calvin Coolidge: Examining the Evidence; A Conference at the John F. Kennedy Library, July 30–31, 1998." *The New England Journal of History* (special issue), Fall 1998, pp. 1–122. Also [Online] http://www.cs.umb.edu/jfklibrary/coolidge_papers.html (accessed on September 8, 2000).

Calvin Coolidge Memorial Foundation, Inc. [Online] http://www.calvin-coolidge.org/ (accessed on August 31, 2000).

Coolidge, Calvin. *The Autobiography of Calvin Coolidge.* New York: Cosmopolitan, 1929. Reprint, Rutland, VT: Academy Books, 1984.

Ferrell, Robert H. *The Presidency of Calvin Coolidge.* Lawrence: University Press of Kansas, 1998.

Feuss, Claude M. *Calvin Coolidge, the Man from Vermont.* Boston: Little, Brown, 1940. Reprint, Westport, CT: Greenwood Publishing Group, 1976.

Fischer, Margaret Jane. *Calvin Coolidge, Jr.* Rutland, VT: Academy Books, 1981.

John Fitzgerald Kennedy. *Calvin Coolidge on the World Wide Web.* [Online] http: www.cs.umb.edu/jfklibrary/coolidge_links.html (accessed on August 31, 2000).

Joseph, Paul. *Calvin Coolidge.* Edina, MN: Abdo Publishing Company, 1999.

Mosley, Leonard. *Lindbergh: A Biography.* Garden City, NY: Doubleday, 1976. Reprint, Mineola, NY: Dover, 2000.

Sobel, Robert. *Coolidge: An American Enigma.* Washington, DC: Regnery Publishing, 1998.

White, William Allen. *A Puritan in Babylon: The Story of Calvin Coolidge.* New York: Macmillan, 1938. Reprint, Gloucester, MA: Patterson Smith, 1973.

Grace Coolidge

Born January 3, 1879
Burlington, Vermont
Died July 8, 1957
Northampton, Massachusetts

Energetic and fun-loving first lady contrasted the president's personality and delighted a nation

Grace Coolidge seemed to be her husband's exact opposite in personality and style. She was outgoing, lively, and spirited, in contrast to the president's famously reserved, almost dour (stern; gloomy) personality. Nevertheless, the Coolidges enjoyed a solid union, for they complemented each other's characters exceedingly well. "For almost a quarter of a century she was borne with my infirmities [faults], and I have rejoiced in her graces," wrote **Calvin Coolidge** (1872–1933; see entry in volume 4) of his wife in his autobiography. Their otherwise happy years in the White House were marked by the tragedy of the death of their son, Calvin Jr., in 1924.

Vermont native

Grace Coolidge, the first graduate of a public university to become a first lady, was born in Burlington, Vermont, in 1879. She was the only child of Andrew Goodhue, a mechanical engineer and steamboat inspector for the Lake Champlain Transportation Company, and Lemira B. Goodhue, a quiet, serious woman. Grace graduated from Burling-

"[I'm] a simple, home-loving woman. I love best of all to gather my little family under my own roof and to stay there. We are just a plain New England family and we like, above all else, to live and do the things that simple New England families do."

Grace Coolidge

Grace Coolidge.
Courtesy of the Library of Congress.

ton High School in 1897 and lived at home during her student years at the University of Vermont. She was a popular student, known for a high-spirited personality, and was a member of Pi Beta Phi, the first Greek organization (sorority) for women.

After graduating in 1902, Grace convinced her parents to allow her to move to another state to begin a career—a rather extreme act for an unmarried young woman at the time, even a college graduate, since few females lived outside households headed by a father or a husband. The sister of a neighbor in Burlington headed the Clarke School for the Deaf in Northampton, Massachusetts, where the inventor of the telephone, Alexander Graham Bell (1847–1922), had once taught. Grace entered the school's teacher training program that fall.

Marriage and the Northampton years

In Northampton, Grace met Calvin Coolidge. A graduate of Amherst College in Northampton, Coolidge was a young attorney who boarded at the home of Amherst's steward, Robert Weir. One day while passing on the street where Weir lived, Grace noticed a man standing in a window wearing a suit of long underwear and a hat while shaving before a mirror. She asked Weir about the man, and he arranged an introduction. Coolidge explained to Grace that he wore the hat when he shaved because of a lock of hair that would not stay in place. The two began dating, though their personalities could not have been more seemingly unsuited: Grace was outgoing and enthusiastic, whereas Calvin was a man of very few words who often wore a gloomy expression upon his face. On the unlikely pair, Weir commented that since Grace had been trained to teach the deaf to hear, perhaps she could now teach a mute to speak.

Lemira Goodhue tried to discourage the relationship between her daughter and the lawyer who was seven years older than her, but Grace did not listen to her advice. She and Calvin were wed at her parents' home in Burlington on October 4, 1905. After returning from a Montreal honeymoon, Coolidge presented his wife with fifty-two pairs of socks that he had been waiting to have mended; incredibly thrifty, he had been saving the socks with the hope that some day a wife would repair them for him. The couple lived in half of a duplex on Massasoit Street in Northampton, where their first son, John, was born in September 1906. A second son, Calvin Jr., arrived in 1908.

Grace was often left alone with her sons in Northampton for long periods of time. Her husband's new political career took him to Boston, and he did not wish to increase his expenses by relocating his household to the far more expensive city. Coolidge became a Massachusetts legislator in 1907, and then returned to Northampton to serve four years as the city's mayor. He went back to Boston when elected to the state senate in 1912. During this period, he came home on weekends; often on Saturday nights he watched the children so that Grace might have time to visit with friends.

An apolitical wife

Grace was an active mother, often playing baseball with her boys. She noted in her autobiography that Coolidge never discussed topics of a political nature or even current events with her; she often learned of his decisions from newspapers, like everyone else. She believed that he considered her education inadequate.

Coolidge's stubbornness about maintaining a cheaper household for his family by having them live in Northampton during his term as governor caused comment among sophisticated Bostonians. Nevertheless, Coolidge was beginning to build a political career upon his reputation as a cost-cutter. Curiously, his penny-pinching did not extend to his wife's clothing expenditures. He even liked to window-shop for her in Boston. Sometimes he bought her extravagant hats and occasionally returned home on the train to Northampton carrying a large hatbox.

When Coolidge became vice president following the victory of **Warren G. Harding** (1865–1923; see entry in volume 4) in the 1920 presidential election, Grace Coolidge suddenly found herself the subject of a great deal of media attention, which she handled with characteristic style. The Coolidges moved to Washington, D.C., while their sons attended Mercersburg Academy, a school about a hundred miles from the District of Columbia. The family journeyed annually to the

The Coolidges enjoyed entertaining celebrities at the White House. Pictured here on October 17, 1924, are (front row) Grace Coolidge, actor John Drew, President Calvin Coolidge, and actor Al Jolson.
Courtesy of the Library of Congress.

Coolidge farmstead in Plymouth Notch, Vermont, where Calvin Coolidge's father still lived. Grace was with her husband there in August 1923 when Harding took ill on the other side of the country; a messenger arrived in Plymouth Notch in the middle of the night with the news that the president had died. Grace stood near as her husband took the oath of office, which was administered by his father, a notary public.

White House tragedy

The Harding administration had been rocked by scandals. As president, Coolidge was determined to restore faith in the Republican leadership. While Coolidge went about his official duties, Grace kept White House social events at a subdued tone, appropriate for a mourning period following the death of Harding and the scandal her husband was helping put to rest. Gradually, the Coolidges began to invite celebrities to official dinners, a practice that continues to the present day.

The new first lady was viewed as a positive attribute in her husband's political career. The press loved her sincerity and unaffectedness, as well as her photogenic qualities. Grace participated enthusiastically in her official duties and at such events as opening rest homes for veterans or ceremoniously laying cornerstones of new buildings.

In 1924, the younger Coolidge son, Calvin, died tragically during the summer his father was nominated to run for a full term on the Republican presidential ticket. Not wearing socks with his sneakers during a tennis game, the youngster developed a blister on his foot that became seriously infected. With an endurance for pain perhaps inherited from his father, the teen said nothing about the wound for a few days and the infection passed into his bloodstream. By the time his septicemia (blood poisoning) was diagnosed, doctors told the Coolidges that the boy's condition was grave. The most modern medical treatments were attempted, but the infection lingered. After two days of severe illness, young Calvin died. The death shocked the country: telegrams and letters of sympathy poured in to Washington from the nation and from around the world.

The Coolidges buried their sixteen-year-old son in Plymouth Notch. They took a small Vermont spruce with them back to Washington. The sapling was planted on the south grounds of the White House, near the tennis courts, and a plaque commemorating the younger Coolidge's brief life was mounted. Grace Coolidge wrote a memorial ode (poem) to her son, "The Open Door," which was published in *Good Housekeeping* magazine in 1929.

Later years

While not a political activist, Grace took advantage of a photographic opportunity staged on the White House lawn in 1925 that showed the first lady completing her absentee ballot for the upcoming elections. She firmly believed that American women were not taking full advantage of their recently won right to vote. Other images of the Coolidge administration reveal the Coolidges as pet lovers: A portrait of Grace, by Howard Chandler Christy (1873–1952), depicts her in a red gown with her white collie, Rob Roy, at her side. **Jacque-**

Grace Coolidge attends a World Series game in 1949. The former first lady loved baseball, and enjoyed listening to the Boston Red Sox on the radio.
Reproduced by permission of the Corbis Corporation.

line Kennedy (1929–1994; see entry in volume 5) liked the painting so much that when she discovered it among warehoused items of the White House, she had it rehung in the Red Room of the White House during her own years as first lady.

After Coolidge declined to run for a second full term in 1928, he and Grace returned to Northampton, where they bought an estate called The Beeches. After a few happy years of retirement, Coolidge died of a heart attack there in January 1933. Grace later sold the house, noting it was too large for one person.

She remained active in many ways over the next two decades, riding in an airplane for the first time and traveling to Europe in 1936. During World War II, she carried food and gifts to the train station for soldiers heading overseas. She also loved to listen to Boston Red Sox baseball games on the radio and spend time with her son, John, his wife Florence, and their two daughters. When Northampton's Forbes Library created a Calvin Coolidge Memorial Room, Grace was invited to the dedication in September 1956. It would be her last public appearance. Grace Coolidge died on July 8, 1957.

Where to Learn More

Coolidge, Grace Goodhue. *Grace Coolidge: An Autobiography.* Edited by Lawrence E. Wikander and Robert H. Ferrell. Worland, WY: High Plains Pub. Co., 1992.

Ross, Ishbel. *Grace Coolidge and Her Era: The Story of a President's Wife.* New York: Dodd, Mead, 1962. Reprint, Plymouth, VT: Calvin Coolidge Memorial Foundation, 1988.

Sayles, Lydia Coolidge. "Grace Coolidge, My Grandmother" in "Calvin Coolidge: Examining the Evidence; A Conference at the John F. Kennedy Library, July 30–31, 1998." *The New England Journal of History* (special issue), Fall 1998, pp. 79–82. Also [Online] http://www.cs. umb.edu/jfklibrary/coolidge_papers.html (accessed on September 8, 2000).

Coolidge's Speech on Government and Business

**Delivered on November 19, 1925;
excerpted from *American Memory* (Web site)**

*"Silent Cal" elaborates on his theme, "the chief business of the
American people is business."*

Calvin Coolidge (1872–1933; see entry in volume 4)
presided during a period of economic prosperity called
"the Roaring 20s." His pro-business administration emphasized few government regulations on business activity. He
lowered taxes, reasoning that the money individuals and
businesses saved on paying taxes could be spent on investments to further encourage business growth.

Because Coolidge did not propose many government
programs, some thought of him as a "do-nothing president,"
content to let the country run on its own. Coolidge believed
that the same freedoms that American citizens enjoyed ought
to be extended to business as well. Not known as a great
speechmaker, he was famous instead for brief remarks, such
as "the chief business of the American people is business," a
quote from a speech the president gave to the American Society of Newspaper Editors on January 17, 1925. Business and
government was the theme of his 1925 address to the New
York State Chamber of Commerce.

> "True business represents
> the mutual organized
> effort of society to
> minister to the economic
> requirements of
> civilization. It is an effort
> by which men provide
> for the material needs of
> each other."
>
> *Calvin Coolidge*

Things to remember while reading an excerpt from President Coolidge's speech on government and business:

- Coolidge was speaking before the state of New York's Chamber of Commerce—a group devoted to promoting and improving businesses within the state. It was an audience that greatly supported the president's policies. In the third paragraph and first sentence of the fourth paragraph in the following speech excerpt, Coolidge defined business in highly respectful terms.

- For Coolidge, the freedoms that individuals enjoyed in a democracy were the same freedoms that allowed business to thrive. He contrasted the freedom that business enjoyed in America with the more governmentally monitored practices abroad. Coolidge maintained that government involvement in business affairs should be focused mainly on "requirements of safety, health, and taxation." Equating business with fairness, Coolidge asserted that government should only interfere with business when unfair practices occurred.

- Near the end of the excerpt, Coolidge addresses the opinion that American prosperity during the 1920s was a result of World War I (1914–18), when many industries and workers helped support the war effort. Coolidge countered that view. He noted that the country spent and lost an enormous amount of money during the war. Coolidge instituted postwar policies of limited government spending, reduction in taxes, and a moderate rise in tariff rates (taxes on foreign goods). That modest and helpful relationship between government and business was, according to Coolidge, the reason for America's prosperity during the 1920s.

Excerpt from President Coolidge's speech on government and business

If a contest could be held to determine how much those who are really prominent in our government life know about business, and *how much those who are really prominent in our business life know about government, it is my firm conviction that the prize would be awarded those who are in government life. This is as it ought to be, for those who have the greater authority ought to have the greater knowledge. But it is my even firmer conviction that the general welfare of our country could be very much advanced through a better knowledge by both of those parties of the multifold problems with which each has to deal. While our system gives an opportunity for great benefit by encouraging **detachment** and breadth of vision which ought not to be sacrificed, it does not have the advantages which could be secured if each had a better conception of their mutual requirements.*

*While I have spoken of what I believed would be the advantages of a more sympathetic understanding, I should put an even stronger emphasis on the desirability of the largest possible independence between government and business. Each ought to be **sovereign** in its own sphere. When government comes unduly under the influence of business, the tendency is to develop an administration which closes the door of opportunity; becomes narrow and selfish in its outlook; and results in an **oligarchy**. When government enters the field of business with its great resources, it has a tendency to extravagance and inefficiency, but, having the power to crush all competitors, likewise closes the door of opportunity and results in **monopoly**. It is always a problem in a republic to maintain on the one side that efficiency which comes only from trained and skillful management without running into **fossilization** and **autocracy**, and to maintain on the other that equality of opportunity which is the result of political and economic liberty without running into **dissolution** and **anarchy**. The general results in our country, our freedom and prosperity, warrant the assertion that our system of institutions has been advancing in the right direction in the attempt to solve these problems. We have order, opportunity, wealth, and progress. . . .*

True business represents the mutual organized effort of society to minister to the economic requirements of civilization. It is an effort by which men provide for the material needs of each other. While it is not an end in itself, it is the important means for the attainment of a supreme end. It rests squarely on the law of service. It has for its main reliance truth and faith and justice. In its larger sense it is one of the greatest contributing forces to the moral and spiritual advancement of the race.

It is the important and righteous position that business holds in relation to life which gives warrant to the great interest which the

Detachment: Separation.

Sovereign: An authority.

Oligarchy: A small group that exercises control over others.

Monopoly: Exclusive ownership of a commodity.

Fossilization: An outmoded existence.

Autocracy: Government in which one person has absolute power.

Dissolution: Disruption or termination.

Anarchy: Absence of government; a state of lawlessness.

National Government constantly exercises for the promotion of its success. This is not exercised as has been the autocratic practice abroad of directly supporting and financing different business projects, except in case of great emergency, but we have rather held to a democratic policy of cherishing the general structure of business while holding its avenues open to the widest competition, in order that its opportunities and its benefits might be given the broadest possible participation. While it is true that the Government ought not to be and is not committed to certain methods of acquisition which, while partaking of the nature of unfair practices try to masquerade under the guise of business, the Government is and ought to be thoroughly committed to every endeavor of production and distribution which is entitled to be designated as true business. Those who are so engaged, instead of regarding the Government as their opponent and enemy, ought to regard it as their vigilant supporter and friend.

It is only in exceptional instances that this means a change on the part of the national administration so much as it means a change on the part of trade. Except for the requirements of safety, health, and taxation, the law enters very little into the work of production. It is mostly when we come to the problems of distribution that we meet the more rigid exactions of legislation. The main reason why certain practices in this direction have been denounced is because they are a species of unfair competition on the one hand or tend to monopoly and restraint of trade on the other. The whole policy of the Government in its system of opposition to monopoly, and its public regulation of transportation and trade, has been animated by a desire to have business remain business. We are a politically free people and must be an economically free people. . . .

*[The] present generation of business almost universally throughout its responsible organization and management has shown every disposition to correct its own abuses with as little intervention of the Government as possible. This position is recognized by the public, and due to the appreciation of the needs which the country has for great units of production in time of war, and to the better understanding of the service which they perform in time of peace, resulting very largely from the discussion of our tax problems, a new attitude of the public mind is distinctly discernible toward great **aggregations** of capital. Their prosperity goes very far to insure the prosperity of all the country. The contending elements have each learned a most profitable lesson.*

This development has left the Government free to advance from the problems of reform and repression to those of economy and con-

Aggregations: A group or body composed of many distinctive parts.

Complete American Presidents Sourcebook

*struction. A very large progress is being made in these directions. Our country is in a state of unexampled and apparently sound and well distributed prosperity. It did not gain wealth, as some might hastily conclude, as a result of the war. Here and there individuals may have profited greatly, but the country as a whole was a heavy loser. Forty billions of the wealth of the Nation was directly exhausted, while the indirect expenditure and depreciation can not be estimated. The Government appreciated that the only method of regeneration lay in economy and production. It has followed a policy of economy in national expenditures. By an enormous reduction in taxation it has released great amounts of capital for use in productive effort. It has sought to stimulate domestic production by a moderate application of the system of protective **tariff duties**. The results of these efforts are known to all the world. . . .*

Great as the accomplishments have been, they are yet but partly completed. We need further improvement in transportation facilities by development of inland waterways; we need railroad consolidations; we need further improvement of our railway terminals for more economical distribution of commodities in the great congested centers; we need reorganization of Government departments; we need still larger extension of electrification; in general, we need still further effort against all the various categories of waste which the Department of Commerce has enumerated and so actively attacked, for in this direction lies not only increased economic progress but the maintenance of that progress against foreign competition. There is still plenty of work for business to do. (American Memory [Web site])

What happened next . . .

America continued to prosper throughout President Coolidge's presidency. His policy of minimal government involvement in business encouraged further economic growth. Coolidge's similar approach to other areas of American life proved more frustrating to many Americans. Many farmers faced bankruptcy with the absence of federal assistance during times of drought or flooding. There were few improvements in civil rights, though some historians believe Coolidge was an improvement over his five predecessors.

Tariff duties: Taxes on imported goods.

Coolidge did not act against risky business practices through which investors bought stocks on margin (meaning they borrowed money in order to buy stocks). Many stocks became over-valued because investors were continually buying, selling, and trading them at ever higher prices. Little more than six months after Coolidge left office, the prices of stock suddenly plummeted. Many people lost money. The collapse of the stock market was the onset of the Great Depression (1929–41), which lasted for over a decade.

Coolidge did not have to face such a formidable challenge during his presidency. His pro-business approach and policy of limited government worked well enough during his administration in a time of peace and prosperity. Doing more to help expand prosperity and to protect against such events as the stock market collapse would have resulted in a different kind of presidency than what Coolidge offered.

Did you know . . .

- President Coolidge's "the chief business of the American people is business" line has often been misquoted as "the business of America is business." William Allen White, author of a 1938 biography on Coolidge, *A Puritan in Babylon,* used the erroneous quote over ten times in books and articles he wrote between 1925 and 1938. In fact, the "chief business" quote, used by the president in a 1925 speech, was followed by this utterance: "Of course the accumulation of wealth cannot be justified as the chief end of existence." And then: "We make no concealment of the fact that we want wealth, but there are many other things that we want very much more. We want peace and honor, and that charity which is so strong an element of all civilization." Taking an incorrect quote out of context has often led to a faulty and negative stereotype of Coolidge—one of a man who valued American materialism above all else.

Where to Learn More

Bittinger, Cyndy. "The Press Under a Free Government." *Calvin Coolidge Memorial Foundation, Inc.* [Online] http://www.calvin-coolidge.org/business_misquote.htm (accessed on September 8, 2000).

Felzenberg, Alvin S. "Calvin Coolidge and Race: His Record in Dealing with the Racial Tensions of the 1920s." In "Calvin Coolidge: Examining the Evidence; A Conference at the John F. Kennedy Library, July 30–31, 1998." *The New England Journal of History* (special issue), Fall 1998. Also [Online] http://www.cs.umb.edu/jfklibrary/coolidge_papers.html (accessed on September 8, 2000).

Ferrell, Robert H. *The Presidency of Calvin Coolidge.* Lawrence: University Press of Kansas, 1998.

Library of Congress. "Prosperity and Thrift: The Coolidge Era and the Consumer Economy, 1921–1929" *American Memory.* [Online] http://memory.loc.gov/ammem/coolhtml/coolhome.html (accessed on September 8, 2000).

McCoy, Donald R. *Calvin Coolidge: The Quiet President.* New York: Macmillan, 1967. Reprint, Newtown, CT: American Political Biography Press, 1999.

Sobel, Robert. *Coolidge: An American Enigma.* Washington, DC: Regnery Pub., 1998.

Herbert Hoover

Thirty-first president (1929–1933)

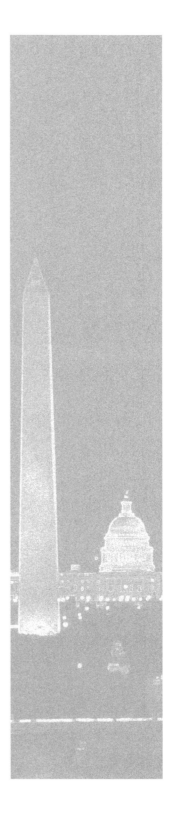

Herbert Hoover . . . 1087

   Fast Facts about Herbert Hoover (box) . . . 1088

   Herbert Hoover Timeline (box) . . . 1089

   Words to Know (box) . . . 1090

   Alfred E. Smith (box) . . . 1094

   Election Results (box) . . . 1096

   Herbert Hoover Administration (box) . . . 1097

   Henry L. Stimson (box) . . . 1100

   A Selection of Hoover Landmarks (box) . . . 1106

Lou Hoover . . . 1109

**Primary source: Hoover's "Rugged Individualism"
Campaign Speech**
   *Presidential candidate Hoover expresses his optimistic views on American
   prosperity one year before the onset of the Great Depression* **. . . 1115**

Herbert Hoover

Born August 10, 1874
West Branch, Iowa
Died October 20, 1964
New York, New York

Thirty-first president of the United States (1929–1933)

Remained optimistic despite the greatest economic crisis in U.S. history— the Great Depression

"I have no fears for the future of our country. It is bright with hope."

Herbert Hoover

Herbert Hoover.
Courtesy of the Library of Congress.

Herbert Hoover had a long and distinguished career in public service and private business. He was a self-made man (one who becomes successful through hard work without the financial help of others). Becoming a millionaire as a mining engineer, Hoover was a world traveler by the time he was thirty and had a narrow escape during a rebellion in China in 1900. When World War I (1914–18) broke out, he used some of his own money to help Americans stranded in Europe. His public service with several war relief agencies earned him a place on a list of "the ten greatest living Americans" published by the *New York Times* shortly after the war.

After serving with distinction as secretary of commerce for presidents **Warren G. Harding** (1865–1923; see entry in volume 4) and **Calvin Coolidge** (1872–1933; see entry in volume 4) during the 1920s, Hoover was elected president in 1928. Hoover's earlier efforts with war relief agencies had earned him a great reputation for "crisis management" (making decisions during a crisis to help improve the situation). During his first year as president, he faced the most serious economic crisis in American history: the stock market crash

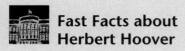
Full name: Herbert Clark Hoover

Born: August 10, 1874

Died: October 20, 1964

Burial site: Herbert Hoover National Historic Site, West Branch, Iowa

Parents: Jesse Clark and Hulda Randall Minthorn Hoover

Spouse: Lou Henry (1875–1944; m. 1899)

Children: Herbert Charles (1903–1969); Allan Henry (1907–1993)

Religion: Society of Friends (Quaker)

Education: Stanford University (B.A., 1895)

Occupation: Mining engineer

Government positions: Public administrator; secretary of commerce under Warren G. Harding and Calvin Coolidge; food relief coordinator

Political party: Republican

Dates as president: March 4, 1929–March 4, 1933

Age upon taking office: 54

(sudden decline in the value of stocks) in October 1929 and the Great Depression (1929–41) that soon followed.

Hoover believed that communities should unite to help themselves during times of crisis. The Great Depression, however, proved to be overwhelming. None of the modest government policies he supported made a significant impact on steadily worsening conditions. He was extremely unpopular by the time he left office in 1933. Hoover regained public respect through his efforts during World War II (1939–45) when he again managed relief efforts for victims of war.

Quaker heritage

Herbert Clark Hoover was born on August 10, 1874, in West Branch, Iowa, a Quaker community. Formally known as the Society of Friends, Quakers believe that each individual can directly feel the presence of God. They value work, community cooperation, spirituality through meditation, and nonviolence. Those values influenced Hoover throughout his life.

Orphaned before he was ten years old, Hoover was sent to Oregon to live with an uncle, Henry Hinthorn, who was a physician and a real estate agent. His uncle planned for Hoover to attend a Quaker college, but Hoover instead entered the newly established Stanford University in California in 1891 to study mining and engineering. To support himself, he earned money with a laundry service and with newspaper routes. He spent summers working for the U.S. Geological Survey and continued to work with the organization after he graduated from Stanford in 1895.

Herbert Hoover Timeline

1874: Born in Iowa

1885: Left an orphan, Hoover travels by train from Iowa to Oregon to live with an uncle

1897: Hired by Bewick-Moreing, a London mining firm, and sent to Australia to search for gold

1900: While working in China, Hoover is trapped along with his wife and other westerners in an uprising against foreigners called the Boxer Rebellion

1908: Forms his own mining and engineering consulting firm

1914: Organizes assistance and safe passages for Americans stranded in Europe at the beginning of World War I; also forms the Commission for the Relief of Belgium during the war

1915–19: Heads the U.S. Food Administration

1921–28: Serves as secretary of commerce under presidents Warren G. Harding and Calvin Coolidge

1929–33: Serves as thirty-first U.S. president

1929: Stock market crashes; Great Depression begins (ends in 1941)

1946: Named head of the international Famine Relief Commission by President Harry S. Truman and visits twenty-five countries in less than two months to supervise relief measures

1964: Dies in New York

In 1897, Hoover was offered a position with Bewick Moreing, a British mining company. He served as a scout searching for mineral deposits in Western Australia. Hoover was soon promoted to become Bewick Moreing's representative in China. Before traveling to China, Hoover returned to California to marry Louise "Lou" Henry (1874–1944; see entry on **Lou Hoover** in volume 4), a geology student he had met at Stanford. After their wedding ceremony in February 1899, the newlyweds boarded a ship and sailed to China.

Living in Beijing, China, the Hoovers soon found themselves in the midst of a dangerous, antiforeigner uprising—the Boxer Rebellion—in 1900. "Boxers" was the Western term for a group of Chinese nationalists, the Righteous and Harmonious Fists, who wanted to rid their country of both

Words to Know

Boxer Rebellion: The Boxers (a term describing a group of Chinese nationalists who called themselves Righteous and Harmonious Fists) were intent on ridding their country of foreign influences. When they began a violent campaign against foreigners, U.S. marines were sent in to fight alongside troops from other Western nations. The Boxers were overcome in August 1900.

Consulting firm: A company made up of experts in a certain field. The firm is hired by businesses to help them improve their operations.

Cooperatives: A group of individuals or businesses with similar interests who pool resources.

Crisis management: The ability to make decisions during a time of crisis to help improve the situation.

Debtors: Those who borrow money from a lending institution and pay back the loan with interest (interest is a charge for borrowing money) over a period of time.

Foreclosing: When a lending institution ends a loan agreement and seizes assets (items of value, such as property) to make up for money owed, after a borrower fails to make agreed upon payments.

Great Depression: The worst financial crisis in American history. Usually dated from 1929, when many investors lost money during a stock market crash, to 1941, when the last Depression-related relief effort to help impoverished and

unemployed people was passed by the government. When America entered World War II (1939–45) in 1941, many more employment opportunities became available in war-related industries.

"Hoovervilles": The nickname given to makeshift camps that homeless people set up during the Depression. The term comes from the name Herbert Hoover, who was president when the Depression set in.

Injunction: A legal maneuver that suspends a certain practice until a legal decision can be reached.

Investors: Those who commit money to an individual or company with the expectation of gaining financial returns as the party they invested in becomes more successful.

Mining engineer: A person who is an expert in minerals and the methods through which the minerals can be mined.

Parliamentary government: A system of government in which executive power resides with Cabinet-level officials responsible to the nation's legislature. The highest-ranking member of the political party with a majority in such a system of government is usually made the nation's chief executive.

Scapegoat: A person unfairly blamed for troubles.

Stock market crash: A sudden decline in the value of stocks that severely affects investors.

foreign influence and foreigners. The Hoovers spent several weeks under siege in the city of Tientsin, where Hoover was working. After the troubles died down, Hoover continued working in China and was soon made a junior partner, a second-level executive involved in strategic planning and decision making, in Bewick Moreing. The Hoovers and son Herbert Charles (1905–1969) spent the next seven years traveling around the world while Hoover supervised company operations in Asia, Africa, and Europe.

Crisis management

Not long after the birth of the Hoovers' second son, Allan Henry (1907–1993), Hoover started his own consulting firm of engineers, with offices in several major cities in the United States and Europe. (A consulting firm is a company that hires out the services of experts in a certain field to other businesses.) When World War I erupted in 1914, thousands of Americans living or traveling in Europe discovered that their money had no value and their ability to travel was restricted. The Hoovers were among those trapped in London, England. When an angry mob of Americans descended on the American consulate (the offices of the representatives of the United States) in London, the U.S. ambassador to England called on Hoover for help. Backed by his personal assets (his own money and property) of over $10 million, Hoover formed the Committee of American Residents in London for Assistance to American Travelers. They organized lodging and food for stranded Americans and arranged for safe passage home within six weeks.

Hoover's feat in London led to his appointment as head of the Committee for Relief of Belgium (CRB). Germany had invaded the country during the first weeks of the war. Since Belgium was heavily dependent on imports for food after being disrupted and occupied by foreign soldiers, the country quickly faced the threat of famine. Hoover accepted the post with reluctance, but he quickly found ways to resume and distribute food supplies for the troubled nation.

Profiled regularly in American newspapers for his efforts in England and Belgium, Hoover was tapped by President **Woodrow Wilson** (1856–1924; see entry in volume 4) in 1917 to head the U.S. Food Administration when America entered World War I. As America's "food czar," Hoover instituted programs and rallied support to conserve (avoid wasteful use of) food resources at home and to ensure that food supplies were available for soldiers. His program, dubbed "Hooverizing," reduced American food consumption by fifteen percent.

After World War I ended in 1919, Hoover was asked to hold several positions in which he could oversee charities dedicated to feeding and clothing millions of European refugees. Hoover himself founded the American Relief Administration (ARA) to fight famine (a great shortage of food) in Europe and was awarded $100 million by Congress to finance the effort. Hoover became a beloved figure in Europe. At a ceremony in Poland, for example, a parade of children greeted him with a banner that read "God Bless Herbert Hoover." At one point, a group of the children scattered, then returned to the procession with a rabbit they caught and presented to Hoover. A *New York Times* poll taken around this time had Hoover listed among the ten greatest living Americans.

More public service

Hoover planned to return to his mining business in 1920 and looked forward to settling into his family's new, large house on a Palo Alto, California, hillside. That changed when Republican Warren G. Harding was elected president in 1920, and asked Hoover to serve as his secretary of commerce.

Hoover took the position and immediately began reorganizing what was then a minor Cabinet (presidential advisory) department. During the next eight years under Harding and his successor, Calvin Coolidge, Hoover instituted a manufacturing code program; that is, he set up a system for regulating manufacturing standards. For example, many common products, such as nuts and bolts, paper, automobile tires, and even milk bottles, were made to follow specific standard sizes under his direction. Similarly, he authored a set of municipal building codes. Such standardization simplified manufacturing processes and made it easier for consumers to become familiar with codes and quality standards. Hoover oversaw the issuing of radio licenses as that medium (means of communication) first came into widespread use during the 1920s. Dur-

ing this period, he worked to expand foreign markets for American products as well.

Hoover was selected by President Coolidge to supervise relief efforts during a particularly severe Mississippi River flood in 1927. Hoover convinced business and industry leaders to lend resources for help. He firmly believed in community cooperation in such situations, a reflection of his Quaker upbringing. He preferred volunteer efforts instead of emergency

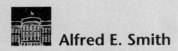

Alfred E. Smith

Alfred Emanuel Smith set two precedents in the presidential election of 1928, which he lost to Republican Herbert Hoover. Smith was the first Roman Catholic candidate for president from a major party, and he won a majority of votes in large urban areas. Big cities had traditionally been won by Republicans, but that trend was reversed by Smith in 1928, and Democratic presidential candidates continued to win in large cities through much of the twentieth century.

Smith was born on December 30, 1873, in a tenement (rental apartment) in New York City. His father, a veteran of the Civil War (1861–65) and owner of a small trucking firm, and Smith's mother grew up in the same New York City neighborhood. Smith attended Catholic schools and developed a reputation as a strong speaker. A month before completing the eighth grade, however, Smith dropped out of school to work as an errand boy for a trucking firm; his father had died when Smith was twelve, and the family had become impoverished. Over the next few years, Smith worked as a clerk, sold fish to merchants and restaurants, and at the age of twenty began working in a boiler manufacturing plant in Brooklyn, New York. In his spare time, he often appeared in productions of his church-sponsored amateur theater group, and occasionally worked as an extra on the stage of a local professional theater. He married Cather-ine Dunn on May 6, 1900; they would have five children.

Along with participation in theater groups, Smith began working for local political causes and became connected with the political machine (a powerful political group able to energize groups of voters for particular candidates). He rose rapidly, eventually winning election to the New York state assembly in 1903. As a state legislator, he backed bills favorable to working class people, and in 1910 he opposed a series of antipolitical machine measures backed by the Republican governor, Charles Evans Hughes (1862–1948; see box in **Warren G. Harding** entry in volume 4). The Triangle Shirtwaist Company fire of 1911, which took 146 lives, most of them women working in a crowded manufacturing building, energized his reform-minded pursuits. He quickly introduced a bill to establish a factory investigating commission, served as vice chairman of the commission, and sponsored its legislation to improve sanitary, health, and fire laws, institute wage and hour regulations for women and children, and improve workmen's compensation laws. Smith gained the distinction of being a social reformer while continuing to be part of an influential political machine.

At the New York constitutional convention of 1915, Smith impressed the press and the majority of Republican delegates with his knowledge of state government

Alfred E. Smith.
Reproduced by permission of Archive Photos.

and his effort to reform government spending practices. He was elected to a two-year term as sheriff of New York City, and in 1918 he was elected the state's governor. Smith continued to support measures sympathetic to people living in crowded urban areas, including an improved worker's compensation law, higher teacher salaries, and improved programs for the sick and mentally ill. After losing the governorship during the countrywide Republican landslide of 1920, he was reelected in 1924 and 1926. Smith was a candidate for the Democratic nomination for president in 1924, but he lost out during a bitterly divided convention that eventually chose former treasury secretary William Gibbs McAdoo (1863–1941) after 103 rounds of voting.

Smith's presidential nomination in 1928 on the first ballot illustrated the growing power of urban Democrats. His opponent, Herbert Hoover, was part of the previous two Republican presidential administrations that governed during a time of great prosperity. Smith did little to distinguish himself from his opponent, though he seemed to be a natural representative for many of the people who did not prosper during the 1920s. His Catholic background was also an issue: many prejudiced voters turned to Hoover, but Smith was also able to draw support from immigrants around the country.

Smith increasingly spoke out against reform measures and government programs after his defeat in 1928. He condemned the New Deal programs of President Franklin D. Roosevelt that began in 1933 and became a charter member of the American Liberty League, an organization of wealthy, conservative industrialists and politicians opposed to the New Deal. Smith eventually broke with the Democratic Party over what he believed was excessive government involvement in the economy. He eventually reconciled with Roosevelt late in the 1930s, and supported the president's foreign policy when World War II broke out in 1939 and America entered the conflict in 1941. Smith died in New York City on October 4, 1944.

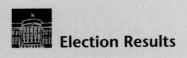

Election Results

1928

Presidential / Vice presidential candidates	Popular votes	Presidential electoral votes
Herbert Hoover / Charles Curtis (Republican)	21,392,190	444
Alfred E. Smith / Joseph T. Robinson (Democratic)	15,016,443	87

Incumbent president Calvin Coolidge chose not to run for another term. He still received seventeen votes for the Republican nomination.

laws and federal cash assistance. Some victims of the flooding claimed that the government did not do enough to help them with their problems. Against the wishes of Hoover and President Coolidge, Congress passed relief legislation that included an expansion of government responsibilities and obligations to states in emergency situations. The crisis, and Hoover's response, would foreshadow events of his presidency.

The election of 1928

When Calvin Coolidge announced in August 1927 that he would not seek another term, Hoover was urged by Republican Party leaders to run for office for the first time in his life. He accepted the Republican Party nomination in 1928; Kansas senator Charles Curtis (1860–1936) was his running mate. Democrat Alfred E. Smith (1873–1944; see box), the progressive governor of New York, was the Democratic Party candidate.

The election of 1928 was one of the uglier campaigns of the era, although both candidates maintained a sense of decency toward each other. Smith met with prejudice over his religion (he was the first Roman Catholic to run for president), and Hoover was opposed by poor people, small farmers, and laborers—those who had not benefited from the economic prosperity of the 1920s. Not a comfortable public speaker, Hoover made only seven speeches during the campaign. Hoover won the election by a large margin, and Curtis became the most prominent government official of Native American heritage.

Hoover took the oath of office from former President **William Howard Taft** (1857–1930; see entry in volume 3), who was chief justice of the Supreme Court. At the time of Hoover's inaugural (swearing-in ceremony), American prosperity and optimism for the future was at an all-time high. He reflected that optimism in his inaugural address, saying, "I have no fears for the future of our country. It is bright with hope."

Throughout the 1920s, the American economy had been robust. Almost everyone was better off it seemed, from businessmen to working-class Americans. There were some warning signs, however. Many Americans borrowed money from banks, and others were all too eager to make investments in risky enterprises.

During his first months in office, Hoover enacted a program of reform aimed at some policies that put investors and debtors in financial jeopardy. (Investors commit money to a company, hoping to make money as the party they invested in becomes more successful. Debtors borrow money from a lending institution—for example, a bank—and pay back the loan plus interest, a charge for borrowing the money, over a period of time.) The Agricultural Marketing Act of 1929, for example, established the Federal Farm Board to ensure that crop prices remained at stable rates and to provide loans for agricultural cooperatives, farmers who pooled their re-

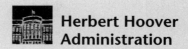

Herbert Hoover Administration

Administration Dates
March 4, 1929–March 4, 1933

Vice President
Charles Curtis (1929–33)

Cabinet

Secretary of State
Henry L. Stimson (1929–33)

Secretary of the Treasury
Andrew W. Mellon (1929–32)
Ogden L. Mills (1932–33)

Secretary of War
James W. Good (1929)
Patrick J. Hurley (1929–33)

Attorney General
William D. Mitchell (1929–33)

Secretary of the Navy
Charles F. Adams (1929–33)

Postmaster General
Walter F. Brown (1929–33)

Secretary of the Interior
Ray L. Wilbur (1929–33)

Secretary of Agriculture
Arthur M. Hyde (1929–33)

Secretary of Labor
James J. Davis (1929–30)
William N. Doak (1930–33)

Secretary of Commerce
Robert P. Lamont (1929–32)
Roy D. Chapin (1932–33)

sources. Farmers of various crops were facing financial ruin during this period of general prosperity.

The crash of 1929

In October 1929, President Hoover took a trip to a museum complex built by automaker Henry Ford (1863–1947) in Dearborn, Michigan. He was there to celebrate the fiftieth anniversary of the invention of electric light. Inventor Thomas Edison (1847–1931) was at the reception held at the laboratory where he invented electric light; the laboratory had been relocated to Ford's museum from Menlo Park, New Jersey. As Hoover returned to Washington, D.C., the value of stocks began to fall on Thursday, October 24.

As news of falling stock prices began to spread through New York City, crowds gathered outside the New York Stock Exchange, where frantic trading and selling of stock was underway. Panic began to sweep the nation. Fortunes were lost, and banks began to fail. Hoover tried to assure the nation by asserting that "the fundamental business of the country, that is, the production and distribution of commodities, is on a sound and prosperous basis."

Secretary of the Treasury Andrew W. Mellon (1855–1937; see box in **Warren G. Harding** entry in volume 4) was sure that the stock market would balance out, an outlook shared by many leading economists of the time. Hoover was concerned, nevertheless. He called a series of meetings in November with top business leaders. He convinced them to pledge that profits, not wages, would be the first victims of an economic depression. Hoover believed that common sacrifice could forestall widespread misery.

Hoover urged state and local governments to expand public works projects to create more jobs. (Public works are items constructed by the government for public use, such as roads and schools.) By early 1930, the stock market tumble seemed to have passed its worst stage, and in February Hoover announced that the worst was over. Still, unemployment continued to rise and many banks were foreclosing on mortgages—that is, ending the loan agreements that people take out and pay back over several years in order to purchase land and homes, and taking back those properties when debtors

could not make payments. The economic crisis worsened when a serious drought struck the Great Plains during the summer of 1930. Thousands of farmers went bankrupt, banks failed in every state, and five million people were without jobs.

Hoover worked tirelessly to find solutions to the economic depression that had set in. He rose before dawn each day, often held dozens of meetings, and put off public appearances that were ceremonious. He urged state and local governments to involve themselves in relief efforts, but funding in those sources had dried up. After rejecting appeals to implement federal aid projects, Hoover became a public scapegoat (a person unfairly blamed and made out to be the symbol of a problem) for the nation's troubles.

Foreign policy

By the summer of 1931, economic depression had set in on Europe as well. Both Great Britain and France were ex-

Soup kitchens were set up during the Great Depression to provide a small measure of relief to the unemployed. This one was opened in Chicago by mobster Al Capone in 1931.
Courtesy of the National Archives and Records Administration.

Henry L. Stimson

Henry Lewis Stimson was born on September 21, 1867, into a wealthy New York City family. His mother died when Stimson was eight years old; his father was a Civil War veteran who established himself as a stock exchange speculator, then as a prominent surgeon. Stimson graduated from Yale University in 1888 and Harvard Law School in 1891. He married Mabel Wellington White on July 6, 1893.

In 1891, Stimson entered the law firm of Root and Clarke. Elihu Root (1845–1937) was a leading New York lawyer who in 1899 would become secretary of war. Stimson and another lawyer started their own successful law firm in 1899. In 1906, President Theodore Roosevelt appointed Stimson the U.S. attorney for the Southern District of New York. Stimson built a staff of excellent young lawyers that included Felix Frankfurter (1882–1965), a future Supreme Court justice. His office won a series of cases against companies that were operating illegally under the terms of the Sherman Antitrust and Elkins Railroad acts.

In 1910, Stimson failed in a bid for governor of New York. From 1911 to 1913, he served as secretary of war for President William Howard Taft, helping to modernize the American military. When World War I broke out, Stimson called for American involvement and advocated the military draft. To prove his "faith by works," as he termed it, he applied for active duty in 1917 and was stationed in France as a lieutenant colonel in the field artillery.

Throughout the 1920s, Stimson worked in his law firm and served his government. In 1927, President Calvin Coolidge sent Stimson to Nicaragua to negotiate peace between warring factions. A treaty was arranged, but a civil war broke out the day after he left the country. A similar experience occurred in the Philippines a year later: Stimson brought conflicting sides together and improved U.S. relations with the nation, but the factions entered into civil war soon after he left.

In 1929, a worldwide economic depression surfaced, partly fueled by international debt created by World War I. The Hoover administration tried several relief efforts, but conditions steadily deteriorated. Attempts to reduce international tensions led to the London Naval Conference of 1930, called to balance naval forces between the United States, England, Japan, France, and Italy. Stimson was the principal U.S. negotiator and a leader in discussions that formed an agreement to eliminate further naval competition, but the agreement was largely ignored. When Japan invaded Manchuria, China, on September 18, 1931, Hoover and Stimson tried several, increasingly forceful ways to encourage the Japanese to withdraw, including "nonrecognition"—a warning that any territorial acquisition not in accord with existing treaties would not be recognized by the United States. However, lacking support from other nations, the efforts failed.

Henry L. Stimson.
Courtesy of the Library of Congress.

Stimson returned to private life in 1933. When World War II began in 1939, he supported those nations opposing Germany and Italy. In June 1940, President Franklin D. Roosevelt appointed him secretary of war. During the war, Stimson organized and directed the war department for a massive effort; oversaw an orderly plan for training troops and assembling materials; surrounded himself with an excellent staff, including George C. Marshall (1880–1959; see box in **Harry S. Truman** entry in volume 4), who would later lead the American postwar effort; and helped plan the administration's foreign policy.

Some of Stimson's efforts were criticized. His outspokenness against Germany and Japan caused some to blame him for the Japanese attack on Pearl Harbor. Stimson made the personally distasteful decision to evacuate all Japanese, whether alien or citizen, from the coastal regions of California, on the grounds of the safety of the nation and military necessity. Stimson's plan for an early invasion of Europe in 1942–43 was overruled in favor of an American focus on North Africa, followed by an attack on Nazi strongholds in Italy, and then the D-Day invasion of Europe (June 6, 1944).

Late in the war, Stimson supervised government activities surrounding the development and manufacture of the atomic bomb. In early 1945, work had progressed far enough to consider the implications of using the bomb. Stimson, like many other American political and military leaders, was convinced that the Japanese would not surrender, and that heavy losses on both sides would occur with a U.S.-led invasion of Japan. Development of the bomb was so secret that Vice President Harry S. Truman did not know about it. When Truman became president after the death of President Roosevelt in April 1945, he learned about the bomb from Stimson. On June 1, 1945, a committee studying the atomic bomb issue recommended that the bomb should be used on Japan. Atomic bombs were dropped on Hiroshima on August 6, and on Nagasaki on August 8. The war ended shortly thereafter, and Stimson retired. He died in 1950.

One of the last events of the Hoover administration was the repeal of Prohibition, which occurred in February 1933. By early April, beer was being sold publicly in the United States for the first time in thirteen years.

periencing difficulties in maintaining their World War I debt payments to the United States. Hoover suspended debt payments, a move he had to make but which meant further economic troubles for the United States. Economic hardships were most difficult in Germany, which faced massive factory closings and widespread unemployment. Germany had tried parliamentary government following World War I with limited success. (In a parliamentary government, executive power resides with Cabinet-level officials responsible to the nation's legislature, and the highest-ranking member of the political party with a majority is usually made the nation's chief executive.) A charismatic leader named Adolf Hitler (1889–1945) and his National Socialist Party gained a majority in parliamentary elections in 1932. In January 1933, Hitler's fascist forces gained control of the government by forcing Germany's aging president, Paul von Hindenburg (1847–1934), to appoint Hitler as chancellor, the chief minister of the state. (Fascism is a political philosophy that places a nation or a particular race of people above individual rights; characteristics of a fascist government include a dictatorial leader, strict control of the economy and of society, and brutal attack of any opposition.)

Meanwhile, a crisis in Asia began in September 1931 when Japan invaded the resource-rich Chinese province of Manchuria. The major U.S. foreign policy move during Hoover's presidency came in 1932, when U.S. secretary of state Henry L. Stimson (1867–1950; see box) formulated what became known as the "Stimson Doctrine." The doctrine stated that nations whose governments were violently overthrown through rebellions would not enjoy formal diplomatic relations with the United States. The Hoover administration then withdrew U.S. troops sent to maintain peace in Nicaragua and Haiti.

Things get worse

In the United States, unemployment rose to over eight million people by the summer of 1931. Thousands of homeless people began camping out in city parks like Chicago's Grant Park, having no other shelter. Riots over scarce food supplies occurred in several cities.

Hoover's initiatives (legislative measures) in 1932 to counteract the Depression only made him more unpopular. Early in the year, Congress passed a bill forming the Reconstruction Finance Corporation, which established a fund of $500 million to provide loans to banks, farmers, and major transportation companies to hold off bankruptcies. Opponents claimed the bill helped business leaders and their companies, not the legions of poor and suffering people. By mid-1932, twelve million Americans were unemployed. Communities of cardboard huts sprang up across the country—in some cases near city garbage dumps to make it easier to scavenge for food. Such makeshift settlements were dubbed "Hoovervilles." In some states, entire school systems stopped operating because of lack of funds.

The worst public relations move by the Hoover administration became known as the Bonus Army March. The event had roots back to 1925, when Congress authorized adjusted-compensation ("bonus") certificates to those who had

The makeshift shack villages of the unemployed (above) during the Great Depression were nicknamed Hoovervilles. The president's name was often used as a negative descriptor: When a jobless man wrapped a blanket around himself it was called a Hoover blanket; a broken down automobile was a Hoover wagon; and an empty pocket turned inside out was a Hoover flag. *Reproduced by permission of Archive Photos.*

served in the U.S. military during World War I. During the Depression, unemployed veterans across the country began petitioning the government for early payoffs on the certificates. Congress passed a bill that would allow certificates to be redeemed for $225 to $400 per veteran, but Hoover vetoed the bill in 1931.

A group of veterans united on the West Coast to begin a march on Washington, D.C. They rode trains across the country toward the nation's capitol during the spring of 1932. By June, over twenty thousand veterans were camped in Washington, D.C. Images of down-and-out veterans begging the government for a few hundred dollars each and cooking skimpy meals over open fires became one of the starkest reflections of the Depression.

Many veterans eventually went home, but about two thousand veterans remained, many of whom were joined by their families. Fearing that the remaining veterans had been influenced by supporters of communism (a political system organized to eliminate private property and to control industrial and agricultural production), Washington, D.C., policemen were called to remove some Bonus Marchers from a building. Shots were fired and one of the veterans was killed. U.S. Army general Douglas MacArthur (1880–1964; see box in **Harry S. Truman** entry in volume 4) was sent in with a military squad to evict Bonus Marchers from their encampment with orders for a restrained show of force. MacArthur ordered tear gas to be fired on the crowd, however, and an unruly mob attacked the veterans and set fire to their cardboard huts. An infant was killed in the struggle.

Reelection fails

When Democratic presidential candidate **Franklin D. Roosevelt** (1882–1945; see entry in volume 4) learned of the riot in Washington, D.C., he said to an advisor, "Well . . . this elects me." Roosevelt quickly emerged as a popular alternative to Hoover. He projected confidence and optimism, while Hoover was harassed. Several campaign stops Hoover made by train were spoiled by crowds throwing eggs and tomatoes, and at least two attempts to sabotage (purposely damage) railroad tracks were discovered. Nearly forty million people cast

votes in the election of 1932, and twenty-three million of them voted for Roosevelt. Hoover received barely forty percent of the popular vote.

After leaving office, the former president established the Hoover Library on War, Revolution and Peace at Stanford University. He became an outspoken critic of President Roosevelt's New Deal program and briefly considered running again for the presidency in 1936.

During World War II, Hoover headed the Polish Relief Commission. His work was expanded in 1946 by President **Harry S. Truman** (1882–1972; see entry in volume 4), who named Hoover to head the international Famine Relief Commission. The seventy-two-year-old Hoover visited twenty-five countries in less than two months to supervise relief measures. Truman also paid tribute to Hoover's engineering background by signing a Congressional resolution that officially named the Hoover Dam on the Colorado River in honor of the former president. (It had been named the Hoover Dam

A Selection of Hoover Landmarks

Herbert Hoover National Historic Site. 210 Parkside Dr., West Branch, IA 52538. (319) 643-5301. Two-hundred-acre site includes Herbert Hoover's birthplace home, his first schoolhouse, a museum, a library, and the gravesite of the president and first lady. See http://hoover.nara.gov/index.html (accessed on September 11, 2000).

Hoover-Minthorn House. 115 S. River St., Newberg, OR 97132. (503) 538-6629. Young Herbert Hoover lived with his aunt and uncle here from 1884 to 1888 after he was orphaned.

while Hoover was in office, but the Roosevelt administration referred to it as Boulder Dam or Boulder Canyon Dam.)

As head of the Hoover Commission, organized to suggest improvements in federal government practices, Hoover made nearly three hundred recommendations that were approved by Congress in 1947. Meanwhile, the former president served as chairman of the Boys' Clubs of America for eight years. In 1962, on his eighty-eighth birthday, Hoover was honored at the dedication ceremony of the Hoover Presidential Library in his birthplace of West Branch, Iowa. He died two years later, on October 20, 1964.

Legacy

Herbert Hoover's reluctance to have the federal government take charge during the early years of the Great Depression led voters to elect Franklin D. Roosevelt president in 1932. Roosevelt's more aggressive federal action made him immensely popular: Voters reelected him president three more times, and he is generally viewed by historians as one of America's greatest presidents. Hoover, on the other hand, is typically ranked as one of America's least effective presidents. He was in charge when economic hard times hit the nation, and he is generally viewed as not having done enough to lift the nation from Depression.

Some economic reforms had been underway during Hoover's administration. In March 1932, for example, the president signed into law the Norris-LaGuardia Anti-Injunction Act, which stopped federal injunctions against strikes (that is, the act stopped legal actions that suspended the strikes). A Revenue Act signed in 1932 increased taxes on corporations and large estates, bringing more money into the government for relief efforts. President Roosevelt's Works Projects Administration, which was praised for providing jobs for the unemployed, was a successor to Hoover's Emergency Relief and Construction Act, which Hoover signed into law in July 1932. The Act authorized $1.5 billion in funds for public works projects.

Hoover's other accomplishments include a program for prison reform. That and some of his other actions are often obscured by the miseries associated with the Great Depression.

Where to Learn More

Burner, David. *Herbert Hoover: A Public Life*. New York: Knopf, 1979. Reprint, New York: Atheneum, 1984.

Fausold, Martin L. *The Presidency of Herbert C. Hoover*. Lawrence: University Press of Kansas, 1985.

Herbert Hoover Presidential Library and Museum. [Online] http://www.hoover.nara.gov/ (accessed on September 28, 2000).

Herbert Hoover Presidential Library Association. [Online] http://www.hooverassoc.org/index.html (accessed on September 28, 2000).

Hoff, Joan. *Herbert Hoover: Forgotten Progressive*. Boston: Little, Brown, 1975.

Hoover, Herbert. *Memoirs*. 3 vols. New York: Macmillan, 1951. Reprint, New York: Garland, 1979.

Lisio, Donald J. *The President and Protest: Hoover, MacArthur, and the Bonus Riot*. New York: Fordham University Press, 1994.

O'Connor, Richard. *The First Hurrah: A Biography of Alfred E. Smith*. New York: Putnam 1970.

Schmitz, David F. *Henry L. Stimson: The First Wise Man*. Wilmington, DE: Scholarly Resources, 2000.

Walch, Timothy, and Dwight M. Miller, eds. *Herbert Hoover and Franklin D. Roosevelt: A Documentary History*. Westport, CT: Greenwood, 1998.

Warren, Harris G. *Herbert Hoover and the Great Depression*. New York: Oxford University Press, 1959. Reprint, Westport, CT: Greenwood, 1980.

Lou Hoover

Born March 29, 1874
Waterloo, Iowa
Died January 7, 1944
New York, New York

**Generous, intelligent, and active first lady
was committed to public service**

The first woman in the United States to earn a degree in geology, Louise (Lou) Henry Hoover led an adventurous life. Whether globetrotting with her husband and two sons or serving actively in Washington, D.C., as the wife of a politician, "Lou" had a wide range of hobbies and interests. Her husband once referred to her as "my good lady who already knows all about a thing or else finds out."

Lou and Bert meet at Stanford

Like her future husband, Lou Hoover was a native of Iowa, born in the town of Waterloo in 1874. Her father, Charles D. Henry, was a banker who inspired in his daughter a love of the outdoors. When Lou was ten, her family moved west to California, hoping that a warmer climate would improve the weak health of her mother, Florence. Living in Monterey, Lou learned to hunt and fish with her father. She also became an expert equestrienne (female horseback rider) and an avid hiker. During hikes, Lou became fascinated by the rocks and minerals she discovered in the hills of Northern

"[Lou was] a symbol of everything wholesome in American life."

Herbert Hoover

Lou Hoover.
Courtesy of the Library of Congress.

California. After attending a lecture on geology while still in high school, Lou abandoned her plans to become a teacher.

Lou enrolled in the geology program at Stanford University in Palo Alto, California. The tall, independent, first-year student first met **Herbert Hoover** (1874–1964; see entry in volume 4) in a laboratory on campus. A senior, he was a member of Stanford's first class when the university opened in 1891. He was studying mining engineering. When he graduated in 1895, Hoover left to work with mining companies. Within two years, he was earning a large salary as a mining engineer in Australia.

Lou and "Bert," as she called him, maintained a correspondence after he left school in 1895. Shortly after Lou graduated in 1898, Bert was offered a position as a mining engineer in China. He sent Lou a letter in which he proposed marriage.

The Hoovers were married on February 10, 1899. Later that day, they boarded a boat bound for China. Lou began learning to speak Chinese, and she often accompanied her husband on mining expeditions. When a group of Chinese began a movement to halt the spread of foreign influences in their country, it turned into a violent uprising in 1900 called the Boxer Rebellion. Military forces from several countries arrived to protect their people and interests. The Hoovers were trapped for two weeks in the town of Tientsin, during which time Lou Hoover carried a pistol for protection.

World travelers

Hoover's responsibilities with the mining company increased. From 1900 to 1907, he and Lou traveled throughout Asia, Europe, and Africa as he inspected or supervised various mining sites. Accompanying them were their two sons, Herbert Charles (1905–1969) and Allan Henry (1907–1993). Hoover started his own mining consulting firm in 1908.

The family was living in London, England, when World War I (1914–18) began. Lou Hoover helped her husband in his work as head of a massive aid project to return tens of thousands of Americans stranded in Europe by the war. To occupy frightened Americans, Lou led them on tours of the English countryside. During the war, she also assisted her husband with famine-relief efforts. She had converted to her husband's Quaker faith shortly after their marriage. Performing acts of charity was among their strong spiritual convictions.

The Hoovers were involved in several relief efforts during World War I, including the Committee for Relief of Belgium (CRB) and the U.S. Food Administration. Following the war, Herbert Hoover founded the American Relief Administration (ARA) to fight famine in Europe. The Hoovers pursued other works as well: For example, they translated a text dating from 1556 on metals, *De Reus Metallica,* from the original Latin, and they designed their home in California.

Twelve years in Washington, D.C.

When Herbert Hoover was appointed secretary of commerce by President **Warren G. Harding** (1865–1923; see entry in volume 4) in 1921, the Hoover family moved to Washington, D.C. Lou Hoover served for three years as president of the Girl Scouts of America beginning in 1922. She had served as a troop leader in the organization, founded in 1912. Since the Girl Scouts of America stressed good citizenship, self-reliance, and outdoor activities for girls, the organization's values matched those of Lou Hoover. When her husband was elected president in 1928, Mrs. Hoover continued to work on behalf of the organization.

During the 1920s, Lou Hoover offered some daring public views for the time. She believed, for example, that a woman could have an active career after marrying and having children. She served in several organizations, including the National Amateur Athletic Federation (as the only woman officer), the National Women's Athletic Association, the American Association of University Women, and the National Geographic Society.

When scandal rocked the White House in the early 1920s over illegal financial deals arranged by several members of the Harding administration, Mrs. Hoover organized the national Women's Conference on Law Enforcement. Addressing over five hundred women from across the country at a meeting in Washington, D.C., Lou Hoover stated that "women of the country are tired of seeing the laws of our land ignored." She added: "We must arouse the whole country to an understanding of the dangerous significance of continued evasion of the law."

Mrs. Hoover took a similarly active position on the role of women in politics. In addition to urging women to vote (after a constitutional amendment in 1918 first permitted women to do so), she encouraged women to become active in politics through community involvement and membership in the League of Women Voters—an organization dedicated to providing voters with information on issues and candidates.

Active first lady

Lou Hoover softened some of her more strident, feminist statements following the election of her husband to president in 1928. Nevertheless, she continued to have an active role in causes she believed in. She maintained her religious value of performing works of charity without expecting public recognition. Among topics she did pursue publicly were health-related issues. For example, she encouraged women to remain active and to enjoy the outdoors during pregnancy (in that era, it was common for pregnant women to be confined indoors).

When the United States faced a financial crisis in 1929 that began the Great Depression (1929–41), the first lady delivered radio speeches in which she urged Americans to share resources and help those in need. Mrs. Hoover usually spent full days in her office addressing pleas that arrived from struggling Americans. She employed a secretary to help answer her mail and to direct those in need to relief agencies. When no aid could be secured, Mrs. Hoover often sent some of her own funds to help a family purchase necessities, like shoes. Many people paid her back later, but Mrs. Hoover never cashed those checks. Her husband never knew of those personal acts of charity until after her death in 1944 when he found the checks hidden among her private papers.

In the White House, the Hoovers personally paid for their secretaries and staffs. Mrs. Hoover oversaw some White House renovations, including the restoration of a sitting room with furniture of the 1820s. That area was named the Monroe Room after the nation's fifth president, **James Monroe**

(1758–1831; see entry in volume 1). Mrs. Hoover also restored a study used by President **Abraham Lincoln** (1809–1865; see entry in volume 2).

As the country faced deeper economic problems, the Hoovers received more bad press reports. Mrs. Hoover endured a controversy stirred in June 1930 when she hosted a tea for the wife of Oscar De Priest (1871–1951), an African American congressman from Illinois. It was a bold move at the time, and the first lady was condemned by southern newspapers that supported racial segregation.

The Hoovers remained deeply supportive of one another during their trying White House years. Whenever the president was away, Mrs. Hoover would send him a telegram to encourage him. When poverty-stricken veterans gathered in Washington, D.C., in 1932, Mrs. Hoover arranged for food and beverages for them—the only gesture of help the veterans received from the government.

After Hoover lost his bid for reelection, he and his wife returned to Palo Alto, California, in 1933. Lou Hoover continued to work with the Girl Scouts and supported the Friends of Music at Stanford. The Hoovers moved to New York City and maintained an apartment at the Waldorf Astoria Hotel during the World War II years. The former first lady continued to assist her husband with relief efforts. In January 1944, Lou Hoover died of a heart attack. She was buried in Palo Alto, but her body was later moved to West Branch, Iowa, where she was buried next to her husband, who died in 1964.

Where to Learn More

Allen, Anne Beiser. *An Independent Woman: The Life of Lou Henry Hoover.* Westport, CT: Greenwood Press, 2000.

Colbert, Nancy A. *Lou Henry Hoover: The Duty to Serve.* Greensboro, NC: Morgan Reynolds, 1998.

Pryor, Helen. *Lou Henry Hoover: Gallant First Lady.* New York: Dodd, Mead, 1969.

Hoover's "Rugged Individualism" Campaign Speech

Delivered on October 22, 1928; excerpted from
The New Day: Campaign Speeches of Herbert Hoover

Presidential candidate Hoover expresses his optimistic views on American prosperity one year before the onset of the Great Depression

During the 1920s, the United States enjoyed a sustained period of economic prosperity. Dubbed the "Roaring '20s," it was an exciting time: cities were growing and the use of automobiles and airplanes became more widespread. There were new forms of popular media, like radio and movies, and new forms of music, like jazz; dance crazes swept through nightclubs, and sports like baseball and golf attracted many more fans. Business was booming, and people were employed.

The nation was not without difficulties during the "Roaring '20s," a period that generally dates from 1920 to 1928. Many rural areas did not enjoy economic prosperity, as farmers faced increasingly challenging market conditions that threatened their livelihood. Urban areas experienced sharp increases in crime. Prohibition—the ban on the manufacture and sale of alcohol—had been in effect since 1919, and criminals were finding ever more resourceful and violent ways to distribute and sell liquor. Many businesses and banks were enjoying large profits, while many citizens were borrowing money from banks to buy houses and land.

"By adherence to the principles of decentralized self-government, ordered liberty, equal opportunity, and freedom to the individual, our American experiment in human welfare has yielded a degree of well-being unparalleled in the world."

Herbert Hoover

Some Americans wanted the government to be more active in addressing the nation's problems. Presidents in the first two decades of the century—**Theodore Roosevelt** (1858–1919; see entry in volume 3), **William Howard Taft** (1857–1930; see entry in volume 3), and **Woodrow Wilson** (1856–1924; see entry in volume 4)—had been successful in enacting policies that regulated business and improved social conditions.

Other Americans warned against increasing government power and influence. They pointed out that government involvement in business and social life in European countries had not been successful in achieving the kind of economic prosperity enjoyed in the United States. Some feared that the U.S. government would control certain industries, or move towards socialism. Russia, for example, had embraced socialism—an economic system where government controls the production and distribution of goods.

Former U.S. secretary of commerce **Herbert Hoover** (1874–1964; see entry in volume 4) was the Republican presidential candidate in 1928. His insistence on limiting government involvement in American business and social affairs won out in the election that year. Americans expected that the good times of the "Roaring '20s" would be sustained by Hoover, whose beliefs were similar to those of his predecessors, **Warren G. Harding** (1865–1923; see entry in volume 4) and **Calvin Coolidge** (1872–1933; see entry in volume 4). Hoover was a self-made millionaire—a man who became wealthy through his own hard work and talent. In 1922, he had published a book called *American Individualism* that praised the American system for encouraging individuals to succeed on their own, without the direction or assistance from government. That theme was prominent in his presidential campaign, where he extolled the value of "rugged individualism."

Things to remember while reading an excerpt from Herbert Hoover's "Rugged Individualism" campaign speech:

- During World War I (1914–18), the U.S. government monitored and controlled businesses and industries that were vital to the war effort. The system worked, but following the war most Americans wanted to return to a normal American relationship between government and business. Traditionally, businesses, like citizens, were independent so long as they followed the laws of the land. Championing such independence, Hoover emphasized the superiority of the "American system of rugged individualism" over European systems where government controlled many businesses and industries.

- Since he was making a campaign speech, Hoover wanted to show that his approach was better than that of his Democratic counterpart, New York governor Alfred E. Smith (1873–1944; see box in **Herbert Hoover** entry in volume 4). Hoover provided three examples of problems America faced, and asserted that his approach to them was superior because the Democratic Party approach involved heavy government involvement. In portions not appearing in the following excerpt, Hoover argued that the Democratic approach to Prohibition would have the government involved in selling liquor; and to assist struggling farmers, Hoover claimed that Democrats would fix the price of agricultural products instead of having them determined by market conditions. Finally, instead of having private companies involved in the construction of dams and other projects that provided energy, Hoover claimed that Democratic policies would turn the government into a business in the energy industry.

- Hoover argued that government involvement in business leads to bureaucracy—a system where several different people or agencies confer on all decisions. Hoover asserted that bureaucracy stifles individual initiative and counters the principle that made America great, which he called "liberalism." (Liberalism is a policy that allows individuals and businesses to operate with few restrictions.) Ironically, beginning in the 1960s, "liberalism" became synonymous with government programs intending to improve social conditions and regulate business.

- Hoover made references to his own experiences near the end of the speech. A self-made millionaire, he asserted that progress could only be attained by the accomplishments of individuals left free to pursue their dreams. That progress, he concluded, was reflected in the prosperity America enjoyed during the period from 1921 to 1928.

Excerpt from Herbert Hoover's "Rugged Individualism" campaign speech

During one hundred and fifty years we have built up a form of self government and a social system which is peculiarly our own. It differs essentially from all others in the world. It is the American system. . . . It is founded upon the conception that only through ordered liberty, freedom and equal opportunity to the individual will his initiative and enterprise spur on the march of progress. And in our insistence upon equality of opportunity has our system advanced beyond all the world. . . .

*When **the war** closed, the most vital of issues both in our own country and around the world was whether government should continue their wartime ownership and operation of many **instrumentalities** of production and distribution. We were challenged with a choice between the American system of rugged individualism and a European philosophy of **diametrically opposed doctrines**—doctrines of **paternalism and state socialism.** The acceptance of these ideas would have meant the destruction of self-government through centralization. . . .*

*When the Republican Party came into full power it went at once **resolutely** back to our fundamental conception of the state and the rights and responsibility of the individual. Thereby it restored confidence and hope in the American people, it freed and stimulated enterprise, it restored the government to a position as an umpire instead of a player in the economic game. For these reasons the American people have gone forward in progress. . . .*

There is [in this election] . . . submitted to the American people a question of fundamental principle. That is: shall we depart from the principles of our American political and economic system, upon which we have advanced beyond all the rest of the world. . . .

When the Federal Government undertakes to go into commercial business it must at once set up the organization and administration of that business, and it immediately finds itself in a

The war: World War I.

Instrumentalities: Components, agencies.

Diametrically opposed doctrines: Complete opposite principles.

Paternalism and state socialism: Governments that strictly oversee business; the word "paternalism" relates to father, so Hoover is asserting that some governments rule over business like a father who serves as the head of a family.

Resolutely: Faithfully.

labyrinth. . . . *Commercial business requires a concentration of responsibility. Our government to succeed in business would need to become in effect a* **despotism**. *There at once begins the destruction of self-government.* . . .

It is a false **liberalism** *that interprets itself into the government operation of commercial business. Every step of bureaucratizing of the business of our country poisons the very roots of liberalism—that is political equality, free speech, free assembly, free press and equality of opportunity. It is not the road to more liberty, but to less liberty. Liberalism should not be striving to spread* **bureaucracy** *but striving to set bounds to it.* . . .

Liberalism is a force truly of the spirit, a force proceeding from the deep realization that economic freedom cannot be sacrificed if political freedom is to be preserved. [An expansion of the government's role in the business world] would cramp and cripple the mental and spiritual energies of our people. It would extinguish equality and opportunity. It would dry up the spirit of liberty and progress. . . . *For a hundred and fifty years liberalism has found its true spirit in the American system, not in the European systems.*

I do not wish to be misunderstood. . . . *I am defining general policy.* . . . *I have already stated that where the government is engaged in public works for purposes of flood control, of navigation, of irrigation, of scientific research or national defense* . . . *it will at times necessarily produce power or commodities as a* **by-product**.

Nor do I wish to be misinterpreted as believing that the United States is a free-for-all and devil-take-the-hindmost. The very essence of equality of opportunity and of American individualism is that there shall be no domination by any group or [monopoly] in this republic. . . . *It is no system of* **laissez faire**. . . .

I have witnessed not only at home but abroad the many failures of government in business. I have seen its tyrannies, its injustices, its destructions of self-government, its undermining of the very instincts which carry our people forward to progress. I have witnessed the lack of advance, the lowered standards of living, the depressed spirits of people working under such a system. . . .

And what has been the result of the American system? Our country has become the land of opportunity to those born without inheritance, not merely because of the wealth of its resources and industry but because of this freedom of initiative and enterprise. Russia has natural resources equal to ours. . . . *But she has not had the*

Labyrinth: Intricate maze.

Despotism: A type of government in which the ruler has unlimited power.

Liberalism: A policy that allows individuals and businesses to operate with few restrictions.

Bureaucracy: A system of administration with a set of strict rules and levels of approval.

By-product: Something that unintentionally remains or is created during a process.

Laissez-faire: A French term (roughly translated as "allow to do") commonly used to describe complete non-interference by government in the affairs of business and the economy.

blessings of one hundred and fifty years of our form of government and our social system.

By adherence to the principles of decentralized self-government, ordered liberty, equal opportunity, and freedom to the individual, our American experiment in human welfare has yielded a degree of well-being unparalleled in the world. It has come nearer to the abolition of poverty, to the abolition of fear of want, than humanity has ever reached before. Progress of the past seven years is proof of it. . . .

The greatness of America has grown out of a political and social system and a method of [a lack of governmental] control of economic forces distinctly its own—our American system—which has carried this great experiment in human welfare farther than ever before in history. . . . And I again repeat that the departure from our American system . . . will jeopardize the very liberty and freedom of our people, and will destroy equality of opportunity not only to ourselves, but to our children. . . . (Hoover, The New Day)

What happened next . . .

Hoover's 1928 speech, delivered just weeks before the presidential election, reflected the feeling of accomplishment and optimism that most Americans felt at the time. However, in October 1929—just over six months after Hoover took office—the United States was plunged into an economic crisis. Many people went bankrupt, banks failed, businesses closed, and people were out of work. The crisis soon turned into the Great Depression (1929–41), where over ten million people were without jobs.

There were many factors that contributed to the economic crisis, which grew worse each year of Hoover's presidency. The situation was further complicated when foreign countries were unable to pay off debts they owed to the United States for assistance during World War I.

Reflecting his dislike of government interference in business affairs and the lives of people, Hoover tried to improve conditions through volunteer efforts. He wanted businesses to sacrifice profits to ensure that they could pay workers their rightful wages, and he urged states and local communities to actively seek ways to improve conditions.

As the Great Depression continued to worsen, Hoover lost support. His opponent in the 1932 presidential election, **Franklin D. Roosevelt** (1882–1945; see entry in volume 4), appealed to voters by presenting plans that had the federal government taking an active role to improve social conditions and to stimulate the growth of employment opportunities. Roosevelt won the election and went on to become largely acknowledged as one of the greatest presidents.

Hoover bore the brunt of blame for the Great Depression, but later historical assessments are generally more positive. His values of individualism and minimal government interference in the affairs of business are still popular, especially in "normal" times when the nation does not face economic crises and is not at war.

Did you know . . .

- Herbert Hoover remained a symbol of the hard times of the Great Depression until after World War II (1939–45). His outspokenness against the New Deal programs of Franklin D. Roosevelt did not help: the Roosevelt administration investigated several alleged scandals of Hoover's administration, but came up empty; and the massive Hoover Dam was frequently referred to as the Boulder Dam or Boulder Canyon Dam during Roosevelt's presidency.

- Hoover's reputation for public service returned in the same manner it had first been established. He had organized massive relief efforts during World War I and made great contributions to create industrial standards as secretary of commerce for presidents Harding and Coolidge during the 1920s. After World War II, presidents **Harry S. Truman** (1884–1972; see entry in volume 4) and **Dwight D. Eisenhower** (1890–1969; see entry in volume 4) both called on Hoover to lead investigations of ways in which the workings of the executive branch of the government could be improved. The presidents approved seventy percent of the Hoover-led commissions' recommendations. In 1947, Truman also paid tribute to Hoover's engineering background by signing a Congressional resolution that officially named the Hoover Dam on the Colorado River in honor of the former president.

Where to Learn More

Barber, William J. *From New Era to New Deal: Herbert Hoover, the Economists, and American Economic Policy.* New York: Cambridge University Press, 1985.

Hoover, Herbert. *American Individualism.* Garden City, NY: Doubleday, Page & Co., 1922. Reprint, West Branch, IA: Herbert Hoover Presidential Library Association, 1989.

Hoover, Herbert. *The New Day: Campaign Speeches of Herbert Hoover.* Stanford, CA: Stanford University Press, 1928.

Nye, Frank T. *Doors of Opportunity: The Life and Legacy of Herbert Hoover.* West Branch, IA: Herbert Hoover Presidential Library Association, 1988.

Wilson, Carol. *Herbert Hoover: A Challenge for Today.* New York: Evans Publishing Company, 1968.

Franklin D. Roosevelt

Thirty-second president (1933–1945)

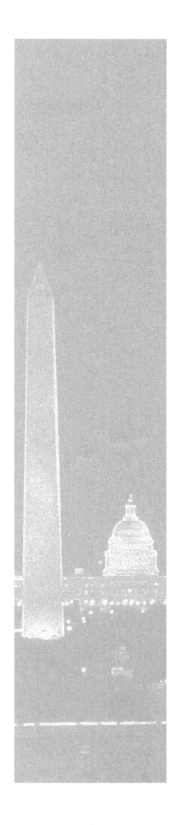

Franklin D. Roosevelt . . . **1125**

    Fast Facts about Franklin D. Roosevelt (box) . . . **1126**

    Franklin D. Roosevelt Timeline (box) . . . **1127**

    Words to Know (box) . . . **1128**

    Physically Challenged Presidents (box) . . . **1132**

    Election Results (box) . . . **1134**

    Franklin D. Roosevelt Administration (box) . . . **1136**

    Major Acts of the New Deal (box) . . . **1138**

    Frances Perkins (box) . . . **1142**

    Inauguration Day Calendar Change (box) . . . **1145**

    Winston Churchill (box) . . . **1148**

    A Selection of Roosevelt Landmarks (box) . . . **1155**

Eleanor Roosevelt . . . **1159**

Primary source: Roosevelt's First Inaugural Address
With the nation in the worst period of the Great Depression, President Roosevelt expresses optimism . . . **1167**

Primary source: Roosevelt's First Fireside Chat
In an informal manner, President Roosevelt explains the nation's banking problems in the first of his "fireside chat" radio broadcasts . . . **1175**

Primary source: Roosevelt's War Message to the American People
President Roosevelt asks Congress for a declaration of war on Japan following the bombing of Pearl Harbor . . . **1181**

Franklin D. Roosevelt

**Born January 30, 1882
Hyde Park, New York
Died April 12, 1945
Warm Springs, Georgia**

**Thirty-second president of the United States
(1933–1945)**

**One of the most popular presidents of all
time, he rose to the challenges of the Great
Depression and World War II**

Franklin D. Roosevelt was president during two of the most serious crises of the twentieth century—the Great Depression (1929–41) and World War II (1939–45). During both ordeals, he was able to make ready massive efforts and rally tremendous support from government and the American people. He was the only president elected more than twice, and he won each of his four presidential elections by wide margins.

Roosevelt was skilled at building coalitions (alliances of support), often among diverse political groups. He favored frequent experimentation and change when progress stalled. His social programs, called the New Deal, offered relief and jobs to struggling Americans during the Depression. The New Deal also reformed financial practices that had contributed to the Depression. Roosevelt's administration instituted such acts as the Social Security program, which guarantees financial support to Americans upon retirement.

The Depression ended as the United States entered World War II in 1941. American industries were revived by manufacturing the materials needed to fight a global war. The large-scale war effort required supervision by many agencies

"When you get to the end of your rope, tie a knot and hang on."

Franklin D. Roosevelt

Franklin D. Roosevelt.
Courtesy of the Franklin D. Roosevelt Library.

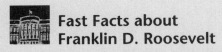

Fast Facts about Franklin D. Roosevelt

Full name: Franklin Delano Roosevelt

Born: January 30, 1882

Died: April 12, 1945

Burial site: Family plot, Hyde Park, New York

Parents: James and Sara Delano Roosevelt

Spouse: Anna Eleanor Roosevelt (1884–1962; m. 1905)

Children: Anna Eleanor (1906–1975); James (1907–1991); Franklin Delano Jr. (1909–1909); Elliott (1910–1990); Franklin Delano Jr. (1914–1988); John Aspinwall (1916–1981)

Religion: Episcopalian

Education: Harvard University (B.A., 1903); attended Columbia Law School

Occupations: Lawyer; banker

Government positions: New York state senator and governor; assistant secretary of the navy under Woodrow Wilson

Political party: Democratic

Dates as president: March 4, 1933–January 20, 1937 (first term); January 20, 1937–January 20, 1941 (second term); January 20, 1941–January 20, 1945 (third term); January 20, 1945–April 12, 1945 (fourth term)

Age upon taking office: 51

and military departments. As commander in chief, Roosevelt worked effectively with American military commanders and leaders of other nations to plan war strategies.

Roosevelt was the first physically challenged president: Stricken by polio at age thirty-nine, he was able to walk only with the use of leg braces and canes for the rest of his life. The public was largely unaware of the severity of his affliction, an infectious disease that attacks skeletal muscles and the spinal cord. The ailment did not rob him of his enthusiasm and energy. Like his efforts against the Depression and American enemies during World War II, he was tireless and persistent against the challenges of living with polio.

Value in public service

Franklin Delano Roosevelt was born January 30, 1882, at his family's estate in Hyde Park, New York. His father, James Roosevelt (1828–1900), headed the family's coal and transportation business. He was a widower of four years with a sixteen-year-old son when he married Sara Delano (1854–1941) in 1880. She was from a wealthy New York family and had traveled widely by the time she married James; she was twenty-six and he was fifty-two on their wedding day.

Roosevelt ancestors stretched back in time in America to the 1640s, when Nicholas Roosevelt (1658–1742) arrived from Holland. Nicholas had two sons, Johannes (1665–1710) and

Jacobus (1692–1776). The family line from Johannes included **Theodore Roosevelt** (1858–1919; see entry in volume 3), who was U.S. president from 1901 to 1909. Franklin D. Roosevelt came from the family line connected with Jacobus.

Roosevelt was raised in wealth on a large estate. He had private schooling and a governess (a teacher hired to work in a private household) until age fourteen. He learned to speak French and German, enjoyed swimming, became an expert sailor, explored nature, and collected stamps as a youth. He often spent summers traveling with his parents in Europe or staying at cottages along the eastern coast of the United States and Canada.

Roosevelt went to a preparatory school (a high school that prepares a person for college) in Massachusetts from 1896 to 1900 with students from other wealthy families. The faculty of the school impressed upon students the virtues of public service, a lesson that helped shape Roosevelt's outlook on life. Roosevelt was only a fair student there and at Harvard University, where he edited the college newspaper.

While in college, he fell in love with Anna Eleanor Roosevelt (1884–1962; see entry on **Eleanor Roosevelt** in volume 4), a distant cousin (she was the daughter of Theodore Roosevelt's brother). Eleanor, as she preferred to be called, came from a troubled background. Her high-society mother had paid little attention to her, and her father was an alcoholic. She was orphaned at age ten.

At the Roosevelts' wedding ceremony on March 17, 1905, President Theodore Roosevelt walked the bride up the

Franklin D. Roosevelt Timeline

1882: Born in New York

1907: Passes bar exam

1910–13: Serves as New York state senator

1913–20: Serves as assistant secretary of the U.S. navy

1914–18: World War I

1914: Runs unsuccessfully as U.S. senate candidate

1920: Runs unsuccessfully as Democratic vice presidential candidate

1921: Stricken with polio

1929–41: Great Depression

1929–33: Serves as New York governor

1933–45: Serves as thirty-second U.S. president

1933: New deal programs begin in Congress

1939–45 World War II

1941: United States enters World War II after Japanese bomb Pearl Harbor

1945: Dies in Georgia; Japanese surrender, ending World War II

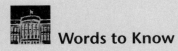
Allies: The countries that fought against Germany, Italy, and Japan during World War II. The makeup of the Allied powers changed over the course of the war. The first major Allied countries were Great Britain and France. Germany defeated France in 1940 but some Free French forces continued to fight with the Allies until the end of the war. The Soviet Union and the United States joined the Allies in 1941.

Axis: The countries that fought together against the Allies. Germany, Italy, and Japan formed the first coalition; eventually, they were joined by Hungary, Romania, Slovakia, Finland, and Bulgaria.

Bar exam: A test lawyers must pass in order to become certified; the bar is a term that encompasses all certified lawyers—those who have passed all official requirements (the bar exam).

"Hoovervilles": The nickname given to makeshift camps that homeless people set up during the Depression. The term comes from the name Herbert Hoover, who was president when the Depression set in.

Midterm elections: Congressional elections that occur midway through a president's term. The elections can change the balance of power in Congress by bringing in more supporters for or challengers to the president.

Military dictatorships: States in which military leaders have absolute power.

Military draft: A mandatory program that requires that all males register for possible military service. Those who pass a medical test receive a draft number. A lottery system is used to determine which available males must serve in the military. Those whose numbers are drawn are "drafted" into military service.

Nazi: The abbreviated name for the National Socialist German Workers' Party,

aisle. The Roosevelts would have six children, one of whom died in infancy. Their family life was prosperous and secure, but not without problems. Franklin Roosevelt had an affair with Eleanor's personal secretary for several years. Later, in 1921, Roosevelt was crippled by polio. Eleanor nursed him and helped him continue an active life.

Name recognition

Roosevelt studied law at Columbia University but left after he passed the bar exam (the test a person must pass to

the political party led by Adolf Hitler, who became dictator of Germany. Hitler's Nazi Party controlled Germany from 1933 to 1945. The Nazis promoted racist and anti-Semitic (anti-Jewish) ideas and enforced complete obedience to Hitler and the party.

New Deal: A series of social programs introduced by President Franklin D. Roosevelt that offered relief and jobs to struggling Americans during the Depression and reformed financial practices that had contributed to the Depression.

Polio: An infectious disease that attacks skeletal muscles and the spinal cord. Victims are often left with permanent disabilities. A vaccine developed in the 1950s proved effective in stopping the spread of polio.

Reciprocal trade agreements: Participating nations promise to trade in a way that will benefit each nation equally.

Socialist and communist: Referring to a political and social philosophy in which private property is banned and goods are available to all based on their needs and distributed by a central governing system.

Transients: People who move from place to place, often in search of work, without having a permanent home. During the Depression, many transients were called "hoboes."

Yalta Conference: A 1944 meeting between Allied leaders Joseph Stalin, Winston Churchill, and Franklin D. Roosevelt in anticipation of an Allied victory in Europe over the Nazis. The leaders discussed how to manage lands conquered by Germany, and Roosevelt and Churchill urged Stalin to enter the Soviet Union in the war against Japan.

become a lawyer) in 1907. He secured a good job with a corporate law firm, but he grew restless. An opportunity to run for state senator in 1910 excited him. His name recognition as a Roosevelt (Theodore Roosevelt had been a popular president and New York governor), his ability to use his own wealth to finance a campaign, and his interest in reform attracted local Democratic leaders.

Campaigning by car and listening to other people as much as making speeches, Roosevelt won in a mostly Republican district. As a state senator, Roosevelt challenged legislation favored by powerful business interests, supported women's suffrage (right to vote), and favored state control instead of private ownership of the energy industry.

In 1912, Roosevelt backed Democrat **Woodrow Wilson** (1856–1924; see entry in volume 4) for president, even though Theodore Roosevelt ran as a third-party candidate. Working closely with aide Louis McHenry Howe (1871–1936), a former journalist, Roosevelt proved an excellent political strategist, helping the Wilson campaign in the East. Following Wilson's victory, Roosevelt accepted an offer for the position of assistant secretary of the navy and moved with his family to Washington, D.C. Theodore Roosevelt had held that same position during the first term of President **William McKinley** (1843–1901; see entry in volume 3).

Stressing preparedness (readiness for war) and expansion of the navy as World War I (1914–18) broke out, Roosevelt displayed a talent for working with a variety of people—from admirals leading fleets of ships to business tycoons negotiating for government contracts. Those people skills, however, did not help him in a failed bid to win the Democratic nomination for the U.S. Senate in 1914.

Hardships and perseverance

After his distinguished service in the Wilson administration, Roosevelt was chosen in 1920 as the Democratic vice presidential running mate of Ohio governor James M. Cox (1870–1957). Young, handsome, energetic, and a proven administrator, Roosevelt worked hard for a losing cause. Cox and Roosevelt were associated with the policies of the Wilson administration, and Americans had turned away from those policies. Republican **Warren G. Harding** (1865–1923; see entry in volume 4), stressing a "return to normalcy," was more in tune with the times than the progressive (forward-thinking, reform-minded) Democrats. Harding and his running mate, **Calvin Coolidge** (1872–1933; see entry in volume 4), won in a landslide. After the election, Roosevelt formed a law firm and became vice president of a bank.

In August 1921, Roosevelt was stricken by polio (see box). Just as he approached nearly every political challenge and social problem in his career, Roosevelt tried many ways to overcome the affliction that paralyzed his legs. He visited

many doctors, tried various medicines, exercised vigorously, and made frequent trips to Warm Springs, Georgia, hoping the warm waters there could help heal him. Roosevelt was unable to walk without the aid of leg braces and a cane.

Remaining a political force, Roosevelt nominated New York governor Alfred E. Smith (1873–1944; see box in **Herbert Hoover** entry in volume 4) for president at the Democratic convention in 1924. Smith was not selected, but Roosevelt helped rally a Democratic Party that was discouraged and losing ground to Republicans. He encouraged Democrats to remain an aggressive alternative to Republicans, stating that "progressivism with the brakes on" is preferable to "conservatism with a move on."

Franklin D. Roosevelt (top right), after being stricken with polio, found relief in the warm mineral waters of Warm Springs, Georgia. After he became president, the site came to be called the Little White House because of the time he spent there.
Reproduced by permission of the Corbis Corporation.

The New Deal

In 1928, he campaigned successfully for Smith's nomination and agreed to run for governor of New York to help

Physically Challenged Presidents

Franklin D. Roosevelt was a physically challenged president. He suffered from paralysis brought on by poliomyelitis, more commonly known as polio. While he was president, Roosevelt never walked without the aid of heavy leg braces, and he often used a cane. He spent most of his working hours in a wheelchair.

The severity of Roosevelt's condition was not widely known. Whenever he appeared in public or was photographed, he would either be sitting or standing, but he was rarely seen moving around. The Secret Service built access ramps around Washington, D.C., to assist in transporting the president. Members of the press agreed that the president's disability was not news. Only among one group, outside of those personally close to him, did Roosevelt freely exhibit his physical challenge: that occurred when he visited with wounded soldiers—he wanted to show that loss of movement in his limbs did not make him less of a person, and that such hardships could be overcome. There was a general feeling at the time, though, that voters might not be so willing to accept a physically challenged president.

A controversy arose during the early 1990s during construction of the FDR memorial in Washington, D.C., over how Roosevelt would be depicted. He was shown sitting, but there were no signs of his disability. Some people felt it was insult-

Smith win that state's electoral votes. (Electoral votes are the votes a presidential candidate receives for having won a majority of the popular vote in a state. Electoral votes are distributed among states in ratios based on population. A candidate must win a majority of electoral votes—over 50 percent—in order to win the presidency.) Smith carried New York but lost the national election to **Herbert Hoover** (1874–1964; see entry in volume 4).

Roosevelt won the governor's race by appealing to a coalition of rural and urban groups. He was an active governor: Rural voters were rewarded by his support for reforestation of land that had been ruined by overuse; workers benefited from his backing of state-financed pensions, unemployment insurance, and regulated working hours; and the public favored his program for state control of the energy industry.

ing to neglect the fact that Roosevelt was physically challenged. Others contended that Roosevelt never made his physical impairments public, and depicting symbols of his impairment in a memorial would not accurately represent the way he was known to the public during his lifetime. In 1998, a decision was made to add a sculpture of Roosevelt sitting in a wheelchair. Only two pictures of wheelchairs that Roosevelt used are known to survive.

Other chief executives faced physical challenges while in office: **Andrew Jackson** (1767–1845; see entry in volume 1) was pained by a bullet lodged in his chest area; **Grover Cleveland** (1837–1908; see entry in volume 3) suffered from a cancer-ous growth in his mouth that was removed secretly while he was in office; and Woodrow Wilson suffered a stroke and spent his final few months in office virtually bedridden. When photographed during those months, Wilson was always positioned to emphasize the right side of his body; his left hand had become almost completely useless, and the left side of his face showed signs of paralysis. In 1955, **Dwight D. Eisenhower** (1890–1969; see entry in volume 4) recovered from a serious heart attack while in office; and in 1981, only two months after becoming president, **Ronald Reagan** (1911– ; see entry in volume 5) was wounded in an assassination attempt. Reagan survived and served two terms as chief executive.

Using the new mass medium of radio, Roosevelt began broadcasting "fireside chats" to inform New Yorkers about issues and policies in a relaxed format. Roosevelt won reelection in 1930 by the largest margin in state history.

As an economic crisis that began in October 1929 worsened into the Great Depression, Roosevelt proved to be a dynamic and imaginative leader. He met with distinguished professors, listened to the ideas of many people, and formed policies that were consistently bold to assist "the forgotten man, " as he called those who had lost their livelihoods. His character traits of persistence and experimentation when dealing with problems helped define him to voters as he sought the Democratic nomination for president in 1932.

Roosevelt led balloting at the Democratic convention during the first three rounds of voting but could not

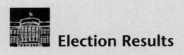 **Election Results**

1932

Presidential / Vice presidential candidates	Popular votes	Presidential electoral votes
Franklin D. Roosevelt / John Nance Garner (Democratic)	22,821,857	472
Herbert Hoover / Charles Curtis (Republican)	15,761,845	59

Roosevelt won the Democratic nomination on the fourth ballot, defeating 1928 nominee Alfred E. Smith. Hoover won the Republican nomination on the first ballot.

1936

Presidential / Vice presidential candidates	Popular votes	Presidential electoral votes
Franklin D. Roosevelt / John Nance Garner (Democratic)	27,476,673	523
Alfred M. Landon / Frank Knox (Republican)	16,679,583	8

1940

Presidential / Vice presidential candidates	Popular votes	Presidential electoral votes
Franklin D. Roosevelt / Henry A. Wallace (Democratic)	27,243,466	449
Wendell L. Willkie / Charles L. McNary (Republican)	22,304,755	82

Roosevelt went against two-term tradition and sought a third term, frustrating such presidential hopefuls as incumbent vice president Garner; Roosevelt easily received the nomination on the first ballot. Newcomer Willkie defeated early ballot leaders Thomas E. Dewey and Robert A. Taft on the sixth ballot.

1944

Presidential / Vice presidential candidates	Popular votes	Presidential electoral votes
Franklin D. Roosevelt / Harry S. Truman (Democratic)	25,602,505	432
Thomas E. Dewey / John W. Bricker (Republican)	22,006,278	99

Amidst World War II, voters opted to keep incumbent Roosevelt in office, despite having already served an unprecedented three terms. Missouri senator Truman replaced Wallace as the vice presidential nominee.

reach the majority he needed to win the nomination. He offered the vice presidency to a main rival, Texas representative and Speaker of the House John Nance Garner (1868–1967). (The Speaker supervises the activity in the

House of Representatives.) Garner freed his delegates, who then supported Roosevelt. Most importantly, Roosevelt had secured a running mate who could appeal to rural and southwestern voters to complement Roosevelt's popularity among urban easterners.

Unlike incumbent (still in office) Republican president Herbert Hoover, who took a cautious approach to economic problems, Roosevelt promised "The New Deal," an aggressive approach to the nation's economic crisis. He would spend federal funds for relief to the unemployed and to create jobs; his farm policy would stop overproduction of some crops that lowered their value; he wanted to conserve public resources and have the government control power utilities; and he promised pensions and regulation of the stock exchange. Many of those pledges were put into effect during Roosevelt's first one hundred days in office.

The one hundred days

Franklin D. Roosevelt easily defeated President Hoover in the 1932 election. When Roosevelt was inaugurated (sworn in as president) in March 1933, more than thirteen million workers were unemployed. One of them, Giuseppe Zangara (1900–1933), an unemployed bricklayer, had attempted to assassinate Roosevelt one month before the inauguration. (Chicago mayor Anton J. Cermak [1873–1933] was killed in the incident.) "Too many people are starving to death!" Zangara shouted. Many of the unemployed were living as transients, people who move from place to place searching for work and a permanent home. Others lived in makeshift camps called "Hoovervilles" (nicknamed in anger after Roosevelt's predecessor, Herbert Hoover). Banks had closed in thirty-eight states, and the economic collapse had spread worldwide. Still, Roosevelt gave a spirited inaugural address (see **Franklin D. Roosevelt** primary source entry in volume 4). Declaring to Americans that "the only thing we have to fear is fear itself," he called a special session of Congress and began acting.

Congress immediately passed the Emergency Banking Act to provide aid to banks. Then, through the Economy Act, the government made cuts in payments to federal work-

Franklin D. Roosevelt Administration

Administration Dates
March 4, 1933–January 20, 1937
January 20, 1937–January 20, 1941
January 20, 1941–January 20, 1945
January 20, 1945–April 12, 1945

Vice President
John Nance Garner (1933–41)
Henry A. Wallace (1941–45)
Harry S. Truman (1945)

Cabinet

Secretary of State
Cordell Hull (1933–44)
Edward R. Stettinius Jr. (1944–45)

Secretary of the Treasury
William H. Woodin (1933–34)
Henry Morgenthau Jr. (1934–45)

Secretary of War
George H. Dern (1933–36)
Harry H. Woodring (1937–40)
Henry L. Stimson (1940–45)

Attorney General
Homer S. Cummings (1933–39)

Francis W. Murphy (1939–40)
Robert H. Jackson (1940–41)
Francis B. Biddle (1941–45)

Secretary of the Navy
Claude A. Swanson (1933–39)
Charles Edison (1940)
William F. Knox (1940–44)
James V. Forrestal (1944–45)

Postmaster General
James A. Farley (1933–40)
Frank C. Walker (1940–45)

Secretary of the Interior
Harold L. Ickes (1933–45)

Secretary of Agriculture
Henry A. Wallace (1933–40)
Claude R. Wickard (1940–45)

Secretary of Commerce
Daniel C. Roper (1933–38)
Harry Lloyd Hopkins (1938–40)
Jesse H. Jones (1940–45)
Henry A. Wallace (1945)

Secretary of Labor
Frances Perkins (1933–45)

ers, freeing up some $500 million that went to local and state agencies as relief grants. People were put to work through agencies that coordinated a range of programs, from large-scale construction projects to conservation and clean-up work.

As confidence in the federal government was being restored, Roosevelt set up agencies that reformed banking policies, helped guide negotiations between management and labor, and established minimum wage and maximum work hours. To help speed legislation, the administration sometimes wrote bills that were quickly debated and passed by Congress and signed by the president—all in one day on several occasions. An amazing amount of legislation was passed during his first one hundred days in office, followed by more legislation in 1934 and 1935 (see box).

Roosevelt worked effectively with Congress and appointed several Republicans to key positions within his administration. Among them was Secretary of the Interior Harold Ickes (1874–1952). Many others were progressive Democrats, including Secretary of Labor Frances Perkins (1880–1965; see box), the first woman to hold a Cabinet position (a position as an advisor to the president); Henry Wallace (1888–1965), originally a Republican, then a Democrat, and Roosevelt's vice president from 1941 to 1945, and later a presidential candidate for the Progressive Party in 1948; and Harry L. Hopkins (1890–1946), Roosevelt's closest advisor. Hopkins was director of the New York State Temporary Relief Administration when Roosevelt was governor of New York, and he also headed the New Deal's Federal Emergency Relief Administration and the Works Progress Administration, served as secretary of commerce from 1938 to 1940, and was an influential advisor during several World War II conferences.

Roosevelt made vast use of his executive powers and drummed up enthusiasm through many press conferences, speeches, and fireside chats. In the chats, broadcast over the radio, he often took time to carefully explain problems to the public (see **Franklin D. Roosevelt** primary source entry in volume 4).

More legislation was passed in Roosevelt's first one hundred days than in the entire administrations of several other presidents. Roosevelt also vetoed over six hundred bills; his vetoes were overridden on nine occasions.

Keep seeking a cure

In 1935, Roosevelt became more progressive. He raised taxes on wealthy individuals and supported a measure that gave the federal banking system, the Federal Reserve, more influence on the economy than private businessmen. He helped establish the Social Security system. Through this program, the federal government pays old-age pensions, pro-

Major Acts of the New Deal

New Deal legislation began in a special session of Congress in 1933. Through the Emergency Banking Act and the Economy Act, Congress authorized sweeping powers for the president to begin implementing New Deal programs after they were passed by Congress. More New Deal programs followed in 1934 and 1935.

Emergency Banking Act: Introduced in Congress, passed, and signed by the president—all in one day—the Act provided sweeping power to the federal government to confront the banking crisis. Roosevelt's first fireside chat described the importance of this Act. Among other measures, the Act greatly increased the authority of the Federal Reserve Board, the government agency that oversees banking activity.

The Economy Act: Reduced government salaries and pensions to provide federal money that could be sent to states to provide relief for unemployed workers. Opposed by many Democratic representatives in Congress, the Act passed with pressure from Roosevelt and support by most Republicans.

The vast scope of New Deal programs are typically organized under the "three R's"—relief, recovery, and reform measures. The following New Deal programs are identified and described in the "three R" arrangement.

Relief measures

Government actions designed to provide immediate relief (in the form of money or work) during the worst period of the Great Depression in 1933 and 1934.

Federal Emergency Relief Administration (FERA): Provided large amounts of money to states (much of it freed for use through the Economy Act). This agency expanded from the Reconstruction Finance Corporation (RFC), established under President Herbert Hoover, Roosevelt's predecessor. The RFC provided loans to financial institutions, railways, and public agencies. FERA reorganized the RFC and simplified and greatly expanded that loan process.

Civil Works Administration (CWA): A subdivision of FERA, it provided work to a large number of men during the winter of 1933 and 1934.

Works Progress Administration (WPA, later renamed the Work Projects Administration): Replaced FERA in 1935, as the government moved from providing immediate economic relief to creating jobs. WPA projects included road repair and construction; building of schools, libraries, and other public structures; and programs to encourage artists, musicians, and writers.

Civilian Conservation Corps (CCC): Provided work for more than 250,000 unemployed and unmarried young men, many of them from city slums. Workers received food, shelter, and pay, lived in camps under the management of army officers, and performed land improvement projects.

National Youth Administration (NYA): Funded part-time jobs at schools for high school and college students and provided part-time employment for other young people.

Recovery measures

Acts designed to revive businesses and provide jobs for the unemployed.

National Industrial Recovery Act (NIRA): Passed Congress in June 1933. Authorized the Public Works Administration and the National Recovery Association (described below).

Public Works Administration (PWA): Greatly expanded a public works program begun by Hoover. Under the authority of Secretary of the Interior Harold L. Ickes, the PWA started slowly (Ickes was careful to avoid having congressmen claim money for projects in their particular state). After careful planning, a massive construction program of public buildings, large dams, and irrigation and flood-control projects began in 1937.

National Recovery Administration (NRA): Designed to provide assistance to businesses by creating codes of fair competition. Suspended laws against combining large businesses in exchange for guarantees to workers (a minimum wage, limited hours, and the right to bargain as a group). By 1934, however, the codes and monitoring practices were excessively complicated. The NRA was unanimously declared unconstitutional by the Supreme Court in 1935.

Agricultural Adjustment Administration (AAA): Established within the Department of Agriculture, the AAA addressed overproduction of crops. Financed by special taxes, the AAA purchased surplus crops and paid farmers to reduce production. These acts helped many farmers out of debt. The AAA was declared unconstitutional by the Supreme Court in 1936. A new and more modest AAA was created by Congress in 1938.

Reform measures

Between 1933 and 1938, the administration and Congress passed the most sweeping reform program since the progressive period of 1901 to 1907.

Federal Deposit Insurance Corporation (FDIC): Insured savings deposits in banks. As Roosevelt explained in his first fireside chat, banks invest money deposited by customers, rather than simply storing that money. As the Depression worsened from 1929 to 1933, customers began withdrawing their savings. Since much of the money had been invested and was lost when stock prices fell, the banks did not have the money available that cus-

$\longrightarrow$

tomers wanted to withdraw. The FDIC ensured that such money would be available in the future.

Securities and Exchange Commission (SEC): An independent agency empowered to monitor the sale of stocks and bonds to ensure that actions are carried out within legal limits.

Reciprocal Trade Agreements Act: Authorized the president to negotiate agreements with other nations for a mutual lowering of import taxes (bypassing the normal process for import tax reduction that had to be approved by Congress). Created the most-favored-nation clause that offers the same import tax rates to all countries that sign a commercial treaty with the United States (if the United States lowers tariffs in a treaty with one nation, all tariffs for other countries with most-favored-nation status have to be reduced as well).

Home Owners' Loan Corporation (HOLC): Assisted individuals with refinancing (changing the payment rates on) their home loans to avoid defaulting on payments and possibly losing their home.

Federal Housing Administration (FHA): Encouraged banks to continue making home loans by insuring loans up to eighty percent of the value of the property.

U.S. Housing Authority: Helped to rebuild slums and encouraged low-cost housing construction—the first direct involvement of the federal government in building houses.

Tennessee Valley Authority (TVA): An independent federal corporation that addressed conditions in an area that reached parts of seven states. The program was designed largely by progressive Republican senator George W. Norris (1861–1944) of Nebraska, who shared Roosevelt's conviction that public utilities (like energy and water companies) should be owned by

---

vides unemployment compensation, and offers relief to the needy and the physically challenged.

The New Deal programs as a whole made modest gains against the devastating effects of the Depression. They brought Roosevelt tremendous support. "He understood," noted historian Garry Wills, "the importance of psychology— that people have to have the courage to keep seeking a cure, no matter what the cure is." Roosevelt was reelected president in 1936 by a margin of eleven million votes over Republican nominee Alf M. Landon (1887–1987), governor of Kansas.

the government since the utilities provide public necessities. The TVA was responsible for dams that provided energy, flood control, and better transportation. Electricity was made available to some areas within the seven states for the first time. Opposed by the country's private-power companies, the TVA was not expanded to other parts of the country, although dams and power plants were constructed with federal help in the western United States.

Social Security Act: After a commission studied problems caused by unemployment, old age, and physical disability, it recommended changes that involved the federal government. Unemployment insurance was established (funded by a federal payroll tax paid in equal parts by employers and employees); an old-age pension system (Social Security) administered by the federal government was enacted and financed by taxes on both employers and employees; and federal money was provided to states to encourage them to care for dependent children and the blind. National health insurance was abandoned, however, when opponents threatened to block the entire Social Security Act legislation.

National Labor Relations Act: Guaranteed workers the right to organize and bargain collectively without interference from employers.

National Labor Relations Board (NLRB): An independent agency established through the National Labor Relations Act that monitors relations between employers and labor and contributed greatly to the rise of unions.

Fair Labor Standards Act: Passed in 1938 as the last significant New Deal legislation, the Act set a minimum wage and limited the number of working hours. Those measures were originally part of the National Recovery Administration that was unanimously declared unconstitutional by the Supreme Court in 1935.

Roosevelt's landslide showed in the Electoral College—46 states and 523 electoral votes to Landon's 2 states and 8 electoral votes. (For more information on the Electoral College, see boxes in **George W. Bush** entry in volume 5.)

Losing ground

Roosevelt noted as he began his second term in 1937 that there was much work to be done—that one third of Americans were still "ill-housed, ill clad, ill nourished." He suggested that Americans had a "rendez-vous [a meeting]

Frances Perkins

Frances Perkins, President Franklin D. Roosevelt's only secretary of labor, drafted important New Deal legislation, including the Social Security Act and the Fair Labor Standards Act. She was born Fannie Coralie Perkins in 1880 in Boston, Massachusetts, to Susan Bean and Frederick W. Perkins. Her father owned a stationery business that also sold books and periodicals. He helped educate her. Fannie attended a largely male preparatory school, then went to Mt. Holyoke College in Massachusetts beginning in 1898. She switched her interest from chemistry and physics to social work after attending meetings of the National Consumers' League and hearing lectures by Florence Kelley (1859–1932), national secretary of the league. The group was dedicated to the elimination of child labor and of low-paying shops that exploited immigrant laborers. Not able to land a job in social work after she graduated from college, Perkins taught briefly in New England and then at a girls' school in Illinois.

Perkins began working with laborers in Chicago, helping them collect their pay from corrupt businessmen and assisting as a nurse. She changed her baptismal name of Fannie to Frances when converting her faith from Congregationalist to Episcopalian. In 1907, she became a professional social worker in Philadelphia, where she joined the Socialist Party and attended classes in economics and sociology at the University of Pennsylvania. Perkins moved to New York in 1909 for training at the New York School of Philanthropy. In 1910, she earned a master's degree in political science from Columbia University and became secretary of the New York City Consumers' League. Her responsibilities involved monitoring sanitary regulations for cellar bakeries, overseeing fire prevention in factories, and limiting the working hours for those under the age of eighteen.

After the 1911 Triangle Shirtwaist Fire in New York City that claimed the lives of 146 workers, mostly young girls, she was named executive secretary of the Committee on Safety of the City of New York. She worked with the Factory Investigating Commission that ordered new fire laws for the state.

In 1913, Perkins married Paul C. Wilson, a New York economist involved in city politics. In the spring of 1915, Perkins suffered a miscarriage; in December of the following year, her daughter Susanna Winslow was born. Perkins was named to the New York State Industrial Commission by New York governor Al Smith in 1919, making her the first woman to hold such a position in the state and the highest paid woman in any state government.

After Smith lost the 1920 election, Perkins served as executive secretary of the Council on Immigrant Education. At Smith's urging, Perkins joined the Democratic Party in 1920. Smith won election again in 1922 and appointed her to the Industrial Board, where she was named chairperson in 1926.

Frances Perkins.
Reproduced by permission of Archive Photos.

In 1929, newly elected governor Franklin D. Roosevelt appointed her industrial commissioner of the state of New York, making her the first woman to serve in a governor's Cabinet. She became the first woman to hold a federal Cabinet post after newly elected president Roosevelt named her secretary of labor in 1933.

"I came to work for God, FDR and the millions of forgotten, plain, common working men," said Perkins about her Cabinet position. She reorganized the Labor Department to increase efficiency. In addition, Perkins advised Roosevelt on key appointments, including Harry Hopkins, who became head of the Federal Emergency Relief Administration.

Perkins played a major role in the government's response to the San Francis-co general strike of 1934. Perkins opposed federal intervention in the strike, believing that it would be quickly resolved. Though it was, she was targeted by some anticommunists for not deporting (expelling from the United States) a union leader suspected but not proved to be a communist. That incident helped fuel an attempt to impeach her in 1938 by the House Un-American Activities Committee (HUAC), formed in the spring of 1937. The impeachment proceedings were very painful for Perkins, and she received hate mail. In March 1938, the Judiciary Committee refused to recommend impeachment, but the HUAC continued to investigate her.

Meanwhile, Perkins aided in drafting legislation for the Social Security Act and the Fair Labor Standards Act. Those achievements, and her negotiating skills in disputes among automobile industry workers and management in the mid-1930s, were the high points of her career. During World War II, she fought for such labor rights as the forty-hour workweek and payment for overtime. She remained in the Cabinet after Roosevelt's death. President Truman later asked her to resign and then appointed her to the Civil Service Commission.

When her husband died in 1952, Perkins began a new career as a college lecturer at the age of seventy-three. She served as a visiting professor at Cornell University until her death on May 14, 1965, at the age of eighty-five.

In his drive to ensure approval of his New Deal programs, President Roosevelt attempted to alter the political makeup of the Supreme Court by adding as many as six judges. This cartoon depicts FDR as a quarterback trying to get the size of his team increased so he can put his own players on it.
Drawing by C. K. Berryman. Courtesy of the Library of Congress.

THE INGENIOUS QUARTERBACK!

with destiny"—a turning point ahead when better things would come. Roosevelt himself would face challenges with the Supreme Court, Congress, and international tensions during his second term.

Some of Roosevelt's New Deal programs were declared unconstitutional by the U.S. Supreme Court. He felt held back by conservative justices who had been appointed by the previous three Republican presidents. Roosevelt sought to add as many as six judges. His attempt to "stack the court" in his favor met with stern resistance, even among his fellow Democrats.

Meanwhile, a series of strikes by workers unhappy with their wages led some to accuse Roosevelt of having been too favorable to labor. On the other hand, the continued desperate economic conditions led others to promote more radical (extreme) solutions to the nation's problems than the New Deal. Over two hundred thousand Americans voted for socialist and communist candidates in the presidential elec-

Complete American Presidents Sourcebook

tions of 1932 and 1936. (Socialists and communists believe that private property should be banned and that goods should be made available to all based on their needs and distributed by a central governing system.)

After slight improvement, the economy worsened in 1936, forcing large cuts in federal spending. Roosevelt was only able to convince Congress to pass small-scale programs related to public housing, fair labor standards, and aid to tenant farmers. In 1938, the midterm congressional elections (elections midway through a president's term) changed the balance of power in Congress; the new congressional term in 1939 brought in enough Republicans to defeat any more legislation for urban welfare.

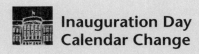

Inauguration Day Calendar Change

The Twentieth Amendment to the Constitution changed the presidential inauguration date from March 4 to January 20; that change was first instituted in 1937, when President Roosevelt was inaugurated after being reelected in 1936. The date change was made to shorten the amount of time between the election and Inauguration Day. This eliminated what was roughly a four-month lame-duck period for an outgoing president. The longer time frame between outgoing and incoming presidents had been needed earlier in history, when the means of communication and travel were more modest.

Foreign affairs

During his first two terms, Roosevelt tried to help stimulate the American economy by increasing foreign trade. He improved diplomatic relations with Russia, which was still struggling to modernize after heavy losses in World War I. Roosevelt instituted a "good neighbor" policy with Latin American countries based on reciprocal trade agreements designed to benefit both sides. (In a reciprocal trade agreement, nations promise to trade in a way that will benefit each nation equally.) He also pledged to end American intervention in Latin American countries that had occurred several times over the previous decades when American business interests were threatened. Meanwhile, the United States did not participate in international attempts to stabilize the world economic crisis. Roosevelt believed that such actions might hinder efforts at home.

Economic hard times led to increasing international tensions. Military dictatorships— states in which military leaders have absolute power—arose during the 1930s in Ger-

President Franklin D. Roosevelt and first lady Eleanor Roosevelt smile at onlookers in 1938.
Reproduced by permission of the Corbis Corporation.

many, Italy, Spain, and Japan. Japan had invaded Manchuria, China, in 1931. Roosevelt maintained the strained diplomatic relations with Japan begun by the Hoover administration. By 1940, Roosevelt had suspended a commercial treaty between the two nations. Italy, led by dictator Benito Mussolini (1883–1945), invaded the east African empire of Ethiopia. The Nazi regime of Adolf Hitler (1889–1945) in Germany teamed with Mussolini to provide aid for the overthrow of the Spanish monarchy. Meanwhile, in March 1938, Germany sent military troops to Austria, occupying and annexing it (making it part of Germany). At the end of August 1939, the Germans concluded a nonaggression pact (a promise not to attack each other) with the Union of Soviet Socialist Republics (USSR). When the Nazis invaded Poland on September 1, 1939, France and Britain declared war on Germany.

To delay American involvement in foreign conflicts, Congress proclaimed American neutrality and placed an embargo (an order preventing trade) on shipping armaments (weapons and war supplies) to warring countries beginning in 1934. The armaments embargo was repealed in 1939 to allow the sale of weapons to nations that could pay cash and transport materials on their own ships. As most of Europe fell under German domination in 1940 and Great Britain was hit by Nazi warplanes with daily aerial bombing, President Roosevelt arranged a trade: Great Britain received fifty American destroyers; in exchange, Britain leased military bases in the Pacific to the United States. The program met with harsh criticism from Americans who wanted to remain neutral. Roosevelt favored the efforts of Britain and France against Nazi Germany.

The United States had entered a state of military preparedness by the late 1930s. A tremendous surge in defense spending provided massive amounts of jobs and sparked industrial expansion, lifting the nation out of the Great Depression. In 1941, responding to pleas for aid from British prime minister Winston Churchill (1874–1965; see box), Roosevelt asked Congress to authorize the Lend-Lease program. This measure, which was expanded to include the thirty-eight countries that formed the Allied powers (those fighting Germany, Italy, and Japan—the Axis powers), sidestepped laws that did not allow the United States to sell arms on credit (future payment). Instead, the United States claimed it was "lending" military hardware and expecting it to be returned.

Franklin D. Roosevelt was the first president in office to appear on television—April 30, 1939, at the opening of the World's Fair in New York City.

Winston Churchill

A celebrated statesman, historian, and Nobel laureate, Winston Churchill is best remembered for his leadership as Britain's prime minister during World War II (1939–45). Born at Blenheim Palace in Oxfordshire, England, Churchill was the son of Lord Randolph Henry Spencer Churchill (1849–1895), a prominent parliamentarian, and Jennie Jerome Churchill (1854–1921), an American socialite. Churchill received his early education in private schools. An unexceptional student, he enrolled at the Royal Military Academy to prepare for a career as a military officer. Graduating with honors in 1894, he was appointed to the Fourth (Queen's Own) Hussars as a sublieutenant in 1895.

During the late 1890s, Churchill traveled to Cuba, India, and the Sudan to report on various military campaigns as a war correspondent for the *London Daily Telegraph* and the *London Morning Post*. His capture by Boer soldiers in 1899 and escape from a South African prison won him renown and helped secure his election to Parliament in 1900. He served continuously in Parliament for more than six decades in several high-ranking positions.

As first lord of admiralty during World War I, Churchill directed a failed campaign in Eastern Europe that resulted in heavy casualties and Churchill's demo-tion. He resigned his office in 1916 to go to the front as a lieutenant colonel in command of the Sixth Royal Fusiliers.

At the outbreak of World War II, Churchill was briefly reappointed first lord of admiralty. Then, after the resignation of Neville Chamberlain (1869–1940), Churchill became prime minister of Great Britain in 1940. Churchill founded the Atlantic Charter with the United States in 1941. The charter grew out of discussions he had with President Roosevelt aboard warships near Newfoundland, Canada. They formed a statement that supported the right of all people to choose their leaders, called for freedom on the seas, and denounced aggressors of war.

Churchill helped orchestrate the Allied victory over Germany with Roosevelt and Soviet leader Joseph Stalin. In 1943, Churchill and Roosevelt agreed that there would be no negotiated peace with the Axis powers. They decided on strategies for winning back Europe from Nazi forces; Allied forces would begin by invading Sicily and Italy in 1943 and then launch a major offensive from western France in 1944. The leaders also agreed to support the founding of the United Nations.

Churchill kept Stalin informed on Allied plans. Churchill, Roosevelt, and Stalin

Winston Churchill.
Reproduced by permission of the Corbis Corporation.

met at the Yalta Conference in 1945 to discuss postwar Europe (Germany's defeat was expected soon) and the war against Japan.

Churchill lost his position as prime minister in 1945 but regained it in 1951. He supported British involvement in international affairs, including the North Atlantic Treaty Organization (NATO) and the Council of Europe (CE). He resigned in 1955, turning over his office to Anthony Eden (1897–1977). He remained active in politics during the last decade of his life and continued to win praise as a writer.

His books revealed Churchill to be an intelligent observer of military campaigns and geopolitical affairs, and he was an excellent biographer and historian. In *The World Crisis,* Churchill provided comprehensive analysis of international affairs and military activities during World War I as a participant in the events he recorded. His later five-volume work, *The Second World War,* provided a general history of the war intermingled with Churchill's recollections and analysis of military and diplomatic events he personally witnessed and directly influenced.

Churchill's sense of the glory of England remained with him all his life. Four times in two centuries, he noted, England had saved Europe from tyrants: Louis XIV (1638–1715), Napoleon I (1769–1821), Kaiser Wilhelm II (1859–1941), and Adolf Hitler. As Churchill saw it, "this island race" was on the side not only of progress and enlightenment but of liberty and justice as well. Churchill regarded history as a question of morality, a struggle between right and wrong, between freedom and tyranny. The purpose of history, according to Churchill, is to teach by example, especially by the examples of great leaders and by the examples of war.

Roosevelt was superstitious: he never traveled on a Friday, and his aversion to the number thirteen prompted him to not sit at a table that held twelve other people. That superstitious nature did not stop him from breaking the custom set by George Washington of a president limiting himself to two terms. FDR won four terms in office. The Twenty-second Amendment to the Constitution (ratified on February 27, 1951) later allowed presidents only two elected terms in office.

Meanwhile, Roosevelt ran for an unprecedented (done for the first time) third term in office. Concern over the war in Europe and Asia made Americans cautious about changing leaders, even though Roosevelt's popularity had fallen. He was reelected by fewer than five million votes—a clear show of support but less than half the margin of his landslide election in 1936. Still, Roosevelt had a sure win over Republican Wendell Willkie (1892–1944) in the Electoral College, 449 votes to 82.

A day of infamy

The United States moved closer to war in September 1941 when a German submarine fired a torpedo at an American destroyer. American warships were authorized for the first time to shoot at German ships. Roosevelt maintained an air of neutrality, but by that time America was clearly offering assistance to Allied powers: American ships, for example, provided information on German naval operations to Great Britain.

Meanwhile, the Roosevelt administration increased aid to China and placed an embargo on the export of iron and steel scrap to Japan. On December 7, 1941, all doubt was lifted over whether the United States would enter World War II. The Japanese air force struck a major blow with a surprise attack on American naval vessels stationed at Pearl Harbor, Hawaii. The action rallied American support against the Japanese, but some wondered about why American forces were open to such an attack as that on Pearl Harbor. Historians generally agree that the attack was a well-executed military maneuver by Japanese forces against a nation they regarded as an enemy and suspected would soon enter World II.

Eight American battleships and ten other naval vessels were sunk or badly damaged, almost two hundred American aircraft were destroyed, and about three thousand military personnel were killed or wounded. The Japanese did not destroy any aircraft carriers nor did they try to invade Hawaii.

Calling December 7 "a day which will live in infamy" in a radio broadcast to the nation (see **Franklin D. Roosevelt** primary source entry in volume 4), Roosevelt asked Congress to declare war on Japan. When Germany and Italy backed

their Japanese ally by declaring war on the United States, Congress declared war on them as well.

New Deal programs were canceled. Issues that might cause political deadlock were addressed quickly if they might affect the war effort. For example, President Roosevelt had delayed civil rights legislation to assure that his other New Deal measures would be enacted without extensive debate. When a

The U.S.S. *Shaw* **was destroyed when the Japanese bombed Pearl Harbor on December 7, 1941.**
Courtesy of the National Archives and Records Administration.

Franklin D. Roosevelt | 1151

march on Washington, D.C., to protest racial injustice was announced, the president acted quickly to empower the Fair Employment Practices Committee (FEPC) to prevent any form of racial discrimination in defense plants.

World War II

As commander in chief, Roosevelt decided on military strategy. The president oversaw the buildup of an enormous army and navy. By the end of the war, more than fifteen million people had served in the armed forces of the United States. At home, people went back to work: Unemployment dropped from seventeen percent in 1939 to one percent in 1944, and personal income doubled. Large numbers of people relocated to urban areas where military-related items were manufactured.

After calling December 7, 1941, the day the Japanese bombed Pearl Harbor, "a date which will live in infamy," President Franklin D. Roosevelt signed the declaration of war against Japan the following day. *Courtesy of the National Archives and Records Administration.*

Executive authority was broadened. An agency called the Selective Service Administration supervised a military draft; that is, a program that required men to register for possible military service. Various agencies monitored industries supporting the war effort. Vital supplies, from tires to foods and even nylon (needed more for tents than for stockings), were rationed; that is, certain goods were made available in limited supplies and purchased with special stamps. As he had with his Cabinet, Roosevelt surrounded himself with aggressive, hardworking administrators and advisors—Democrat and Republican alike. His secretary of the navy, Frank Knox (1874–1944), had been outspoken against the New Deal and was the Republican vice presidential candidate in 1936. Henry L. Stimson (1867–1950; see box in **Herbert Hoover** entry in volume 4), who had served in the Cabinets of three Republican presidents, was named secretary of war.

In 1942, the United States defeated the Japanese navy at the Battle of Midway in the mid-Pacific and assisted the Al-

lied invasion of North Africa. Meanwhile, struggling Russian forces stopped the German advance on their nation in the Battle of Stalingrad.

Roosevelt met with Churchill in January 1943 in Casablanca, Morocco, to make further plans and to announce that they insisted on unconditional surrender by the enemy. In November 1943, the president met with Churchill and Chinese leader Chiang Kai-shek (1887–1975) in Cairo, Egypt, to prepare plans for the war against Japan. Roosevelt made plans with Soviet leader Joseph Stalin (1879–1953) in Tehran, Iran, agreeing to an offensive against Germany, beginning with an invasion of Nazi-occupied France by Allied forces in the spring of 1944. That invasion—D-Day—began on June 6, 1944. From there, the Allies moved methodically toward Germany.

The Big Three (left to right): Prime Minister Winston Churchill of Great Britain, President Franklin D. Roosevelt of the United States, and Premier Joseph Stalin of the USSR meet at Yalta on the Crimean Peninsula in February 1945. *Courtesy of the Library of Congress.*

Final weeks

Roosevelt was in weak health in the election year of 1944. He had not often appeared in public during the war years. Still popular and bolstered by American success in the war in Europe, he won election for an unprecedented fourth term. His victory margin was the smallest of his four presidential wins—just over two and a half million popular votes, but he won by an overwhelming 432 votes to 99 votes in the Electoral College over Republican candidate Thomas E. Dewey (1902–1971).

Victory over Nazi Germany was expected soon. After his inauguration in January 1945, President Roosevelt traveled in February to attend the Yalta Conference, held in the Crimea region of the Soviet Union. Roosevelt discussed war strategies and the fate of postwar Europe with Churchill and Stalin. Roosevelt secured Stalin's agreement to enter the war against Japan once the Nazis were defeated. He also obtained a promise by Stalin to ensure that free elections would be held in East European nations occupied by the USSR as the Soviet military pushed toward Germany. That promise was broken soon after the war.

Roosevelt returned to Washington, D.C., but he immediately left for his vacation home in Warm Springs, Georgia, on March 30. Two weeks later, on April 12, 1945, Roosevelt was dead of a cerebral hemorrhage. He was laid to rest in the rose garden in the family estate at Hyde Park. The defeat of the Nazis occurred less than a month later.

Legacy

Franklin D. Roosevelt effectively used broad presidential authority to organize massive efforts to combat the Depression as well as the Axis powers. On the homefront, New Deal programs benefited millions of people and helped restore confidence in the American economic system. While the New Deal did not end the Depression, its progressive legislation brought about many needed changes. Several New Deal programs were still in place at the end of the twentieth century.

Critics argue that Roosevelt could have been more aggressive in attacking the nation's economic woes, whereas others contend his powers were too broad. The debate over the role of the federal government in the daily lives of citizens continues. Many Americans strongly identify the mod-

A Selection of Roosevelt Landmarks

Eleanor Roosevelt National Historic Site. 4079 Albany Post Rd., Hyde Park, NY 12538. (845) 229-8114. President Roosevelt had a smaller home built for Eleanor Roosevelt. She lived the rest of her life here following the president's death in 1945. See http://www.nps.gov/elro/elrohome.html and http://www.ervk.org/index.htm (accessed on September 13, 2000).

Franklin D. Roosevelt Presidential Library and Museum. 4079 Albany Post Rd., Hyde Park, NY 12538. (845) 229-8114. First presidential library and first used by a sitting president. Artifacts and the president and first lady's personal papers are housed at the museum and library. See http://www.fdrlibrary.marist.edu/ (accessed on September 13, 2000).

Franklin Delano Roosevelt Memorial. West Basin Drive, Washington, DC (202) 426-6841. A four-room memorial—each room representing one of Roosevelt's terms in office and consisting of sculptures, water cascades, trees, and engraved quotes—pays tribute to the late president. See http://www.nps.gov/fdrm/home.htm (accessed on September 13, 2000).

Home of Franklin D. Roosevelt National Historic Site. 4079 Albany Post Rd., Hyde Park, NY 12538. (845) 229-8114. Seventeen-room house where the president was born and raised. Franklin and Eleanor are buried in the Rose Garden. See http://www.nps.gov/hofr/hofrhome.html (accessed on September 13, 2000).

Little White House State Historic Site. 399 Little White House Rd., Warm Springs, GA 31830. (706) 655-5870. The polio-stricken president enjoyed vacationing in Warm Springs and swimming in its waters. Roosevelt died in this house. The famous unfinished portrait of the president is among the items on display.

Roosevelt Campobello International Park. 459 Route 774, Welshpool, Campobello, New Brunswick, E5E 1A4 Canada. (506) 752-2922. Also, P.O. Box 129, Lubec, ME 04652. Roosevelt family vacation home, garden, and grounds are near the U.S.-Canada border, just outside Lubec, Maine. A visitors center highlights Roosevelt's association with the island. See http://www.nps.gov/roca/ and http://www.fdr.net/ (accessed on September 13, 2000).

ern-day Democratic Party with Roosevelt's belief in using the powers of government to address the country's problems.

Roosevelt's role as commander in chief has also been much analyzed. Some commentators suggest that aggressive

U.S. actions toward Japan invited the attack on Pearl Harbor or that the United States was not prepared for the surprise assault. Others view the attack as a strategic, well-coordinated first strike by Japan. During the war, government agencies closely supervised American industries to direct work toward the war effort. That domination of industry by government was quickly stopped once the emergency of war had ended.

Roosevelt's foreign policy clearly favored the Allied powers during events leading up to America's involvement in World War II. After the war, the agreements Roosevelt and Stalin forged at the Yalta Conference became controversial. Russia's promise of free elections in the Eastern European countries it occupied during the war was not kept. Those nations fell under Russian domination—behind an "iron curtain," as the boundary was called. Although they were allies during the war, it was not long before the United States and the Soviet Union were engaged in what was called the "Cold War"—a tense period of strained diplomatic relations, military buildup, and the constant threat of war that lasted until the late 1980s.

The continuing debate about Roosevelt's policies reflects the tremendous impact of his administrations on United States history. He is regularly ranked by presidential historians among the greatest presidents.

Where to Learn More

Alsop, Joseph. *FDR, 1882–1945: A Centenary Remembrance.* New York: Viking, 1982. Reprint, New York: Gramercy Books, 1998.

Burns, James MacGregor. *Roosevelt: The Lion and the Fox.* New York: Harcourt, 1956.

Franklin D. Roosevelt Presidential Library and Museum. [Online] http://www.fdrlibrary.marist.edu/ (accessed on September 28, 2000).

Freedman, Russell. *Franklin Delano Roosevelt.* New York: Clarion Books, 1990.

Larsen, Rebecca. *Franklin D. Roosevelt: Man of Destiny.* New York: Franklin Watts, 1991.

Leuchtenburg, William E. *The FDR Years: On Roosevelt and His Legacy.* New York: Columbia University Press, 1995.

Manchester, William. *The Last Lion: Winston Spencer Churchill.* Boston: Little, Brown, 1983.

Martin, George W. *Madam Secretary, Frances Perkins.* Boston: Houghton Mifflin, 1976.

Pasachoff, Naomi E. *Frances Perkins: Champion of the New Deal.* New York: Oxford University Press, 1999.

Perret, Geoffrey. *Old Soldiers Never Die: The Life of Douglas MacArthur.* New York: Random House, 1996.

Schlesinger, Arthur M., Jr. *The Age of Roosevelt.* 3 vols. Boston: Houghton Mifflin, 1957.

Severance, John B. *Winston Churchill: Soldier, Statesman, Artist.* New York: Clarion Books, 1996.

Eleanor Roosevelt

**Born October 11, 1884
New York, New York
Died November 7, 1962
New York, New York**

**Redefined the role of first lady, advising
her husband, developing programs, and
pursuing her own interests in social reform**

"We cannot wait until
tomorrow. Tomorrow is
now."

Eleanor Roosevelt

Eleanor Roosevelt.
*Reproduced by permission of
AP/Wide World Photos.*

E leanor Roosevelt was the most politically active first lady.
She held weekly press conferences and wrote newspaper
and magazine columns. She consistently worked on programs
to help the less-advantaged, was active in promoting civil
rights, lobbied for positions and equal pay for qualified
women, and helped influence some of the New Deal programs of her husband's administration. After the death of
Franklin D. Roosevelt (1882–1945; see entry in volume 4) in
1945, she served with the United Nations.

Her transformation from a timid child to a self-re-
liant, energetic, and outspoken woman developed through
several life crises. Eleanor Roosevelt was orphaned at ten, felt
out of place and unattractive as a teen in the New York high-
society life of her family and social circle, endured a bossy
mother-in-law, confronted her husband's unfaithfulness, and
helped Roosevelt continue to be energetic after he suffered
physical impairment.

As first lady, her outspokenness for humanitarian
causes was sometimes ridiculed by opponents. Eleanor Roosevelt received hate mail among the three hundred thousand

letters written to her during her first year as first lady. Many others, including her husband, admired her tireless work: "My missus," he said, "goes where she wants to, talks to everybody and does she learn something!"

Born into wealth

Anna Eleanor Roosevelt was born on October 11, 1884, in New York City. Her mother, Anna, was an attractive socialite, and her father, Elliott, was the wealthy and handsome brother of **Theodore Roosevelt** (1858–1919; see entry in volume 3). Her mother, who died when Eleanor was eight, did not pay much attention to Eleanor and her two brothers. Her father doted on her, but he was an alcoholic. He was often away, either on binges of drinking or seeking treatment for his addiction. He died when she was ten. Eleanor and her brothers moved in with their grandmother, a strict disciplinarian.

Shy and self-conscious about her looks, feeling gangly and unattractive, Eleanor found enjoyment in riding horses, learning French, and writing. Her life changed for the better when she attended a finishing school in England beginning at age fifteen. The school's leader, Marie Souvestre (1834–1905), noticed Eleanor's intelligence and encouraged her to speak out. She took Eleanor with her on trips to the European continent, challenged her intellectually, and developed her practical skills through such tasks as having her make travel arrangements.

In 1902, as she approached her eighteenth birthday, Eleanor was back in New York. Typical of girls from wealthy families, she had a "coming out" party, attended balls, teas, luncheons, dinners, and parties. In that social setting, she became reacquainted with Franklin Roosevelt, a Harvard student making the society rounds. Distantly related, they had occasionally played together as children.

The following year, Franklin drove Eleanor to Groton, a preparatory school that Franklin had attended and where Eleanor's younger brother was enrolled. Franklin proposed marriage to her there. Roosevelt's mother was against the engagement and arranged a Caribbean vacation for him, hoping that he would change his mind. Instead, the engagement was officially announced in the fall of 1904. Roosevelt began studying law at Columbia University, and Eleanor taught classes in an impoverished area of New York. When they were married on March 17, 1905, President Theodore Roosevelt walked the bride up the aisle.

Social purpose

While in their teens and away at school, Eleanor and Franklin both had mentors—older, trusted counselors, who helped inspire them to work for social improvements. In 1910, when Roosevelt first entered politics, they were both interested in pursuing that goal. As Roosevelt began writing speeches for a state senate campaign, Eleanor found that she agreed with many of his progressive views. His election in 1910 and the family's move to the state capital of Albany, New York, stimulated Eleanor's interest in politics. The move also took her away from a life of privilege on a large estate, where she had often felt dominated by Roosevelt's mother, who lived nearby. Managing a household and raising three children (Anna Eleanor was born in 1906, James was born in 1907, the first Franklin Jr. was born and died in 1909, and Elliott was born in 1910) proved liberating for Eleanor. The Roosevelts would have two more children: the second Franklin Jr. was born in 1914, and John in 1916.

The family moved to Washington, D.C., in 1913, when Roosevelt was appointed to a position in the administration of President **Woodrow Wilson** (1856–1924; see entry in volume 4). In addition to hosting parties and socializing, Eleanor became active with the Red Cross following the outbreak of World War I (1914–18). In 1918, however, her marriage was threatened when she discovered her husband had been involved with her social secretary. Roosevelt ended the affair and Eleanor forgave him. The couple remained married, admired each other's strengths, but were more partners than husband and wife.

Eleanor became more involved in social causes. She regularly visited wounded soldiers, attended meetings of the International Congress for Women Workers, took classes in typing and shorthand, and prepared monthly reports on Congress for the League of Women Voters. Roosevelt ran as a vice presidential candidate in 1920, but the Democrats lost that election.

Great suffering, greater sympathy

In August 1921, Franklin Roosevelt was stricken with polio, an infectious disease that attacks skeletal muscles and the spinal cord. The disease left him partially paralyzed: He could not walk without the aid of leg braces and a cane. Eleanor helped him continue to lead an active political career. When she was later first lady, she was once challenged after a speech with the question of whether her husband's ailment had affected his mental capacity: "Yes," she replied. "Anyone who has gone through great suffering is bound to have a greater sympathy and understanding of the problems of mankind."

She would drive him to speeches and drive voters to the polls. Overcoming her own shyness, Eleanor would occasionally substitute for him at speeches and began giving her own talks as well. Additionally, she worked as a teacher in private schools, served as editor of the *Women's Democratic News,* and was a board member of several charitable foundations.

When Franklin Roosevelt was elected governor of New York in 1928, Eleanor became even more active politically. Her political role expanded further in 1932 when her husband ran for the presidency. Eleanor helped write biographical profiles of Roosevelt, worked with the women's division of the Democratic Party, and helped her husband campaign. He read his speeches to her for advice and commentary.

Humanitarian and columnist

As first lady, Eleanor Roosevelt presided graciously over the usual festive occasions in the White House. She traveled extensively—over thirty-eight thousand miles in 1933, and even more in 1934. With the country in the grips of the Great Depression (1929–41), Eleanor used her travel experiences to provide the president with first-hand reports of conditions throughout the country. She became involved in several causes: Her report on poor neighborhoods in Washington, D.C., led Congress to appropriate money for social improvement in the

nation's capital; she spoke out for equal pay for women and for consumer protection; and she became involved in projects connected with her husband's New Deal program (see box in **Franklin D. Roosevelt** entry in volume 4).

Eleanor Roosevelt is credited with having expanded two New Deal projects: She lobbied successfully to have artists and entertainers included in appropriations for work through the Civil Works Administration; and she championed the National Youth Administration that funded part-time jobs at schools for high school and college students and part-time employment for other young people. She promoted the program after becoming concerned that young people would become dispirited and restless over their future prospects during the Depression years. She also lobbied to have noted educator Mary McLeod Bethune (1875–1955) named head of that administration.

Her support for Bethune was among many examples of Eleanor Roosevelt's activism on the part of African Americans, who were regularly invited to dinners and policy discussions on a scale far exceeding those of previous administrations. For example, the National Association for the Advancement of Colored People (NAACP) was consulted regularly for input into administration policies. Eleanor resigned from the Daughters of the American Revolution when that group refused to allow noted African American singer Marian Anderson (1897–1993) to perform at one of the group's functions. When Eleanor attended a lecture in Alabama and found that the seating was segregated, with whites on one side and blacks on the other, she picked up her chair and moved it to an open area between the two groups.

Among her many humanitarian causes, Eleanor founded the homestead community of Arthurdale, West Virginia, after having visited poor miners and discovering their horrible living conditions. From impoverished regions to Japanese internment camps (places where Japanese Americans were held while the United States was at war with Japan) to military bases in Europe and the Pacific, Eleanor Roosevelt seemed to be everywhere. A cartoon of the day showed a thick black box representing a mine with light cast by a miner who exclaims, "For gosh sakes, here comes Mrs. Roosevelt."

Eleanor Roosevelt was also busy as a columnist, contributing "Mrs. Roosevelt's Column" regularly to *Woman's Home Companion* beginning in 1934. Another feature, "If You Ask Me," ran in the *Ladies Home Journal* beginning in 1942 and in *McCalls* beginning in 1944. In 1935, she wrote a syndicated newspaper column, "My Day," that moved from general chatter to commentary on social issues of the day. In 1937, she published her autobiography, *This Is My Story,* which became a bestseller. In 1940, she spoke out in defense of the novel *The Grapes of Wrath* when it was banned in several cities.

Tomorrow is now

When Franklin D. Roosevelt died in April 1945, Eleanor broke the news to Vice President **Harry S. Truman** (1884–1972; see entry in volume 4). She remained active, especially in association with the United Nations. She was part of the committee that drafted the U.N. Declaration of Human Rights and served as a delegate under presidents Truman and **John F. Kennedy** (1917–1963; see entry in volume 5). Her other responsibilities during the Kennedy administration included membership on the board that developed the Peace Corps and on the President's Commission on the Status of Women. She was slowed by a blood disease and died of the ailment on November 7, 1962.

"The future is literally in our hands to mold as we like," she wrote in *Tomorrow Is Now,* a book published shortly after her death. "But we cannot wait until tomorrow. Tomorrow is now." That is how she lived her life.

Where to Learn More

Freedman, Russell. *Eleanor Roosevelt: A Life of Discovery*. New York: Clarion, 1993.

Roosevelt, Eleanor. *The Autobiography of Eleanor Roosevelt*. Boston: G. K. Hall, 1984. Reprint, New York : Da Capo Press, 1992.

Roosevelt, Eleanor. *If You Ask Me*. New York: D. Appleton-Century, 1946.

Roosevelt, Eleanor. *This Is My Story*. New York: Harper, 1937.

Roosevelt, Eleanor. *Tomorrow Is Now*. New York: Harper, 1963.

Youngs, J. William T. *Eleanor Roosevelt: A Personal and Public Life*. Edited by Oscar Handlin. Boston: Little, Brown, 1985. Reprint, New York: Longman, 2000.

Roosevelt's First Inaugural Address

Delivered on March 4, 1933; excerpted from
Bartleby.com: Great Books Online **(Web site)**

With the nation in the worst period of the Great Depression,
President Roosevelt expresses optimism

When **Franklin D. Roosevelt** (1882–1945; see entry in volume 4) was sworn into office as president, the nation was at the worst point in the Great Depression (1929–41). Over thirteen million people were out of work. Just a month earlier, millions of people were so worried about the nation's economy and their own ability to survive that they tried to withdraw their savings from the nation's banks. By the time of the inauguration a month later, banks were closed in thirty-eight states.

Roosevelt had a plan of action to combat the Depression. He called it the New Deal (see box in **Franklin D. Roosevelt** entry in volume 4) during his campaign for the presidency. Roosevelt had already fought the effects of the Depression as governor of New York from 1928 to 1932. As governor, he had consulted with business leaders, scholars, and many other people to take an aggressive approach to the woes of common people in New York. As president, he planned an even more ambitious program.

President Roosevelt took the occasion of his inauguration to try and rally the people of the nation. He spoke can-

"The only thing we have to fear is fear itself—nameless, unreasoning unjustified terror. . . ."

Franklin D. Roosevelt

didly about problems, and inspirationally about the challenge ahead. "The only thing we have to fear is fear itself," he assured the nation.

Things to remember while reading an excerpt from President Roosevelt's first inaugural address:

- In the opening words of the speech, Roosevelt quickly assured Americans that the nation would triumph over the terrible economic conditions of the times. His remark, "the only thing we have to fear is fear itself—nameless, unreasoning unjustified terror . . ." became immediately famous. He proceeded to state in plain terms the challenges the nation faced, remaining upbeat but not overly optimistic: "Only a foolish optimist," he stated, "can deny the dark realities of the moment."

- In the middle portion of the address, Roosevelt focused on some of the circumstances that caused economic hardships. Then, he began to present his plans.

- In portions of the speech not in the following excerpt, Roosevelt made two key points: "Happiness," he stated, "lies not in the mere possession of money; it lies in the joy of achievement, in the thrill of creative effort"; and he announced his plan to focus on America's problems instead of connecting America's recovery with international improvement of the economic crisis. Regarding the first point, he blamed much of the financial crisis on "money changers" (investment brokers and bankers) who were motivated only by possessing money.

- Roosevelt used the metaphor of war in describing his program for fighting the Depression. The courage, sacrifice, and discipline it would take to overcome the hardship were likened to a "sacred obligation."

Excerpt from President Roosevelt's first inaugural address

*I am certain that my fellow Americans expect that on my induction into the Presidency I will address them with a candor and a decision which the present situation of our Nation impels. This is preeminently the time to speak the truth, the whole truth, frankly and boldly. Nor need we shrink from honestly facing conditions in our country today. This great Nation will endure as it has endured, will revive and will prosper. So, first of all, let me assert my firm belief that the only thing we have to fear is fear itself—nameless, unreasoning unjustified terror which paralyzes needed efforts to **convert retreat into advance**. In every dark hour of our national life a leadership of frankness and **vigor** has met with that understanding and support of the people themselves which is essential to victory. I am convinced that you will again give that support to leadership in these critical days.*

*In such a spirit on my part and on yours we face our common difficulties. They concern, thank God, only material things. **Values** have shrunken to fantastic levels; taxes have risen; our ability to pay has fallen; government of all kinds is faced by serious **curtailment** of income; the means of exchange are frozen in the currents of trade; the withered leaves of industrial enterprise lie on every side; farmers find no markets for their produce; the savings of many years in thousands of families are gone.*

*More important, a host of unemployed citizens face the grim problem of existence, and an equally great number **toil** with little return. Only a foolish optimist can deny the dark realities of the moment.*

*Yet our distress comes from no failure of substance. We are stricken by no plague of locusts. Compared with the perils which our forefathers conquered because they believed and were not afraid, we have still much to be thankful for. Nature still offers her bounty and human efforts have multiplied it. Plenty is at our doorstep, but a generous use of it **languishes** in the very sight of the supply.*

*Primarily this is because the rulers of the exchange of mankind's goods have failed, through their own stubbornness and their own incompetence, have admitted their failure, and **abdicated**. Practices*

Convert retreat into advance: Change avoidance to progress.

Vigor: Energy.

Values: Prices.

Curtailment: Decrease.

Toil: Work.

Languishes: Is neglected.

Abdicated: Given up power and responsibility.

of the **unscrupulous money changers** stand indicted in the court of public opinion, rejected by the hearts and minds of men. True they have tried, but their efforts have been cast in the pattern of an out-worn tradition. Faced by failure of credit they have proposed only the lending of more money. Stripped of the lure of profit by which to induce our people to follow their false leadership, they have resorted to **exhortations**, pleading tearfully for restored confidence. They know only the rules of a generation of self-seekers. They have no vision, and when there is no vision the people perish. . . .

Our greatest primary task is to put people to work. This is no unsolvable problem if we face it wisely and courageously. It can be accomplished in part by direct recruiting by the Government itself, treating the task as we would treat the emergency of a war, but at the same time, through this employment, accomplishing greatly needed projects to stimulate and reorganize the use of our natural resources.

Hand in hand with this we must frankly recognize the overbalance of population in our industrial centers and, by engaging on a national scale in a redistribution, endeavor to provide a better use of the land for those best fitted for the land. The task can be helped by definite efforts to raise the values of agricultural products and with this the power to purchase the output of our cities. It can be helped by preventing realistically the tragedy of the growing loss through **foreclosure** of our small homes and our farms. It can be helped by insistence that the Federal, State, and local governments act **forthwith** on the demand that their cost be drastically reduced. It can be helped by the unifying of relief activities which to-day are often scattered, uneconomical, and unequal. It can be helped by national planning for and supervision of all forms of transportation and of communications and other utilities which have a definitely public character. There are many ways in which it can be helped, but it can never be helped merely by talking about it. We must act and act quickly.

Finally, in our progress toward a resumption of work we require two safeguards against a return of the evils of the old order; there must be a strict supervision of all banking and credits and investments; there must be an end to speculation with other people's money; and there must be provision for an adequate but sound **currency**.

There are the lines of attack. I shall presently urge upon a new Congress in special session detailed measures for their fulfillment, and I shall seek the immediate assistance of the several States.

Unscrupulous money changers: Unprincipled banks and other institutions that invest the money of their customers.

Exhortations: Emphatic expressions of beliefs.

Foreclosure: When a lending institution ends a loan agreement and seizes assets (such as property) to make up for money owed, after a borrower fails to make agreed upon payments.

Forthwith: Immediately.

Currency: Money—bills and coins.

Complete American Presidents Sourcebook

Through this program of action we address ourselves to putting our own national house in order and making income balance outgo. Our international trade relations, though vastly important, are in point of time and necessity secondary to the establishment of a sound national economy. I favor as a practical policy the putting of first things first. I shall spare no effort to restore world trade by international economic readjustment, but the emergency at home can not wait on that accomplishment. . . .

*If I read the **temper** of our people correctly, we now realize as we have never realized before our interdependence on each other; that we can not merely take but we must give as well; that if we are to go forward, we must move as a trained and loyal army willing to sacrifice for the good of a common discipline, because without such discipline no progress is made, no leadership becomes effective. We are, I know, ready and willing to submit our lives and property to such discipline, because it makes possible a leadership which aims at a larger good. This I propose to offer, pledging that the larger purposes will bind upon us all as a sacred obligation with a unity of duty **hitherto** evoked only in time of armed strife.*

With this pledge taken, I assume unhesitatingly the leadership of this great army of our people dedicated to a disciplined attack upon our common problems. . . .

I am prepared under my constitutional duty to recommend the measures that a stricken nation in the midst of a stricken world may require. These measures, or such other measures as the Congress may build out of its experience and wisdom, I shall seek, within my constitutional authority, to bring to speedy adoption. But in the event that the Congress shall fail to take one of these two courses and in the event that the national emergency is still critical, I shall not evade the clear course of duty that will then confront me. I shall ask the Congress for the one remaining instrument to meet the crisis—broad Executive power to wage a war against the emergency, as great as the power that would be given to me if we were in fact invaded by a foreign foe.

*For the trust **reposed** in me I will return the courage and the devotion that **befit** the time. I can do no less.* (Bartleby.com: Great Books Online [Web site])

Temper: Frame of mind.

Hitherto: Previously.

Reposed: Placed.

Befit: Are proper to.

What happened next . . .

President Roosevelt called a special session of Congress. Congress had been adjourned and was not scheduled to begin meeting again until December 1933. Congress granted Roosevelt special powers and helped him enact dozens of measures to provide relief, jobs, and reforms of financial systems. Through the end of June—a period called The Hundred Days—Congress and the president acted together to bring the country out of the worst stage of the Depression.

Many people benefited from the government programs enacted by the federal government. In general, the economy of the nation improved modestly until more problems began in 1936, but the worst was over. New Deal programs were dismantled by 1941, when the United States entered World War II (1939–45) and millions of people worked in positions that helped the war effort.

Did you know . . .

- Many elements of President Roosevelt's New Deal program were quickly enacted during his first one hundred days in office, and several more important programs were launched over the next two years. Some programs, however, were challenged and were ruled unconstitutional by the Supreme Court. The National Industrial Recovery Act (NIRA) was ruled unconstitutional as a "federal intervention in intrastate affairs," meaning that the national government was attempting to control some businesses engaged in commerce that were supposed to be governed by individual states, as outlined in the Constitution. Other New Deal programs struck down by the court were the Agricultural Adjustment Administration (AAA), which paid farmers to decrease crop production in order to stop overproduction of certain goods; and the Railroad Pension Act and the Guffey-Snyder Act, because the government was attempting to change the terms of agreements already negotiated and adopted.

- In 1937, Roosevelt introduced a bill that would allow him to appoint additional Supreme Court justices and to limit the terms of justices (to get rid of the "old men," as he called them, who were blocking his plans). However, he had not consulted with fellow Democrats about the proposal, and when Republicans roundly accused Roosevelt of trying to "stack the court" in his favor and generally becoming too powerful, Roosevelt found little support. His proposal was soundly defeated and led to an erosion of his popularity.

• Despite Roosevelt's unpopular attempt to "stack the court," he was elected president for the third time in 1940. Voters continued to appreciate his efforts, and the government system of checks and balances worked to limit his powers appropriately. Roosevelt was one of the most active presidents in using his authority to influence events and legislation. Some believe that he overextended the powers of the presidency, while many others credit him with effectively using presidential power during times of emergency—the Great Depression and World War II. He is generally ranked by historians with the greatest presidents.

Where to Learn More

"Franklin D. Roosevelt: First Inaugural Address." *Bartleby.com: Great Books Online.* [Online] http://www.bartleby.com/124/pres49.html (accessed on September 15, 2000).

Lawson, Don. *FDR's New Deal.* New York: Crowell, 1979.

Sargent, James E. *Roosevelt and the Hundred Days: Struggle for the Early New Deal.* New York: Garland Publishers, 1981.

Shebar, Sharon Sigmond. *Franklin D. Roosevelt and the New Deal.* New York: Barron's Educational Series, 1987.

Roosevelt's First Fireside Chat

Delivered on March 12, 1933; excerpted from
Fireside Chats of Franklin D. Roosevelt **(Web site)**

In an informal manner, President Roosevelt explains the nation's banking problems in the first of his "fireside chat" radio broadcasts

Radio first emerged as a major national medium during the 1920s. **Franklin D. Roosevelt** (1882–1945; see entry in volume 4) was one of the first politicians to make use of radio to broadcast messages to the general public. While he was governor of New York from 1928 to 1932, Roosevelt began broadcasting "fireside chats"—using common language to address issues of concern to citizens of New York. Roosevelt continued that practice after he was elected president in 1932.

The first of his fireside chats as president focused on the banking crisis—when a large number of banks closed because they could not meet the demand of people withdrawing their savings. In the chat, Roosevelt carefully explained the nature of the crisis, urged people to be calm, and announced his intention to call a bank holiday—to close all banks while the government could arrange funds necessary to keep the banks in business.

"You people must have faith; you must not be stampeded by rumors or guesses. Let us unite in banishing fear."

Franklin D. Roosevelt

Things to remember while reading an excerpt from President Roosevelt's first fireside chat:

- President Roosevelt wanted to help raise confidence among Americans to help ease the banking crisis. He was careful to describe the situation, and he used upbeat language. For example, the closing of banks was called a "holiday," rather than a term that might create further panic—such as a banking "emergency."

- The upbeat language continued as Roosevelt described the ways in which the government reacted to the crisis and helped ease the problems. By the end of the address, he was expressing confidence that the situation had improved.

Excerpt from President Roosevelt's first fireside chat

I want to talk for a few minutes with the people of the United States about banking—with the comparatively few who understand the mechanics of banking but more particularly with the overwhelming majority who use banks for the making of deposits and the drawing of checks. I want to tell you what has been done in the last few days, why it was done, and what the next steps are going to be. . . .

First of all, let me state the simple fact that when you deposit money in a bank the bank does not put the money into a safe deposit vault. It invests your money in many different forms of credit— bonds, commercial paper, mortgages and many other kinds of loans. In other words, the bank puts your money to work to keep the wheels of industry and of agriculture turning around. A comparatively small part of the money you put into the bank is kept in **currency**—*an amount which in normal times is wholly sufficient to cover the cash needs of the average citizen. In other words, the total amount of all the currency in the country is only a small fraction of the total deposits in all of the banks.*

What, then, happened during the last few days of February and the first few days of March? Because of **undermined** *confidence on the part of the public, there was a general rush by a large portion of*

Currency: Money—bills and coins.

Undermined: Weakened.

our population to turn bank deposits into currency or gold—a rush so great that the **soundest** banks could not get enough currency to meet the demand. The reason for this was that on the spur of the moment it was, of course, impossible to sell perfectly sound **assets** of a bank and convert them into cash except at **panic prices** far below their real value.

By the afternoon of March 3rd scarcely a bank in the country was open to do business. Proclamations temporarily closing them in whole or in part had been issued by the Governors in almost all the States. It was then that I issued the proclamation providing for the nationwide bank holiday, and this was the first step in the Government's reconstruction of our financial and economic **fabric**.

The second step was the legislation promptly and patriotically passed by the Congress confirming my proclamation and broadening my powers so that it became possible in view of the requirement of time to extend the holiday and lift the ban of that holiday gradually. This law also gave authority to develop a program of **rehabilitation** of our banking facilities. I want to tell our citizens in every part of the Nation that the national Congress—Republicans and Democrats alike—showed by this action a devotion to public welfare and a realization of the emergency and the necessity for speed that it is difficult to match in our history.

The third stage has been the series of regulations permitting the banks to continue their functions to take care of the distribution of food and household necessities and the payment of payrolls.

This bank holiday, while resulting in many cases in great inconvenience, is affording us the opportunity to supply the currency necessary to meet the situation. No sound bank is a dollar worse off than it was when it closed its doors last Monday. . . .

We had a bad banking situation. Some of our bankers had shown themselves either incompetent or dishonest in their handling of the peoples funds. They had used the money entrusted to them in **speculations** and unwise loans. This was, of course, not true in the vast majority of our banks, but it was true in enough of them to shock the people for a time into a sense of insecurity and to put them into a frame of mind where they did not differentiate, but seemed to assume that the acts of a comparative few had tainted them all. It was the Government's job to straighten out this situation and do it as quickly as possible. And the job is being performed. I do not promise you that every bank will be reopened or that individual

Soundest: Most solid, secure.

Assets: Items that have value.

Panic prices: When an item is sold at an amount below its value.

Fabric: Structure.

Rehabilitation: Restoration of something that has been injured.

Speculations: Purchases that a buyer believes will increase in value, allowing him or her to sell them later for profit.

losses will not be suffered, but there will be no losses that possibly could be avoided; and there would have been more and greater losses had we continued to drift. I can even promise you salvation for some at least of the sorely pressed banks. We shall be engaged not merely in reopening sound banks but in the creation of sound banks through reorganization.

It has been wonderful to me to catch the note of confidence from all over the country. I can never be sufficiently grateful to the people for the loyal support they have given me in their acceptance of the judgment that has dictated our course, even though all our processes may not have seemed clear to them.

After all, there is an element in the readjustment of our financial system more important than currency, more important than gold, and that is the confidence of the people. Confidence and courage are the essentials of success in carrying out our plan. You people must have faith; you must not be stampeded by rumors or guesses. Let us unite in banishing fear. We have provided the machinery to restore our financial system; it is up to you to support and make it work.

It is your problem no less than it is mine. Together we cannot fail. (Fireside Chats of Franklin D. Roosevelt *[Web site]*)

What happened next . . .

The Emergency Banking Act passed by Congress (the second step noted by Roosevelt to address the banking crisis) provided the funds necessary for banks to operate normally. Governors of some states had been closing banks beginning in late February, and the nationwide bank holiday occurred on Friday, March 10. On Monday, March 13, banks were beginning to open again for business.

Within a week, the federal government passed several more acts to confront the economic crisis: federal workers had their pay cut by fifteen percent, government pensions were reduced, and taxes on beer and wine went into effect. Those acts provided the government with money to help banks and provide funds for states to use for job programs.

The bank holiday, and the New Deal program of President Roosevelt in general, marked the greatest government involvement in the American economy during a time of peace. The programs helped lift the morale of the nation and provided many Americans with temporary jobs. The Depression ended after the United States entered World War II (1939–45) in 1941 and industries began massive production of materials needed for the war.

President Franklin D. Roosevelt (right) sits with his wife, Eleanor Roosevelt (left), and his mother, Sara Roosevelt (center), before the radio broadcast of a 1936 fireside chat.
Reproduced by permission of Archive Photos.

Did you know . . .

President Roosevelt used the format of fireside chats regularly during his four terms as president. Other chats included an outline of his New Deal program (May 7, 1933); a report on drought conditions that especially hurt the southwest (September 6, 1936); his plan to reorganize the judiciary (March 9, 1937), which eventually failed; and reports on the outbreak of World War II (September 3, 1939), the progress of the war after the United States became involved (February 23, 1942), peace plans (July 28, 1943), and international conferences (December 24, 1943).

Where to Learn More

Mid Hudson Regional Information Center. "On the Bank Crisis." *Fireside Chats of Franklin D. Roosevelt.* [Online] http://www.mhrcc.org/fdr/chat1.html (accessed on September 15, 2000).

Robinson, Edgar Eugene. *The Roosevelt Leadership, 1933–1945.* Philadelphia: Lippincott, 1955. Reprint, New York: Da Capo Press, 1972.

Sullivan, Lawrence. *Prelude to Panic: The Story of the Bank Holiday.* Washington, DC: Statesman Press, 1936.

Tugwell, Rexford G. *Roosevelt's Revolution: The First Year, A Personal Perspective.* New York: Macmillan, 1977.

Roosevelt's War Message to the American People

Delivered on December 8, 1941; excerpted from *A Chronology of US Historical Documents* (Web site)

President Roosevelt asks Congress for a declaration of war on Japan following the bombing of Pearl Harbor

World War II (1939–45) began in September 1939. The United States maintained neutrality—a policy of not taking either side in a dispute. Despite that official policy, government actions on the part of the United States were often supportive of the Allied nations—Great Britain, France, and the Soviet Union—in their struggle against Nazi Germany. Meanwhile, the United States had strained relations with Japan since 1931, when that nation invaded and occupied the Manchuria region of China. Tensions between the United States and Japan grew worse after World War II began and the Japanese army occupied several other countries. In 1941, the United States announced a trade embargo against Japan.

The nations continued to make occasional attempts at negotiation, but that ended on December 7, 1941, when the Japanese military launched a surprise attack on the American naval base at Pearl Harbor, on Oahu in the Hawaiian Islands. In response to the attack, President **Franklin D. Roosevelt** (1882–1945; see entry in volume 4) asked for and received from Congress a declaration of war on Japan. He announced his request for a declaration of war to the Ameri-

"Yesterday, December 7, 1941—a date which will live in infamy—the United States of America was suddenly and deliberately attacked by naval and air forces of the Empire of Japan."

Franklin D. Roosevelt

can public in a nationally broadcast radio address on December 8, 1941.

Things to remember while reading President Roosevelt's war message to the American people:

- President Roosevelt coined several remarkable phrases during his presidency, including "the only thing we have to fear is fear itself" during his first inaugural address, and Americans have "a rendez-vous with destiny" in his second inaugural address. The opening sentence of his war message to the American people contained another of those memorable phrases—"a date which will live in infamy"—which he used to firmly establish the theme of an important speech.

- Roosevelt immediately focused on the Pearl Harbor attack as a surprise and a betrayal, noting that the United States was still engaged in negotiations with Japan. The speech developed from depicting the United States as being in a state of peace to having become a victim of war (in the fourth paragraph). Roosevelt then took a dramatic tone, listing a series of other aggressive actions taken by the Japanese military.

- After assuring the nation that American military defenses were prepared against further attack, Roosevelt began rallying the people for war—using such words as "confidence" ("in our armed forces") and determination.

President Roosevelt's War Message to the American people

*Yesterday, December 7, 1941—a date which will live in **infamy**—the United States of America was suddenly and deliberately attacked by naval and air forces of the Empire of Japan.*

*The United States was at peace with that nation and, at the **solicitation** of Japan, was still in conversation with its Government*

Infamy: Disgrace, brought about by a shocking, evil act.

Solicitation: Request.

and its Emperor looking toward the maintenance of peace in the Pacific. Indeed, one hour after Japanese air squadrons had **commenced** bombing Oahu, the Japanese Ambassador to the United States and his colleague delivered to the Secretary of State a formal reply to a recent American message. While this reply stated that it seemed useless to continue the existing **diplomatic negotiations**, it contained no threat or hint of war or armed attack.

It will be recorded that the distance of Hawaii from Japan makes it obvious that the attack was deliberately planned many days or even weeks ago. During the **intervening** time, the Japanese Government has deliberately sought to deceive the United States by false statements and expressions of hope for continued peace.

The attack yesterday on the Hawaiian Islands has caused severe damage to American naval and military forces. Very many American lives have been lost. In addition, American ships have been reported torpedoed on the high seas between San Francisco and Honolulu.

Yesterday the Japanese Government also launched an attack against Malaya.

Last night Japanese forces attacked Hong Kong.

Last night Japanese forces attacked Guam.

Last night Japanese forces attacked the Philippine Islands.

Last night the Japanese attacked Wake Island.

This morning the Japanese attacked Midway Island.

Japan has, therefore, undertaken a surprise **offensive** extending throughout the Pacific area. The facts of yesterday speak for themselves. The people of the United States have already formed their opinions and well understand the **implications** to the very life and safety of our nation.

As Commander-in-Chief of the Army and Navy, I have directed that all measures be taken for our defense.

Always will we remember the **character of the onslaught** against us.

No matter how long it may take us to overcome this **premeditated** invasion, the American people in their **righteous might** will win through to absolute victory.

I believe I interpret the will of the Congress and of the people when I assert that we will not only defend ourselves to the uttermost

Commenced: Begun.

Diplomatic negotiations: Talks of a possible compromise between the United States and Japan.

Intervening: Time frame in between events.

Offensive: Attack.

Implications: Consequences.

Character of the onslaught: Roosevelt is referring to the underhanded nature of the Japanese attack.

Premeditated: Planned.

Righteous might: Strength or power that goes with being right, just, and good.

*but will make very certain that this form of **treachery** shall never endanger us again.*

Hostilities exist. There is no blinking at the fact that our people, our territory and our interests are in grave danger.

*With confidence in our armed forces—with the **unbounding** determination of our people—we will gain the **inevitable** triumph—so help us God.*

*I ask that the Congress declare that since the **unprovoked** and **dastardly** attack by Japan on Sunday, December 7, a state of war has existed between the United States and the Japanese Empire.* (A Chronology of US Historical Documents *[Web site]*)

What happened next . . .

Congress declared war on Japan the same day as Roosevelt's speech to the nation. After Germany, an ally of Japan, declared war on the United States, the United States declared war on Germany on December 11, 1941. Against Japan, the United States used a strategy of "island hopping," engaging Japanese forces in a series of isolated battles while the United States also fought Nazi forces in North Africa and Europe. There were many battles in the Pacific Ocean, including the famous battles of Midway and Okinawa, but the U.S. military did not give full attention to the war against Japan until after victory was assured in Europe. That occurred in June 1945, two months after President Roosevelt died.

American military experts were certain that the Japanese military would not surrender, and that five hundred thousand soldiers might die during a military invasion of Japan. Those factors weighed heavily on the decision by Roosevelt's successor as president, **Harry S. Truman** (1884–1972; see entry in volume 4). He decided to use the atom bomb on Japan to bring that nation to surrender. Atomic bombs were dropped on the Japanese cities of Hiroshima and Nagasaki in August 1945, causing massive destruction and loss of life. The Japanese military officially surrendered days later.

Did you know . . .

- Debate about Japan's attack on Pearl Harbor is among the most intriguing of military issues. It is generally viewed as a mistake, since the attack brought the United States into World War II and the American military proved decisive for the Allied forces in winning the war in both Europe and Asia.

- Some military historians note that Japan succeeded in launching a devastating attack that hurt the American military and caused some Americans to question whether or not the nation was prepared for war. They also note that diplomatic hostilities between the two nations, and several American actions that supported the Allied cause in general, indicated that the United States was already involved in World War II and likely to officially enter the conflict.

Where to Learn More

Beard, Charles A. *President Roosevelt and the Coming of the War, 1941.* New Haven, CT: Yale University Press, 1948. Reprint, Hamden, CT: Archon Books, 1968.

Goodwin, Doris Kearns. *No Ordinary Time: Franklin and Eleanor Roosevelt: The Home Front in World War II.* New York: Simon & Schuster, 1994.

Larrabee, Eric. *Commander in Chief: Franklin Delano Roosevelt, His Lieutenants, and Their War.* New York: Harper & Row, 1987.

University of Oklahoma Law Center. "Franklin D. Roosevelt's Infamy Speech." *A Chronology of US Historical Documents.* [Online] http://www.law.ou.edu/hist/infamy.html (accessed on September 15, 2000).

Harry S. Truman

Thirty-third president (1945–1953)

Harry S. Truman . . . 1189

    Fast Facts about Harry S. Truman (box) . . . 1190

    Harry S. Truman Timeline (box) . . . 1191

    Words to Know (box) . . . 1192

    Truman Becomes President (box) . . . 1196

    Harry S. Truman Administration (box) . . . 1197

    George C. Marshall (box) . . . 1200

    Election Results (box) . . . 1205

    Douglas MacArthur (box) . . . 1208

    A Selection of Truman Landmarks (box) . . . 1211

Bess Truman . . . 1215

Primary source: Truman's Address to the Nation About the Bombing of Japan
President Truman describes "a new weapon"—the atomic bomb—that has been dropped on Hiroshima, Japan, in an effort to end World War II . . . **1221**

Primary source: Truman's Executive Order Banning Segregation in the Military
President Truman's executive order is a landmark in the expansion of civil rights . . . **1229**

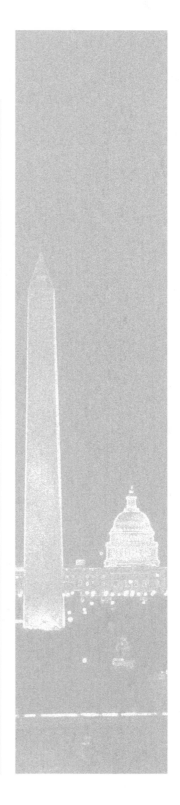

Harry S. Truman

Born May 8, 1884
Lamar, Missouri
Died December 26, 1972
Kansas City, Missouri

Thirty-third president of the United States (1945–1953)

Came to power near the end of World War II and continued Roosevelt's New Deal programs

"The buck stops here."

From a sign on Harry S. Truman's desk

Decisive, blunt, fair-minded, and well-informed, Harry S. Truman was the "common man" president. He had worked as a farmer, a clerk, and a salesman, among other jobs; he served his country during World War I (1914–18); and he became a straight-talking and honest politician who continually beat the odds to win elections.

As president, Truman had to face some of the most profound issues of the twentieth century. He was the first leader to authorize the use of nuclear weapons—the atomic bomb. He supported war crimes trials against Nazi leaders following World War II (1939–45). (Nazi is the term commonly used to refer to members of the National Socialist Party of Germany.) Truman fought aggressively through diplomatic and military means to check the spread of communism (theory that holds that private property should be banned and that goods should be made available to all based on their needs and distributed by a central governing system).

Seeking fairness at home, he proposed strict economic measures and civil rights legislation as part of his adminis-

Harry S. Truman.
Reproduced by permission of AP/Wide World Photos.

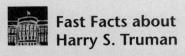

Fast Facts about Harry S. Truman

Full name: Harry S. Truman

Born: May 8, 1884

Died: December 26, 1972

Burial site: Courtyard of the Truman Presidential Library, Independence, Missouri

Parents: John Anderson and Martha Ellen Young Truman

Spouse: Elizabeth "Bess" Virginia Wallace (1885–1982; m. 1919)

Children: Mary Margaret (1924–)

Religion: Baptist

Education: Attended Kansas City School of Law

Occupations: Bank clerk; farmer; soldier

Government positions: Jackson County, Missouri, judge; U.S. senator from Missouri

Political party: Democratic

Dates as president: April 12, 1945–January 20, 1949 (first term); January 20, 1949–January 20, 1953 (second term)

Age upon taking office: 60

tration's Fair Deal program to help the nation make a smooth transition from wartime conditions.

Truman's sweeping foreign and domestic programs met stern resistance from opponents in Congress. His tough measures increasingly lost public support as well. When he ran for election in 1948, some members of his own Democratic Party turned elsewhere. Persisting with determination and conviction, Truman scored a stunning upset victory. His campaign theme was borrowed from a remark shouted by a supporter at one of his rallies: "Give 'em hell, Harry!" was the remark. Truman would say later, "Well, I never gave anybody hell—I just told the truth on those fellows and they thought it was hell."

Avid reader

Born in Lamar, Missouri, on May 8, 1884, Harry S. Truman was the oldest of three children of Martha Ellen Young Truman and John Anderson Truman. He had no middle name, but his parents added the initial "S." as a compromise between his grandfathers' names: "Shipp" for his father's father, Anderson Shipp Truman, and "Solomon" for his mother's father, Solomon Young. The Truman family moved to Independence, Missouri, in 1890. Wearing glasses with thick lenses to correct extreme nearsightedness, Truman began attending school and enjoyed playing piano. An avid reader, he completed an amazing number of biographies, histories, and accounts of great military battles.

After he graduated from high school in 1901, Truman did not have enough money to attend college, and his nearsightedness kept him from being accepted into the West Point Military Academy. He worked a series of odd jobs—clerking for the Santa Fe Railroad, for the Kansas City *Star* newspaper, and at a bank—before helping his parents run a farm they inherited in Grandview, Missouri, in 1906. Truman trained with the national guard, farmed for ten years, and joined a Kansas City Democratic organization run by the politically powerful Pendergast family. In 1914, Truman became the Grandview postmaster. When the United States entered World War I in 1917, Truman's national guard unit was mobilized (assembled and prepared for military duty). He trained at Fort Sill, Oklahoma, then returned to Missouri as a recruiter (someone who signs people up for military service) before being elected first lieutenant by the men of Missouri's Second Field Artillery.

Truman was promoted to captain by March 1918 and commanded a unit that fought with distinction in several battles in France. By the time he was discharged and returned home in the spring of 1919, he had reached the rank of major. That summer, he married Elizabeth Virginia Wallace (1885–1982; see entry on **Bess Truman** in volume 4). Bess, as she was called, had known Harry since the fifth grade. Their only child, Mary Margaret, was born in 1924.

Political career begins

Truman was part owner of a men's clothing store in Kansas City, Missouri, through 1922. That year, he was the surprising winner of an election for a Jackson County, Mis-

Harry S. Truman Timeline

1884: Born in Missouri

1906–16: Works on family farm in Grandview, Missouri

1918: Leads army units with distinction in France and Italy during World War I

1919–22: Works at a men's clothing store in Independence, Missouri

1923–33: Serves as judge in Jackson County Court, Missouri

1934–45: Serves as U.S. senator from Missouri

1939–45: World War II

1945: Serves as vice president under Franklin D. Roosevelt; assumes the office of president after Roosevelt dies; World War II ends

1945–53: Serves as thirty-third U.S. president

1950–54: Korean War

1953: Retires to Independence, Missouri

1972: Dies in Missouri

Words to Know

Allies: A term describing alliances of countries in military opposition to another group of nations. Twenty-eight nations made up the Allied and Associated powers in World War I. In World War II, the Allied powers included Great Britain, the United States, and the Soviet Union.

Atomic bomb: An explosive device that releases nuclear energy (energy that comes from an atom's core). All previous explosive devices were powered by rapid burning or decomposition of a chemical compound; they only released energy from the outermost electrons of an atom. Nuclear explosives are energized by splitting an atom, a process called fission.

Cold War: Tense conflicts and failed diplomacy between the United States and the Soviet Union.

Korean War: A war from 1950 to 1953 fought between communist North Korea and non-communist South Korea; China backed North Korea and the United Nations backed South Korea.

Marshall Plan: A post–World War II program led by Secretary of State George C. Marshall that helped rebuild European economies (also benefiting U.S. trade) and strengthened democratic governments.

Nazi: A member of the Nationalist Socialist Party of Germany. The term generally also refers to the army.

New Deal: A series of programs initiated by the administration of President Franklin D. Roosevelt to create jobs and stimulate the economy during the Great Depression (1929–41).

North Atlantic Treaty Organization (NATO): An alliance for collective security created by the North Atlantic Treaty (1949) and originally involving Belgium, Canada, Denmark, France, Great Britain, Iceland, Italy, Luxembourg, the Netherlands, Norway, Portugal, and the United States.

Taft-Hartley Act: Act that outlawed union-only workplaces, prohibited certain union activities, forbade unions to contribute to political campaigns, established loyalty oaths for union leaders, and allowed court orders to halt strikes that could affect national health or safety.

Truman Doctrine: A Cold War–era program designed by President Truman that sent aid to anticommunist forces in Turkey and Greece. The Union of Soviet Socialist Republics (U.S.S.R.) had naval stations in Turkey, and nearby Greece was fighting a civil war with communist-dominated rebels.

Yalta Conference: A 1944 meeting between Allied leaders Joseph Stalin, Winston Churchill, and Franklin D. Roosevelt in anticipation of an Allied victory in Europe over the Nazis. The leaders discussed how to manage lands conquered by Germany, and Roosevelt and Churchill urged Stalin to enter the Soviet Union in the war against Japan.

souri, position as supervisor of roads and buildings. He had won without the backing of the powerful Pendergast political machine (a highly organized political group that controls local political action), and he had beaten a popular candidate who was supported by the local Ku Klux Klan, an organization based on white supremacy. Truman had little authority in his position, but he managed to improve roads as well as the county's finances. Meanwhile, he studied at the Kansas City Law School and drilled with the national guard. He was beaten for reelection by a Klan-supported candidate after Truman refused to join the group; it proved to be his only election defeat. After jobs selling memberships to automobile clubs and working for a bank, Truman returned to politics in 1926 with the backing of Tom Pendergast (1872–1945).

Elected to a position with authority over county roads, buildings, and taxes, Truman greatly improved the local construction system and fired officials (including many Pendergast supporters) who were pocketing tax money. Nevertheless, Pendergast continued to support him and he was reelected in 1930 to a second four-year term. Although the Pendergast machine became associated with gangsters, Truman maintained his integrity (honesty and independence) as an honest official. Based on that reputation, he was elected to the U.S. Senate in 1934.

In the Senate, Truman was a solid supporter of the New Deal programs (see box in **Franklin D. Roosevelt** entry in volume 4) of President **Franklin D. Roosevelt** (1882–1945; see entry in volume 4). When a federal investigation into illegal activities of the Pendergast political machine was launched, Truman was considered by many guilty by association. The investigation uncovered evidence of corruption and intimidation (dishonesty and violence) by Pendergast associates. Tom Pendergast was jailed in 1939 for income tax evasion (purposely not paying taxes owed to the government), but Truman was not connected with even a single act of wrongdoing. Instead of turning his back on the organization, Truman told a reporter, "Tom Pendergast has always been my friend, and I don't desert a sinking ship."

Meanwhile, Senator Truman was named to the Appropriations Committee, a group in charge of distributing federal funds, and the Interstate Commerce Committee. He cowrote the Truman-Austin bill, creating the Civil Aeronautics Board that supervises the airplane industry. He was also a major force for the Transportation Act of 1940, which brought needed reform and regulation to railroads.

Surprising reelection

Despite his fine record in the Senate, Truman was an underdog (the predicted loser) in his bid for reelection. He was opposed for the Democratic nomination by Missouri governor Lloyd Stark (1886–1972), who had the backing of President Roosevelt for helping bring down the Pendergast political machine. Running behind Stark and another popular candidate and having little money to campaign with, Truman drove around Missouri in his own car. He made speeches in plain language that concentrated on his record of public service.

Truman barely won the Democratic nomination. He defeated Manvel H. Davis, a Republican opponent who had consistently mentioned Truman's ties with the Pendergast organization. Truman's surprising reelection showed that an honest and straightforward politician could win even with meager resources. His U.S. Senate colleagues gave him a standing ovation when he returned to begin his second term.

At the time, the United States was facing the prospect of entering World War II. After discovering poor conditions in military camps and defense plants in his home state, Truman drove around neighboring areas. He discovered similarly overstaffed operations and poor-quality equipment financed by tax dollars. After reporting his findings on the Senate floor and demanding an inquiry, Truman was named the head of a Senate investigation later called the Truman Committee. The committee's detailed report, supported by many witnesses, uncovered widespread fraud and waste: at a cost of $400,000 in taxpayer money over three years, the Truman committee is estimated to have saved the country $15 billion. Truman became a national political figure.

As the 1944 presidential election neared, President Roosevelt was in ill health. The outspokenness of his vice president, Henry A. Wallace (1888–1965), was considered a disadvantage. At the Democratic National Convention that year, no clear vice presidential candidate emerged. Truman won the

nomination on the second round of voting. He proved to be an excellent campaigner while Roosevelt made few appearances to protect his health and to focus on steering the country through wartime. The United States had entered World War II in 1941; in 1944, the Allies were pushing across Europe toward Germany against retreating Nazi forces. (The Allies included Great Britain, the United States, and the Soviet Union.)

Truman was active as vice president, though he saw little of Roosevelt. After the inauguration in January 1945, President Roosevelt traveled to Eastern Europe in February to attend the Yalta Conference. At the conference, Roosevelt discussed war strategies and how the Allies would manage lands they reconquered from Nazi occupation with British prime minister Winston Churchill (1874–1965; see box in **Franklin D. Roosevelt** entry in volume 4) and Soviet leader Joseph Stalin (1879–1953). Roosevelt returned in March, but he did not share information with Truman about war plans.

Harry S. Truman (center) places his hand on the Bible as he takes the presidential oath of office from U.S. Supreme Court chief justice Harlan Fiske on April 12, 1945, following Franklin D. Roosevelt's death. New first lady Bess Truman is to his left.
Photograph by Abbie Rowe. Reproduced by permission of the Corbis Corporation.

Truman Becomes President

Harry S. Truman became president of the United States following the death of Franklin D. Roosevelt. (See Roosevelt entry for election results from the Roosevelt/Truman campaign.) This marked the seventh time in U.S. history that a vice president became president following the death of his predecessor. Truman's victory in 1948 marked the third time that a former vice president finishing his predecessor's term was elected as president on his own in the next election.

Roosevelt left for his vacation home in Warm Springs, Georgia, on March 30. Two weeks later, Truman was called to the White House, where he met with Eleanor Roosevelt (1884–1962; see entry in volume 4), the president's wife. She said to him, "Harry, the president is dead." Truman asked if there was anything he could do for her, and she responded, "Is there anything we can do for *you?* For you are the one in trouble now." Truman had been vice president of the United States for fewer than ninety days. He was sworn into the office of president on April 12, 1945.

A new weapon

Truman met with Roosevelt's Cabinet officials and asked them to remain in their positions. Secretary of War Henry L. Stimson (1867–1950; see entry in **Herbert Hoover** entry in volume 4) stayed in the room after the other officials left. He informed Truman about a new weapon the United States had successfully devised—the atomic bomb, an explosive device that releases nuclear energy (energy that comes from an atom's core); it was the first time Truman had heard that the weapon was available. Meanwhile, the Nazi defeat became official on May 8, 1945—Truman's sixty-first birthday. He proclaimed it Victory-in-Europe Day (V-E Day).

Foreign affairs issues dominated Truman's time. In June, he addressed the final session of the founding conference of the United Nations (UN) in San Francisco and then presented the United Nations Charter to the Senate for ratification (approval). From July 17 to August 2, 1945, he attended the Potsdam Conference in Germany. Meeting with Stalin, Churchill, and Clement Attlee (1863–1967), Churchill's successor, Truman proposed the establishment of an international council to settle issues related to World War II and to conduct trials against Nazis for war crimes. He secured Stalin's promise to enter the war against Japan.

Harry S. Truman Administration

Administration Dates
April 12, 1945–January 20, 1949
January 20, 1949–January 20, 1953

Vice President
None (1945–49)
Alben W. Barkley (1949–53)

Cabinet

Secretary of State
Edward R. Stettinius Jr. (1945)
James F. Byrnes (1945–47)
George C. Marshall (1947–49)
Dean G. Acheson (1949–53)

Secretary of the Treasury
Henry Morgenthau Jr. (1945)
Frederick M. Vinson (1945–46)
John W. Snyder (1946–53)

Secretary of War
Henry L. Stimson (1945)
Robert P. Patterson (1945–47)
Kenneth C. Royall (1947)

Attorney General
Francis B. Biddle (1945)
Thomas C. Clark (1945–49)
James H. McGrath (1949–52)

James P. McGranery (1952–53)

Secretary of Defense
James V. Forrestal (1947–49)
Louis A. Johnson (1949–50)
George C. Marshall (1950–51)
Robert A. Lovett (1951–53)

Secretary of the Navy
James V. Forrestal (1945–47)

Secretary of the Interior
Harold L. Ickes (1945–46)
Julius A. Krug (1946–49)
Oscar L. Chapman (1949–53)

Secretary of Agriculture
Claude R. Wickard (1945)
Clinton P. Anderson (1945–48)
Charles F. Brannan (1948–53)

Secretary of Commerce
Henry A. Wallace (1945–46)
William Averell Harriman (1946–48)
Charles Sawyer (1948–53)

Secretary of Labor
Frances Perkins (1945)
Lewis B. Schwellenbach (1945–48)
Maurice J. Tobin (1948–53)

Truman issued the Potsdam Declaration on July 26; it called for Japan's unconditional surrender. Meanwhile, members of his administration convened a committee of distinguished citizens to debate moral and military issues concerning use of the atomic bomb. Military leaders reported that war against Japan would result in the probable loss of another five hundred thousand lives. They believed that using the atom bomb could force a quick Japanese surrender. After

Japan did not respond to the Potsdam surrender ultimatum
(the final request for surrender), Truman authorized use of
the atomic bomb. Dropped on Hiroshima, Japan, on August
6, 1945, at 9:15 A.M. Tokyo time, the atomic explosion virtually destroyed the city. According to Supreme Allied Headquarters, almost 130,000 people were killed, injured, or missing, and another 175,000 were homeless. (See **Harry S.
Truman** primary source entry in volume 4.)

While Soviet forces invaded Japanese strongholds in Manchuria, China, and Korea, a second atomic bomb was dropped on the city of Nagasaki on August 9. One-third of that city was destroyed and nearly seventy thousand people were killed or injured. On August 14, Japan requested peace. The official Japanese surrender took place on September 2, 1945, aboard the U.S.S. *Missouri* anchored in Tokyo Bay.

Japanese leaders sign surrender documents aboard the U.S.S. *Missouri* on September 2, 1945. *Reproduced by permission of AP/Wide World Photos.*

The Cold War begins

The end of World War II was quickly followed by the beginning of another kind of war, this time between the United States and the Soviet Union. The two nations never directly engaged in battle, but tense conflicts and failed diplomacy came to be known as the Cold War. The Soviet Army controlled much of Eastern Europe after World War II and the Soviet government refused to hold free elections. The Union of Soviet Socialist Republics (U.S.S.R.) moved "to protect" naval

George C. Marshall

George Catlett Marshall Jr. was born on December 31, 1880, in Uniontown, Pennsylvania. Socially awkward and a poor student, he gradually developed a strong drive to succeed. His father had served in the Civil War (1861–65), and Marshall decided to attend the Virginia Military Institute. He thrived in the disciplined environment, graduating as the top cadet in his class. He married Elizabeth Carter Coles shortly after he received a commission as a second lieutenant in the U.S. Army in 1902. After serving in the Philippines, he returned to the United States to attend an infantry training school and then the army's command and general staff school. He taught for two years at Fort Leavenworth, Kansas.

During World War I, Marshall was among the first members of the American Expeditionary Force sent to France in 1917 when the United States entered the war. He served as chief of operations at the American headquarters in France and earned the nickname "Wizard" for his ability to make plans with firm details for commanders. Winning the respect of General John J. Pershing (1860–1948; see box in **Woodrow Wilson** entry in volume 4), America's supreme commander in World War I, Marshall worked as Pershing's personal aide from 1919 to 1924. After a tour of duty in China, Marshall was left a widower when his wife died unexpectedly in 1927. In 1930, Marshall met and married Katherine Tupper Brown.

During the middle of the Great Depression in the 1930s, Marshall supervised Illinois National Guard units and Civilian Conservation Corps (CCC) camps. One of many New Deal government programs designed to combat the Depression, the CCC was run in military fashion and gave unemployed young men work on conservation projects. In 1938, Marshall was appointed to manage the War Plans Division of the army, then he became army chief of staff after World War II began in 1939. He is credited with helping the U.S. military rebound effectively from the Japanese attack at Pearl Harbor in December 1941. (See **Franklin D. Roosevelt** primary source entry in volume 4.)

As a trusted military advisor to President Franklin D. Roosevelt, Marshall participated in all major wartime policy-making conferences. Marshall was responsible for elevating General Dwight D. Eisenhower to command early military moves against Germany. Marshall was expected to command what became the Allied, D-Day invasion of 1944, but Eisenhower headed the invasion instead; Roosevelt said he "could not sleep well at night with Marshall out of Washington." Marshall became *Time* magazine's "Man of the Year" in 1944.

Marshall began a well-earned retirement after the war ended in 1945, but President Harry S. Truman asked him to mediate an end to the long civil war in China. A firm and patient negotiator, Mar-

George Marshall.
Courtesy of the Library of Congress.

shall accomplished more than previous American leaders had, but in the end his mission failed. Nevertheless, in 1947, Truman asked Marshall to become his secretary of state. With Europe still reeling from the destruction of World War II and a threat of communist expansion by the Soviet Union and China looming, Marshall developed a plan to help bolster European nations. What became known as the Marshall Plan succeeded grandly. The United States provided money and materials while noncommunist Europeans worked together to solve their problems. An economically healthy Western Europe defeated postwar hunger, resumed trade with the United States, and rejected communism. Marshall went on to win the Nobel Peace Prize for his efforts.

Marshall resigned as secretary of state early in 1949, but when North Korean communists invaded South Korea in June 1950, Truman convinced Marshall to take the recently created post of secretary of defense. The president thought that only Marshall had sufficient prestige to get Congress, Cabinet departments, and different branches of the military to cooperate in the United Nations effort to stop communist aggression in Korea.

When President Truman rejected General Douglas MacArthur's plan to expand the war to Communist China, MacArthur publicly criticized the president's policies, and Truman relieved him of command. MacArthur's supporters were outraged. Senator Joseph McCarthy of Wisconsin claimed that the U.S. government, as represented by Roosevelt, Truman, and Marshall, had allowed the Soviets to take over Eastern Europe and had "lost China" to communism as well. McCarthy published a book proving, he claimed, that Marshall was the leader of a communist conspiracy. But in 1954, it was McCarthy, not Marshall, who was disgraced during nationally televised hearings concerning communist infiltration of the American military. McCarthy's accusations, many of them exaggerated and false, hurt the reputations of many respectable Americans, including Marshall. Marshall's reputation was quickly restored with McCarthy's downfall. Marshall died on October 16, 1959.

stations in Turkey, and nearby Greece was embroiled in a civil war with communist-dominated rebels. The president responded with the Truman Doctrine, which sent aid to anticommunist forces in Greece and Turkey. Truman wanted to inspire American public sentiment for fighting the Cold War. Congress backed his request for $250 million for Greece and $150 million for Turkey.

World War II had left much of Europe in ruin. Truman worked closely with his secretary of state, General George C. Marshall (1880–1959; see box), to create the European Recovery Plan. Better known as the Marshall Plan, the program helped rebuild European economies (also benefiting U.S. trade) and strengthened democratic governments. Under the Marshall Plan, the United States spent more than $12.5 billion over a four-year period, helping spur a quick recovery throughout Western Europe, including West Germany. The Soviet Union called the Marshall Plan an "imperialist plot to enslave Europe." (Imperialism is the policy of creating an empire: expanding a nation by taking over foreign lands or by establishing economic and political dominance over other nations.)

The U.S.S.R. established its own plan for Eastern Europe, which was dominated by communist governments allied with the Soviet Union. The Soviets closed Allied access to the city of Berlin and helped create a communist state called East Germany. Truman countered by ordering ongoing airlifts of essential supplies in Berlin—a policy that lasted for nearly a year. War was distinctly possible, with each side waiting for the other to make the first military move. Truman's humanitarian gesture toward Berlin helped solidify anti-Soviet sentiments among noncommunist nations.

Problems at home

At home, the end of the war was greeted with much joy and celebration. But it took time for life to become normal again. For nearly a decade and a half—from the beginning of the Great Depression (1929–41) in 1929 to the end of World War II in 1945—Americans had either lived in poor economic times or faced limited supplies and food rationing to help the war effort. Having noted that economic problems occurred in the United States after World War I in 1919, Truman was determined to avoid a similar period of inflation (a time when money loses some of its value, in relation to the goods and services, which become more expensive) and unemployment.

In his attempt to take decisive action, Truman proposed wage controls, price controls, and rent controls; he wanted to expand public housing and extend old-age benefits; and he supported a national health insurance program, a higher minimum wage, and a permanent Fair Employment Practices Commission to assist minorities. The sweeping proposals met quick opposition from Congress and stalled. Prices for goods soon increased. Workers then began striking for higher wages. Always a labor sympathizer, Truman nevertheless used executive orders (orders issued by the president and having the force of law) and court injunctions (court orders that prohibit or require a certain action) to ensure that strikes would not hurt the nation.

President Harry S. Truman enjoyed playing the piano. Here, actress Lauren Bacall lounges on the piano as he plays at a Press Club function.
Reproduced by permission of Archive Photos.

Truman's actions were widely criticized, even by members of his own party. With rising prices, strikes, and scarce supplies, the midterm elections of 1946 turned into a clear-cut victory for Republicans, who gained majorities in both houses of Congress for the first time since 1930. (Midterm elections are congressional elections that occur halfway through a presidential term. These elections can affect the president's dealings with Congress. A president is elected every four years; House representatives, every two years; and senators, every six years.) In 1947, the new Congress promptly passed the Taft-Hartley Act, which outlawed union-only workplaces, prohibited certain union activities, forbade unions to contribute to political campaigns, established loyalty oaths for union leaders (public pledges that they were not communists), and allowed court orders to halt strikes that could affect national health or safety. Truman vetoed (rejected) the bill, but it passed over his veto. When Truman called for legislation to control rising prices, Congress instead voted a tax-cut bill that favored more wealthy people.

Several other Truman measures failed to be enacted, including his fair employment and national health measures.

The morning after the 1948 presidential election, President Harry S. Truman holds up an early edition of the *Chicago Tribune* that announced a victory for Thomas Dewey. However, Truman upset his Republican opponent and was reelected.

Reproduced by permission of the Corbis Corporation.

Truman ordered desegregation of the armed forces. (See **Harry S. Truman** primary source entry in volume 4.) But when he called for an end to "Jim Crow" state laws that maintained racial segregation in the South, he lost support—even within his own party. Southern Congressional Democrats abandoned their party when those policies were written into the 1948 Democratic presidential platform. (A platform is a declaration of policies that a candidate or a political party intends to follow if elected.) South Carolina governor J. Strom Thurmond (1902–) formed the States' Rights Democrats, or Dixiecrats. Meanwhile, former vice president Henry Wallace formed the Progressive Party.

With the Democratic Party disunited and Republicans enjoying increasing support, Truman's popularity was at a low: laborers were angry at his interference in strikes (almost a million workers went on strike in 1945, and another million joined them in 1946); businesses bristled at his insistence on

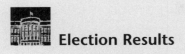

Election Results

1948

Presidential / Vice presidential candidates	Popular votes	Presidential electoral votes
Harry S. Truman / Alben W. Barkley (Democratic)	24,105,695	303
Thomas E. Dewey / Earl Warren (Republican)	21,969,170	189
J. Strom Thurmond / Fielding L. Wright (States' Rights Democratic)	1,169,021	39

Incumbent president Truman upset Dewey, who had also lost in the 1944 presidential election. Two factions of the Democratic Party broke off: one, the States' Rights Democratic (Dixiecrat) Party, led by South Carolina governor Thurmond, won four states; the other, the Progressive Party, led by former vice president Henry A. Wallace, was less successful. Popular World War II general Dwight D. Eisenhower was wooed by both parties, but he declined to enter the race.

maintaining wartime controls on the economy; and his civil rights policies angered some white voters.

"DEWEY DEFEATS TRUMAN"

After receiving the Democratic Party nomination, Truman played a master political stroke. He reconvened Congress on July 26 to give Republicans a chance to carry out their party's platform pledges. When the special session ended without any important legislation, Truman embarked on an extensive cross-country whistle-stop tour (a campaign by train that stops in all depots along the way) defending his record and blasting the "do-nothing" Republican Congress. When someone responded "Give 'em hell, Harry!" at a stop in Albuquerque, New Mexico, the phrase became his campaign slogan.

Nearly everyone, from political commentators to registered Democrats, thought that Republican candidate Thomas E. Dewey (1902–1971), governor of New York, would win the 1948 election. Truman campaigned hard to the end. A few hours after the polls closed, the *Chicago Tribune* issued an early edition with the headline "DEWEY DEFEATS TRUMAN." But as the image of a smiling Truman holding up that issue of the *Tribune* showed the next day, he had proved many wrong. His whistle-stop tour had energized small town, rural, and minority voters, and he was reelected.

Cold War hits home

A Democratic majority was elected to Congress, but Truman had only modest success with his domestic programs during his second term. Increased public housing, expanded social security coverage, increased minimum wages, and stronger farm price support bills were parts of his Fair Deal domestic program that passed Congress. His request for repeal of the Taft-Hartley Act, plans for constructing public hydroelectric companies, and proposals for civil rights legislation were rejected. He managed to strengthen civil rights in the Justice Department and appointed a few African Americans to government positions.

Meanwhile, the Cold War hit home in 1948. Writer and editor Whittaker Chambers (1901–1961) testified before California representative **Richard Nixon** (1913–1994; see entry in volume 5) and the House Committee on Un-American Activities that he had been a communist in the 1920s and 1930s. He charged that Alger Hiss (1904–1996), a member of the State Department, had given him classified documents to send to the Soviet Union. Hiss denied the charges, but microfilm copies of documents identified as classified and bearing Hiss's handwriting were revealed. Hiss was indicted for perjury (lying under oath) by the Department of Justice. The jury failed to reach a verdict, but Hiss was convicted after a second trial in January 1950.

In February 1950, Wisconsin senator Joseph R. McCarthy (1908–1957) charged in a speech in Wheeling, West Virginia, that the State Department knowingly employed over two hundred communists. He consistently reduced the number, but an investigation revealed that all the charges were false. McCarthy continued to accuse many government officials and private citizens of having communist sympathies. He held hearings that implicated hundreds of people, many of whom lost their jobs and were deprived of their rights. Not one spy was revealed, and McCarthy was eventually discredited, but not until after he had damaged many lives, careers, and reputations. He was so powerful at one point that two senators who dared to challenge him lost their bids for reelection.

Also in 1950, Congress passed the Internal Security Act, also called the McCarran Act, over Truman's veto. The act forced all communist organizations to register with the government, allowed the government to intern communists during national emergencies, prohibited communists from working in defense positions, and denied entrance into the United States of anyone who was a member of a totalitarian organization (a group that supports a form of government ruled by one party that tolerates no opposition and exercises absolute control over every part of human life).

When the White House underwent a major renovation during Truman's second term, the family lived at Blair House, a large house across the street from the White House. Work, entertaining, and Truman's brisk daily walks all proceeded as usual during the three years it took to reconstruct the White House. Truman escaped an assassination attempt at Blair House when two gunmen tried to kill him on November 1, 1950. A secret service agent and one of the gunmen were killed. The second gunman was found guilty of attempted murder and sentenced to execution, but Truman commuted the sentence (reduced the penalty) to life in prison. Twenty-nine years later, President **Jimmy Carter** (1924– ; see entry in volume 5) commuted the life sentence, freeing the prisoner. (Presidents have the power to issue an executive pardon or to commute a sentence in certain cases where a federal crime was committed.)

The Korean War

In foreign affairs, Truman supported the United Nations and continued the Marshall Plan. Seeking to establish a collective defense against communist aggression, he supported the development of the North Atlantic Treaty Organization (NATO), a regional defense alliance created by a 1949 treaty. The Senate ratified the treaty after extensive debate. World War II hero **Dwight D. Eisenhower** (1890–1969; see entry in volume 4) was selected to command NATO.

In China, the government of Chiang Kai-shek (1887–1975), which was supported by the United States, was

Douglas MacArthur

Douglas MacArthur was born on January 26, 1880, in Little Rock, Arkansas, where MacArthur's father, Arthur, was stationed. His father had fought in the Civil War, earned the Congressional Medal of Honor for heroism, and served as military governor of the Philippines. By then, Douglas MacArthur was beginning his own distinguished military career.

A 1903 graduate of West Point, MacArthur rose rapidly in the military, beginning in the Philippines as an aide to his father. Douglas MacArthur became a captain in 1911, was promoted to major in 1914, and was on the general staff (the group that oversees all army operations) of the army when the United States entered World War I in 1917. MacArthur backed a plan to enlist state National Guard units to strengthen the small and inexperienced army, proposing to form a single battalion from volunteers of every state; he called it the Rainbow Battalion, and he argued that it was a practical military plan as well as a way to help unite the nation in the war effort. President Woodrow Wilson approved the idea, and MacArthur was elevated to the rank of colonel. He led the former guardsmen into battle as a brigadier general, and won medals for his bravery and leadership. One of his officers was future president Harry S. Truman.

After the war, MacArthur served as superintendent of West Point, went on an assignment to the Philippines, and com-manded several army posts. In 1930, he became chief of staff of the army. MacArthur had an unsuccessful marriage in the 1920s, but in 1937 he wed Jean Marie Faircloth and they had a son. General MacArthur retired from the U.S. Army in 1937. Philippines president Manuel Quezon (1878–1944) asked him to serve as a military adviser. He became a field marshall in the Philippine army and had as his assistant a young major named Dwight D. Eisenhower.

The Philippines had been a U.S. territory since the Spanish-American War in 1898. It was about to become a free country when World War II began. In 1941, MacArthur was promoted to lieutenant general in charge of the U.S. forces in the Pacific. He believed that the Philippines was not threatened by the war even after Japanese airplanes struck Pearl Harbor on December 7, 1941. But ten hours later, the Japanese struck Clark Field in the Philippines, destroying most of MacArthur's planes. A huge Japanese invasion force hit the Philippines, and MacArthur's troops were penned up in jungles with little possibility of escape or reinforcement. MacArthur took personal command of his army's defenses and refused to leave the desperate situation until he was commanded to by President Franklin D. Roosevelt. MacArthur sent a last message to the Japanese and Filipinos: "I shall return." The army had recommended that his official pronouncement should be, "We shall return."

Douglas MacArthur.
Courtesy of the Library of Congress.

Two years after he left, and now in command of the army in the Pacific, MacArthur did return to the Philippines. MacArthur made his base on the island nation and directed the army in the final days of the war. As commander of the U.S. forces and of the Allied forces in the Pacific, General MacArthur accepted the Japanese surrender in 1945. He was then charged with helping the transformation of Japan from rule by an emperor to an elected government.

For five years after the war, General MacArthur held several positions—commander of the U.S. forces in the Pacific, commander of the Allied and then the UN forces, and military commander of Japan. An uprising in Korea in 1950 caught the general, and the United States, by surprise.

The attack was so sudden by the communist North Korean military against the democratic South that within a few days the South Korean capital city of Seoul was threatened and U.S. forces were fleeing south. The American army, now joined by UN troops, established a defense line in the far south of the peninsula nation, but this was soon threatened.

MacArthur designed a counter-offensive that put North Korean forces in retreat. It appeared that the war would end quickly with a UN victory. The North Koreans, however, regrouped and were joined by thousands of volunteers from China; together they again pushed back South Korea's defenders. MacArthur carried out an excellent battle plan and repelled the invaders. He proposed to bombard China and help non-communist Chinese to rebel. Such action would lead to war with China and perhaps the Soviet Union. President Truman, meanwhile, directed all military leaders to refrain from making any plans contrary to the specific police action in Korea. When MacArthur began to speak out against the president's policies, Truman found it harmful and fired his most famous and popular general.

MacArthur returned to Washington, D.C., where twenty thousand admirers welcomed him. On April 19, 1951, he addressed Congress and uttered the famous words: "Old soldiers never die; they just fade away." MacArthur died on April 5, 1964.

overwhelmingly defeated by communist forces led by Mao Tse-tung (also spelled Mao Ze-dong, 1893–1976) in 1949 and was forced into exile on Taiwan, a Pacific island off the coast of Mainland China. The People's Republic of China was formed, with Mao as chairman.

The nation of Korea was divided after World War II with a communist regime in the north and an anticommunist government in the south. Civil strife in South Korea inspired North Korea's leader, Kim Il Sung (1912–1994), to try to reunite Korea. The North Korean army, equipped mainly by the U.S.S.R., invaded South Korea in June 1950. The United States immediately sent supplies to South Korea and sponsored a UN resolution for military sanctions against North Korea. Then President Truman ordered U.S. troops stationed in Japan to move to Korea. American and South Korean forces were joined by units from fifteen other nations under UN command, with U.S. general Douglas MacArthur (1880–1964; see box) as leader.

Originally a policekeeping effort to protect South Korea, the mission changed as the American and UN forces repulsed a North Korean invasion, moved into North Korea, and approached the Chinese border. After several warnings, Chinese forces pushed the UN contingent back toward the South. General MacArthur requested an extension of the war into Communist China, but the Truman administration returned to the original peacekeeping mission. When MacArthur publicly attacked that policy, Truman relieved him of his command in April 1951 and replaced him with Lieutenant General Matthew B. Ridgway (1885–1993).

MacArthur, who had been a hero for his efforts in the Pacific during World War II, returned home to a rousing welcome. On the same day that MacArthur received a ticker-tape parade in New York City, President Truman was heavily booed when he threw out the ceremonial first pitch of the 1951 baseball season in Washington, D.C.

Near the end of Truman's second term, the president tried to prevent a steel mill strike. Just hours before the scheduled strike, Truman announced to a nationwide radio audience that Secretary of Commerce Charles Sawyer (1887–1979) had been directed to seize the mills to maintain production for the war effort. However, on June 2, 1952, the Supreme

A Selection of Truman Landmarks

Harry S. Truman Birthplace State Historic Site. 1009 Truman Ave., Lamar, MO 64759. (417) 682-2279. Small restored farmhouse is where Truman was born in 1884.

Harry S. Truman Library and Museum. 500 W. U.S. Highway 24, Independence, MO 64050. (800) 833-1225. Museum includes exhibits on the Truman presidency, the famous 1948 election, and the Korean War. Harry and Bess Truman are buried in the courtyard. See http://www.trumanlibrary.org/ (accessed on September 18, 2000).

Harry S. Truman Little White House. 111 Front St., Key West, FL 33040. (305) 294-9911. Harry Truman stayed in this former naval officers' quarters during his many visits to the Florida Keys while president. It is now a museum full of Truman artifacts, and is also open to the public for lodging. See http://www.trumanlittlewhitehouse.com/ (accessed on September 18, 2000).

Harry S. Truman National Historic Site. 223 North Main St., Independence, MO 64050-2804. (816) 254-9929. Site consists of a visitors center; the childhood home of Bess Truman, in which she lived after her marriage to Harry; and the Missouri Pacific Depot, where a museum commemorates Truman's 1948 whistle-stop train tour. A walking tour through various Truman neighborhoods is also available. See http://www.nps.gov/hstr/ (accessed on September 18, 2000).

Truman Farm Home. 12301 Blue Ridge Blvd., Grandview, MO. (816) 254-9929. Home in which Harry Truman lived while working on his family's farm from 1906 to 1917. Part of the Harry S. Truman National Historic Site. See http://www.nps.gov/hstr/ (accessed on September 18, 2000).

Court declared the seizure unconstitutional in *Youngstown Sheet and Tube Co. v. Sawyer.* Truman could have used the Taft-Hartley Act to delay the strike, but he disliked the law too much to use it. By that time, Truman had declared that he would not seek reelection.

Truman retired to Independence, Missouri, where in 1957 he dedicated the Harry S. Truman Library. He published *Memoirs, Year of Decisions* (1955) and *Years of Trial and Hope, 1946–1952* (1956) and recounted the events of his administration in a nationally televised series, *Decision—The Conflicts of Harry S. Truman* (1964). Truman died in 1972 and is buried on the grounds of the Truman Library and Museum.

Legacy

Harry S. Truman assumed the office of president during World War II and left with the Korean War (1950–54) still in progress. The Cold War occupied his time in between. Through his support for the United Nations and NATO, the United States became involved in international organizations that could respond to acts of aggression. Truman's attempts to contain communism (not allow it to spread) were continued by his successors, as reflected by the Vietnam War. (But there, as in Korea, fighting in another nation's civil war proved costly and unsuccessful.) Truman's successor, Dwight D. Eisenhower, fulfilled his campaign pledge to end U.S. involvement in Korea.

Truman's success with promoting civil rights was mixed. Progress was made in desegregating the military after an executive order, but civil rights legislation did not pass through Congress. Truman's attempts to regulate the postwar economy also met only modest success. A prolabor president, Truman nevertheless took action against labor when strikes threatened to slow the nation.

Discussion of Truman's presidency always considers his decision to use the atomic bomb. It brought a quick end to the war and likely resulted in fewer deaths than in prolonged conflict. The new weapon brought fears of mass destruction as well. Its influence on history has been immense.

Where to Learn More

Cochran, Bert. *Harry Truman and the Crisis Presidency.* New York: Funk & Wagnalls, 1973.

Cray, Ed. *General of the Army: George C. Marshall, Soldier and Statesman.* New York: Norton, 1990.

Donovan, Robert J. *Conflict and Crisis: The Presidency of Harry S. Truman, 1945–1948.* New York: Norton, 1977. Reprint, Columbia, MO: University of Missouri Press, 1996.

Ferrell, Robert H. *Harry S. Truman: A Life.* Columbia: University of Missouri Press, 1994.

Hamby, Alonzo L. *Man of the People: A Life of Harry S. Truman.* New York: Oxford University Press, 1995.

Harry S. Truman Library and Museum. [Online] http://www.trumanlibrary.org/ (accessed on September 18, 2000).

Leavell, J. Perry. *Harry S. Truman.* New York: Chelsea House Publishers, 1988.

McCoy, Donald R. *The Presidency of Harry S. Truman.* Lawrence, KS: University Press of Kansas, 1984.

Project WhistleStop. [Online] http://www.whistlestop.org/index.html (accessed on September 28, 2000).

Ross, Irwin. *The Loneliest Campaign: The Truman Victory of 1948.* New York: New American Library, 1968. Reprint, Westport, CT: Greenwood Press, 1977.

Schuman, Michael. *Harry S. Truman.* Springfield, NJ : Enslow Publishers, 1997.

Truman, Margaret. *Harry S. Truman.* New York: William Morrow, 1973. Reprint, New York: Quill, 1984.

Bess Truman

Born February 13, 1885
Independence, Missouri
Died October 18, 1982
Independence, Missouri

Small-town first lady stayed behind the scenes

When **Harry S. Truman** (1884–1972; see entry in volume 4) opened a men's store in Kansas City, Missouri, in 1919, his wife Bess helped behind the scenes. She was responsible for advertising and for inventory for the store. Bess was content with a similar behind-the-scenes role during her husband's political career in Washington, D.C., where Truman was a senator beginning in 1935. Bess handled mail, performed some research on issues, and advised Truman on his speeches.

Shunning publicity and living quietly, Bess Truman was not comfortable in her role as first lady, which she assumed in 1945. She announced early on, for example, that she would not speak out on issues, nor would she hold regular press conferences: "I am not the one who was elected," she remarked. "I have nothing to say to the people." She came to Washington, D.C., as a small-town woman. She maintained her modest lifestyle throughout the nearly twenty years she spent in the capital, and then returned to her small town, where she lived for almost another thirty years.

"I am not the one who was elected. I have nothing to say to the people."

Bess Truman

Bess Truman.
Courtesy of the Library of Congress.

1215

Who's that playing third base?

Harry and Bess first crossed paths at Sunday School in a Presbyterian church in 1890. His family had recently moved to Independence, Missouri, where Bess was born Elizabeth Virginia Wallace to Margaret "Madge" and David Wallace on February 13, 1885. Six-year-old Harry immediately developed a crush on Bess.

It was not until they were both in fifth grade that they became friends, although they had little in common. Bess's family, who owned a flour mill, was wealthy and lived in a large house. Harry's family was poor, and he worked in a drugstore as a boy. Small in stature and very nearsighted, Harry preferred playing piano and reading. Bess was active riding horses or skating, and she enjoyed playing sports. She was remembered as "a marvelous athlete—the best third baseman in Independence, a superb tennis player, a tireless ice skater—and she was pretty besides," by townspeople interviewed by daughter Margaret and quoted in her book many years later.

Both families were struggling when Bess and Harry graduated from high school in 1901. Harry moved to Kansas City and took on a series of jobs. Bess's father became distraught by business failures. He killed himself in the family's bathroom, an event that deeply affected Bess. She refused to ever talk about the event again. Daughter Margaret would say later that her mother feared the suicide would be brought up as an issue in her husband's political campaigns. It never was, but she remained disturbed over the incident for the rest of her life.

Bess, her mother, and three younger brothers moved to their grandparent's house in 1904, when she was nineteen. The following year, her grandfather arranged for Bess to attend a nearby finishing school—a school at which young women learn social graces, domestic tasks, and briefly continue their education. After returning home from school, she settled into a quiet life, playing bridge, doing needlework, and riding horses.

A persistent suitor

Truman, meanwhile, had moved to Grandview, Missouri, where he worked on his family farm. In 1910, he was visiting an aunt and cousins in nearby Independence when an opportunity arose to renew his acquaintance with Bess. His aunt had borrowed a cake plate from Bess's mother. Harry volunteered to return the plate, met Bess, and they resumed their friendship. Working long hours on the farm, Harry wrote letters to Bess and returned to Independence whenever he could. One letter in 1911 included a marriage proposal. Truman admitted that he was struggling, but he asserted, "I've always had a sneakin' notion I'd amount to something."

Bess turned down his proposal, but she did not dismiss him. "The best girl in the universe" and "an ordinary gink [slang for guy]," as Truman referred to Bess and himself, gradually became closer. She had not planned to get married, but in 1917 she was ready. This time it was Truman who delayed; America was about to enter World War I (1914–18), and Truman's national-guard unit was being prepared for military service. Truman promised to return to her after the war.

Truman did return to Bess and Independence in the spring of 1919, and the couple married that June. Truman opened his men's store that year and then was elected to a local office in 1922. The couple's daughter, Margaret, was born in 1924. Truman's political reputation improved so much over the next ten years that he was elected to the U.S. Senate in 1934.

Life in the capital

When the Trumans moved to Washington, D.C., it was the first time Bess lived anywhere but Independence (except for her time at the finishing school). With her daughter and mother, Bess spent time sightseeing and shopping. She began working in her husband's senate office, helping with mail and providing advice. When the fact that she was on his payroll became a political issue, Truman quickly defended her work—"she earned every cent I pay her."

Truman won reelection in 1940 by traveling around Missouri by car and making unplanned speeches wherever he could find a crowd. That same method was expanded in the presidential election of 1948 to a whistle-stop, cross-country train tour. Stopping in any small or large town that had a depot, Truman spoke plainly to people who shared his expe-

The Trumans stand outside their Independence, Missouri, home in 1967. *Reproduced by permission of the Corbis Corporation.*

riences as a hard-working person from a small town. He often ended his campaign talks by introducing his wife as "the Boss" and his daughter, Margaret, as "the Boss's Boss."

Truman had become vice president in 1944. Three months later, he assumed the presidency when **Franklin D. Roosevelt** (1882–1945; see entry in volume 4) died. The Trumans took part in the ritual of social functions and entertained in simple and unassuming ways.

Bess Truman handled White House bookkeeping and supervised the daily menu. She advised the president on strategies for reelection and fulfilled the social obligations of her position. When the White House underwent a major renovation during Truman's second term, the family lived in nearby Blair House and kept social life to a minimum.

Back home again

The Trumans retired to Independence after Truman's presidency ended in 1953. Bess was happy to return to a quiet life, but the streets of Independence were jammed in celebration of their arrival. After things quieted down, she enjoyed reading and watching sports, and she helped arrange the wedding of her daughter Margaret in 1956. Truman wrote his memoirs and occasionally spoke out on political issues. In 1957, the couple dedicated the Harry S. Truman Library in Independence. Truman died in 1972 and was buried on the library grounds.

Bess Truman's last public appearance came in 1976, when she joined President **Gerald Ford** (1913– ; see entry in volume 5) to dedicate an expansion of the Harry S. Truman Library. When she died in 1982 at the age of ninety-seven, Bess Truman was buried next to her husband on the grounds of the library in her hometown.

Where to Learn More

Robbins, Jhan. *Bess & Harry: An American Love Story.* New York: Putnam, 1980.

Sandak, Cass R. *The Trumans.* New York: Crestwood House, 1992.

Truman, Margaret. *Bess W. Truman.* New York: Macmillan, 1986.

Truman's Address to the Nation About the Bombing of Japan

Broadcast on radio and issued as a press release on August 6, 1945; excerpted from *Project WhistleStop* (Web site)

*President Truman describes "a new weapon"—
the atomic bomb—that has been dropped on
Hiroshima, Japan, in an effort to end World War II*

From July 17 to August 2, 1945, President **Harry S. Truman** (1884–1972; see entry in volume 4), British prime minister Winston Churchill (1874–1965; see box in **Harry S. Truman** entry in volume 4), his successor, Clement Attlee (1863–1967), and Soviet premier Joseph Stalin (1879–1953) met in Potsdam, Germany, to discuss the future of Germany and to plan strategies against Japan. It was more than two months after Germany had surrendered; World War II (1939–45) in the European Theater was over. Truman received a promise from Stalin that the Soviet Union (USSR) would enter the war against Japan.

Meanwhile, the first atomic bomb was tested on July 16, 1945, at Alamogordo, New Mexico. Truman informed Churchill that the United States had successfully detonated the weapon and had built several more.

On July 26, the Allied Powers meeting at Potsdam issued an ultimatum to Japan demanding its unconditional surrender. On July 29, the Japanese government decided not to comment on the ultimatum. The silence was interpreted as rejection. An American Air Force unit in the Pacific possessed

"[The] atomic bomb . . . is a harnessing of the basic power of the universe. The force from which the sun draws its power has been loosed against those who brought war to the Far East."

Harry S. Truman

two atomic bombs. President Truman directed them to use one of the bombs at the first opportunity if Japan did not surrender by August 3, 1945. On the morning of August 6, an atomic bomb was dropped on the city of Hiroshima. Sixteen hours later, President Truman addressed the American nation in a radio broadcast.

Things to remember while reading President Truman's address to the nation about the bombing of Japan:

- The decision to drop the atomic bomb remains one of the most profound issues any world leader has faced. The United States entered World War II in 1941 following the Japanese attack on American ships stationed at Pearl Harbor, Hawaii. Americans viewed the attack as a pure act of aggression; Japanese leaders believed that America would soon enter World War II and wanted to strike an early blow. When the United States entered World War II, American military leaders decided to concentrate first on the war in Europe. Meanwhile, the strategy in the Pacific Theater focused on keeping Japan from expanding its area of control.

- The United States lost over four hundred thousand military personnel during the war, and Japan's military losses totaled over a million and a half people. America was planning a final assault on Japan at the time of the Potsdam Conference. Military leaders expected another half-million people would die before Japan could be successfully invaded and overcome. Faced with those staggering additional losses but prepared to bring World War II to conclusion with the invasion of Japan, President Truman demanded a Japanese surrender. When Japan did not respond, President Truman decided to use the atomic bomb, rather than to prolong the war.

- At the time President Truman delivered this message, the United States and Japan were still at war—even after the destruction of Hiroshima, where the atomic bomb was dropped. His language in his address to the American people indicated that the United States was prepared to use all of its might to bring about a Japanese surrender.

- In 1939, Albert Einstein (1879–1955) and several other physicists wrote a letter to President **Franklin D. Roosevelt** (1882–1945; see entry in volume 4) explaining the possibility of making an atomic bomb and the likelihood that the German government was attempting to construct one. Einstein regarded the Nazi regime in Germany as a terrible threat to humankind. He had left Germany for America after the Nazi regime came to power. The atomic bomb was developed through the Manhattan Project, a massive, secret effort by the United States established in August 1942.

- German chemists Otto Hahn (1879–1968) and Fritz Strassmann (1902–1980) had successfully split the uranium atom into two roughly equal parts by bombardment with neutrons, a key development toward the release of atomic energy. A secret race was on to see which nation could build the first successful atom bomb.

President Truman's address to the nation about the bombing of Japan

*Sixteen hours ago an American airplane dropped one bomb on Hiroshima, an important Japanese Army base. That bomb had more power than 20,000 tons of **T.N.T.** It had more bomb power than two thousand times the blast power of the **British "Grand Slam,"** which is the largest bomb ever yet used in the history of warfare.*

The Japanese began the war from the air at Pearl Harbor. They have been repaid many fold. And the end is not yet. With this bomb we have now added a new and revolutionary increase in destruction to supplement the growing power of our armed forces. In their present form these bombs are now in production and even more powerful forms are in development.

*It is an **atomic bomb**. It is a harnessing of the basic power of the universe. The force from which the sun draws its power has been **loosed** against those who brought war to the Far East.*

Before 1939, it was the accepted belief of scientists that it was theoretically possible to release atomic energy. But no one knew any

T.N.T.: Trinitrotoluene—better known as dynamite, a powerful, explosive substance.

British "Grand Slam": A bomb first used by Great Britain on March 14, 1945, against Germany.

Atomic bomb: An explosive device that releases nuclear energy (energy that comes from an atom's core).

Loosed: Released, fired.

*practical method of doing it. By 1942, however, we knew that the Germans were working feverishly to find a way to add atomic energy to the other engines of war with which they hoped to enslave the world. But they failed. We may be grateful to **Providence** that the Germans got the **V-1's and V-2's** late and in limited quantities and even more grateful that they did not get the atomic bomb at all.*

The battle of the laboratories held fateful risks for us as well as the battles of the air, land and sea, and we have now won the battle of the laboratories as we have won the other battles.

*Beginning in 1940, before Pearl Harbor, scientific knowledge useful in war was pooled between the United States and Great Britain, and **many priceless helps** to our victories have come from that arrangement. Under that general policy the research on the atomic bomb was begun. With American and British scientists working together we entered the race of discovery against the Germans.*

The United States had available the large number of scientists of distinction in the many needed areas of knowledge. It had the tremendous industrial and financial resources necessary for the project and they could be devoted to it without undue impairment of other vital war work. In the United States the laboratory work and the production plants, on which a substantial start had already been made, would be out of reach of enemy bombing, while at that time Britain was exposed to constant air attack and was still threatened with the possibility of invasion. For these reasons Prime Minister Churchill and President Roosevelt agreed that it was wise to carry on the project here.

We now have two great plants and many lesser works devoted to the production of atomic power. Employment during peak construction numbered 125,000 and over 65,000 individuals are even now engaged in operating the plants. Many have worked there for two and a half years. Few know what they have been producing. They see great quantities of material going in and they see nothing coming out of these plants, for the physical size of the explosive charge is exceedingly small. We have spent two billion dollars on the greatest scientific gamble in history—and won.

But the greatest marvel is not the size of the enterprise, its secrecy, nor its cost, but the achievement of scientific brains in putting together infinitely complex pieces of knowledge held by many men in different fields of science into a workable plan. And hardly less marvelous has been the capacity of industry to design, and of labor

Providence: Divine guidance. When an event is believed to have happened through an act of God, it is called providence.

V-1's and V-2's: Guided missle bombs developed by Germany during the 1930s.

Many priceless helps: Much valuable assistance.

to operate, the machines and methods to do things never done before so that the brain child of many minds came forth in physical shape and performed as it was supposed to do. Both science and industry worked under the direction of the United States Army, which achieved a unique success in managing so diverse a problem in the advancement of knowledge in an amazingly short time. It is doubtful if such another combination could be got together in the world. What has been done is the greatest achievement of organized science in history. It was done under high pressure and without failure.

We are now prepared to **obliterate** more rapidly and completely every productive enterprise the Japanese have above ground in any city. We shall destroy their docks, their factories, and their communications. Let there be no mistake; we shall completely destroy Japan's power to make war.

It was to spare the Japanese people from utter destruction that the ultimatum of July 26 was issued at Potsdam. Their leaders promptly rejected that ultimatum. If they do not now accept our terms they may expect a rain of ruin from the air, the like of which has never been seen on this earth. Behind this air attack will follow sea and land forces in such numbers and power as they have not yet seen and with the fighting skill of which they are already well aware.

The Secretary of War [Henry L. Stimson], who has kept in personal touch with all phases of the project, will immediately make public a statement giving further details.

His statement will give facts concerning the sites at **Oak Ridge near Knoxville, Tennessee, and at Richland near Pasco, Washington, and an installation near Santa Fe, New Mexico.** Although the workers at the sites have been making materials to be used in producing the greatest destructive force in history they have not themselves been in danger beyond that of many other occupations, for the utmost care has been taken of their safety.

The fact that we can release atomic energy ushers in a new era in man's understanding of nature's forces. Atomic energy may in the future supplement the power that now comes from coal, oil, and falling water, but at present it cannot be produced on a basis to compete with them commercially. Before that comes there must be a long period of intensive research.

It has never been the habit of the scientists of this country or the policy of this Government to withhold from the world scientific

Obliterate: Destroy all trace of.

Oak Ridge near Knoxville, Tennessee, and at Richland near Pasco, Washington, and an installation near Santa Fe, New Mexico: Sites where industrial plants and laboratories were built in the early 1940s that contributed to the development of nuclear weapons.

knowledge. Normally, therefore, everything about the work with atomic energy would be made public.

But under present circumstances it is not intended to divulge the technical processes of production or all the military applications, pending further examination of possible methods of protecting us and the rest of the world from the danger of sudden destruction.

I shall recommend that the Congress of the United States consider promptly the establishment of an appropriate commission to control the production and use of atomic power within the United States. I shall give further consideration and make further recommendations to the Congress as to how atomic power can become a powerful and forceful influence towards the maintenance of world peace. (Project WhistleStop *[Web site]*)

What happened next . . .

A second atomic bomb was detonated over the Japanese city of Nagasaki on August 9. Meanwhile, the U.S.S.R. declared war on Japan on August 8 and invaded Japanese military strongholds in Manchuria, China, the next day. On August 14, Japan announced its surrender; the formal surrender took place on September 2 in Tokyo Bay aboard the battleship U.S.S. *Missouri*.

In the United States, President Truman transferred control and development of nuclear energy from the military to the civilian Atomic Energy Commission. The authority to use the atomic bomb was placed solely with the president. When the Soviet Union announced that it had developed nuclear weapons, the threat of wide-ranging destruction became possible and frightening. That possibility remains; at the end of the twentieth century, at least six nations had successfully detonated atom bombs in tests.

Did you know . . .

- All previous explosive devices were powered by rapid burning or decomposition of a chemical compound; they only released energy from the outermost electrons of an atom. Nuclear explosives release nuclear energy (energy that comes from an atom's core); they are energized by splitting an atom, a process called fission.

- The Manhattan Project and the successful testing of the atomic bomb were so secret that Vice President Harry S. Truman did not learn about it until after he assumed the office of president in 1945, following the death of Franklin D. Roosevelt (1882–1945). At that time, Secretary of War Henry L. Stimson (1867–1950; see entry in **Herbert Hoover** entry in volume 4) informed Truman about the new weapon.

Where to Learn More

"Draft of a White House press release, 'Statement by the President of the United States,' ca. August 6, 1945 (3 pages)." *Project WhistleStop.* [Online] http://www.whistlestop.org/study_collections/bomb/small/mb10.htm (accessed on September 19, 2000).

Ferrell, Robert H. *Harry S. Truman and the Bomb: A Documentary History.* Worlland, WY: High Plains Publishing, 1996.

Haynes, Richard F. *The Awesome Power: Harry S. Truman as Commander in Chief.* Baton Rouge: Louisiana State University Press, 1973.

Moskin, J. Robert. *Mr. Truman's War: The Final Victories of World War II and the Birth of the Postwar World.* New York: Random House, 1996.

O'Neal, Michael. *President Truman and the Atomic Bomb: Opposing Viewpoints.* San Diego: Greenhaven Press, 1990.

Truman's Executive Order Banning Segregation in the Military

Issued on July 26, 1948; excerpted from
Harry S. Truman Library & Museum **(Web site)**

President Truman's executive order is a landmark in the expansion of civil rights

During the World War II years (1939–45), racial segregation was practiced in the military as well as in areas of the American South. African Americans often trained in separate facilities than whites, and some units of the military were off-limits to non-whites. Calling segregation in the military "the most un-American activity in the whole government," President **Harry S. Truman** (1884–1972; see entry in volume 4) issued Executive Order 9981 on July 26, 1948. To pursue desegregation of the military, Truman created the President's Committee on Equality of Treatment and Opportunity in the Armed Services to recommend a process that would ensure the executive order was carried out.

Things to remember while reading President Truman's executive order banning segregation in the military:

- The Constitution authorizes the president to exercise important legislative functions by issuing executive orders that have the force of law and by authorizing administra-

"It is hereby declared to be the policy of the President that there shall be equality of treatment and opportunity for all persons in the armed services without regard to race, color, religion or national origin."

Harry S. Truman

tive agencies to "promulgate [make known to the public] rules in conformity with law."

- The President's Committee on Equality of Treatment and Opportunity in the Armed Services was the administrative agency created by the president to promulgate rules in conformity with law.

President Truman's executive order banding segregation in the military

Establishing the President's Committee on Equality of Treatment and Opportunity In the Armed Forces.

WHEREAS it is essential that there be maintained in the armed services of the United States the highest standards of democracy, with equality of treatment and opportunity for all those who serve in our country's defense:

*NOW THEREFORE, by virtue of the authority vested in me as President of the United States, by the Constitution and the **statutes** of the United States, and as Commander in Chief of the armed services, it is hereby ordered as follows:*

*1. It is hereby declared to be the policy of the President that there shall be equality of treatment and opportunity for all persons in the armed services without regard to race, color, religion or national origin. This policy shall be put into effect as rapidly as possible, having due regard to the time required to **effectuate** any necessary changes without impairing efficiency or morale.*

2. There shall be created in the National Military Establishment an advisory committee to be known as the President's Committee on Equality of Treatment and Opportunity in the Armed Services, which shall be composed of seven members to be designated by the President.

3. The Committee is authorized on behalf of the President to examine into the rules, procedures and practices of the Armed Services in order to determine in what respect such rules, procedures and practices may be altered or improved with a view to carrying out the policy of this order. The Committee shall confer and advise the Sec-

Statutes: Laws enacted by the legislative branch of a government.

Effectuate: Put into practice.

retary of Defense, the Secretary of the Army, the Secretary of the Navy, and the Secretary of the Air Force, and shall make such recommendations to the President and to said Secretaries as in the judgment of the Committee will effectuate the policy hereof.

4. All executive departments and agencies of the Federal Government are authorized and directed to cooperate with the Committee in its work, and to furnish the Committee such information or the services of such persons as the Committee may require in the performance of its duties.

5. When requested by the Committee to do so, persons in the armed services or in any of the executive departments and agencies of the Federal Government shall testify before the Committee and shall make available for use of the Committee such documents and other information as the Committee may require.

6. The Committee shall continue to exist until such time as the President shall terminate its existence by Executive order. (Harry S. Truman Library & Museum *[Web site]*)

What happened next . . .

Executive Order 9981 and Truman's support for civil rights legislation in 1946 were issues in the 1948 campaign, as much among members of Truman's own party as it was for his opponents. Southern Democrats against Truman's policies on civil rights defected from the party and supported South Carolina governor Strom Thurmond (1902–) for president on the State's Rights Democratic (Dixiecrat) ticket.

Truman won the presidential election of 1948, but he was unable to pass any significant civil rights legislation through Congress. The executive order banning segregation in the military, however, was a significant step in the growing civil rights movement. During the 1950s, professional baseball was integrated, the Supreme Court (in *Brown v. Board of Education*) declared that any laws racially segregating public schools were unconstitutional, and acts of civil disobedience (peaceful protest) were staged against racist practices. The momentum developed further during the 1960s, culminating with the Civil Rights Act of 1964 that made it illegal to discriminate against people based on race, religion, and ethnic origin.

Did you know . . .

- The Tuskegee Institute in Alabama had programs through which qualified African Americans could receive the military training denied to them in the segregated armed forces, including an opportunity to train as pilots and officers for the Army Air Corps. During the war, the all-black Ninety-ninth Pursuit Squadron flew an unprecedented number of successful bomber missions, suffering fewer casualties and garnering more decorations than almost any other unit on the European front. They were known as the Tuskegee Airmen.

Where to Learn More

Berman, William C. *The Politics of Civil Rights in the Truman Administration.* Columbus: Ohio State University Press, 1970.

"Executive Order 9981: 50th Anniversary of the Desegregation of the Armed Services." *Harry S. Truman Library & Museum.* [Online] http://www.trumanlibrary.org/9981.htm (accessed on September 20, 2000).

McCoy, Donald R., and Richard T. Ruetten. *Quest and Response: Minority Rights and the Truman Administration.* Lawrence: University of Kansas, 1973.

Dwight D. Eisenhower

Thirty-fourth president (1953–1961)

Dwight D. Eisenhower . . . 1235

    Fast Facts about Dwight D. Eisenhower (box) . . . 1236

    Dwight D. Eisenhower Timeline (box) . . . 1237

    Words to Know (box) . . . 1238

    Election Results (box) . . . 1244

    Adlai E. Stevenson (box) . . . 1246

    Dwight D. Eisenhower Administration (box) . . . 1250

    Nikita Khrushchev (box) . . . 1252

    The Iron Curtain (box) . . . 1254

    A Selection of Eisenhower Landmarks (box) . . . 1255

Mamie Eisenhower . . . 1257

Primary source: Eisenhower's Farewell Address to the Nation
America's World War II hero warns the nation to be responsible with its economic, military, and technological power **. . . 1263**

Dwight D. Eisenhower

Born October 14, 1890
Denison, Texas
Died March 28, 1969
Washington, D.C.

Thirty-fourth president of the United States (1953–1961)

A brilliant World War II general became an enormously popular president

> "Dollars and guns are no substitutes for brains and willpower."
>
> *Dwight D. Eisenhower*

Dwight D. Eisenhower. *Courtesy of the Library of Congress.*

After heroic service in World War II (1939–45), Dwight D. Eisenhower was so popular that he was courted as a presidential candidate by both the Democratic *and* the Republican parties. A brilliant military officer, he served as supreme commander of the Allied forces in Europe from 1942 until the end of the war. Eisenhower then proved equal to the task of running the United States during the 1950s. The country enjoyed an extended period of prosperity during his two terms in office. Despite the Cold War, tensions between the United States and its postwar allies and Communist governments in the Soviet Union and China and their allies, Eisenhower managed to keep America out of armed conflict.

During his eight years in the White House, Eisenhower was sometimes criticized as an inactive leader who surrounded himself with a weighty bureaucracy and allowed advisors to dictate policy. (A bureaucracy is a government or big business set up to be run by bureaus, or departments, that strictly follow rules and regulations and a chain of authority.) That view, widely held in the 1950s and 1960s, was reversed when Eisenhower's presidential papers were released for

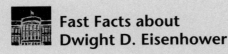

Fast Facts about Dwight D. Eisenhower

Full name: Dwight David Eisenhower

Born: October 14, 1890

Died: March 28, 1969

Burial site: Place of Meditation, on the grounds of the Eisenhower Presidential Center, Abilene, Kansas

Parents: David Jacob and Ida Elizabeth Stover Eisenhower

Spouse: Marie "Mamie" Geneva Doud (1896–1979; m. 1916)

Children: Doud Dwight (1917–1921); John Sheldon Doud (1923–)

Religion: Presbyterian

Education: U.S. Military Academy at West Point (B.S., 1915); graduate of several military colleges

Occupations: Soldier; general; Columbia University president

Government positions: None

Political party: Republican

Dates as president: January 20, 1953–January 20, 1957 (first term); January 20, 1957–January 20, 1961 (second term)

Age upon taking office: 62

scholarly review in the 1970s. Only then was he regarded as a decision-making chief executive. During his tenure (time in office), he seemed effective and projected a good-natured image to the public while the country seemed to run on its own. But Eisenhower was able to balance the political and the public demands of the presidency very well while leading the nation into a new era of scientific and economic advances and concern for civil rights. A grateful electorate (the voting public) recognized his contributions and rallied behind his campaign slogan, "I like Ike."

A Kansas boyhood

Dwight David Eisenhower was born on October 14, 1890, in Denison, Texas. He was the third of seven sons born to David and Ida Stover Eisenhower. While Dwight was still young, the family moved to Abilene, Kansas, where David Eisenhower supported them by working as a merchant. The Eisenhowers were not wealthy: The seven brothers found themselves crowded together in a series of small houses where they were forced to share bedrooms and help with many chores that were at that time considered "woman's work." Young Dwight learned to cook at an early age, a talent he enjoyed practicing throughout his life.

"Little Ike" was an above-average student who loved sports, especially football and baseball. His best subjects were mathematics and history. An avid reader of military histories, he was particularly interested in ancient battles of Greece and Rome. After graduating from high school in 1909, he tried to

Dwight D. Eisenhower Timeline

1890: Born in Texas

1915: Graduates from West Point

1917: Supervises training of the Tank Corps in Fort Meade, Maryland, during World War I

1925: Attends the U.S. Army's Command and General Staff School, graduating first in his class

1930s: Serves as chief military aide to General Douglas MacArthur

1939–45: World War II

1943–45: Serves as supreme commander of the Allies during the latter half of World War II

1944: Plans the successful invasions of German strongholds in North Africa and Italy; directs the D-Day invasion of France

1945: Commands the Battle of the Bulge, effectively ending Nazi aggression in Western Europe

1948–50: Serves as president of Columbia University

1950–52: Serves as commander of the NATO Forces in Europe

1953–61: Serves as thirty-fifth U.S. president

1954: Supreme Court calls for an end to racial segregation in schools in the *Brown v. Board of Education of Topeka* case, and Eisenhower orders regular army units to escort African American students to class at Central High School in Little Rock, Arkansas

1955: Suffers a serious heart attack; recovers fully and is reelected in 1956

1969: Dies in Washington, D.C.

gain entrance into the U.S. Naval Academy—only to discover that he was too old; he had been forced to repeat his first year of high school due to an injury. For two years, he worked in the Belle Springs Creamery in Abilene. Then he received a much-desired appointment to the U.S. Military Academy at West Point. He entered the academy in June 1911.

Never a brilliant student, Eisenhower found West Point demanding. He excelled in athletics, but he disliked the academy's many rules and regulations. Upon graduation in 1915, he was ranked at about the middle of the class academically and in the bottom fourth for discipline. He received the rank of second lieutenant in the infantry and was assigned to a post at Fort Sam Houston in Texas. During this first tour of

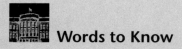

Words to Know

Allied forces: Alliances of countries in military opposition to another group of nations. Twenty-eight nations made up the Allied and Associated powers in World War I. In World War II, the Allied powers included Great Britain, the United States, and the Soviet Union.

Armistice: Truce.

Battle of the Bulge: Battles surrounding the last German offensive (1944–45) during World War II. Allied forces moving toward Germany from France following the D-Day invasion were stalled by bad weather along the German border. Germans launched a counteroffensive to divide American and British forces. Germans created a "bulge" in the Allied lines, but they were halted and then withdrew.

Bureaucracy: A government or big business set up to be run by bureaus, or departments, that strictly follow rules and regulations and a chain of authority.

Central Intelligence Agency: A U.S. government agency charged with accumulating information on foreign countries.

Cold War: A period of tension between two groups of nations from 1945 through 1989, with the United States and its allies on one side and a group of nations led by the Soviet Union on the other.

Communist: One who believes in a system of social and political ideas that bans private property and makes goods available to all based on their needs and distributed by a central governing system.

D-Day: A military term that describes the day when an event can be scheduled. D-Day in World War II was June 6, 1944,

duty, he met and married Denver socialite Mamie Doud (1896–1979; see entry on **Mamie Eisenhower** in volume 4).

On the move

A career army officer can expect to move frequently and to undertake a wide variety of duties. In his first seven years with the U.S. Army, Eisenhower moved almost a dozen times. He served in such locales as Texas, Georgia, Maryland, Pennsylvania, and New Jersey. Promoted to captain in 1917, he was eager to go to Europe to fight in World War I (1914–18). Instead, his orders were to supervise training of the Tank Corps in Fort Meade, Maryland. Although disap-

when Allied forces landed in Normandy, France.

Five-star general: The highest rank in the American military.

Integration: The bringing together of people of all races and ethnic backgrounds without restrictions; desegregation.

Iron Curtain: A term describing Eastern European nations dominated by the Soviet Union.

North Atlantic Treaty Organization: An alliance for collective security (the security of all the nations in the organization) created by the North Atlantic Treaty (1949). The treaty originally involved Belgium, Canada, Denmark, France, Great Britain, Iceland, Italy, Luxembourg, the Netherlands, Norway, Portugal, and the United States.

Nuclear test ban treaty: An agreement to stop testing nuclear weapons.

Pearl Harbor: An American naval station in Hawaii attacked without warning by Japanese forces in December 1941.

Segregation: The policy of keeping groups of people from different races, religions, or ethnic backgrounds separated.

South East Asia Treaty Organization: An alliance of nations founded in 1954 to prevent the spread of communism in Asian and Pacific island nations. Original members included Australia, France, Great Britain, New Zealand, Pakistan, the Philippines, Thailand, and the United States. The alliance disbanded in 1977.

Theater: A large area where military operations are occurring.

pointed with this position at the time, he learned a great deal about tanks and their deployment (how they should be used in battle). He put this knowledge to good use in World War II. He also participated in a transcontinental convoy (a group, usually with a protective escort) of army tanks and trucks in 1919. Watching the machines make their way slowly over substandard roadways convinced him of the need for better highways to link the nation's cities.

Shortly after World War I ended in 1919, Eisenhower was promoted to major and sent to serve as an executive assistant to General Fox Conner (1874–1951) in the Panama Canal Zone, a U.S.-controlled strip of land (from 1903 to 1999) ten miles wide that runs across Panama. Conner believed that the world was headed for another major war, and he urged Eisenhower to prepare for it. Taking his superior's warnings to heart, Eisenhower applied himself completely to every task at hand. From 1925 to 1926, he attended the army's Command and General Staff School, graduating first in his class of 245. By 1929, he had finished courses at the Army War College and was serving as executive officer to Assistant Secretary of War George Moseley (1874–1960). One of Eisenhower's more unusual orders during this period was to visit France and write a guidebook on the major battle sites of World War I.

Emerges as a military leader

During the Great Depression (1929–41), Eisenhower served as chief military aide to General Douglas MacArthur (1880–1964; see box in **Harry S. Truman** entry in volume 4), who was charged with the task of preparing the Philippines for independence. Like so many of Eisenhower's superiors, MacArthur was impressed with him. In one performance evaluation, MacArthur wrote of Eisenhower: "This is the best officer in the U.S. Army. When the next war comes, move him right to the top." By the 1940s, MacArthur's words proved an accurate prediction.

After serving with MacArthur in the Philippines until 1939, Eisenhower returned to the United States as a lieutenant colonel. By that time, aggressive actions by Nazi Germany were underway in Europe. Eisenhower had been expecting to retire from the military, but he continued serving as the war broadened into a global (worldwide) conflict. On December 7, 1941, Japanese forces bombed the American naval station at Pearl Harbor, Hawaii, and the United States entered World War II.

Eisenhower was a colonel at the time of Pearl Harbor. He had only recently come into the public eye as the chief of staff for the Third Army. It was noted how quickly and efficiently he could organize troops and maintain their welfare. He certainly could not have predicted the role he was about to play in the war. Just five days after the Pearl Harbor attack, Eisenhower was summoned to Washington, D.C., by Army chief of staff George C. Marshall (1880–1959; see box in **Harry S. Truman** entry in volume 4). He placed Eisenhower in charge of the War Plans Division and ordered him to devise a strategy for U.S. deployment in the war.

Eisenhower recommended that the United States concentrate its forces in the African and European theaters (areas of military operation), with the goal of first defeating Germany and Italy. His plan called for America to fight a defensive war against Japan in the Pacific theater until Europe could be reconquered by the Allies. To his surprise, Eisenhower was placed in command of American troops. Based in England, he soon found himself debating strategy with President **Franklin D. Roosevelt** (1882–1945; see entry in volume 4) and British prime minister Winston Churchill (1874–1965; see box in **Franklin D. Roosevelt** entry in volume 4). Both leaders were so impressed with Eisenhower that when battle plans were finally agreed upon, Eisenhower was named supreme commander of all the Allied forces.

General Dwight D. Eisenhower in France during World War II.
Reproduced by permission of AP/Wide World Photos.

A victorious general

From the time the Allies invaded French North Africa in May 1942 until Germany formally surrendered on May 7, 1945, Eisenhower directed Allied forces. He successfully planned invasions of German strongholds in North Africa and Italy. He was the architect (chief planner) of the D-Day (June 6, 1944) invasion of Normandy Beach in France, where Allied troops landed to push towards Germany. He commanded the bloody "Battle of the Bulge" that effectively ended Nazi aggression in Western Europe. (In a counteroffensive against American and British forces, Germans created a "bulge" in the Allied lines, but they were halted and then withdrew.)

Eisenhower proved to be decisive and quick to act, displaying great expertise at moving large numbers of troops and implements of war. Never was this more important than in the Battle of the Bulge, when he smashed a German counteroffensive by rushing armies to the front and overwhelming the Nazi's last efforts.

From the beginning of his time as supreme commander, Eisenhower realized that along with an enemy to conquer he had to keep peace among his various commanders and battalions from numerous Allied nations. He devised the strategy of a "broad front" that did not allow any single Allied country or general to emerge triumphant at the cost of others. Furthermore, as the forces of the Allies closed in on Berlin, Germany, he ordered that the Soviet forces moving in from the east would be allowed to occupy Germany's capital. All those moves seemed diplomatic and politically advantageous at the time. However, many observers were voicing distrust of the Soviets and their communist agenda. (Communists believe that private property should be banned and goods distributed by a central government should be available for all according to their needs.)

When Eisenhower cabled the news of victory in Europe to the army chief of staff Marshall in Washington, D.C., he received a reply that praised his accomplishments in no small measure: "You have completed your mission with the greatest victory in the history of warfare. You have commanded with outstanding success the most powerful military force that has ever been assembled. . . . You have made history, great history for the good of mankind and you have stood for all we hope for and admire in an officer of the United States Army." Eisenhower returned to a hero's welcome in America.

The accomplishments that had made him one of the most famous men in the world did not make Eisenhower wealthy—nor was he lighthearted about a victory that had been enormously costly in terms of human suffering. He spent two post-war years as the army's chief of staff and then retired from the military in 1948 as a five-star general—the highest rank given in the U.S. military.

Road to the presidency

After serving for two years as the president of Columbia University (during which time he published a best-selling book about World War II, *Crusade in Europe*), Eisenhower was

called back into service by President **Harry S. Truman** (1884–1972; see entry in volume 4). Truman sent him to Europe as supreme commander of Allied forces. This time, Eisenhower was to organize a multinational army for the new North Atlantic Treaty Organization (NATO). While in Europe, he observed with dismay the advances being made in Eastern Europe by the Soviet Union.

By that time, both Democrats and Republicans were urging Eisenhower to run for president even though his political views were unknown. When he finally agreed to campaign, Eisenhower revealed that he was a Republican. Democrats had held the White House for the past twenty years. It hardly mattered. Eisenhower won the Republican Party nomination, and with thirty-nine-year-old running mate **Richard Nixon** (1913–1994; see entry in volume 5), he easily defeated Democratic nominee Adlai Stevenson (1900–1965; see box) in the 1952 election.

President Harry S. Truman (left) speaks with Dwight D. Eisenhower (right), supreme commander of the Allied Forces.
Reproduced by permission of Archive Photos.

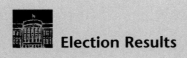 **Election Results**

1952

Presidential / Vice presidential candidates	Popular votes	Presidential electoral votes
Dwight D. Eisenhower / Richard M. Nixon (Republican)	33,778,964	442
Adlai E. Stevenson / John J. Sparkman (Democratic)	27,314,992	89

1956

Presidential / Vice presidential candidates	Popular votes	Presidential electoral votes
Dwight D. Eisenhower / Richard M. Nixon (Republican)	35,581,003	457
Adlai E. Stevenson / C. Estes Kefauver (Democratic)	25,738,765	73

During his campaign, Eisenhower promised to seek an end to the Korean War (1950–53). A bloody stalemate had developed despite U.S. support for South Korea. (A stalemate is a deadlock, a situation in which no progress can be made.) The once-united nation of Korea had divided into two countries—North Korea, which was communist, and South Korea, which was democratic. Shortly after his inauguration (swearing-in ceremony) as president on January 20, 1953, Eisenhower began negotiating an armistice—a truce—that was completed in July. With the end of that war, the former general began to scale back conventional military forces. He wanted to cut military costs in an effort to balance the federal budget. Mindful of the Cold War, however, he increased spending on nuclear weapons and missiles, escalating (stepping up) an arms race that would continue for decades.

The Cold War

Americans were generally experiencing a period of prosperity during the 1950s: New homes were being built in suburban areas, and jobs were plentiful. Even so, the Cold War caused a great deal of uneasiness. Concern about the spread of communist values had become more acute following World War II. Eisenhower backed covert (secret) actions by the Central Intelligence Agency (CIA) to discredit communist governments in the Middle East and Central America. The CIA is the U.S. government agency charged with accumulating information on foreign countries.

Wisconsin senator Joseph McCarthy (1908–1957) began a much-publicized investigation into communist activity in America. He claimed that there was widespread communist infiltration (gradual or secret entrance) into American cultural and political institutions. But America watched as McCarthy's widely publicized hearings turned into mockeries of justice, full of false accusations and conspiracy theories. Eisenhower quietly worked behind the scenes to challenge the combative senator after McCarthy began investigating the army.

As proliferation (rapid increase) of nuclear weapons began, Eisenhower took a public stand urging peaceful applications of nuclear technology. His administration sponsored an "Atoms for Peace" campaign that educated the public about positive uses of nuclear energy. He also called for serious diplomatic conferences with the Soviet Union. The death of Soviet dictator Joseph Stalin (1879–1953) ushered in a slight thaw in relations between the United States and the Soviet Union, and Eisenhower was able to arrange face-to-face meetings with Stalin's successor, Nikita Khrushchev (1894–1971; see box). Nevertheless, as deep distrust continued between the two nations, Eisenhower initiated a secret program of high-altitude aerial surveillance (close observation) of the Soviet Union. That program would have serious consequences during Eisenhower's second term.

Meanwhile, procommunist activity spread to yet another country, the small southeast Asian nation of Vietnam. France had held Vietnam as a colony for decades, but representatives there were attacked and routed by communist rebels. Eisenhower's advisors urged him to intervene (interfere with force) in Vietnam, fearing that if Vietnam fell to the communists, other neighboring nations would follow. Eisenhower was not eager to involve American troops in another foreign war, especially for a French colony. Instead, he supported the partition (division) of Vietnam into a communist-controlled North Vietnam and an independent South Viet-

"I Like Ike" automobile sticker. This was a popular 1952 campaign slogan for Dwight D. Eisenhower. *Reproduced by permission of the Corbis Corporation.*

Adlai E. Stevenson

He lost two presidential elections to Dwight D. Eisenhower by wide margins, but Adlai Stevenson remained a popular and respected figure in American politics. Unlike Ike, Stevenson favored progressive politics of social programs and expansion of civil rights. Americans preferred their World War II hero, Eisenhower, and his more conservative policies. Had Stevenson won either election of 1952 or 1956, the course of American history would have been different. Instead, the more cautious approach of Eisenhower at home, and his tougher stance against communism abroad, won out and influenced the 1950s.

Born Adlai Ewing Stevenson in Los Angeles, California, on February, 5, 1900, to Lewis Green Stevenson, a former secretary of state for Illinois, and Helen Louise Davis, Stevenson was part of a prominent family in Bloomington, Illinois, where they returned to live after he was born. His grandfather, Adlai E. Stevenson (1835–1914), was vice president during the second term of **Grover Cleveland** (1837–1908; see entry in volume 3), and a great grandfather was a close friend and avid supporter of **Abraham Lincoln** (1809–1865; see entry in volume 2). Graduating from the public schools, young Adlai Stevenson attended an eastern private school, graduated from Princeton University in 1922 (where he edited and wrote for the school newspaper), and earned a law degree from Northwestern University in 1926. Admitted that year to the Illinois bar, he began practicing law in Chicago.

Stevenson's interest in politics blossomed as he became familiar with the needs of farmers around Bloomington, and as he became active in the Chicago Council on Foreign Relations. On December 1, 1928, he married Ellen Borden. They had three sons, one of whom, Adlai E. Stevenson III (1930–), served as a U.S. senator from Illinois from 1970 to 1981. The Stevensons were divorced in 1949.

In 1933, Stevenson went to Washington, D.C., to work for President Franklin D. Roosevelt's Agricultural Adjustment Administration. In 1934, he rejoined his Chicago law firm, and the following year was elected president of the Chicago Council on Foreign Relations. He developed a reputation as a speechmaker, and became involved in many causes, including protecting the rights of immigrants, minorities, and disadvantaged children. In 1940, he became chairman of the Chicago Chapter of the Committee to Defend America by Aiding the Allies, a group that pursued vigorous support for enemies of Nazi Germany during World War II, which the United States had not yet entered. In June 1941, Secretary of the Navy Frank Knox (1874–1944) appointed Stevenson as his agency's principal attorney.

Stevenson became a special assistant to Secretary of State Edward R. Stettinius Jr. (1900–1949), under President Harry Truman. Stevenson was appointed senior adviser to the U.S. delegation for the

Adlai E. Stevenson.
Courtesy of the Library of Congress.

first session of the General Assembly of the United Nations (UN) in 1946. In 1948, Stevenson was elected governor of Illinois. His administration was modestly successful, facing opposition from Republicans and a sharp division between rural and industrial regions of Illinois. Nevertheless, he attracted wide attention with speeches and articles. Early in January 1952, Stevenson announced that he would seek reelection as governor, but three weeks later President Truman asked him to seek the presidential nomination. Stevenson refused. As the Democratic Party's convention approached, some party leaders urged him to announce that he would accept the nomination if it were offered him. On the third ballot, Stevenson was drafted as the nominee because the convention wanted him and nobody else.

Stevenson conducted a high-spirited and dignified campaign: his speeches became best-selling books at home and abroad. Still, Stevenson was overwhelmed in the election by popular war hero Dwight D. Eisenhower. Stevenson then went on an international tour, wrote articles for *Look* magazine, and published *Call to Greatness* (1954).

During his second presidential campaign in 1956, Stevenson supported a suspension of nuclear testing in the atmosphere; reduction of tensions with the Soviet Union; increased assistance to underdeveloped countries through the UN; and substantial federal assistance to education, to the poor, and to the elderly. After his second election defeat—again to Eisenhower—Stevenson helped found the Democratic Advisory Council to issue policy statements, traveled around the world, and formed his own law firm.

Stevenson was pressed again to run for president in 1960, but he refused. After John F. Kennedy's victory, Stevenson hoped to be appointed secretary of state; instead, Kennedy offered him the UN ambassadorship. He wanted the UN to be the center of U.S. foreign policy, but this concept was not accepted. During his time in the UN, Stevenson represented American interests during tense confrontations between the United States and the Soviet Union over events in Cuba, the near bankruptcy of the UN, and many other international crises. Stevenson died of a heart attack in 1965.

nam. Meanwhile, he helped organize the South East Asia Treaty Organization (SEATO). The SEATO alliance, dedicated to preventing the spread of communism in Asian and Pacific Island nations, gave the United States expanded responsibilities in South Vietnam.

Shortly after meeting Soviet leaders at a conference in Geneva, Switzerland, in the summer of 1955, Eisenhower suffered a serious heart attack. He was very ill for three months. Republicans despaired that their most popular candidate might not be well enough to run for a second term. However, by the early spring of 1956, Eisenhower had fully recovered his health and announced he would seek a second term as president.

New challenges

In the 1956 presidential election, Eisenhower again defeated Adlai Stevenson. His second term was more difficult than his first. Successes included passage of a huge public works bill to create the nation's first interstate highway program. (Interstate highways continue from state to state.) In foreign affairs, his administration played a key role in the peaceful settlement of an international dispute centered on Egypt's Suez Canal, a vital shipping link between the Mediterranean Ocean and the Red Sea.

Several serious domestic and foreign crises contributed further to Cold War tensions. An uprising against Soviet influence in Hungary was crushed by Soviet tanks and military power. The Soviet Union's domination of Eastern Europe came to be known as the Iron Curtain, as Sir Winston Churchill called it in a speech. Borders of Soviet-dominated nations were closed, and travel and means of communication, such as radio and newspapers, as well as free speech, severely restricted. When the Soviet Union launched a man-made satellite called *Sputnik* into orbit around the Earth, it sparked concern about America's military and educational systems. Democratic leaders in particular claimed that Eisenhower had allowed a "missile gap"—they claimed that the Soviets had gained superior strength in production of air weapons. The satellite launch led some Americans to criticize the nation's educational system. They felt the system was falling behind in preparing students in science and mathematics.

Other issues concerning education developed. Racial segregation (the policy of keeping groups of people from different races separated), was practiced in schools. The Supreme Court's 1954 decision in the case of *Brown v. Board of Education of Topeka* called for an end to racial segregation in schools and led to a series of tense civil rights confrontations. Though Eisenhower never made a distinct pronouncement for or against segregation, he had helped to further the integration of the armed forces (opening the armed forces to people of all races without any restrictions). (In 1948, Eisenhower's predecessor, Harry S. Truman, had ordered desegregation of the armed forces. [See **Harry S. Truman** primary source entry in volume 4.]) When African American students were refused admittance to Central High School in Little Rock, Arkansas, in 1957, President Eisenhower ordered regular army units to escort them to class. He sent a clear signal that court-ordered integration would not be compromised. During this period, Eisenhower proposed and signed into law a civil rights bill; however, it was so weakened by Senate amendments that its provisions were useless.

Dwight D. Eisenhower Administration

Administration Dates
January 20, 1953–January 20, 1957
January 20, 1957–January 20, 1961

Vice President
Richard M. Nixon (1953–61)

Cabinet

Secretary of State
John F. Dulles (1953–59)
Christian A. Herter (1959–61)

Secretary of the Treasury
George M. Humphrey (1953–57)
Robert B. Anderson (1957–61)

Attorney General
Herbert Brownell Jr. (1953–57)
William P. Rogers (1957–61)

Postmaster General
Arthur E. Summerfield (1953–61)

Secretary of the Interior
Douglas McKay (1953–56)

Frederick A. Seaton (1956–61)

Secretary of Agriculture
Ezra T. Benson (1953–61)

Secretary of Labor
Martin P. Durkin (1953)
James P. Mitchell (1953–61)

Secretary of Commerce
C. Sinclair Weeks (1953–58)
Frederick H. Mueller (1959–61)

Secretary of Defense
Charles E. Wilson (1953–57)
Neil H. McElroy (1957–59)
Thomas S. Gates Jr. (1959–61)

**Secretary of Health, Education and
    Welfare**
Oveta Culp Hobby (1953–55)
Marion B. Folsom (1955–58)
Arthur S. Flemming (1958–61)

To strengthen education in America, Eisenhower launched the National Defense Education Act, which awarded college scholarships to students specializing in mathematics and the sciences. He created the first President's Science Advisory Committee, and he supervised the birth of the National Aeronautics and Space Agency (NASA), ordering it to catch up with the Soviets in the space race.

As for defense, Eisenhower was well aware that the "missile gap" theory was wrong. Informed by reports from high-altitude U-2 planes that flew over the Soviet Union, Eisenhower knew that the United States was ahead of the Soviets in sophisticated military weaponry. He could not make this information public, however, without jeopardizing the U-2 flights, which violated international law.

International tour and tension

During the last two years of his presidency, Eisenhower emerged from the White House on an international tour for peace. Using the new presidential jet, Air Force One, he visited many foreign nations and many parts of America, speaking to the public in a more personable manner than he had before. A summit meeting with Nikita Khrushchev was planned for Paris in the spring of 1960, but before it could be undertaken, Eisenhower faced the biggest international scandal of his career.

Just prior to the Paris Summit, the Soviet military shot down one of the U-2 spy planes that had been supplying the Eisenhower administration with classified information about enemy defenses. Leaving no room for doubt, Soviet soldiers recovered the plane, photographs of sensitive government installations, and a frightened pilot, Francis Gary Powers (1929–1977). Khrushchev was furious. The Soviet leader canceled the summit talks, which were to have included steps toward the first nuclear test ban treaty, an agreement to stop testing nuclear weapons.

The cancellation of the Paris Summit was the biggest disappointment of Eisenhower's presidency. The Cold War worsened and drew closer to home. On the island of Cuba just off the coast of Florida, communist rebel leader Fidel Castro (1927–) took control of the government.

A Gettysburg address

Eisenhower completed his term in office on January 20, 1961. Two months later, President **John F. Kennedy** (1917–1963; see entry in volume 5) reinstated him as an army general, but Eisenhower served in little more than an advisory capacity. Eisenhower and his wife Mamie were ready to settle down on a farm they had bought near Gettysburg, Pennsylvania—the only permanent home the two had ever owned. From there, Eisenhower could visit the nation's capital when needed, but he was in his seventies and eager to

An avid golfer, President Eisenhower had a putting green installed on the White House lawn, and he could also be found putting in the Oval Office. He once claimed that his happiest moment occurred on February 6, 1968, when he shot a hole in one at the Seven Lakes Country Club in Palm Springs, California.

Nikita Khrushchev

Nikita Khrushchev was born in Kalinovka, Russia, on April 17, 1894. After working as a coal miner, he received education and political training in schools for young workers set up by the Communist Party during the 1920s. He joined the Communist Party of the Ukraine, and from 1925 to 1953 he was connected with the political career of Joseph Stalin. In 1929, Khrushchev went to Moscow, the center of national power, and moved up the ranks of Moscow's Party organization. In 1934, he became head of the Moscow branch of the Communist Party and was appointed to the Central Committee of the Soviet Communist Party, which consisted of the most powerful Party figures.

Khrushchev helped strengthen Stalin's fierce dictatorship over Soviet society. From 1934 to 1938, Khrushchev oversaw construction of Moscow's subway system and helped Stalin purge political figures he found threatening. (Most of Khrushchev's Central Committee colleagues were executed.) In 1938, he became the leader of the Communist Party of the Ukraine, the nation's most important agricultural region and a center of resistance to Stalin's farm policy. Stalin had ordered all farm property to be nationalized (made part of the nation's property) to form a collective agricultural program supervised by the government. From 1938 to 1941, Khrushchev directed mass arrests and downgraded the Ukrainian language and culture in favor of Russian, a cultural policy used by Stalin to bring all regions of the Soviet Union under Moscow's control.

When Germany attacked the Ukraine during World War II, Khrushchev was a lieutenant general in the Soviet army. After the war, Khrushchev remained in the Ukraine to supervise reconstruction. He developed into a different kind of Party leader, one who circulated among the population and who was interested in agriculture. As the powerful head of an important region, Khrushchev maintained as much of an independent position as anyone could in Stalin's dictatorial system.

In 1949, Khrushchev returned to lead the Communist Party in the Moscow region. A rivalry to succeed Stalin was underway. Stalin died in 1953, but it took Khrushchev about two years to solidify his power. This occurred in February 1956, when he called for "de-Stalinization." Khrushchev recounted Stalin's crimes against Party members during the 1930s and condemned Stalin's mistakes during World War II. As a result, some Eastern Europe countries, under Soviet Union control since the end of World War II, sought changes in their own countries. Poles and Hungarians attempted to oust their ruling Communist governments. A settlement was made with Poland, but the Soviet Union army crushed a Hungarian rebellion in 1956 by killing thousands of rebels.

In October 1957, the Soviet Union launched *Sputnik*, the first space satellite, leading many foreign observers to view the Soviet Union as the world leader in advanced technology. The success of *Sputnik*

Nikita Khrushchev.
Courtesy of the Library of Congress.

spawned a space race against the much wealthier United States. Meanwhile, friction developed between the Soviet Union and the People's Republic of China. Faced with growing competition from both communist and non-communist countries, Khrushchev freed many of Stalin's victims from prison and ended a constant threat of police terror that had arisen in the 1930s. Americans continued to eye the Soviet Union suspiciously. Khrushchev's efforts to reduce political and military tensions were mixed with aggressive moves, such as threats made to the Western-controlled parts of Berlin in 1958 and 1961.

To boost his position at home, Khrushchev matched his political reforms with colorful promises of economic abundance. By the early 1960s, he spoke of Russia overtaking and surpassing the standard of living of the United States in the near future. However, his farm program did not produce results after an early, promising start.

Khrushchev had his own record of brutality, and he sometimes presented himself as a bully by threatening Berlin or angrily banging his shoe on a desk during a United Nations debate. In the fall of 1961, a military clash with the United States seemed likely when Khrushchev, reacting to the growing departure of East Germans to West Berlin, built the wall separating the communist and non-communist sectors of the city. The following fall brought about the most dangerous confrontation of the Cold War. The Soviet Union placed missiles in Cuba. The United States demanded that the missiles be removed. After a tense week in which the world stood on the edge of nuclear war, Khrushchev—unable or unwilling to risk a military clash with the United States—agreed to remove the missiles.

The aftermath of the missile crisis of 1962 brought a new wave of Soviet-American cooperation. The arms race was modified by a ban on nuclear testing in the atmosphere. The Soviet Union began to buy large quantities of food from the United States. Khrushchev's failures in agriculture and foreign policy, however, weakened his stature. He was removed from his position by Party leaders in October 1964, and lived in Moscow until his death in 1971.

The Iron Curtain

A year after the end of World War II, a new term emerged that described the Eastern European nations dominated by the Soviet Union. Borders of those nations were sealed, travel and communication severely restricted, and the nations were subject to censorship. The term came into popular usage after former British prime minister Winston Churchill described post-World War II Eastern Europe in a speech in Fulton, Missouri, on March 5, 1946: "From Stettin in the Baltic to Trieste in the Adriatic an iron curtain has descended across the continent."

relax and work on his golf game. He once claimed that his happiest moment came in February 1968 when—at age seventy-seven—he shot his first and only hole in one.

A year later, the thirty-fourth president died of heart trouble at Walter Reed Army Hospital in Washington, D.C. After lying in state at the White House, Eisenhower's remains were flown to Abilene, Kansas, where he was buried in the Place of Meditation at the Eisenhower Center.

Legacy

The 1950s are often depicted historically as a time of calm, when not much happened to compare with the Great Depression of the 1930s, World War II during the 1940s, and the political idealism and civil strife of the 1960s. President Eisenhower, who was often content to delegate authority and did not initiate bold new plans, reflected the times. Yet, he was able to maneuver successfully through a period marked by tense Cold War relations and the frightening prospect of nuclear war.

The nation enjoyed a general period of prosperity and growth, with a building boom in housing (and the creation of many new suburbs) and roads, including new interstate highway systems. The U.S. space program was started, and programs like social security retirement benefits were expanded.

If the Eisenhower administration did not initiate many bold programs, officials also did not hinder progress. In the area of civil rights, for example, the administration waited for the Supreme Court to make decisions. When the 1954 *Brown v. Board of Education of Topeka* case ended segregation of schools, the Eisenhower administration backed the ruling, even sending in federal troops to Arkansas when officials there refused to allow integration of public schools.

Americans seemed to want firm leadership when needed, and mostly to be left alone, without much govern-

A Selection of Eisenhower Landmarks

Dwight D. Eisenhower Library & Museum. 200 Southeast Fourth St., Abilene, KS 67410. (785) 263-4751. The Eisenhower Center includes the house the president lived in from 1898 to 1946; a museum that includes exhibits depicting his childhood, World War II, and his presidency; the presidential library; and the final resting place of President and Mrs. Eisenhower and their first child. See http://www.eisenhower.utexas.edu/ (accessed on September 20, 2000).

Eisenhower Birthplace State Historical Park. 208 E. Day, Denison, TX 75020. (903) 465-8908. Birthplace house of the president in 1890 sits in a ten-acre park. See http://www.eisenhowerbirthplace.org/ (accessed on September 20, 2000).

Eisenhower National Historic Site. 97 Taneytown Rd., Gettysburg, PA 17325. (717) 338-9114. Retirement home of Dwight and Mamie Eisenhower, purchased by them in 1950. See http://www.nps.gov/eise/home.htm (accessed on September 20, 2000).

Mamie Doud Eisenhower Birthplace. 709 Carroll St., Boone, IA 50036. (515) 432-1896. Birthplace of the first lady. A museum and library are on the first floor. See http://www.booneiowa.com/mamie/ (accessed on September 20, 2000).

ment interference in their lives. They liked Ike for those reasons, and he governed in that manner. He was anti-communist, but he did not support the excessive investigations of Senator Joseph McCarthy. Eisenhower was a military man, but he preferred to use military power for diplomacy, rather than using it as force (as reflected in the subtitle of his White House memoirs, *Waging Peace*). He was certainly not the most active president, but a majority of Americans seemed to like it that way.

Where to Learn More

Albertson, Dean, ed. *Eisenhower as President*. New York: Hill and Wang, 1963.

Allen, Craig. *Eisenhower and the Mass Media: Peace, Prosperity, and Prime-Time TV*. Chapel Hill: University of North Carolina Press, 1993.

Baker, Jean H. *The Stevensons: A Biography of an American Family*. New York: W. W. Norton & Co., 1996.

Brandon, Piers. *Ike: His Life and Times*. New York: Harper & Row, 1986.

Brown, D. Clayton. *Dwight D. Eisenhower.* Springfield, NJ: Enslow, 1998.

Burk, Robert F. *Dwight D. Eisenhower, Hero and Politician.* Boston: Twayne, 1986.

Eisenhower, Dwight D. *At Ease: Stories I Tell to My Friends.* Garden City, NY: Doubleday, 1967. Reprint, Blue Ridge Summit, PA: TAB Books, 1988.

Eisenhower, Dwight D. *Crusade in Europe.* Garden City, NY: Doubleday, 1948. Reprint, Baltimore: Johns Hopkins University Press, 1997.

Eisenhower, Dwight D. *Selected Speeches of Dwight David Eisenhower, 34th President of the U.S.; Selected from the Three Principal Periods of His Life.* Washington, DC: Government Printing Office, 1970.

Eisenhower, Dwight D. *The White House Years: Waging Peace.* Garden City, NY: Doubleday, 1963–65.

Farrell, Robert H., ed. *The Eisenhower Diaries.* New York: Norton, 1981.

Jacobs, William Jay. *Dwight David Eisenhower: Soldier and Statesman.* New York: Franklin Watts, 1995.

Khrushchev, Sergei. *Nikita Khrushchev: Creation of a Superpower.* University Park: Pennsylvania State University Press, 2000.

Krieg, Joann P., ed. *Dwight D. Eisenhower: Soldier, President, Statesman.* Westport, CT: Greenwood, 1987.

Pach, Chester J. Jr., and Elmo Richardson. *The Presidency of Dwight D. Eisenhower.* Lawrence: University Press of Kansas, 1991.

Stevenson, Adlai. *Call to Greatness.* New York: Harper, 1954.

Taubman, William, Sergei Khrushchev, and Abbott Gleason, eds. *Nikita Khrushchev.* New Haven, CT: Yale University Press, 2000.

Warshaw, Shirley Anne, ed. *Reexamining the Eisenhower Presidency.* Westport, CT: Greenwood, 1993.

Mamie Eisenhower

Born November 14, 1896
Boone, Iowa
Died November 1, 1979
Washington, D.C.

Charming hostess was active in charitable work, not politics

Mamie Eisenhower's husband was one of the nation's most popular presidents, and she was a beloved and admired first lady. During the eight years she spent in the White House, Mrs. Eisenhower in many ways reflected conservative social values of the 1950s in her appearance and behavior: A gracious hostess, she was always smartly dressed and ready to lend her name and time to charitable concerns. In matters of public policy, however, she was almost completely inactive. She did not play a significant part in the presidential administration of **Dwight D. Eisenhower** (1890–1969; see entry in volume 4)—other than her flawless performance at social functions; even in that respect, she was a feminine ideal of her era.

"She's a career woman. Her career is 'Ike'."

Headline in the Washington Post

Valentine engagement

Born Mamie Doud on November 14, 1896, in Boone, Iowa, she was one of four daughters of a businessman who had made a fortune in the meatpacking business. The family moved to Denver, Colorado. Mamie was educated at public schools in Denver. Following her high school graduation, she

Mamie Eisenhower.
Reproduced by permission of Archive Photos.

Dwight D. Eisenhower, then a lieutenant, and Mamie Eisenhower on their wedding day, July 1, 1916. *Reproduced by permission of the Corbis Corporation.*

attended Miss Woolcott's, a private "finishing school" where young ladies learned social graces and foreign languages in preparation for upper-class marriages.

The Doud family often spent the winters in San Antonio, Texas, where they kept a vacation home. In October 1915, they were staying in Texas when Mamie met Second Lieutenant Dwight Eisenhower at Fort Sam Houston. Both Dwight and Mamie recalled years later that the attraction was mutual: She found him "just about the handsomest male I had ever seen," while he was dazzled by the "saucy look about her face and in her whole attitude." A courtship followed; on Valentine's Day 1916, Eisenhower presented Mamie with a miniature copy of his West Point ring as he proposed marriage.

The couple was married on July 1, 1916, at Mamie's family home in Denver. After a brief honeymoon, Mrs. Eisenhower moved into her husband's two-room apartment at Fort Sam Houston—the first of more than thirty temporary quarters they would share during his long service in the military. For a young society woman raised in upper-class comfort, the transition was sometimes difficult. "Ike" had to teach his bride how to cook and to live on a budget. They endured frequent separations when he was ordered away on maneuvers (military training exercises). Nevertheless, the marriage proved solid. A son, Doud Dwight Eisenhower, was born on September 24, 1917.

The family faced tragedy when little Doud (nicknamed "Icky") died of scarlet fever on January 2, 1921. Mamie in particular grieved the loss of her child, her spirits lifting again only when she delivered a second son on August 3, 1922. From this son, John Sheldon Doud Eisenhower (1922–), who himself would have a distinguished military and diplomatic career, the Eisenhowers would eventually have four grandchildren and eight great-grandchildren. (One of the grandchildren, David, would marry Julie Nixon, the daughter of Dwight Eisenhower's vice president, **Richard Nixon** [1913–1994; see entry in volume 5].)

On the move

The Eisenhower family moved frequently. Mamie and John followed Dwight to the Panama Canal Zone, the Philippines, and France, and to numerous posts in America. The first lady once estimated that she packed up her household twenty-seven times in thirty-seven years. Throughout the 1920s and 1930s, Dwight Eisenhower was advancing rapidly within the army ranks as a highly respected and efficient officer. Mrs. Eisenhower stayed out of the public eye, caring for her husband and son.

Soon after the Japanese military bombed Pearl Harbor, Hawaii, in December 1941, Dwight Eisenhower was called to Washington, D.C., to head the army's War Plans Division. Mrs. Eisenhower took an apartment at the Wardman Park Hotel in Washington. She lived there throughout the rest of World War II (1939–45) while her husband served as supreme commander of the Allied forces in Europe. Separated for all but twelve days over three years, Mamie was anxious about her husband and her son. John was a student at West Point. Mrs. Eisenhower shunned the publicity that might have come to her as the wife of the nation's most famous general. She preferred to volunteer hours with the United Service Organization (USO) and the Red Cross. The USO, formed by a variety of agencies, is most well known for providing entertainment for American armed services personnel; the organization maintains hospitality centers and social and spiritual programs as well. The Red Cross is an international organization concerned with relieving suffering and improving health.

Victory in World War II did not put an end to the couple's moving. After serving as president of Columbia University for two years, the general was called back to Europe to supervise the creation of a North Atlantic Treaty Organization (NATO) military force. Although they had purchased a farm near Gettysburg, Pennsylvania, in 1949, Dwight and Mamie Eisenhower were not able to live there for eleven more years. Eight of those years were spent in the White House, their last of many temporary residences.

First lady

Like so many first ladies before her, Mamie Eisenhower was not thrilled by the loss of privacy she experienced as the president's wife. Especially embarrassing were questions about her use of alcohol. Mrs. Eisenhower was afflicted with Ménière's disease, a disorder of the inner ear that sometimes caused her to stagger and stumble as if she had been drinking. Mrs. Eisenhower was content to say very little about her private life during the campaign and after beginning her two terms as first lady.

As wife of the president, Mamie Eisenhower reflected the traditions of her times. She made a point of dressing elegantly, and she was a distinct influence on fashion during the 1950s. Equally elegant were the dinners and parties she presided over at the White House, events that mirrored the nation's prosperity and its place in world affairs. Only when President Eisenhower suffered a serious heart attack in 1955 did her duties become slightly more official, as she answered her husband's correspondence, supervised his recovery, and reassured the public about his condition.

When President Eisenhower had regained his health enough to seek a second term, Mrs. Eisenhower supported his decision. She was aware that her husband still needed to be active, and she had discovered that she genuinely enjoyed the role of first lady. However, the Eisenhowers' second term was not as lively with parties as the first term: the couple traveled frequently and were mindful of the president's ailing heart.

"I Like Ike" was a popular slogan for the Eisenhower campaign. Mamie Eisenhower, in fun, had worn a button that said "Ike Likes Me." And Ike, in turn, pinned on a button that said, "I Like Mamie."
Reproduced by permission of the Corbis Corporation.

At the end of her eight years in the White House, Mrs. Eisenhower had never given a press conference on a national issue, nor had she contributed in any serious way to her husband's domestic or foreign policy decisions. Nevertheless, she was a celebrity in her own right, admired as a loving wife, mother, and grandmother, and copied from her clothing to her hairstyle.

When Dwight Eisenhower's presidency ended in 1961, the couple retired to their farm in Gettysburg, where they lived quietly until Dwight died in 1969. Mamie continued to live at the farm for much of the next decade, continuing her work for charitable causes in her husband's name. She died on November 1, 1979, in Washington, D.C., and was buried next to her husband in a chapel—the Place of Meditation—located at the Eisenhower Center, in Abilene, Kansas.

Where to Learn More

David, Lester, and Irene David. *Ike and Mamie: The Story of the General and His Lady.* New York: Putnam, 1981.

Eisenhower, Susan. *Mrs. Ike: Memories and Reflections on the Life of Mamie Eisenhower.* New York: Farrar, Straus and Giroux, 1996.

Sinnott, Susan. *Mamie Doud Eisenhower, 1896–1979.* New York: Children's Press, 2000.

Eisenhower's Farewell Address to the Nation

Delivered to Congress and broadcast on radio and television on January 17, 1961; excerpted from *Dwight D. Eisenhower Library & Museum* (Web site)

America's World War II hero warns the nation to be responsible with its economic, military, and technological power

During his eight years in the White House, President Dwight D. Eisenhower (1890–1969; see entry in volume 4) presided over an America that was experiencing a postwar economic boom. In the years following World War II (1939–45), jobs were plentiful, many new homes and roads were constructed, and confidence in the American system was high. There were profound concerns as well: Americans were disturbed by communist values abroad and the threat of nuclear war. (Communists believe that private property should be banned and goods distributed by a central government should be available for all according to their needs.) At home, racial inequalities continued to challenge American ideals.

President Eisenhower was a popular president who could have bid a fond farewell to the nation and rested on his high public rating. Instead, he used the occasion of his farewell address to discuss issues of concern. He urged Americans to be responsible with their economic, military, and technological power.

"Good judgment seeks balance and progress; lack of it eventually finds imbalance and frustration."

Dwight D. Eisenhower

Things to remember while reading President Eisenhower's farewell address to the nation:

- The tense relationship between the United States and communist nations—a situation often referred to as the Cold War—was evident early in the speech: referring to communism as "a hostile ideology," Eisenhower urged Americans to be wary of communist expansionism. Setting the theme of his address, Eisenhower called for Americans to be responsible and remain on a course of "peace and human betterment."

- After World War II, the American defense industry began to flourish. Prior to that time, when large amounts of war materials were needed, they were produced by converting industrial production to the manufacturing of war supplies. For example, automobile factories stopped producing cars during World Wars I and II in order to make military vehicles, airplanes, boats, and even helmets and bullets. Eisenhower cautioned Americans about the new defense industry: while recognizing that it was necessary, he insisted that Americans should ensure that the industry support "our peaceful methods and goals."

- Eisenhower supported limiting the influence of the federal government. Rather than believing that more government involvement could solve problems, he expressed concern that individual initiative might become overwhelmed. Just as he urged Americans to be aware of the growing defense industry, he warned about advances sponsored by the government in science and technology that could prove more harmful than beneficial. Computer technology, in its early stage at the time, was among the areas in which Eisenhower called for responsible development.

- Eisenhower concluded by stressing the importance of balance (through judgment and responsibility) and respect toward other nations and to people of all faiths and races. Eisenhower became world famous through his conduct of war; he officially ended his public career with a long sentence expressing the aspiration for peace "guaranteed by the binding force of mutual respect and love."

President Eisenhower's farewell address to the nation

*America is today the strongest, the most influential and most productive nation in the world. Understandably proud of this **pre-eminence,** we yet realize that America's leadership and prestige depend, not merely upon our unmatched material progress, riches and military strength, but on how we use our power in the interests of world peace and human **betterment.***

Throughout America's adventure in free government, such basic purposes have been to keep the peace; to foster progress in human achievement, and to enhance liberty, dignity and integrity among peoples and among nations.

To strive for less would be unworthy of a free and religious people.

Any failure traceable to arrogance or our lack of comprehension or readiness to sacrifice would inflict upon us a grievous hurt, both at home and abroad.

*Progress toward these noble goals is persistently threatened by the conflict now **engulfing** the world. It commands our whole attention, absorbs our very beings. We face a **hostile ideology** global in scope, **atheistic** in character, **ruthless** in purpose, and **insidious** in method. Unhappily the danger it poses promises to be of indefinite duration. To meet it successfully, there is called for, not so much the emotional and transitory sacrifices of crisis, but rather those which enable us to carry forward steadily, surely, and without complaint the burdens of a prolonged and complex struggle—with liberty the stake. Only thus shall we remain, despite every **provocation,** on our charted course toward permanent peace and human betterment.*

Crises there will continue to be. In meeting them, whether foreign or domestic, great or small, there is a recurring temptation to feel that some spectacular and costly action could become the miraculous solution to all current difficulties. A huge increase in the newer elements of our defenses; development of unrealistic programs to cure every ill in agriculture; a dramatic expansion in basic and applied research—these and many other possibilities, each possibly promising in itself, may be suggested as the only way to the road we wish to travel.

Pre-eminence: Superiority.

Betterment: Improvement.

Engulfing: Overwhelming.

Hostile ideology: Eisenhower is referring to communism.

Atheistic: Denial of the existence of God.

Ruthless: Cruel.

Insidious: Gradually harmful.

Provocation: Intended fight.

But each proposal must be weighed in light of a broader consideration; the need to maintain balance in and among national programs—balance between the private and the public economy, balance between the cost and hoped for advantages—balance between the clearly necessary and the comfortably desirable; balance between our essential requirements as a nation and the duties imposed by the nation upon the individual; balance between the actions of the moment and the national welfare of the future. Good judgment seeks balance and progress; lack of it eventually finds imbalance and frustration.

The record of many decades stands as proof that our people and their Government have, in the main, understood these truths and have responded to them well in the face of threat and stress.

But threats, new in kind or degree, constantly arise.

Of these, I mention two only.

A vital element in keeping the peace is our military establishment. Our arms must be mighty, ready for instant action, so that no potential aggressor may be tempted to risk his own destruction.

Our military organization today bears little relation to that known by any of my predecessors in peacetime, or indeed by the fighting men of World War II or Korea.

Until the latest of our world conflicts, the United States had no **armaments industry**. *American makers of* **plowshares** *could, with time and as required, make swords as well. But now we can no longer risk emergency improvisation of national defense; we have been compelled to create a permanent armaments industry of vast proportions. Added to this, three and a half million men and women are directly engaged in the defense establishment. We annually spend on military security more than the net income of all United States corporations.*

This conjunction of an immense military establishment and a large arms industry is new in the American experience. The total influence—economic, political, even spiritual—is felt in every city, every Statehouse, every office of the Federal government. We recognize the imperative need for this development. Yet we must not fail to comprehend its grave implications. Our toil, resources and livelihood are all involved; so is the very structure of our society.

In the councils of government, we must guard against the acquisition of **unwarranted** *influence, whether sought or unsought, by*

Armaments industry: Industry manufacturing products of war.

Plowshares: Farm cutting tools.

Unwarranted: Unreasonable.

the **military-industrial complex.** The potential for the disastrous rise of misplaced power exists and will persist.

We must never let the weight of this combination endanger our liberties or democratic processes. We should take nothing for granted. Only an alert and knowledgeable citizenry can compel the proper **meshing** of the huge industrial and military machinery of defense with our peaceful methods and goals, so that security and liberty may prosper together.

Akin to, and largely responsible for the sweeping changes in our industrial-military posture, has been the technological revolution during recent decades.

In this revolution, research has become central, it also becomes more formalized, complex, and costly. A steadily increasing share is conducted for, by, or at the direction of, the Federal government.

Today, the solitary inventor, tinkering in his shop, has been overshadowed by task forces of scientists in laboratories and testing fields. In the same fashion, the free university, historically the **fountainhead** of free ideas and scientific discovery, has experienced a revolution in the conduct of research. Partly because of the huge costs involved, a government contract becomes virtually a substitute for intellectual curiosity. For every old blackboard there are now hundreds of new electronic computers.

The prospect of domination of the nation's scholars by Federal employment, project **allocations**, and the power of money is ever present—and is gravely to be regarded.

Yet, in holding scientific research and discovery in respect, as we should, we must also be alert to the equal and opposite danger that public policy could itself become the captive of a scientific-technological **elite.**

It is the task of statesmanship to mold, to balance, and to integrate these and other forces, new and old, within the principles of our democratic system—ever aiming toward the supreme goals of our free society.

Another factor in maintaining balance involves the element of time. As we peer into society's future, we—you and I, and our government—must avoid the impulse to live only for today, **plundering,** for our own ease and convenience, the precious resources of tomorrow. We cannot mortgage the material assets of our grandchildren without asking the loss also of their political and spiritual heritage.

Military-industrial complex: Industries that build weapons and other items used by the military.

Meshing: Coordination.

Fountainhead: Source.

Allocations: Portions of money provided by one source, in this case the government.

Elite: A group of people who wield power and influence.

Plundering: Stealing.

*We want democracy to survive for all generations to come, not to become the **insolvent phantom** of tomorrow.*

Down the long lane of the history yet to be written America knows that this world of ours, ever growing smaller, must avoid becoming a community of dreadful fear and hate, and be, instead, a proud confederation of mutual trust and respect.

Such a confederation must be one of equals. The weakest must come to the conference table with the same confidence as do we, protected as we are by our moral, economic, and military strength. That table, though scarred by many past frustrations, cannot be abandoned for the certain agony of the battlefield.

***Disarmament**, with mutual honor and confidence, is a continuing imperative. Together we must learn how to compose differences, not with arms, but with intellect and decent purpose. Because this need is so sharp and apparent I confess that I lay down my official responsibilities in this field with a definite sense of disappointment. As one who has witnessed the horror and the lingering sadness of war—as one who knows that another war could utterly destroy this civilization which has been so slowly and painfully built over thousands of years—I wish I could say tonight that a lasting peace is in sight.*

Happily, I can say that war has been avoided. Steady progress toward our ultimate goal has been made. But, so much remains to be done. As a private citizen, I shall never cease to do what little I can to help the world advance along that road.

So—in this my last good night to you as your President—I thank you for the many opportunities you have given me for public service in war and peace. I trust that in that service you find some things worthy; as for the rest of it, I know you will find ways to improve performance in the future.

You and I—my fellow citizens—need to be strong in our faith that all nations, under God, will reach the goal of peace with justice. May we be ever unswerving in devotion to principle, confident but humble with power, diligent in pursuit of the Nations' great goals.

To all the peoples of the world, I once more give expression to America's prayerful and continuing aspiration: We pray that peoples of all faiths, all races, all nations, may have their great human needs satisfied; that those now denied opportunity shall come to enjoy it to the full; that all who yearn for freedom may experience its spiritual blessings; that those who have freedom will understand, also, its

Insolvent phantom: Ghost; a being without life.

Disarmament: Giving up weapons.

heavy responsibilities; that all who are insensitive to the needs of others will learn charity; that the scourges of poverty, disease and ignorance will be made to disappear from the earth, and that, in the goodness of time, all peoples will come to live together in a peace guaranteed by the binding force of mutual respect and love. (Dwight D. Eisenhower Library & Museum *[Web site]*)

What happened next . . .

The American defense industry continued to grow, as the arms race (amount of weapons) between the Soviet Union and the United States dominated government spending in both nations through the 1980s. In an effort to stop the spread of communism, the United States became involved in several conflicts, including the Vietnam War.

Advances in science and technology were abundant through the end of the twentieth century. In general, those developments have been greatly beneficial to improving the quality of life. The potential for less desirable results remains, making Eisenhower's call for all Americans to remain informed and responsible continually relevant.

Eisenhower's call for more limited government was not heeded. The promise of a "new frontier," inspired by Eisenhower's successor, **John F. Kennedy** (1917–1963; see entry in volume 5), faded by the mid-1960s with violence and social unrest: Kennedy was assassinated; America became deeply involved in an unpopular war in Vietnam; the civil rights movement enjoyed success, but racial tensions, violence, and inequality persisted; and government attempts to cure social ills, such as poverty and urban decay, did not produce lasting improvement.

Did you know . . .

- "You do not lead by hitting people over the head," was one of Eisenhower's favorite sayings. As president, he remained above party politics and threw his support to programs he believed were beneficial, including the expansion of social security. He excelled as a military leader, but he hated war "as only a soldier who has lived it can." And in his final speech as president, he warned the nation about the temptation of using military power excessively, and of the growing business of manufacturing weapons.

Where to Learn More

"Farewell Address." *Dwight D. Eisenhower Library & Museum* [Online] http://www.eisenhower.utexas.edu/farewell.htm (accessed on September 20, 2000).

Medhurst, Martin J. *Dwight D. Eisenhower: Strategic Communicator.* Westport, CT: Greenwood Press, 1993.

Pach, Chester J., and Elmo Richardson. *The Presidency of Dwight D. Eisenhower.* Lawrence: University of Kansas Press, 1991.

Stassen, Harold, and Marshall Houts. *Eisenhower: Turning the World Toward Peace.* St. Paul: Merrill/Magnus, 1990.

Where to Learn More

The following list of resources focuses on material appropriate for middle school or high school students. Please note that the web site addresses were verified prior to publication, but are subject to change.

Books

Bailey, Thomas A. *The Pugnacious Presidents: White House Warriors on Parade.* New York: Free Press, 1980.

Barber, James David. *The Presidential Character: Predicting Performance in the White House.* 4th ed. Englewood Cliffs, NJ: Prentice-Hall, 1992.

Barzman, Sol. *Madmen and Geniuses: The Vice-Presidents of the United States.* Chicago: Follett, 1974.

Berube, Maurice. *American Presidents and Education.* Westport, CT: Greenwood Press, 1991.

Boller, Paul F., Jr. *Presidential Anecdotes.* Rev. ed. New York: Oxford, 1996.

Boller, Paul F., Jr. *Presidential Campaigns.* Rev. ed. New York: Oxford, 1996.

Boller, Paul F. Jr. *Presidential Wives: An Anecdotal History.* Rev. ed. New York: Oxford, 1998.

Brace, Paul, Christine B. Harrington, and Gary King, eds. *The Presidency in American Politics.* New York: New York University Press, 1989.

Brallier, Jess, and Sally Chabert. *Presidential Wit and Wisdom.* New York: Penguin, 1996.

Brinkley, Alan, and Davis Dyer, eds. *The Reader's Companion to the American Presidency*. New York: Houghton Mifflin, 2000.

Brogan, Hugh, and Charles Mosley. *American Presidential Families*. New York: Macmillan Publishing Co., 1993.

Bumann, Joan. *Our American Presidents: From Washington through Clinton*. St. Petersburg, FL: Willowisp Press, 1993.

Campbell, Colin. *The U.S. Presidency in Crisis: A Comparative Perspective*. New York: Oxford University Press, 1998.

Clotworthy, William G. *Presidential Sites*. Blacksburg, VA: McDonald & Woodward, 1998.

Cook, Carolyn. *Imagine You Are the . . . President*. Edina, MN: Imaginarium, 1999.

Cooke, Donald Ewin. *Atlas of the Presidents*. Maplewood, NJ: Hammond, 1985.

Cronin, Thomas, ed. *Inventing the American Presidency*. Lawrence: University of Kansas Press, 1989.

Cunliffe, Marcus. *American Presidents and the Presidency*. New York: Houghton Mifflin, 1986.

Dallek, Robert. *Hail to the Chief: The Making and Unmaking of American Presidents*. New York: Hyperion, 1996.

Davis, James W. *The American Presidency*. 2nd ed. Westport, CT: Praeger, 1995.

DeGregorio, William. *The Complete Book of U.S. Presidents*. 4th ed. New York: Barricade Books, 1993.

Fields, Wayne. *Union of Words: A History of Presidential Eloquence*. New York: The Free Press, 1996.

Fisher, Louis. *Presidential War Power*. Lawrence: University of Kansas Press, 1995.

Frank, Sid, and Arden Davis Melick. *Presidents: Tidbits and Trivia*. Maplewood, NJ: Hammond, 1986.

Frost, Elizabeth, ed. *The Bully Pulpit: Quotations from America's Presidents*. New York: Facts On File, 1988.

Genovese, Michael. *The Power of the American Presidency, 1789–2000*. New York: Oxford, 2001.

Gerhardt, Michael J. *The Federal Impeachment Process: A Constitutional and Historical Analysis*. 2nd ed. Chicago: University of Chicago Press, 2000.

Goehlert, Robert U., and Fenton S. Martin. *The Presidency: A Research Guide*. Santa Barbara, CA: ABC-Clio Information Services, 1985.

Havel, James T. *U.S. Presidential Candidates and the Elections: A Biographical and Historical Guide*. New York: Macmillan Library Reference USA, 1996.

Henry, Christopher E. *The Electoral College*. New York: Franklin Watts, 1996.

Henry, Christopher E. *Presidential Elections*. New York: Franklin Watts, 1996.

Hess, Stephen. *Presidents and the Presidency: Essays*. Washington, DC: The Brookings Institution, 1996.

Israel, Fred L., ed. *The Presidents*. Danbury, CT: Grolier Educational, 1996.

Jackson, John S. III, and William Crotty. *The Politics of Presidential Selection*. 2nd ed. New York: Longman, 2001.

Jamieson, Kathleen Hall. *Packaging the Presidency: A History and Criticism of Presidential Campaign Advertising*. 3rd ed. New York: Oxford, 1996.

Kessler, Paula N., and Justin Segal. *The Presidents Almanac*. Rev. ed. Los Angeles: Lowell House Juvenile, 1998.

Kruh, David, and Louis Kruh. *Presidential Landmarks*. New York: Hippocrene Books, 1992.

Kunhardt, Philip B. Jr., Philip B. Kunhardt III, and Peter W. Kunhardt. *The American President*. New York: Penguin, 1999.

Laird, Archibald. *The Near Great—Chronicle of the Vice Presidents*. North Quincy, MA: Christopher Publishing House, 1980.

Mayer, William G., ed. *In Pursuit of the White House: How We Choose Our Presidential Nominees*. Chatham, NJ: Chatham House, 1996.

Murray, Robert K., and Tim H. Blessing. *Greatness in the White House: Rating the Presidents*. 2nd ed. University Park: Pennsylvania State University Press, 1994.

Neustadt, Richard E. *Presidential Power and the Modern Presidents: The Politics of Leadership from Roosevelt to Reagan*. New York: The Free Press, 1990.

Patrick, Diane. *The Executive Branch*. New York: Franklin Watts, 1994.

Presidents of the United States. A World Book Encyclopedia. Chicago: Field Enterprises Educational Corp., 1973.

Riccards, Michael, and James MacGregor Burns. *The Ferocious Engine of Democracy: A History of the American Presidency. Vol I: From the Origins through William McKinley. Vol. II: Theodore Roosevelt through George Bush*. Lanham, MD: Madison Books, 1996.

Robb, Don. *Hail to the Chief: The American Presidency*. Watertown, MA: Charlesbridge, 2000.

Rose, Gary L. *The American Presidency Under Siege*. Albany: State University of New York Press, 1997.

Sanders, Mark C. *The Presidency*. Austin, TX: Steadwell Books, 2000.

Shenkman, Richard. *Presidential Ambition: How the Presidents Gained Power, Kept Power, and Got Things Done*. New York: HarperCollins, 1999.

Shogan, Robert. *The Double-Edged Sword: How Character Makes and Ruins Presidents, from Washington to Clinton*. Boulder, CO: Westview Press, 2000.

Sisung, Kelle S., ed. *Presidential Administration Profiles for Students*. Detroit: Gale Group, 2000.

Smith, Nancy Kegan, and Mary C. Ryan, eds. *Modern First Ladies: Their Documentary Legacy*. Washington, DC: National Archives and Records Administration, 1989.

Stier, Catherine. *If I Were President*. Morton Grove, IL: Albert Whitman, 1999.

Suid, Murray I. *How to Be President of the U.S.A.* Palo Alto, CA: Monday Morning Books, 1992.

Truman, Margaret. *First Ladies: An Intimate Group Portrait of White House Wives*. New York: Ballantine, 1995.

Vidal, Gore. *The American Presidency*. Monroe, ME: Odonian Press, 1998.

Wheeless, Carl. *Landmarks of American Presidents*. Detroit: Gale, 1995.

Video

The American President. Written, produced, and directed by Philip B. Kunhardt Jr., Philip B. Kunhardt III, and Peter W. Kunhardt. Co-production of Kunhardt Productions and Thirteen/WNET in New York. 10 programs.

Web Sites

The American Presidency: Selected Resources, An Informal Reference Guide (Web site). [Online] http://www.interlink-cafe.com/uspresidents/ (accessed on December 11, 2000).

C-Span. *American Presidents: Life Portraits.* [Online] http://www.american presidents.org/ (accessed on December 11, 2000).

Grolier, Inc. *Grolier Presents: The American Presidency.* [Online] http://gi.grolier. com/presidents/ea/prescont.html (accessed on December 11, 2000).

Internet Public Library. *POTUS: Presidents of the United States.* [Online] http:// www.ipl.org/ref/POTUS/index.html (accessed on December 11, 2000).

Public Broadcasting System. "The American President." *The American Experience.* [Online] http://www.pbs.org/wgbh/amex/presidents/nf/intro/intro. html (accessed on December 11, 2000).

University of Oklahoma Law Center. *A Chronology of US Historical Documents.* [Online] http://www.law.ou.edu/hist/ (accessed on December 11, 2000).

White House. *Welcome to the White House.* [Online] http://www.whitehouse. gov/ (accessed on December 11, 2000).

The White House Historical Association. [Online] http://www.whitehousehistory. org/whha/default.asp (accessed on December 11, 2000).

Yale Law School. *The Avalon at the Yale Law School: Documents in Law, History and Diplomacy.* [Online] http://www.yale.edu/lawweb/avalon/avalon. htm (accessed on December 11, 2000).

Index

A

Abolitionists, *2:* 410, 483, 502–3, 513
  Adams, John Quincy, *1:* 234
  Brown, John, *2:* 526–27, 528–29, 529 (ill.), 540, 559
  Buchanan's warning, *2:* 540
  Fugitive Slave Law, *2:* 496–97
  Hayes, Lucy and Rutherford B., *3:* 685, 700–701
  Stowe, Harriet Beecher, *2:* 467, 470–71, 471 (ill.), 513
Abortion, *5:* 1425, 1477
Absentee ballots, election of 2000, *5:* 1614
Adams, Abigail, *1:* **75–80,** 75 (ill.), 221
  correspondence, *1:* 89, 222–23
  life as first lady, *1:* 78–79
  life in England and France, *1:* 77–78
  marriage and family, *1:* 76
  opinion of Louisa Adams, *1:* 239, 241
  "Presidential Palace," *1:* 79
  Revolutionary War, *1:* 76–77
Adams, Anne Abbott, *4:* 977
Adams, Charles Francis, election of 1848, *2:* 439

Adams, George, *1:* 243
Adams, John, *1:* **53–74,** 55 (ill.), 63 (ill.), 133 (ill.)
  administration, *1:* 62
  Alien and Sedition Acts, *1:* 66–70
  American Revolution, *1:* 58–60
  Boston attorney, *1:* 57–58
  Committee of Five, *1:* 126
  Continental Congress, *1:* 59
  correspondence with Abigail, *1:* 89
  Defence of the Constitutions of Government of the United States of America, *1:* 59
  diplomatic career, *1:* 59
  election of 1789, *1:* 19
  election of 1792, *1:* 19
  election of 1796, *1:* 61; *5:* 1612
  election of 1800, *1:* 109
  first vice president, *1:* 18, 60–62
  government moves to Washington, D.C., *1:* 70–71
  inaugural speech, *1:* 62
  Jefferson, Thomas, *1:* 108–9, 110, 119
  marriage and family, *1:* 57, 76, 78, 80
  minister to Britain, *1:* 59
  presidency, *1:* 62–71
  Puritan legacy, *1:* 56–57

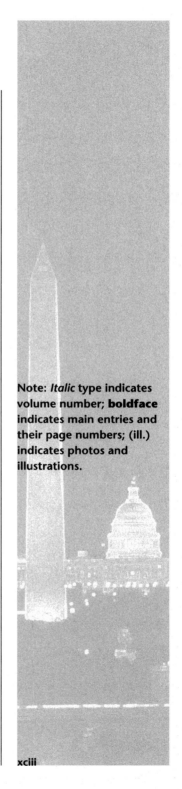

Note: *Italic* type indicates volume number; **boldface** indicates main entries and their page numbers; (ill.) indicates photos and illustrations.

retirement, *1:* 71–72
"Thoughts on Government," *1:* 59, **81–89**
Adams, John II, *1:* 243
Adams, John Quincy, *1:* 67, 211 (ill.), **217–37**, 219 (ill.); *5:* 1279, 1618
  abolitionist, *1:* 234–35, 246
  Amistad case, *1:* 235, **245–53**
  ancestry, *1:* 221
  Calhoun, John C., *1:* 270
  Clay, Henry, *1:* 226–27, 266
  contested election, *1:* 226–27
  daily routine, *1:* 232
  death, *1:* 235
  diplomatic career, *1:* 220, 224–25, 241–42
  early years, *1:* 221–23
  election of 1820, *1:* 193
  election of 1824, *1:* 227, 266, 298; *2:* 399; *5:* 1612
  election of 1828, *1:* 232, 266, 267, 298
  European travels, *1:* 223–25
  Harrison, William Henry, *2:* 334–35
  Jackson, Andrew, *1:* 219–20, 226–27, 236, 265; *2:* 519
  legal and writing careers, *1:* 224
  marriage and family, *1:* 224, 225–26, 233, 240
  Monroe years, *1:* 203
  "Old Man Eloquent," *1:* 233–35
  presidency, *1:* 227–32
  Van Buren, Martin, *1:* 246, 297
Adams, Louisa, *1:* **239–44**, 239 (ill.), 243 (ill.)
  British heritage, *1:* 239, 240
  diplomatic travel, *1:* 241–44
  family tragedies, *1:* 243
  London years, *1:* 240–41
  marriage and family, *1:* 240–41, 242
  writer, *1:* 240, 244
Adams, Nabby, *1:* 80
Adams, Samuel Hopkins, *3:* 924
Address to Congress on the Crisis in Kuwait (George Bush), *5:* **1537–44**
Adenauer, Konrad, *4:* 994 (ill.)
Advisory Committee on Government Organization, *5:* 1412
AEF. *See* American Expeditionary Force (AEF) (World War I)
Aerial surveillance, of Soviet Union by United States, *4:* 1245, 1250–51
Afghanistan, *5:* 1467
African Americans. *See also* Civil rights

Brown v. Board of Education of Topeka, *2:* 561; *4:* 1249; *5:* 1292
  Carter, Jimmy, *5:* 1444
  cavalry unit, *4:* 970
  Jim Crow laws, *3:* 871
  Kennedy, John F., *5:* 1290–91
  Missouri Compromise, *1:* 199
  Populists, *3:* 823
  Reconstruction, *3:* 655–56
  Roosevelt, Eleanor, *4:* 1164
  segregation, *2:* 596; *4:* 1045
  World War II, *4:* 1232
African Game Trails (Theodore Roosevelt), *3:* 899
Africans, slave trade cases, *1:* 246
"Age of Jackson," *1:* 257; *2:* 603
The Age of Reason (Paine), *1:* 191
Agnew, Spiro T., *5:* 1380, 1406, 1408
  election of 1968, *5:* 1366
  election of 1972, *5:* 1366
Agrarian movement. *See* Populism
Agricultural Adjustment Administration (AAA), *4:* 1172
Agricultural Marketing Act, *4:* 1097–98
Agriculture, Populism, *3:* 823
Air Commerce Act, *4:* 1067
Air Force One, *4:* 1251
Air strikes, North Vietnam, *5:* 1334
Air traffic controllers strike, *5:* 1481
Airplane, *3:* 901
Alabama, *2:* 562
  King, Martin Luther, Jr., *5:* 1293
  Wallace, George, *5:* 1291
Alabama, *2:* 611; *3:* 654–55, 656
Alaska, *2:* 611, 613
  Gold Rush, *3:* 849, 860
  Harding tour, *4:* 1030
Albanians, in Serbia, *5:* 1564
Albany Regency, *1:* 297, 312
Albright, Madeleine, *5:* 1561, 1562–63, 1563 (ill.), 1564, 1565
Alcoa (Aluminum Company of America), *4:* 1022
Alcoholic beverages. *See also* Prohibition; Temperance movement
  Coolidge, Calvin, *4:* 1059–60
  Grant, Ulysses S., *3:* 643
  Harding, Warren G., *4:* 1020
  Harrison, William Henry, *2:* 335, 337
  Johnson, Andrew, *2:* 607
  Pierce, Franklin, *2:* 489–90
Alden, John and Priscilla, *1:* 221
Algiers Treaty, *1:* 26, 29
Alien Acts, *1:* 67, 68–69, 108
Alien and Sedition Acts, *1:* 66–70, 68–69, 108–9, 154
  Alien Act, *1:* 68–69

Alien Enemies Act, *1:* 67, 68
    Naturalization Act, *1:* 67
    Sedition Act, *1:* 69
Alien Enemies Act, *1:* 67, 68
Alliance for Progress, *5:* 1284
Allied Powers (World War I), *4:*
    973–76, 1004, 1005, 1010,
    1046
Allied Powers (World War II), *4:*
    1147, 1150, 1181, 1221, 1235,
    1241, 1242
Alternative energy sources, *5:* 1448
Aluminum Company of America
    (Alcoa), *4:* 1022
Alzheimer's disease, *5:* 1489,
    1493–94, 1499
Amendment(s). *See* Bill of Rights;
    Constitution; specific amend-
    ment, e.g., Twelfth Amend-
    ment
"America First," *4:* 1025
American Ballet Theater, *5:* 1329–30
American Colonization Society, *1:*
    198
American Expeditionary Force (AEF)
    (World War I), *4:* 971, 1002–3
American imperialism. *See* Imperial-
    ism
American Indians. *See* Native Amer-
    icans
American Individualism (Hoover), *4:*
    1116
American (Know Nothing) Party, *2:*
    469, 484
An American Life (Reagan), *5:* 1489
American military, World War I, *4:*
    971, 976, 1002–3
"American Prince of Wales." *See*
    Adams, John Quincy
American Relief Administration
    (ARA), *4:* 1092, 1093 (ill.),
    1111
American Revolution, *1:* 10–16, 11
    (ill.), 82
    Adams, John and Abigail, *1:* 76
    Adams, John Quincy, *1:* 223
    Anti-British sentiment, *1:* 9
    Declaration of Independence, *1:*
        125–34
    Franklin, Benjamin, *1:* 17
    Jackson, Andrew, *1:* 260–61
    Jefferson, Thomas, *1:* 98–99,
        101–2
    Lafayette, Marquis de, *1:* 33 (ill.),
        186–87, 187 (ill.)
    Marshall, John, *1:* 64–65
    Monroe, James, *1:* 182–83, 205–6
    Paine, Thomas, *1:* 190
    privateers, *1:* 205
    Randolph, Edmund Jennings, *2:*
        362

Washington, George, *1:* 10–16,
    11 (ill.)
Washington, Martha, *1:* 32–34
"American System" (Clay), *1:* 228,
    230–31
Americans, Reagan's view, *5:* 1502
Americans with Disabilities Act, *5:*
    1521
Americas, Monroe Doctrine, *1:* 200
Ames, Oakes, *3:* 657
Amistad case, *1:* 234, 245–46
    closing argument (John Quincy
        Adams), *1:* **245–53**
Anderson, John, election of 1980, *5:*
    1477, 1478
Anderson, Marian, *4:* 994 (ill.),
    1164
Andropov, Yuri, *5:* 1484
Angola, *5:* 1415
Annexation, Texas, *1:* 308
Annual Address to Congress. *See
    also* State of the Union Address
    Arthur, Chester A., *3:* **769–74**
    Buchanan, James, *2:* **539–48**
    Fillmore, Millard, *2:* **479–84**
    Grant, Ulysses S., *3:* 659
    Johnson, Andrew, *2:* **629–36**
    Roosevelt, Theodore, *3:* **909–16**
    Taft, William Howard, *3:* **949–56**
    Taylor, Zachary, *2:* **451–56**
Antelope case, *1:* 246
Anthony, Susan B., *3:* 785, 786–87,
    787 (ill.)
Anti-American sentiment, Iran, *5:*
    1450–51
Anti-Communism, *4:* 1143
Antidrug campaign, *5:* 1493
Antietam, Battle of, *2:* 568, 582
Anti-Federalist(s), *1:* 45, 60, 135–36,
    141, 153. *See also* Democratic-
    Republican Party; Federalist(s)
    vs. Anti-Federalist(s)
Anti-Imperialism League, *3:* 791
Anti-Jacksonians, *1:* 51; *2:* 364
Anti-Masonic Party, *1:* 300; *2:*
    461–62, 608
Antislavery. *See* Abolition
Antitrust laws, *3:* 915
Anti-union legislation, *4:* 1203
Antiwar (Vietnam War) protests, *5:*
    1334, 1335, 1337, 1366,
    1391–92, 1396–97
    Reagan, Ronald, *5:* 1475–76
    "Silent Majority" Speech
        (Nixon), *5:* **1391–97**
Apaches, *4:* 970
Apartheid, *5:* 1522
Appleton, Jane Means. *See* Pierce,
    Jane
Appleton, Jesse, *2:* 505

Appomattox Court House, *2:* 570, 596; *3:* 645, 649, 650, 671, 672–73
Appropriations bills, *3:* 736
Appropriations committee
　Garfield, James A., *3:* 717
　Truman, Harry S., *4:* 1193
Apshur, Abel, *2:* 380
Arafat, Yasser, *5:* 1565 (ill.), 1568
Argonne Forest, *4:* 971
Argument in Defense of William Freeman (Seward), *2:* 612
Arista, Mariano, *2:* 406
Arizona, *2:* 503
　O'Connor, Sandra Day, *5:* 1486–87
Arkansas
　Clinton, Bill, *5:* 1549, 1553–54, 1583
　Clinton, Hillary Rodham, *5:* 1583
　joins Confederacy, *2:* 563
Arkansas Education Standards Committee, *5:* 1583
Arlington National Cemetery, *3:* 948
"Armed neutrality," *4:* 998
Armenia, *5:* 1485
Armistice, World War I, *4:* 1003
Arms race, *4:* 1244, 1264, 1269. *See also* Cold War
Army
　Confederate. *See* Confederate Army
　Union. *See* Union Army
　World War I, *4:* 971, 976, 1002–3
　World War II, *4:* 1232
Army Appropriations Act, *2:* 618
Arnold, Benedict, *1:* 13, 15
Art and arts
　Harrison, Caroline, *3:* 827
　Kennedy, John F., *5:* 1312–13
　Lane, Harriet, *2:* 537, 538
　Mellon, Andrew W., *4:* 1023
　White House, *4:* 1075–76
　Wilson, Ellen, *4:* 989
Arthur, Chester A., *3:* 745–63, 747 (ill.), 754 (ill.), 755 (ill.), 759 (ill.)
　administration, *3:* 760
　civil rights, *3:* 750–51
　civil service reform, *3:* 697, 748, 760, 782
　Civil War service, *3:* 751, 766
　crier for Clay, *3:* 749
　customs collector, *3:* 695, 697, 753, 766
　early years, *3:* 748–50
　effectiveness as president, *3:* 761
　election of 1880, *3:* 718, 754–55, 767

"Elegant Arthur," *3:* 747, 761, 765
First Annual Message to Congress, *3:* 769–74
Garfield assassination, *3:* 758–59
marriage and family, *3:* 751, 758, 766–67
political career, *3:* 750–58
political patronage, *3:* 747, 748, 781
presidency, *3:* 758–61
Arthur, Ellen, *3:* 758, 765 (ill.), 765–68
　Chester's sister as White House hostess, *3:* 768
　marriage and family, *3:* 766–67
　tributes from Chester, *3:* 767
　untimely death, *3:* 767
Articles of Confederation, *1:* 37–44, 183
　authority of Congress, *1:* 38, 43
　failure leads to Constitution, *1:* 38, 43
Articles of Impeachment, *5:* 1377
Ash Lawn (Monroe), *1:* 188, 201, 208, 214
Asia, *3:* 935–36, 955
Asia (Southeast), Eisenhower, Dwight D., *4:* 1245–48
Asian Americans, *5:* 1338
"Ask not what your country can do for you" (Kennedy), *5:* 1307
Assassination attempts
　Ford, Gerald R., *5:* 1414
　Reagan, Ronald, *5:* 1479, 1479 (ill.), 1493, 1518
　Roosevelt, Franklin D., *4:* 1135
　Roosevelt, Theodore, *3:* 900
　Truman, Harry S., *4:* 1207
　Wallace, George C., *5:* 1366
Assassinations
　Garfield, James A., *3:* 722–23, 731–32, 752, 758–59
　Kennedy, John F., *5:* 1273, 1291–94, 1304, 1312, 1317, 1323–25
　Kennedy, Robert F., *5:* 1289, 1305, 1335
　King, Martin Luther, Jr., *5:* 1293, 1334–35
　Lincoln, Abraham, *2:* 570, 571, 578, 596, 607
　McKinley, William, *3:* 858–59, 859 (ill.), 866–67
Assertive militarism, *5:* 1564
Astronomical observatory, *1:* 230
Atchison, David Rice, *2:* 436
Atlantic Charter, *4:* 1148
Atomic bomb
　development, *4:* 1223, 1226
　Kennedy, John F., *5:* 1309

Stimson, Henry L., *4:* 1101
Truman, Harry S., *4:* 1196,
  1197–99, 1212, 1221
Atomic Energy Commission, *4:*
  1226
"Atoms for Peace" campaign, *4:*
  1245; *5:* 1412
Attlee, Clement, *4:* 1196, 1221
Attorney general. *See also* adminis-
  tration of specific president
  first, *1:* 20
Atzerodt, George, *2:* 635
Audiotapes, Watergate, *5:* 1360,
  1376, 1379 (ill.), 1379–80,
  1407, 1432
Austria, *1:* 194–95
  World War I, *4:* 1025
  World War II, *4:* 1147
Austria-Hungary, World War I, *4:*
  972–73
Aviation
  commercial, *4:* 1067
  Lindbergh, Charles A., *4:*
    1064–65
  Truman-Austin bill, *4:* 1194
Axis Powers, World War II, *4:* 1147
Axson, Ellen Louise. *See* Wilson,
  Ellen

B

Babbitt, Bruce, *5:* 1487
Babcock, Orville E., *3:* 657, 658
Bacall, Lauren, *4:* 1203 (ill.)
Bache, Benjamin Franklin, *1:* 67
Bad Axe River Massacre, *2:* 435
Baker, Howard H., *5:* 1376–77
Baker, Newton D., *3:* 901
Baldwin, Roger S., *1:* 234
Ballots, election of 2000, *5:* 1614,
  1615
The Ballpark in Arlington (Texas
  Rangers), *5:* 1602, 1623
Bancroft, George, *2:* 590
Bank notes, Civil War, *3:* 695. *See
  also* Greenbacks
Bank of the United States
  First, *1:* 21, 25, 141
  Second, *1:* 269, 273, 276, 300; *2:*
    367, 400
**Bank of the United States, Veto
  Message Regarding** (Jackson),
  1: 285–90
"Bank War," *1:* 286, 289
Banking, New Deal legislation, *4:*
  1138–39, 1175–80
Banking and Currency committee,
  3: 717
Banking houses, *3:* 793

**Banning Segregation in the Mili-
  tary: Executive Order** (Tru-
  man), *4:* **1229–32**
Baptists (Southern Convention), *5:*
  1453–54
Barbara Bush: A Memoir (Barbara
  Bush), *5:* 1533
Barbara Bush Foundation for Family
  Literacy, *5:* 1531
Barbary Coast pirates, *1:* 26, 29,
  111, 154
Barkley, Alben W., election of 1948,
  4: 1205
Barnett, Ross R., *5:* 1291
Baseball, *3:* 935
Battle(s)
  Battle of Antietam, *2:* 568, 582
  Battle of Bloody Angle, *3:* 645
  Battle of Brandywine Creek, *1:*
    13, 14
  Battle of Buena Vista, *2:* 433 (ill.),
    436, 564
  Battle of Bull Run, First (Battle of
    First Manassas), *2:* 566
  Battle of Bull Run, Second (Battle
    of Second Manassas), *2:* 566
  Battle of Bunker Hill, *1:* 223
  Battle of Chancellorsville, *3:* 649
  Battle of Chattanooga, *2:* 589; *3:*
    645
  Battle of Chickamauga, *3:* 717
  Battle of Cold Harbor, *3:* 645
  Battle of Concord, *1:* 10, 12
  Battle of Contreras, *2:* 491
  Battle of Fallen Timbers, *2:* 328,
    332
  Battle of First Manassas), *2:* 566
  Battle of Five Forks, *3:* 650
  Battle of Fredericksburg, *3:* 649
  Battle of Gettysburg, *2:* 565, 568,
    588, 589; *3:* 650
  Battle of Little Big Horn, *3:* 770
  Battle of Monterrey, *2:* 433–34,
    436
  Battle of New Orleans, *1:* 263–64,
    265 (ill.)
  Battle of Palo Alto, *2:* 433
  Battle of San Jacinto, *2:* 385
  Battle of Saratoga, *1:* 13
  Battle of Second Manassas (Sec-
    ond Battle of Bull Run), *2:* 566
  Battle of Shiloh, *2:* 566; *3:* 644,
    647, 650
  Battle of South Mountain, *3:* 686
  Battle of Thames, *1:* 157; *2:* 331,
    333
  Battle of the Bulge, *4:* 1241
  Battle of Tippecanoe, *1:* 306; *2:*
    330 (ill.), 330–31
  Battle of Trenton, *1:* 11, 13
  Battle of Veracruz, *4:* 969

Battle of Vicksburg, *2:* 568; *3:* 640, 644, 650, 667
Battle of Wisconsin Heights, *2:* 435
Seven Days' Battles, *2:* 566; *3:* 649
Baudelaire, Charles-Pierre, *5:* 1301
Bay of Pigs invasion (Cuba), *5:* 1283–84
"Bayonet Constitution," *3:* 831
Beanes, William, *1:* 158
"The Beauty of America" project, *5:* 1344
Bedtime for Bonzo (film), *5:* 1473
Beecher, Catherine, *2:* 470
The Beeches (Coolidge), *4:* 1076
Begin, Menachem, *4:* 1146–47, 1148 (ill.); *5:* 1445
Belgium, World War I, *4:* 973, 1091–92
Belknap, William W., *3:* 658
Bell, Alexander Graham, *3:* 724–25, 725 (ill.)
Bell, John, *2:* 468 (ill.), 562
    election of 1860, *2:* 562
"Belle of Canton." *See* McKinley, Ida
Benton, Thomas Hart, *2:* 408, 468 (ill.)
Bentsen, Lloyd, *5:* 1515
    election of 1988, *5:* 1519
Berlin airlifts, *4:* 1202
Berlin Wall, *4:* 1253; *5:* 1285, 1490 (ill.)
BEST Foundation for a Drug-Free Tomorrow, *5:* 1499
Bethune, Mary McLeod, *4:* 1163 (ill.), 1164
Betty Ford Center, *5:* 1425
Bewick Moreing, *4:* 1089
Bicentennial Celebration, *5:* 1417
Bierce, Ambrose, *3:* 854
"Big Bill" ("Big Lub"). *See* Taft, William Howard
"Big stick" foreign policy, *3:* 891–94, 895–96
Big Three (Paris, 1919), *4:* 975 (ill.)
Big Three (Potsdam, 1945), *4:* 1198 (ill.)
Bill of Rights, *1:* 20, 99, 106, 151, 152, 177
Bill of Rights proposal (Madison), *1:* 169–78
Bimetallism
    Cleveland, Grover, *3:* 789, 860
    McKinley, William, *3:* 795, 845–46, 848
Birmingham, Alabama, segregation protest, *5:* 1293
Birney, James G., *2:* 404
"Black Codes," *2:* 612, 635
Black Hawk, *2:* 434, 554

Black Hawk War, *1:* 275, 305; *2:* 431; *3:* 770
Black, Jeremiah, *2:* 526 (ill.)
"Black Monday" stock market crash, 1566–67
Blaine, James G., *2:* 442; *3:* 660, 689, 721, 722, 754, 756–57, 757 (ill.), 781 (ill.), 782–83
    "Blaine from Maine," *3:* 756
    election of 1884, *3:* 782, 783
    Garfield's eulogy, *3:* 723
Blair, Francis P., Jr., election of 1868, *3:* 651
Blair House, *4:* 1207
"Bleeding Kansas," *2:* 500 (ill.), 501, 528
Bliss, Alexander, *2:* 590
Bliss, Mary Elizabeth (Betty), *2:* 448, 449
Bloody Angle, Battle of, *3:* 645
Bloomer, Amelia, *3:* 786
Bloomer, Elizabeth Ann. *See* Ford, Betty
Bolívar, Simon, *2:* 335
Bone, Scott C., *4:* 1029 (ill.)
Bones, Helen Woodrow, *4:* 992
Bonus Army March, *4:* 1103–4
Boom and bust cycles, *1:* 293, 309; *3:* 663
Booth, John Wilkes, *2:* 570 (ill.), 571, 578, 596, 610, 635; *3:* 677
Bootleg liquor, *4:* 1059
"Border states," *2:* 563
Borie, Adolph E., *3:* 652
Bork, Robert, *5:* 1379
Bosnia (Bosnia and Herzegovina), *5:* 1563, 1564
"The Boss." *See* Truman, Bess
"The Boss's Boss." *See* Truman, Margaret
Boston, Massachusetts
    Adams, John, *1:* 57–58
    during American Revolution, *1:* 10, 12, 33
    police strike (1919), *4:* 1054
Boston Tea Party, *1:* 9, 76, 77 (ill.)
Boutwell, George S., *3:* 652
Boxer Rebellion (Righteous and Harmonious Fists), *3:* 858; *4:* 1089–91, 1110
Boys' Clubs of America, *4:* 1106
Braddock, Edward, *1:* 8
Brady, James, *5:* 1479 (ill.)
Brady, John R., *3:* 755 (ill.)
Braintree, Massachusetts, *1:* 223
Branch Davidians, *5:* 1570
Brandeis, Louis, *3:* 936 (ill.)
Brandt, Willy, *5:* 1295
Brandywine Creek, Battle of, *1:* 13, 14
Brazil, *3:* 900

Rockefeller, Nelson, *5:* 1412
Breckinridge, John C., *2:* 562
  election of 1856, *2:* 523
  election of 1860, *2:* 562
Brezhnev, Leonid, *5:* 1369 (ill.),
  1371, 1416 (ill.), 1484
Briand, Aristide, *4:* 1061, 1063
Bricker, John W., election of 1944,
  4: 1134
Bristow, Benjamin H., *3:* 658
Britain. *See* Great Britain
British Guiana, *3:* 791
Britton, Nan, *4:* 1015
Brokaw, Tom, *5:* 1609
Broward County, Florida, election
  of 2000, *5:* 1610, 1614
Brown, Benjamin G., election of
  1872, *3:* 651
Brown, Edmund G. "Pat," Sr., *5:*
  1365, 1474
Brown, John, *2:* 526–27, 528–29,
  529 (ill.), 540, 559; *3:* 648
*Brown v. Board of Education of Tope-
  ka, 2:* 561; *4:* 1249, 1254; *5:*
  1292
Bryan, Charles W., election of 1924,
  4: 1060
Bryan, William Jennings, *3:* 856–57,
  857 (ill.)
  anti-imperialist, *3:* 807
  "Cross of Gold" speech, *3:* 823
  election of 1896, *3:* 823, 848
  election of 1900, *3:* 848
  election of 1908, *3:* 932, 933
  election of 1912, *4:* 966
  foreign relations, *3:* 956; *4:* 972
  relationship with Woodrow Wil-
    son, *4:* 989
Brzezinski, Zbigniew, *5:* 1562
Buchanan, James, *2:* 469 (ill.), 493,
  497, 500 (ill.), **515–33,** 517
  (ill.), 521 (ill.), 522 (ill.), 526
  (ill.)
  administration, *2:* 525
  early years, *2:* 518
  election of 1856, *2:* 469, 501,
    523, 558
  **Final Annual Address to Con-
    gress,** *2:* 539–48
  foreign policy, *2:* 519–22
  Lincoln, Abraham, *2:* 540
  political career, *2:* 518–19, 536
  presidency, *2:* 523–30
  "Save the Union" campaign, *2:*
    522–23
  slavery issue, *2:* 523–25, 531
  South Carolina secedes, *2:*
    530–31
Buchanan, Pat, *5:* 1610
"The buck stops here" (Truman), *5:*
  1428

Buckner, Simon Bolivar, *3:* 646–47
Budget and Accounting Act, *4:* 1025
Buena Vista, Battle of, *2:* 433 (ill.),
  436, 564
Buffalo, New York
  Cleveland, Grover, *3:* 779, 781
  Fillmore, Millard, *2:* 472
Bulge, Battle of the, *4:* 1241
"Bull Moose" (Progressive) Party, *3:*
  900, 937
Bull Run, First Battle of (Battle of
  First Manassas), *2:* 566
Bull Run, Second Battle of (Battle of
  Second Manassas), *2:* 566
"Bully pulpit," *3:* 918
Bulwer, Sir William, *2:* 442
Bunker Hill, Battle of, *1:* 223
Bunyan, John, *3:* 918
Bureaucracy, Hoover's view on, *4:*
  1117
Burgoyne, John, *1:* 13
Burnside, Ambrose, *2:* 569
Burr, Aaron, *1:* 116, 116 (ill.), 117
  (ill.)
  duel with Hamilton, *1:* 25
  election of 1796, *1:* 61
  election of 1800, *1:* 109, 110; *5:*
    1612
  introduces Madisons, *1:* 164
  treason trial, *1:* 65, 304; *2:* 363
Burr Conspiracy, *1:* 116, 117
Bush, Barbara, *5:* 1381 (ill.),
  1531–35, 1534 (ill.), 1603
  active retirement, *5:* 1534–35
  "everybody's grandmother," *5:*
    1531, 1533–35
  family literacy, *5:* 1531–32,
    1533–34
  marriage and family, *5:* 1532
  role as first lady, *5:* 1533
Bush, Barbara (daughter of George
  W.), *5:* 1601, 1623
Bush, Dorothy, *5:* 1513
Bush Exploration, *5:* 1602
Bush, George, *5:* 1381 (ill.), 1488
  (ill.), **1509–30,** 1511 (ill.), 1517
  (ill.), 1599–1600, 1603
  acting president, *5:* 1518
  **Address to Congress on the Cri-
    sis in Kuwait,** *5:* **1537–44**
  administration, *5:* 1520
  CIA, *5:* 1414
  early accomplishments, *5:*
    1512–15
  early years, *5:* 1512–15
  economic troubles, *5:* 1525, 1554
  election of 1980, *5:* 1477, 1478,
    1516–18
  election of 1984, *5:* 1477
  election of 1988, *5:* 1489,
    1519–20

election of 1992, *5:* 1525, 1555
father of a president, *5:* 1528
foreign policy, *5:* 1512, 1522–23
Gulf War, *5:* 1512, 1523–25, 1537–38, 1543–44
Iran-Contra arms sales scandal, *5:* 1518–19
marriage and family, *5:* 1513, 1532
military service, *5:* 1513, 1532
Nixon, Richard, *5:* 1516
Operation Desert Storm, *5:* 1523–24
parachute jump, *5:* 1528
political career, *5:* 1515–19
presidency, *5:* 1520–28
retirement, *5:* 1528
Bush, George W., *5:* **1595–1619,** 1597 (ill.), 1604 (ill.), 1608 (ill.)
campaign 2000, *5:* 1604–15
domestic policy, *5:* 1598–99, 1626
early years, *5:* 1599–1601
election of 2000, *5:* 1605–17, 1630–31
governor of Texas, *5:* 1602–5
marriage and family, *5:* 1601
political career, *5:* 1601–5
president-elect, *5:* 1617–18
Presidential Nomination Acceptance Speech, *5:* **1625–32**
Texas Air National Guard, *5:* 1600
Bush, Jeb, *5:* 1611–12
Bush, Jenna, *5:* 1601, 1623
Bush, Laura, *5:* 1604 (ill.), **1621–24,** 1621 (ill.)
first lady of Texas, *5:* 1624
literacy and libraries, *5:* 1623–24
marriage and family, *5:* 1622–23
reading teacher, *5:* 1622–23
Bush, Prescott, *5:* 1512–13, 1599
Business and government
Business and Government speech (Coolidge), *4:* **1077–83**
Coolidge, Calvin, *4:* 1057, 1077–78, 1081–82
Harding, Warren G., *4:* 1040, 1045
interstate, *3:* 911
Roosevelt, Theodore, *3:* 890, 895, 911, 928
"Rugged Individualism" campaign speech, *4:* **1115–22**
Taft, William Howard, *3:* 933–35
Business monopolies. *See* Trusts
Butler, Pierce, *3:* 936 (ill.)
Butler, William O., election of 1848, *2:* 439
Butterfield, Alexander, *5:* 1376

C

Cabinet. *See also* administration of each president
first, *1:* 20, 22 (ill.), 62
"Cabinet Government in the United States" (Wilson), *4:* 963
Cable News Network (CNN), Gulf War coverage, *5:* 1544
Caledonia Furnace, *2:* 608
Calhoun, Floride, *2:* 417
Calhoun, John C., *1:* 156, 211 (ill.), 230, 270–71, 271 (ill.)
election of 1828, *1:* 267
nullification, *1:* 267–68
Van Buren, Martin, *1:* 299, 300
Whig Party, *2:* 370
California
acquisition from Mexico, *2:* 404, 405–6
counterculture youth and anti-war protests, *5:* 1475
free state, *1:* 271; *2:* 371, 439–40, 452, 465, 466
Frémont, John C., *2:* 408–9
Nixon, Richard, *5:* 1360–61, 1365
Reagan, Ronald, *5:* 1474–76
Call to Greatness (Stevenson), *4:* 1247
Cambodia, *5:* 1287, 1331, 1370, 1371, 1373, 1375, 1396, 1415, 1417
"Camelot" (Kennedy White House), *5:* 1287–90, 1299
Camelot (play), *5:* 1299
Camp David Accords, *5:* 1417, 1446–47, 1447 (ill.)
Carter, Jimmy, *5:* 1445
Campaign banners
Hayes and Wheeler, *3:* 688 (ill.)
Polk and Dallas, *2:* 402 (ill.)
Whig Party, *2:* 463 (ill.)
Campaign posters
Buchanan, James, *2:* 521 (ill.)
Frémont, John C., *2:* 524 (ill.)
Garfield and Arthur, *3:* 754 (ill.)
McKinley, William, *3:* 847 (ill.)
Whig candidate, *2:* 437 (ill.)
Campaign slogans
"54°40' or Fight!," *2:* 403, 405
"Give 'em hell, Harry!," *4:* 1190, 1205
"He kept us out of war," *4:* 973 (ill.), 974
"I Like Ike," *4:* 1236, 1245 (ill.), 1261 (ill.)
"It's the economy, stupid," *5:* 1558
"Keep cool with Coolidge," *4:* 1056

"Keep the ball rolling," *2:* 334 (ill.)

"Read my lips: no new taxes," *5:* 1519

"Return to normalcy," *4:* 1016, 1024

"Save the Union," *2:* 523

"Tippecanoe and Tyler Too!," *1:* 306; *2:* 325, 364, 376

Campaign speeches, **"Rugged Individualism"** (Hoover), *4:* **1115–22**

Canada
  in Articles of Confederation, *1:* 43–44
  The Caroline incident, *1:* 303–4
  North American Free Trade Agreement (NAFTA), *5:* 1525, 1560

Canal Ring, *3:* 690

Canals. *See* Infrastructure

Cape Kennedy, *5:* 1305

Capital, location of, *1:* 21

Caribbean, *3:* 891; *5:* 1483

Caricatures, Campaign of 1884, *3:* 781 (ill.)

The Caroline incident, *1:* 303–4

Carow, Edith Kermit. *See* Roosevelt, Edith

Carranza, Venustiamo, *4:* 969, 972

Carter Center, *5:* 1436, 1453, 1467

Carter, Jimmy, *4:* 1207; *5:* 1381 (ill.), **1433–55,** 1435 (ill.), 1439 (ill.), 1441 (ill.), 1448 (ill.), 1449 (ill.), 1453 (ill.), 1562
  administration, *5:* 1443
  Camp David Accords, *5:* 1445
  domestic policy, *5:* 1445–48
  early years, *5:* 1436–39
  election of 1976, *5:* 1418, 1442
  election of 1980, *5:* 1451, 1452, 1477, 1478, 1518
  family peanut business, *5:* 1440
  Ford, Gerald R., *5:* 1419
  foreign policy, *5:* 1436, 1444–45, 1448, 1462, 1466–67
  governor of Georgia, *5:* 1440–41
  "Human Rights and Foreign Policy" Speech, *5:* **1461–68**
  human rights efforts, *5:* 1436, 1452–53
  inaugural speech, *5:* 1419
  inflation problems, *5:* 1445
  Iran hostage crisis, *5:* 1448–52, 1449, 1450–51, 1452 (ill.)
  life after the presidency, *5:* 1436, 1452–54, 1459–60
  marriage and family, *5:* 1439, 1458, 1459
  naval career, *5:* 1439–39

political career, *5:* 1440–42, 1458–59
  presidency, *5:* 1442–52, 1459
  Soviets invade Afghanistan, *5:* 1467
  trouble with Congress, *5:* 1444

Carter, "Miss Lillian," *5:* 1437, 1444

Carter, Rosalynn, *5:* 1381 (ill.), 1457 (ill.), **1457–68**
  human rights efforts, *5:* 1453, 1459–60
  navy wife, *5:* 1458
  peanuts and politics, *5:* 1458–59
  role as first lady, *5:* 1457, 1459

Cartoons, political
  "Bleeding Kansas," *2:* 500 (ill.)
  Campaign of 1884, *3:* 781 (ill.)
  1856 presidential campaign, *2:* 522 (ill.)
  Garfield, James A., *3:* 720 (ill.)
  Johnson, Andrew, *2:* 618 (ill.)
  Kennedy vs. Khrushchev and Castro, *5:* 1285 (ill.)
  Lusitania, *4:* 974 (ill.)
  Nixon tapes, *5:* 1379 (ill.)
  Polk and Webster, *2:* 407 (ill.)
  Roosevelt, Franklin D., *4:* 1144 (ill.)
  Scott and Pierce, *2:* 494 (ill.)
  Stevens and Johnson, *2:* 614 (ill.)
  Taft and Roosevelt, *3:* 932 (ill.)
  Wilson, Woodrow, *4:* 965 (ill.)

Casablanca conference, *4:* 1153

Cass, Lewis, *1:* 309; *2:* 440–41, 441 (ill.), 468 (ill.), 493, 500 (ill.), 526 (ill.)
  election of 1848, *2:* 349, 439

Castro, Fidel, *4:* 1251; *5:* 1283, 1285 (ill.), 1416

Center for National Policy, *5:* 1562

Central America, *2:* 443, 526; *3:* 894, 935–36, 955

Central government. *See* Federal government

Central High School (Little Rock, Arkansas), *4:* 1249

Central Intelligence Agency (CIA), *4:* 1245
  Bay of Pigs invasion (Cuba), *5:* 1283–84
  Bush, George, *5:* 1516
  Ford's overhaul, *5:* 1416

Central Powers (World War I), *4:* 997–99, 1003, 1004, 1005, 1010

Cermak, Anton J., *4:* 1135

Chads, "dimpled," *5:* 1614, 1615

Chamber of Commerce (New York), *4:* 1078

Chamberlain, Neville, *4:* 1148

Chamberlayne, Richard, *1:* 32

Chambers, Whittaker, *4:* 1206; *5:* 1363
Chancellorsville, Battle of, *3:* 649
Charbonneau, Toussaint, *1:* 115
A Charge to Keep (George W. Bush), *5:* 1601–2
Charles I, king of England, *3:* 813
Chase, Salmon P., *2:* 470
Chattanooga, Battles of, *2:* 589; *3:* 645
"Checkers" speech (Nixon), *5:* 1364
"Checks and balances," *1:* 59, 103, 150; *5:* 1380
  Roosevelt, Franklin D., *4:* 1173
  wartime, *4:* 997
Cheney, Dick, *5:* 1544, 1604 (ill.), 1605, 1606–7, 1607 (ill.), 1626
  election of 2000, *5:* 1609
  Gulf War, *5:* 1607
  Noriega, Manuel, *5:* 1607
  political career, *5:* 1606–7
  Reagan, Ronald, *5:* 1607
Cheney, Lynne, *5:* 1604 (ill.), 1606
Chernenko, Konstantin, *5:* 1484
Cherokee, *1:* 232, 274, 305, 306, 307 (ill.); *2:* 332, 440
Cherry blossom trees, *3:* 947
Chesapeake, 1: 270
Chiang Kai-shek, *4:* 1207–8; *5:* 1278
  World War II, *4:* 1153
Chicago Tribune, 4: 1205
  "Dewey Defeats Truman," *4:* 1204 (ill.), 1205–6
Chickamauga, Battle of, *3:* 717
"The chief business of America is business" (Coolidge), *4:* 1050, 1082
"Chief Executive." *See* Harding, Florence
Chief Joseph, *3:* 770
Child labor, *3:* 883; *4:* 969
Children's Defense Fund (CDF), *5:* 1582
Childress, Sarah. *See* Polk, Sarah
Chile, *3:* 820
  Rockefeller, Nelson, *5:* 1412
China. *See also* People's Republic of China
  Boxer Rebellion, *3:* 858; *4:* 1089–91, 1110
  Chiang Kai-shek, *4:* 1207–8
  Manchurian invasion, *4:* 1100, 1102, 1147, 1181
  McKinley, William, *3:* 851, 858
  World War I, *4:* 978
China collection (White House), *3:* 827
Chinese immigration, *3:* 696, 761, 762
Choate, Pat, election of 1996, *5:* 1555

Chou En-lai, *5:* 1372
"Chowder and Marching Society," *5:* 1404
Christian, Letitia. *See* Tyler, Letitia
Christopher, Warren, *5:* 1563
Christy, Howard Chandler, *4:* 1075–76
Churchill, Winston, *4:* 1147, 1148–49, 1149 (ill.), 1153 (ill.), 1195, 1196, 1198 (ill.), 1221
  Eisenhower, Dwight D., *4:* 1241
Cider, *2:* 335, 337
  at William Henry Harrison's campaign rallies, *2:* 335
Cincinnati, Ohio
  Hayes, Rutherford B., *3:* 685, 686–87
  Taft, William Howard, *3:* 928–30
Cinque, *1:* 253
Cities, vs. suburbs, *5:* 1329
Civil Aeronautics Board, *4:* 1194
Civil rights
  Arthur, Chester A., *3:* 750–51
  Eisenhower, Dwight D., *4:* 1249, 1254
  Humphrey, Hubert H., *5:* 1336–37
  Johnson, Lyndon B., *5:* 1325–26
  Kennedy, John F., *5:* 1290–91, 1312
  Kennedy, Robert F., *5:* 1288–89
  King, Martin Luther, Jr., *4:* 1292–93
  legislation, *2:* 596; *4:* 1151–52
  limitations on, *2:* 612
  Marshall, Thurgood, *5:* 1332–33
  Truman, Harry S., *4:* 1204, 1229–32
Civil Rights Act (1875), *3:* 659
Civil Rights Act (1964), *4:* 1232; *5:* 1289, 1293, 1325
Civil Service Commission, *3:* 726, 760, 885
Civil service reform
  Arthur, Chester A., *3:* 748, 761–62
  Garfield, James A., *3:* 713
  Hayes, Rutherford B., *3:* 689, 694–95
Civil War, *2:* 546–47, 562–70, 573, 581–82; *3:* 644–45
  Arthur, Chester A., *3:* 751, 766
  Cleveland rejects pensions, *3:* 784
  Confederate surrender, *3:* 671–78
  Davis, Jefferson, *2:* 564–65, 565 (ill.)
  Emancipation Proclamation (Lincoln), *2:* 456, 514, 567–68, **581–86,** 582 (ill.)
  Garfield, James A., *3:* 717, 718

Gettysburg Address (Lincoln), *2:*
587–90
Grant, Ulysses S., *3:* 644–50,
667–68, 671–78
Johnson, Andrew, *2:* 606–7,
624–25
Lee, Robert E., *3:* 648–49
McKinley, William, *3:* 843–44
money supply, *3:* 652–53
reparations from Great Britain, *2:*
611
Second Inaugural Address (Lin-
coln), *2:* 593–97
southern states secede, *2:* 562
Tyler, Julia, *2:* 382–83
Weaver, James B., *3:* 824
Wilson, Woodrow, *4:* 961
Civil Works Administration (CWA),
4: 1138
Civilian Conservation Corps (CCC),
4: 1138–39, 1200
Clark, James B. "Champ," *4:* 965–66
Clark, William, *1:* 112, 114–15
Clarke School for the Deaf, *4:* 1072
Clay, Henry, *1:* 156, 228–29, 229
(ill.), 266, 272, 285
Adams, John Quincy, *1:* 226–27
"American System," *1:* 228,
230–31
Compromise of 1850, *1:* 229; *2:*
371, 441–42, 464
election of 1824, *1:* 227
election of 1832, *1:* 267, 272
election of 1844, *2:* 372, 401,
403–4
Harrison, William Henry, *2:* 337,
339, 365
Whig Party, *2:* 370
Clayton-Bulwer Treaty, *2:* 442
Clayton, John M., *2:* 442, 456
Clean Air Act, *5:* 1330, 1338, 1521
"Clear and present danger," *3:* 893
Clemenceau, Georges, *4:* 975 (ill.),
1011
Clemency for draft-dodgers (Vietnam Era Reconciliation Program), *5:* 1412–14
Clemens, Samuel (Mark Twain), *3:*
661, 669
Cleveland, Frances, *3:* 797–801,
797 (ill.), 799 (ill.)
curious courtship, *3:* 797–98
marriage and family, *3:* 799, 800
popular first lady, *3:* 800
youngest-ever first lady, *3:* 798
Cleveland, Grover, *3:* 775–95, 777
(ill.), 781 (ill.), 799 (ill.)
administrations, *3:* 785
annexation of Hawaii, *3:* 778,
789, 803, 832, 834
Civil War replacement, *3:* 779, 783

early years, *3:* 778–79
election of 1884, *3:* 762, 782–83
election of 1888, *3:* 788, 818,
819; *5:* 1556, 1613
election of 1892, *3:* 782, 789,
800, 821, 830
family, *3:* 800
foreign policy, *3:* 778
"His Obstinacy," *3:* 790
marriage in White House, *3:* 788,
798–99 (ill.), 799 (ill.)
**Message to Congress Opposing
the Annexation of Hawaii**, *3:*
803–8
political appointments, *3:* 784
political career, *3:* 779–83, 798
presidency (first term), *3:* 783–90
presidency (second term), *3:*
790–91
presidential romance, *3:* 797–98
retirement, *3:* 791–94, 800–801
"veto mayor," *3:* 781
Cleveland, Rose Elizabeth "Libbie,"
3: 785, 798–99
Clinton, Bill, *5:* 1381 (ill.),
1545–80, 1547 (ill.), 1552 (ill.),
1565 (ill.), 1569 (ill.), 1584 (ill.)
administration, *5:* 1559
domestic policy, *5:* 1560–61,
1578
early years, *5:* 1549–51
election of 1992, *5:* 1525,
1554–55, 1557, 1558
election of 1996, *5:* 1555, 1557,
1561
federal budget surplus, *5:* 1568
**Final State of the Union Ad-
dress**, *5:* 1587–93
foreign policy: assertive militarism, *5:* 1561–68, 1578–79
governor of Arkansas, *5:* 1553
impeachment, *5:* 1547, 1548,
1569, 1573 (ill.), 1574–76
improper conduct, *5:* 1555,
1574–75
Kennedy, John F., *5:* 1549
marriage and family, *5:* 1553,
1583
military draft avoided, *5:*
1550–51
national reputation, *5:* 1554
political career, *5:* 1552–54
presidency, *5:* 1558–69
Reno, Janet, *5:* 1571
Whitewater scandal, *5:* 1569–72
Clinton, Chelsea, *5:* 1584 (ill.)
Clinton, DeWitt, *1:* 297
election of 1812, *1:* 155, 156
Clinton, George, *1:* 157
election of 1792, *1:* 19
election of 1804, *1:* 109, 115

election of 1808, *1:* 155

Clinton, Hillary Rodham, *5:* 1381
(ill.), 1569 (ill.), **1581–86**, 1581
(ill.), 1584 (ill.)
conference on women in Beijing,
5: 1585
health insurance plan, *5:* 1560,
1585
legal career, *5:* 1581, 1582–83
marriage and family, *5:* 1583
media attention, *5:* 1583–85
most traveled first lady, *5:* 1585
New York's first female U.S. senator, *5:* 1586
role as first lady, *5:* 1583–86
support for Bill Clinton, *5:* 1586

Clinton, Sir Henry, *1:* 14

Clintonians, *1:* 297

**Closing Argument in *Amistad
Case*** (John Quincy Adams), *1:*
245–53

CNN (Cable News Network), Gulf
War coverage, *5:* 1544

Coal mining, federal regulation, *3:*
899

"Coattail" effect, *2:* 354

Cobb, Howell, *2:* 526 (ill.), 537

Cobb, Mary Ann, *2:* 537

Cockerill, John A., *3:* 852

Cogswell, William, *3:* 817 (ill.)

Colby, William, *5:* 1414, 1416

Cold Harbor, Battle of, *3:* 645

Cold War, *4:* 1156
defense industry, *4:* 1264, 1270
Eisenhower, Dwight D., *4:* 1235,
1244–48, 1248, 1251, 1264
Kennedy, John F., *5:* 1283–86
Khrushchev, Nikita, *4:* 1253
Nixon, Richard, *5:* 1372–73
Reagan, Ronald, *5:* 1490
Truman, Harry S., *4:* 1199–1202,
1206–7

Coleman, Anne, *2:* 519

Coleman, Julia, *5:* 1437

Colfax, Schuyler, *3:* 658
election of 1868, *3:* 651

Colombia
Harrison, William Henry, *2:* 335,
343
Panama revolution, *3:* 894
Roosevelt, Theodore, *3:* 894, 903

Colonial Convention, *1:* 88

Colson, Charles, *5:* 1378

Commerce
international, *4:* 1061
regulation, *1:* 136

Commercial aviation, *4:* 1067

Commission on Economy and Efficiency, *3:* 941

Committee for Relief of Belgium
(CRB), *4:* 1091, 1111

Committee of American Residents
in London for Assistance to
American Travelers, *4:* 1091

Committee of Five, *1:* 126, 133 (ill.)

Committee on Un-American Activities, *4:* 1143, 1206; *5:* 1363,
1372, 1474

Committee to Defend America by
Aiding the Allies, *4:* 1246

Committee to Re-Elect the President (CREEP), *5:* 1378, 1406,
1407

Common Americans, Reagan's view,
5: 1502

The Common Law (Holmes Jr.), *3:*
892, 893

Common Sense (Paine), *1:* 190

Commonwealth of Independent
States, *5:* 1485

Communications technology, *4:*
1040

Communism, *4:* 1143, 1189. *See
also* Cold War
elections of 1932 and 1936, *4:*
1144–45
House Committee on Un-American Activities, *4:* 1206–7; *5:*
1363
U.S. foreign policy, *5:* 1462

Communist Party
Gorbachev, Mikhail, *5:* 1485
Khrushchev, Nikita, *4:* 1252

"Compassionate conservatism," *5:*
1603

Compromise of 1850, *1:* 229; *2:*
371, 455, 464–67, 472, 487,
493, 495–97, 509, 513, 608

Compromise of 1877, *3:* 693

Computer technology, *4:* 1264

Concerning Human Understanding
(Locke), *1:* 102

Confederacy. *See* Confederate States
of America (CSA)

Concord, Battle of, *1:* 10, 12

Confederate Army, *2:* 547, 565; *3:*
673
amnesty, *2:* 612
Battle of Gettysburg, *2:* 588
Lee, Robert E., *3:* 648–49
terms of surrender, *2:* 570; *3:* 650,
671–78

Confederate Congress, *2:* 614

Confederate States of America
(CSA), *2:* 531, 562, 581
Davis, Jefferson, *2:* 564–65, 565
(ill.)
**Grant's recollection of surren-
der,** *3:* **671–78**
Texas, *2:* 391

**The Confederate Surrender, Recol-
lection of** (Grant), *3:* **671–78**

Congregationalism, *1:* 56

Congress, *2:* 621, 629. *See also* Annual Address; Confederate Congress; Continental Congress; House of Representatives; Senate; State of the Union Address

Articles of Confederation, *1:* 38

Budget Office, *5:* 1411

declarations of war, *4:* 997

declares war on Axis powers, *4:* 1150–51

declares war on Japan, *4:* 1181–82, 1184

election of 1876, *3:* 693

Emergency Banking Act, *4:* 1178

Fourteen Points (Wilson), *4:* **1005–11**

gag rule on slavery, *1:* 234–35

Great Depression, *4:* 1103

Hayes, Rutherford B., *3:* 696, 719

impeachment of Andrew Johnson, *2:* 616–17

impeachment of Bill Clinton, *5:* 1548

Jackson censure, *1:* 273, 300–301; *2:* 364

legislation freeing slaves, *2:* 547

Message Opposing the Annexation of Hawaii (Cleveland), *3:* **803–8**

Missouri Compromise, *1:* 198

Native Americans, *3:* 753–54

New Deal legislation (The Hundred Days), *4:* 1137, 1138–41, 1172

president's relationship, *1:* 298; *2:* 354

Reconstruction, *2:* 610, 629–30

relationship to president (1970s), *5:* 1419

riders (legislative), *3:* 736

Speech to a Special Session (Harding), *4:* **1013–32**

Tariff of Abominations, *1:* 232

War Message to Congress (Wilson), *4:* **997–1004**

Watergate babies, *5:* 1411–12

Watergate scandal, *5:* 1406–7

Congressional Government (Wilson), *4:* 959, 968

Conkling, Roscoe, *3:* 721, 722, 751, 752, 752 (ill.), 753, 758, 781–82

Connally, John C., *5:* 1291

Connecticut Plan, *1:* 150

Conner, Fox, *4:* 1239

Conscription, *1:* 297

Conservation

Carter, Jimmy (fuel), *5:* 1445–48

Johnson, Lady Bird, *5:* 1346

Roosevelt, Theodore, *3:* 896–99

Conservatives, Republican, *5:* 1419, 1474, 1476–77, 1483, 1507, 1511, 1521, 1525

Constitution, *1:* 18, 43, 88, 106

Bill of Rights, *1:* 106, 151, 152, 169–71

central ideas, *1:* 82

commander in chief, *4:* 997

Congress and Andrew Johnson, *2:* 630–31

constructionists, *1:* 136

Electoral College, *5:* 1610, 1612–13

federal government, *1:* 135–37

Fifteenth Amendment, *3:* 652, 655–56, 687

Fourteenth Amendment, *2:* 609, 615; *3:* 787

Great Depression, *4:* 1027

"high crimes and misdemeanors," *5:* 1572

Lee, Richard Henry, *1:* 100

Madison, James, *1:* 170–71

Marshall, John, *1:* 65

Nineteenth Amendment, *3:* 787

presidential succession, *2:* 338, 357–58

ratification, *1:* 18, 150–54, 169–70, 178, 188

removal of a chief executive, *5:* 1383

"Revolution Against" speech (Garfield), *3:* **735–43**

slavery issue, *2:* 452, 510, 518, 540–41

Thirteenth Amendment, *2:* 568, 570, 596, 611, 612; *3:* 677

treaties, *2:* 386

Twelfth Amendment, *1:* 73, 115

Twentieth Amendment, *4:* 1145

Twenty-third Amendment, *5:* 1613

vs. Articles of Confederation, *1:* 37, 43

Constitutional Conventions, *1:* 18, 43, 149, 151; *2:* 362

Madison's role, *1:* 169–71, 177–78

Washington's role, *1:* 52, 169

Constitutionality

appropriations riders, *3:* 736

Constitutionality of a National Bank (Jefferson), *1:* **135–42**

Emancipation Proclamation, *2:* 583

New Deal legislation, *4:* 1139, 1141, 1144

Constitutionality of a National Bank (Jefferson), *1:* **135–42**

Constructionists, *1:* 107, 112, 136, 137; *2:* 357

Continental Army, *1:* 11, 12

Continental Congress, *1:* 9, 12. *See also* Congress
  Articles of Confederation, *1:* 37–38, 38
  Canada as American colony, *1:* 43–44
  Continental Army, *1:* 59
  Declaration of Independence, *1:* 125–26
  Jefferson, Thomas, *1:* 98
  Lee, Richard Henry, *1:* 100
Continental System, *1:* 195
"Contract with America," *5:* 1560
Contras (El Salvador), *5:* 1483
Contreras, Battle of, *2:* 491
Convention, Constitutional. *See* Constitutional Convention
Convention of 1800, *1:* 70
Cook, Captain James, *3:* 808
Coolidge, Calvin, *4:* 1030, **1047–69,** 1049 (ill.), 1050 (ill.), 1057 (ill.), 1059 (ill.), 1066 (ill.), 1074 (ill.)
  administration, *4:* 1058
  death of Calvin Jr., *4:* 1056, 1075
  death of Harding, *4:* 1030, 1054, 1055–56
  domestic issues, *4:* 1066–67
  early years, *4:* 1051–53
  election of 1920, *4:* 1021, 1055, 1073
  election of 1924, *4:* 1056–57, 1060
  election of 1928, *4:* 1096
  foreign policy, *4:* 1060–61
  Harding, Warren G., *4:* 1055
  legal career, *4:* 1053–54
  Lindbergh, Charles, *4:* 1066
  marriage and family, *4:* 1054, 1056, 1072–73
  political career, *4:* 1054–55, 1073
  presidency, *4:* 1057–67
  pro-business economic policy, *4:* 1077–78, 1081–82
  Prohibition, *4:* 1058–60
  retirement, *4:* 1067
  Speech on Government and Business, *4:* **1077–83**
  succeeds Harding, *4:* 1055–56
  thrifty nature, *4:* 1072, 1073
Coolidge, Calvin, Jr., *4:* 1056, 1059 (ill.), 1075
Coolidge, Grace, *4:* 1059 (ill.), **1071–76,** 1071 (ill.), 1074 (ill.), 1076 (ill.)
  baseball fan, *4:* 1076
  marriage and family, *4:* 1072–73
  supporter of women's suffrage, *4:* 1075
  unexpected loss of teenaged son, *4:* 1075

Coolidge, John, *4:* 1059 (ill.)
Coonskin hats, *2:* 337
Cooper, Thomas, *2:* 377
"Cooper Union" speech (Lincoln), *2:* 559
Cornwallis, Charles, *1:* 14, 16, 186
Corporate income tax, first, *3:* 933
Corporate monopolies. *See* Trusts
Corporation for Public Broadcasting, *5:* 1330
"Corrupt bargain," *1:* 227
Cortelyou, George B., *3:* 867
Coulon, Joseph, *1:* 7
Council of Europe (CE), *4:* 1149
Court system, *1:* 20. *See also* Judiciary
"Cover up" (Watergate), *5:* 1378
Cox, Archibald, *5:* 1376, 1378, 1379
Cox, James M., election of 1920, *4:* 979, 1011, 1021, 1024, 1039
Crash of 1929, *3:* 663; *4:* 1082, 1098–99
Crawford, William H., *1:* 211 (ill.)
  election of 1824, *1:* 227, 266
"Credibility gap," *5:* 1335, 1338
Credit and currency, *1:* 274, 302
Crédit Mobilier of America scandal, *3:* 657–58
  Garfield, James A., *3:* 718
Creek, *2:* 332
Creek nation, *1:* 232, 263
CREEP, *5:* 1378, 1406, 1407
Crier, *3:* 749
Crimes, "high," *5:* 1572
The Crisis (Paine), *1:* 190
Crittendon, John J., *2:* 468 (ill.)
Cromwell, Oliver, *3:* 813
Crop rotation, *1:* 8
"Cross of Gold" speech (Bryan), *3:* 823
Crusade in Europe (Eisenhower), *4:* 1242
Cuba, *4:* 1251
  Amistad case, *1:* 245
  Clinton, Bill, *5:* 1564
  Cuban missile crisis, *4:* 1253; *5:* 1273, 1286
  Gonzalez, Elian, *5:* 1571
  Kennedy, John F., *5:* 1283–84, 1286
  Monroe Doctrine, *1:* 214; *3:* 791
  Ostend Manifesto, *2:* 497, 521–22
  Spanish American War, *3:* 849–51, 887–88; *4:* 970
  Taft negotiates settlement, *3:* 931
  Virginius incident, *3:* 655, 659–60
Cukor, George, *5:* 1495
Cumberland Road, *1:* 231
Curley, James M., *5:* 1278
Currency supply, *1:* 274, 300; *2:* 404; *3:* 717, 789, 791, 824, 848

Curtis, Charles
  election of 1928, *4:* 1096
  election of 1932, *4:* 1134
"Custer's Last Stand," *3:* 770
Custis, Daniel Park, *1:* 32
Custis, Martha Dandridge. *See*
  Washington, Martha
Custis, Mary Anne Randolph, *3:*
  648
Czechoslovakia, democratization, *5:*
  1482, 1522
Czolgosz, Leon F., *3:* 859, 859 (ill.),
  860 (ill.), 866

D

Dade County, Florida, election of
  2000, *5:* 1610, 1614
Dakota Territory, *3:* 884
Dallas, George M., *2:* 402 (ill.)
  election of 1844, *2:* 401
Dana, Francis, *1:* 223
Darrow, Clarence, *3:* 857
Darwin, Charles, *3:* 892
"A date which will live in infamy"
  speech (Franklin D. Roosevelt),
  4: 1150, 1181, 1182
Daugherty, Harry M., *4:* 1019, 1020,
  1021, 1024, 1025 (ill.),
  1025–26
Daughters of the American Revolu-
  tion, *3:* 827, 829; *4:* 1164
Davie, William Richardson, *1:* 260
Davies, Dale, *3:* 693
Davis, Henry G., *3:* 894–95
  election of 1904, *3:* 895
Davis, Jefferson, *2:* 448, 495, 527,
  563, 564–65, 565 (ill.); *3:* 649
Davis, John W., election of 1924, *4:*
  1056, 1060
Davis, Manvel H., *4:* 1194
Davis, Nancy. *See* Reagan, Nancy
Dawes Act (General Allotment Act),
  3: 773–74, 784
Dawes, Charles G., election of 1924,
  4: 1060
Dawes Plan (German reparations),
  4: 1027, 1063
Dayton, William L., election of
  1856, *2:* 523
D-Day, World War II, *4:* 1153, 1241
De Priest, Mrs. Oscar, *4:* 1113
De Reus Metallica (Hoover, Herbert
  and Lou), *4:* 1111
De Wolfe, Henry, *4:* 1034
Deaf, education, *3:* 724–25
Dean, John, *5:* 1376, 1377 (ill.),
  1378
Death of presidents

by assassination. *See* Assassinations
  on July 4, *1:* 71–72, 119, 201
Debt, national, *1:* 21–22
*Decision—The Conflicts of Harry S.
  Truman* (TV series), *4:* 1211
Declaration of Independence, *1:*
  81, 88, 98–99, **125–34**
  central ideas, *1:* 82
  charges against George III, *1:*
    127–28
  Committee of Five, *1:* 126, 133
    (ill.)
  introduction, *1:* 127
  Jefferson, Thomas, *1:* 125–34
  preamble, *1:* 127
  signers, *1:* 133–34
Declaration of Independence Com-
  mittee, *1:* 13, 133 (ill.)
Declaration of the Rights of Man
  and the Citizen (initiative of
  Lafayette), *1:* 186
*Defence of the Constitutions of Gov-
  ernment of the United States of
  America* (John Adams), *1:* 59
"The Defense of Fort McHenry"
  (Key), *1:* 159
"Defense of the Constitutionality of
  the Bank" (Hamilton), *1:* 140
Defense spending
  post–World War II, *4:* 1264, 1270
  Reagan era, *5:* 1481–82
  World War II, *4:* 1147
Deism, *1:* 191
Delahanty, Thomas, *5:* 1479 (ill.)
Delaware, *1:* 169
Delaware River, *1:* 10, 11
Democratic Advisory Council, *4:*
  1247
Democratic Leadership Council, *5:*
  1554
Democratic National Convention
  (1968), *5:* 1335, 1337, 1367
Democratic National Headquarters
  committee offices (Watergate
  burglary), *5:* 1375, 1405, 1516
Democratic Party, *1:* 272; *2:* 489; *3:*
  661–62
  Bryan, William Jennings, *3:*
    856–57
  Hayes, Rutherford B., *3:* 696, 719
  post–Civil War, *3:* 735
  Van Buren, Martin, *1:* 300, 309
Democratic-Republican Party, *1:* 46,
  51, 67, 71, 107, 272, 296, 297.
  See also Anti-Federalist(s)
  Adams, John Quincy, *1:* 225
  election of 1800, *1:* 109–10
  Jacksonian Democrats, *1:* 272,
    297–98, 300–301, 309; *2:* 399,
    519, 603–4

Demonstrations (1968), *5:* 1334
Dent, Julia. *See* Grant, Julia
Department of Energy, *5:* 1448
Department of Health, Education, and Welfare, *5:* 1412
Department of Housing and Urban Development, *5:* 1329
Department of Public Welfare, *4:* 1040
Department of State. *See* State Department
Department of Welfare, *4:* 1045
Depression. *See* Great Depression
Desegregation (integration)
    Eisenhower, Dwight D., *4:* 1249
    Kennedy, Robert F., *5:* 1288–89
    Marshall, Thurgood, *5:* 1332
    Truman, Harry S., *4:* 1229–32
"De-Stalinization," *4:* 1252
Détente, *5:* 1372–73
Detroit, Michigan, *2:* 440
Developing countries, *3:* 949, 950
"Dewey Defeats Truman," *4:* 1204 (ill.), 1205–6
Dewey, George, *3:* 887
Dewey, Thomas E.
    election of 1944, *4:* 1134, 1154
    election of 1948, *4:* 1205; *5:* 1336
Diaghilev, Serge, *5:* 1300
Dickens, Charles, *2:* 377
Dickinson, John, *1:* 37
"Digital divide," *5:* 1568
Dimmick, Mary Scott Lord (Mary Harrison), *3:* 822, 825 (ill.)
"Dimpled chads," *5:* 1614, 1615
Dingley Tariff, *3:* 875
Dinwiddie, Robert, *1:* 6, 8
Disaster relief, federal, *4:* 1060, 1096
Disciples of Christ, *3:* 714, 730
Discrimination
    Marshall, Thurgood, *5:* 1332, 1333
    O'Connor, Sandra Day, *5:* 1486–87
District of Columbia, *1:* 21, 110, 242
Dixiecrats (States' Rights Democratic Party), *4:* 1204, 1231; *5:* 1336–37
DNA testing, Jefferson-Hemings, *1:* 105
Dole, Elizabeth, *5:* 1381 (ill.)
Dole, Robert (Bob), *5:* 1381 (ill.), 1417, 1528
    election of 1976, *5:* 1442
    election of 1996, *5:* 1555, 1561
Dole, Sanford B., *3:* 832
"Dollar Diplomacy," *3:* 936, 949–50
"Domestic tranquility," *5:* 1428

Dominican Republic, *3:* 656–57, 937
Donelson, Andrew Jackson, election of 1856, *2:* 523
Donelson, Emily, *1:* 282
Donelson, John, *1:* 261
Donelson, Rachel. *See* Jackson, Rachel
"Don't ask, don't tell" policy, *5:* 1558
Doud, Mamie. *See* Eisenhower, Mamie
Douglas, Stephen A., *2:* 468 (ill.), 493, 498, 500 (ill.), 557
    election of 1860, *2:* 562
    Kansas-Nebraska Bill, *2:* 499–500
    Lincoln-Douglas debates, *2:* 559, 560–61, 561 (ill.)
Douglass, Frederick, *2:* 528, 596–97
Draft (military)
    draft-dodgers clemency (Vietnam Era Reconciliation Program), *5:* 1412–14
    World War II, *4:* 1152
Dred Scott v. Sandford, *2:* 523–24, 558, 560, 561
Drew, John, *4:* 1074 (ill.)
Drop of Milk program, *3:* 945
Drought, Great Plains (1930), *4:* 1099
Drug-abuse awareness
    Ford, Betty, *5:* 1425
    Reagan, Nancy, *5:* 1497, 1498–99
"Dubya." *See* Bush, George W.
Dufree, Amos, *1:* 306
Dukakis, Michael, election of 1988, *5:* 1519, 1554, 1557, 1562
"Duke of Braintree," *1:* 67
Dustin, Daniel, *3:* 817 (ill.)

E

Eagle Claw, *5:* 1451
Early Childhood Development Initiative, *5:* 1624
Earth in the Balance (Gore), *5:* 1557
East Germany, *5:* 1285
    democratization, *5:* 1482, 1485, 1522
Eastern Europe. *See also* Europe
    break-up of Soviet Union, *5:* 1485, 1522
    Cold War, *4:* 1248, 1252
    Iron Curtain, *4:* 1248, 1254
Eaton, Dorman B., *3:* 760
Eaton, John, *1:* 272, 283
Eaton, Margaret (Peggy), *1:* 272
Ecology issues, *5:* 1346
Economic crises

crisis of 1907, *3:* 934
energy crisis (1970s), *5:* 1445
Great Depression, *4:* 1027,
1098–99
Panic of 1837, *1:* 276, 289, 293,
302
Panic of 1873, *3:* 658–59, 695
Panic of 1893, *3:* 790, 793
stock market crash of 1929, *3:*
663; *4:* 1082, 1098–99
stock market crash of 1987, *5:*
1481, 1566–67
Economic Opportunity Act of 1964,
5: 1327–28
Economic Recovery Tax Act of
1981, *5:* 1480
Economics
supply-side, *5:* 1481
"voodoo," *5:* 1517
Economy. *See also* Boom and bust
cycles
North, *2:* 547, 589; *3:* 869
pre-Depression, *4:* 1097
South, *2:* 547, 564–65; *3:* 869
Economy Act, *4:* 1135, 1138
Edelman, Marian Wright, *5:* 1582
Eden, Anthony, *4:* 1149
Edison, Thomas, *4:* 1098
Education
Bell, Alexander Graham, *3:*
724–25
Carter, Jimmy, *5:* 1454
Clintons' Arkansas program, *5:*
1553, 1583
Eisenhower, Dwight D., *4:* 1250
Garfield, James A., *3:* 715–16
Garfield, Lucretia, *3:* 729, 730
Johnson, Lyndon B., *5:* 1319,
1328
Wilson, Woodrow, *4:* 963–65
Edward VIII, prince of Wales, *2:* 537
Egypt
Camp David Accords, *5:* 1446–47,
1466
Carter, Jimmy, *5:* 1445
Ford, Gerald, *5:* 1417
Kissinger, Henry, *5:* 1371
Ehrlichman, John, *5:* 1369, 1378,
1380
Einstein, Albert, *4:* 1223
Eisenhower, Dwight D., *3:* 801; *4:*
1207, **1233–56,** 1235 (ill.),
1241 (ill.), 1243 (ill.), 1258
(ill.), 1261 (ill.); *5:* 1308 (ill.)
administration, *4:* 1250
civil rights, *4:* 1249
domestic policy, *4:* 1245,
1248–50
early years, *4:* 1236–38
election of 1952, *4:* 1243, 1244
election of 1956, *4:* 1244

Farewell Address to the Nation,
4: **1263–70**
foreign affairs, *4:* 1245, 1248,
1250–51
golfer, *4:* 1251
heart attack, *4:* 1248, 1261
"I Like Ike," *4:* 1245 (ill.)
limited federal government, *4:*
1264
marriage and family, *4:* 1238,
1259
military career, *4:* 1238–42,
1259–60
National Cultural Center, *5:* 1313
postwar prosperity, *4:* 1244,
1254, 1261, 1263
presidency, *4:* 1242–51
retirement, *4:* 1251–52
Vietnam, *5:* 1287, 1331–32
Eisenhower, John Sheldon Doud, *4:*
1259
Eisenhower, Mamie, *4:* 1257 (ill.),
1257–62, 1258 (ill.)
marriage and family, *4:* 1259
military moves, *4:* 1259
stylish first lady, *4:* 1260–61
World War II, *4:* 1260
El Salvador, *5:* 1483
Elba, *1:* 195
Election of 2000, *5:* 1598, 1605–17,
1611 (ill.)
absentee ballots, *5:* 1611
Florida law on recounts, *5:*
1610–11
machine recounts, *5:* 1611
Election results. *See* e.g., Carter,
Jimmy, election of 1976; other
years under each president by
election year
Electoral College, history, *5:* 1610,
1612–13
Electoral Commission (1877), *3:*
691, 693, 718–19; *5:* 1613
Electoral vote(s), *1:* 18, 19, 61, 109,
197, 227; *5:* 1610, 1613. *See
also* election results under each
president
election of 2000, *5:* 1557, 1598
Electors, first, *1:* 18
Electronic Data Systems (EDS), *5:*
1526
"Elegant Arthur." *See* Arthur,
Chester A.
Elementary and Secondary Educa-
tion Act, *5:* 1328
Elizabeth II, queen of Great Britain,
5: 1301
Elk Hill, California, *4:* 1030
Elkhorn Ranch (Theodore Roo-
sevelt), *3:* 884
Ellsberg, Daniel, *5:* 1375–78

Emancipation, gradual, *2:* 581
Emancipation Proclamation (Lincoln), *2:* 456, 514, 567–68, **581–86**, 582 (ill.)
Embargo Act (1807), *1:* 117, 155, 189, 304
Emergency Banking Act, *4:* 1135, 1138, 1178
Emergency Relief and Construction Act, *4:* 1107
Emerson, Ralph Waldo, *3:* 685
Emma, queen of Hawaii, *2:* 625
Empiricism, *1:* 102
The End of Reconstruction, Speech on (Hayes), *3:* **705–10**
Energy crisis, *5:* 1445–48
Energy resources, *5:* 1448
Enforcement Act, *3:* 655–56
England
    Churchill, Winston, *4:* 1149
    World War I, *4:* 973, 978, 1091
English, William H., election of 1880, *3:* 718
Enlightenment (philosophical movement), *1:* 190
Environmental movement, *5:* 1346
Environmental Protection Agency, *5:* 1367
Equal rights
    for African Americans. *See under* African Americans; Civil rights for Filipinos, *3:* 944–45
    for immigrants. *See under* particular immigrant group, e.g., Chinese immigration
    for women. *See* Women's rights
Equal Rights Amendment (ERA), *5:* 1425
"Era of Good Feelings," *1:* 181, 182, 193, 196–99
Erie Canal, *1:* 231 (ill.)
Erwin committee, *5:* 1376–77, 1377 (ill.), 1378
Erwin, Sam, *5:* 1376
Estaing, Jean-Baptiste-Charles-Henri-Hector d', *1:* 14
"Ethnic cleansing," *5:* 1564
Europe. *See also* Eastern Europe
    Cold War, *4:* 1248
    Great Depression, *4:* 1099
    Marshall, George C., *4:* 1201
    military governments (1930s), *4:* 1145–46
    Monroe Doctrine, *1:* 200, 210
    Monroes' diplomacy tour, *1:* 207
    post–World War II, *4:* 1154, 1202
    World War I, *3:* 955–56; *4:* 972–74, 1091–92
    World War II, *4:* 1147
European Recovery Plan (Marshall Plan), *4:* 1201, 1202

Everett, Edward, *2:* 587, 590
    election of 1860, *2:* 562
"Evil empire," *5:* 1482
Evolution, *3:* 857, 892
Excise Tax, *1:* 21–22, 23
Executive branch, *1:* 34
    limitations, *2:* 349
    powers, *3:* 860; *4:* 1003. *See also* Presidential powers
    during World War II, *4:* 1152
Executive orders
    Banning Segregation in the Military (Truman), *4:* **1229–32**
    Constitutional authorization, *4:* 1229–30
    intelligence services, *5:* 1416–17
Executive privilege, *1:* 28; *5:* 1376, 1380
Exit polls, *5:* 1608
Expansionism. *See also* Native Americans
    Adams, John Quincy, *1:* 230
    effect on Native Americans, *3:* 769–70
    Frémont, John C., *2:* 408
    Grant, Ulysses S., *3:* 652
    Harrison, Benjamin, *3:* 811
    Jay's Treaty, *1:* 26
    Lincoln, Abraham, *2:* 568
    Lodge, Henry Cabot, *4:* 980–81
    McKinley, William, *3:* 795, 851
    Polk, James K., *2:* 404–10, 419–21, 451
    Van Buren, Martin, *1:* 316
    World War I era, *4:* 972
Exploration
    Frémont, John C., *2:* 408–9
    Lewis and Clark, *1:* 112–13, 114–15
Exposé journalism, *3:* 917

F

Factions, Washington's view, *1:* 51
Fair Deal, *4:* 1206
Fair Employment Practices Commission (FEPC), *4:* 1152
Fair Housing Act of 1968, *5:* 1328
Fair Labor Standards Act, *4:* 1141, 1143; *5:* 1329
Fairbanks, Charles W., *3:* 894
    election of 1904, *3:* 895
    election of 1916, *4:* 966
Fairfax, George, *1:* 5
Fall, Albert, *4:* 1024, 1029–30, 1055
Fallen Timbers, Battle of, *2:* 328, 332
Family and Medical Leave Act of 1993, *5:* 1560

Family literacy, *5:* 1531–32, 1533–34

Famine Relief Commission, *4:* 1105

Farewell Address of 1796 (Washington), *1:* **45–52**

Farmer, James, *5:* 1325 (ill.)

Farmers, *4:* 1097–98
McNary-Haugen Bill, *4:* 1066–67, 1068
Populism, *3:* 823

Farmers' Alliance, *3:* 824

Fascism, *4:* 1102

"Father of the Constitution." *See* **Madison, James**

"Fear itself" speech (Franklin D. Roosevelt), *4:* 1135, 1168

"The Fed." *See* Federal Reserve System ("the Fed")

Federal banking system, *1:* 228, 272–73, 273 (ill.), 275 (ill.), 285–86, 289, 300, 302; *2:* 367, 399–401. *See also* Federal Reserve

Federal budget
Clinton administration, *5:* 1561, 1567, 1568
Greenspan, Alan, *5:* 1566–67

Federal budget deficit, *5:* 1472, 1507, 1511–12
Bush, George, *5:* 1521, 1538–39, 1567

Federal budget surplus, *3:* 788; *5:* 1568

Federal Bureau of Investigation (FBI), *5:* 1380, 1406

Federal circuit court system, *3:* 931

Federal Conscription Act, *3:* 779

Federal Deposit Insurance Corporation (FDIC), *4:* 1139–40

Federal disaster relief, *4:* 1060

Federal Emergency Relief Administration (FERA), *4:* 1138

Federal Espionage Act, *3:* 893

Federal Farm Board, *4:* 1097–98

Federal government. *See also* States' rights
Articles of Confederation, *1:* **37–44,** 46, 135
branches, *1:* 59, 103, 150
Constitution, *1:* 135–37
deregulation of business (Reagan era), *5:* 1481
early financial system, *1:* 21, 24–25
Garfield's view, *3:* 737
Hamilton's view, *1:* 24, 152–53
limitations, *1:* 37–44, 150; *4:* 1116
Madison's view, *1:* 150, 152–53
Morgan, J. P., *3:* 793

Reagan's view, *5:* 1472, 1501, 1502, 1507
regulation of business and banking. *See* Fair Deal; Great Society; New Deal
Washington's Farewell Address of 1796, *1:* **45–52**
World War II, *4:* 1154–55

Federal Housing Administration, *4:* 1140

Federal oil deposits, *4:* 1030

Federal Reserve Act (1913), *1:* 141, 276, 289

Federal Reserve System ("the Fed"), *1:* 289, 302; *4:* 968, 1137, 1138
Greenspan, Alan, *5:* 1566–67

Federal spending, *5:* 1411

Federal Trade Commission, *4:* 968–69

Federalist(s)
decline, *1:* 71
financial system, *1:* 107
Hamilton, Alexander, *1:* 24–25, 25 (ill.), 60, 152–53
taxes, *1:* 21–22
vs. anti-Federalists, *1:* 45, 60, 106–7, 141, 152–53, 188
vs. Democratic-Republicans, *1:* 225
Webster, Daniel, *2:* 370

The Federalist Papers, *1:* 24, 27, 152

Federalist Party, *1:* 107

Federalist Plan (Hamilton), *1:* 152–53

Feminist movement, *5:* 1397

Ferraro, Geraldine, election of 1984, *5:* 1477

Field, James G., election of 1892, *3:* 782

Fifteenth Amendment, *3:* 652, 655–56, 687

"54°40' or Fight!," *2:* 403, 405

Fillmore, Abigail, *2:* 461, 469, **475–77,** 475 (ill.)
schoolteacher, *2:* 475–76
White House library, *2:* 476–77

Fillmore, Caroline Carmichael McIntosh, *2:* 472, 472 (ill.)

Fillmore, Millard, *2:* **457–73,** 459 (ill.), 463 (ill.), 468 (ill.), 469 (ill.), 522 (ill.)
administration, *2:* 465–66
Annual Message to Congress, First, *2:* **451–56**
Compromise of 1850, *2:* 443, 455, 466–68
early years, *2:* 460–61
election of 1848, *2:* 439
election of 1852, *2:* 468
election of 1856, *2:* 469, 523

foreign and domestic policy, *2:* 480

Johnson, Andrew, *2:* 472

Lincoln, Abraham, *2:* 472

marriage and family, *2:* 461, 469, 472, 475–76

political career, *2:* 462–65, 476

presidency, *2:* 465–69

retirement, *2:* 469, 472

trade and industry growth, *2:* 468

vice presidency, *2:* 464–65

Financial system, Federalists' view, *1:* 21

"Fire in a theater" scenario, *3:* 893

Fireside chats (Franklin D. Roosevelt), *4:* 1133, 1137, 1138, 1139, 1175, 1179 (ill.), 1179–80

First Fireside Chat, First, *4:* 1175–80

First lady

called first lady, *2:* 535

first accompanies husband at inaugural, *3:* 946

first press conferences, *4:* 1033, 1035

First Lady from Plains (Rosalynn Carter), *5:* 1458

First Manassas, Battle of (Battle of Bull Run), *2:* 566

First National Bank, *1:* 21, 24–25, 141, 285

Fish, Hamilton, *3:* 652, 654–55, 655 (ill.)

Fisk, Jim, *3:* 653

Fiske, Harlan, *4:* 1195 (ill.)

Five Forks, Battle of, *3:* 650

Florida, *2:* 562. *See also* Seminole nation

election of 1876, *3:* 692

election of 2000, *5:* 1598, 1605–17

law on recounts, *5:* 1610–11

purchase, *1:* 197, 265

Reno, Janet, *5:* 1570–71

Spanish possession, *1:* 196

Stowe, Harriet Beecher, *2:* 471

Florida State Canvassing Board, *3:* 692

Florida Supreme Court, election of 2000, *5:* 1614

Floyd, John B., *2:* 526 (ill.)

Folsom, Frances. *See* Cleveland, Frances

Food, war relief, *4:* 1091–92

Food and Drug Act, *3:* 924

Food and drug legislation, *3:* 895, 915

Forbes, Charles, *4:* 1024, 1029, 1036

Ford, Betty, *5:* 1381 (ill.), **1421–26,** 1421 (ill.), 1424 (ill.)

breast cancer, *5:* 1421, 1424–25

comfort with the press, *5:* 1425

demands of political life, *5:* 1423

marriage and family, *5:* 1422–23

role as first lady, *5:* 1423–24, 1425

substance-abuse awareness, *5:* 1423, 1426

Ford, Gerald R., *5:* 1380, 1381 (ill.), **1399–1420,** 1401 (ill.), 1402 (ill.), 1411 (ill.), 1416 (ill.), 1424 (ill.), 1429 (ill.), 1517 (ill.)

administration, *5:* 1410

anti-inflation program, *5:* 1414–15

as athlete, *5:* 1402 (ill.), 1414

Carter, Jimmy, *5:* 1419

clemency for draft-dodgers (Vietnam Era Reconciliation Program), *5:* 1412–14

domestic policy, *5:* 1414–15

early years, *5:* 1401–3

election of 1976, *5:* 1417–18, 1425–26, 1432, 1442

election of 1980, *5:* 1418, 1518

foreign affairs, *5:* 1415–17

foreign intelligence, *5:* 1416–17

marriage and family, *5:* 1403–4, 1422–23

military service, *5:* 1403

Nixon, Richard, *5:* 1404, 1406–9

pardon backlash, *5:* 1410–11, 1431

Pardon of Richard Nixon, *5:* 1381, 1408–9, **1427–33,** 1429 (ill.)

political career, *5:* 1404–6, 1422–23

presidency, *5:* 1407–17, 1423–24

"Remarks on Taking the Oath of Office as President" (excerpt), *5:* 1408–9

retirement, *5:* 1418

vice presidency, *5:* 1406–7, 1423

Vietnam War, *5:* 1412–14, 1415

Watergate, *5:* 1405–7

Ford, Henry, *4:* 1065, 1098

"Foreign Policy and Human Rights" Speech (Carter), *5:* **1461–68**

Foreign relations

Adams, John Quincy, *1:* 220

Articles of Confederation, *1:* 43

Monroe Doctrine, *1:* 200

Nixon, Richard, *5:* 1372–73

Foreign Service, *3:* 935

Forest Reserve Act, *3:* 897

Forest Service, *3:* 897

"The forgotten middle class," *5:* 1558

Forsyth, John, *1:* 246
Fort Crawford, *2:* 431
Fort Detroit, *2:* 333
Fort Donelson, *3:* 644, 646
Fort Duquesne, *1:* 7–8
Fort La Boeuf, *1:* 7
Fort McHenry, *1:* 157, 158–59
Fort Necessity, *1:* 7
Fort Sumter, *2:* 563
Forty-ninth parallel, *2:* 405, 520
Foster Grandparents Program, *5:* 1496
Fourteen Points (Wilson), *4:* 976, 977, **997–1004**
Fourteenth Amendment, *2:* 609, 615; *3:* 787
Fourth World Conference on Women (United Nations, Beijing, China), *5:* 1585
Fox tribe, *2:* 431, 434
France
  Adams, John, *1:* 59
  American Revolution, *1:* 14, 16
  French Revolution, *1:* 22, 62, 105–6
  Great Depression, *4:* 1099
  Indochina, *5:* 1287, 1302, 1331, 1373
  Kennedys' tour, *5:* 1284, 1303
  Lafayette, Major General, *1:* 186–87, 187 (ill.)
  Lafayette, Marquise de, *1:* 206–7
  Mexico, *2:* 611
  Monroe, Elizabeth, *1:* 206–7
  Monroe, James, *1:* 188
  Napoleon I (Napoleon Bonaparte, emperor of France), *1:* 111–12, 189, 194–95
  Napoleonic war reparations, *1:* 274, 298–99
  Quasi-War, *1:* 66, 70
  Vietnam, *4:* 1245, *5:* 1287, 1331, 1373
  World War I, *4:* 973, 978
  XYZ affair, *1:* 66
Frankfurter, Felix, *4:* 1100
Franklin, Benjamin, *1:* 14, 15–16, 17, 17 (ill.), 133 (ill.), 190
  Committee of Five, *1:* 126
Franz Ferdinand, Archduke, *4:* 973
Frederick William III, *1:* 241
Fredericksburg, Battle of, *3:* 649
Free blacks, *1:* 199
"Free silver," *3:* 789, 845
Free Soil Party, *1:* 308; *2:* 439, 493
Free states
  California, *2:* 371, 439–40
  New Mexico, *2:* 439–40
Free trade policies, *3:* 858, 860
Freedmen's Bureau, *2:* 614

Freedom of speech, World War I, *3:* 893
Freedoms of individuals, applied to business, *4:* 1078
Freemasons, *2:* 462
Frelinghuysen, Theodore, election of 1844, *2:* 401
Frémont, John C., *2:* 408–9, 409 (ill.), 410, 469 (ill.), 522 (ill.), 524 (ill.); *3:* 792
  election of 1856, *2:* 409, 522, 523, 558
French and Indian War, *1:* 7–8, 8 (ill.)
French Empire, *1:* 194–95
French Revolution, *1:* 22–23, 62, 105–6
  Lafayette, Major General, *1:* 186–87, 187 (ill.)
  Lafayette, Marquise de, *1:* 206–7
  Napoleon I (Napoleon Bonaparte, emperor of France), *1:* 194
  Paine, Thomas, *1:* 190–91
Friedman, Milton, *5:* 1481
Fromme, Lynette "Squeaky," *5:* 1414
"Front porch" campaigns
  Bush, George W., *5:* 1631
  Garfield, James A., *3:* 742–43
  Harding, Warren G., *4:* 1024
  McKinley, William, *3:* 858; *5:* 1631
Frontier
  Homestead Act, *2:* 568, 573
  political development, *1:* 258, 275
Fuel conservation, *5:* 1445–48
Fugitive Slave Act, *2:* 371, 442, 455, 466–67, 479, 496–97, 509, 513, 541, 608
  Stowe, Harriet Beecher, *2:* 470
Fulbright, J. William, *5:* 1550
Fundamentalism, *3:* 856–57

G

Gable, Clark, *5:* 1495
Gadsden Purchase, *2:* 497–98, 503, 564
Gaines, Edmund, *1:* 304
Galt, Edith Bolling. *See* Wilson, Edith
Galt, Norman, *4:* 992
Gandhi, Mohandas, *5:* 1292
Gardiner, Julia. *See* Tyler, Julia
Gardiner, Lion, *2:* 379
Garfield, James A., *3:* **711–27,** 713 (ill.), 720 (ill.), 723 (ill.), 754 (ill.)

administration, *3:* 719
assassination, *3:* 722–23, 731–32, 752, 758–59
civil service reform, *3:* 713, 721, 722, 758
congressional career, *3:* 713–14, 717–20, 731
early years, *3:* 714–16
election of 1876, *3:* 718–20, 735–36
election of 1880, *3:* 718, 742, 754–55, 757
Lincoln, Abraham, *3:* 716
marriage and family, *3:* 716, 729, 730, 732
military service, *3:* 717, 731
political career, *3:* 713–14
presidency, *3:* 722–23, 731
"Revolution Against the Constitution" speech, *3:* 735–43
Garfield, Lucretia, *3:* 729–33, 729 (ill.)
assassination of husband, *3:* 731–32
progressive-minded schoolteacher, *3:* 729
Garner, John Nance, *4:* 1134
GATT (General Agreement on Tariffs and Trade), *5:* 1560
General Agreement on Tariffs and Trade (GATT), *5:* 1560
General Allotment Act (Dawes Act), *3:* 773–74
General Electric Company, *5:* 1474
General Motors (GM), *5:* 1526–27
General Paper Company, *4:* 1062
George II (king of England), *1:* 6–7
George III (king of England), *1:* 125, 127, 127 (ill.)
Georgia (Soviet), *5:* 1485
Georgia (U.S.), *2:* 562
Carter, Jimmy, *5:* 1436–37, 1440–41
Cherokee, *1:* 274, 305
Seminoles, *1:* 231–32, 264
German Americans, *4:* 999
Germany
Berlin Wall, *5:* 1285
Cold War, *5:* 1285
Einstein, Albert, *4:* 1223
Great Depression, *4:* 1102
Lindbergh, Charles A., *4:* 1065
reunification, *5:* 1485
World War I, *4:* 973–76, 978, 984, 997–99, 1003, 1005–6, 1011, 1025
World War II, *4:* 1147, 1184, 1195, 1223
Gerry, Elbridge, *1:* 63, 155, 156
election of 1812, *1:* 155

Gettysburg Address (Lincoln), *2:* 569, **587–91,** 589
manuscript copies, *2:* 590
Gettysburg, Battle of, *2:* 565, 568, 588, 589; *3:* 650
Ghent, Treaty of, *1:* 226, 264
"The Gipper." *See* Reagan, Ronald
Girl Scouts of America, *4:* 1111
Glasnost ("openness"), *5:* 1482, 1484
Gold reserve, *3:* 653–55, 791, 793
Gold standard, *1:* 274; *3:* 695, 717, 789, 791, 845, 856, 860
Gold Standard Act, *3:* 875
Goldwater, Barry M., *5:* 1334, 1474
election of 1964, *5:* 1326, 1496
Gompers, Samuel, *4:* 1054, 1055 (ill.)
"Good neighbor" policy, *4:* 1145
Goodhue, Grace. *See* Coolidge, Grace
GOP ("Grand Old Party"). *See* Republican Party
Gorbachev, Mikhail, *5:* 1482, 1484–85, 1485 (ill.), 1522
Gorbachev, Raisa, *5:* 1484, 1533
Gordy, Tom, *5:* 1437
Gore, Al, Jr., *5:* 1554, 1555, 1556–57, 1557 (ill.)
election of 1992, *5:* 1555
election of 1996, *5:* 1555
election of 2000, *5:* 1557, 1577, 1597, 1605–17, 1608–17, 1630–31
Gore, Al, Sr., *5:* 1556
Gore, Albert, III, *5:* 1557
Gore, Tipper, *5:* 1556
Gould, Jay, *3:* 653
Government, John Adams' Thoughts on, *1:* 81–89
Government and business
Government and Business speech (Coolidge), *4:* **1077–83**
Harding, Warren G., *4:* 1040, 1045
Roosevelt, Theodore, *3:* 890, 895, 911, 928
"Rugged Individualism" campaign speech (Hoover), *4:* **1115–22**
Taft, William Howard, *3:* 933–35
Government deficit. *See* Federal budget deficit
Government pensions, *3:* 784
Government social programs. *See* Great Society; New Deal
Graduated income tax, *4:* 968
Graham, Billy, *5:* 1603
Graham, Martha, *5:* 1422
Graham, William A., election of 1852, *2:* 495

Grand Canyon National Monument, *3:* 899

"Grand Old Party" (GOP). *See* Republican Party

Granger, Francis, election of 1836, *1:* 301

Grant, Julia, *3:* 661, **665–69,** 665 (ill.)
  happy as first lady, *3:* 668
  military wife, *3:* 666–67
  world tour, *3:* 668

Grant, Nellie, *3:* 660, 668

Grant, Ulysses S., *2:* 568; *3:* **637–64,** 639 (ill.), 646 (ill.), 647 (ill.), 661 (ill.), 673 (ill.), 752
  Annual Address to Congress (1874), *3:* 659
  Civil War, *2:* 568, 569–70, 589; *3:* 640, 644–50, 665
  early years, *3:* 641–43
  election of 1868, *3:* 651–52
  election of 1872, *3:* 651
  election of 1880, *3:* 660, 668
  greenbacks, *3:* 653–55
  Johnson, Andrew, *2:* 619; *3:* 650–51
  Lee, Robert E., *3:* 649
  marriage and family, *3:* 643, 665, 666
  memoirs, *3:* 661
  Mexican War, *2:* 425; *3:* 643
  military career, *3:* 644–50, 665, 666–67
  patronage system, *3:* 663, 753
  presidency, *3:* 639–40, 651–60, 665
  Recollection of the Confederate Surrender, *3:* **671–78**
  Reconstruction, *3:* 640–41, 655–56, 659
  retirement, *3:* 660–61, 669
  world tour, *3:* 660, 668

Grayson, Cary T., *4:* 992

The Great American Fraud (S. M. Adams), *3:* 924

Great Britain
  Adams, John, *1:* 59
  Adams, John Quincy, *1:* 242
  Alabama, *2:* 611; *3:* 654–55, 656
  American Revolution, *1:* 9, 12, 16, 23, 97
  Atlantic Charter, *4:* 1148
  The Caroline incident, *1:* 303–4
  Civil War, *2:* 611
  Embargo Act of 1807, *1:* 117, 155, 189, 304
  fishing rights dispute, *3:* 819–20
  Great Depression, *4:* 1099
  Jay's Treaty, *1:* 26
  Kennedy, John F., *5:* 1275

Monroe Doctrine, *1:* 200, 209
  Northern Ireland, *5:* 1568
  Seminole raids, *1:* 196
  taxes American colonies, *1:* 57–58
  War of 1812, *1:* 146, 156–59, 166–67
  World War I, *4:* 973, 978, 997–98, 1147
  World War II, *4:* 1147

"The Great Commoner." *See* Bryan, William Jennings

"The Great Communicator." *See* Reagan, Ronald

"The Great Compromiser." *See* Clay, Henry

Great Depression, *3:* 663; *4:* 1067–68, 1098–1104, 1112, 1147
  Hoover, Herbert, *4:* 1023, 1120–21
  Hoover, Lou, *4:* 1112
  Hoovervilles, *4:* 1103, 1103 (ill.), 1135
  Hughes, Charles Evans, *4:* 1027
  Marshall, George C., *4:* 1200
  Mellon, Andrew W., *4:* 1023
  relief agencies, *4:* 1136–37
  relief, recovery, and reform legislation, *4:* 1138–41
  Roosevelt, Eleanor, *4:* 1162–63
  Roosevelt, Franklin D., *4:* 1135–45, 1167–68, 1172, 1179
  Soup kitchens, *4:* 1099 (ill.)

"The Great Dissenter." *See* Holmes, Oliver Wendell, Jr.

Great Northern Railroad, *3:* 793

"The Great Nullifier." *See* Calhoun, John C.

"The Great Pathfinder." *See* Frémont, John C.

Great Plains drought (1930), *4:* 1099

Great Society, *5:* 1326–30, 1343–44, 1349–50, 1354–55
  arts and humanities, *5:* 1329–30
  economic opportunity (Act and Office), *5:* 1327–28
  education, *5:* 1328
  "Great Society" speech (Lyndon B. Johnson), *5:* **1349–56**
  housing, *5:* 1328–29
  labor, *5:* 1329
  medical care, *5:* 1328
  "War on Poverty," *5:* 1326

Great Wall of China, *5:* 1273 (ill.)

"The Greatest Generation," *5:* 1626

Greece, *4:* 1202

Greeley, Horace, election of 1872, *3:* 651

Greenback Party, *3:* 824

Greenbacks, *3:* 652–55, 659, 695
Greenspan, Alan, *5:* 1566–67, 1567 (ill.), 1568
Greenville Treaty, *2:* 332; *3:* 769
Grenada, *5:* 1483
"Gridlock," *5:* 1525
Grouseland (William Henry Harrison), *2:* 329
Guffey-Snyder Act, *4:* 1172
Guiteau, Charles J., *3:* 722, 722 (ill.), 723 (ill.), 758
Gulf of Tonkin incident, *5:* 1330–31
Gulf Oil Corporation, *4:* 1022
Gulf War, *5:* 1512, 1523–25, 1524 (ill.), 1537–38, 1543–44
   Bush, George, *5:* 1524, 1537–38, 1607
   Cheney, Dick, *5:* 1607
   clearly defined mission, *5:* 1524, 1543

H

Habitat for Humanity, *5:* 1436, 1453, 1453 (ill.)
Hahn, Otto, *4:* 1223
Haig, Alexander M., Jr., *5:* 1408
"Hail to the Chief" (Sanderson), *2:* 380, 381; *5:* 1407
Haiti, *3:* 656–57; *5:* 1563
Haldeman, H. R., *5:* 1369, 1378, 1380
Half-Breeds, *3:* 721, 758
   Blaine, James G., *3:* 756
   election of 1880, *3:* 754–55, 757
Halliburton Company, *5:* 1607
Hamer, Thomas, *3:* 642
Hamilton, Alexander, *1:* 20, 21, 22 (ill.), 24–25, 25 (ill.), 117 (ill.)
   Adams, John, *1:* 60, 61, 71
   Burr, Aaron, *1:* 25, 115–17, 117 (ill.)
   Jefferson, Thomas, *1:* 106–7, 135–36, 140
   Madison, James, *1:* 152–53
   Washington, George, *1:* 140
Hamlin, Hannibal, election of 1860, *2:* 562
Hammerschmidt, John Paul, *5:* 1553
Hampton, Wade, *3:* 694
Hance, Kent R., *5:* 1602, 1603
Hancock, John, *1:* 133
Hancock, Winfield Scott, election of 1880, *3:* 718, 722, 743
Hanna, Mark, *3:* 848; *5:* 1631
"Happiness," *1:* 81, 127; *4:* 1168
Hard cider, *2:* 335, 337

"The Hard Cider Quick Step" (campaign song), *2:* 335
"Hard money." *See* Gold standard
Harding, Florence, *4:* 1029 (ill.), **1033–37,** 1033 (ill.), 1035 (ill.)
   active first lady, *4:* 1035–36
   early independence, *4:* 1034
   marriage, *4:* 1034–35
Harding, Warren G., *4:* **1013–32,** 1015 (ill.), 1029 (ill.), 1035 (ill.)
   administration, *4:* 1024
   Coolidge, Calvin, *4:* 1055
   death of, *4:* 1030, 1054, 1055–56
   early years, *4:* 1016–17
   economic policy, *4:* 1025, 1040, 1045
   election of 1912, *4:* 1019
   election of 1920, *4:* 979, 981, 1011, 1021, 1039
   League of Nations, *4:* 1030, 1039, 1041
   Lodge, Henry Cabot, *4:* 981
   marriage, *4:* 1017, 1034
   political career, *4:* 1018–24, 1034–35
   presidency, *4:* 1024–30, 1035–36
   publishing career, *4:* 1017, 1034
   scandal-ridden administration, *4:* 1025–30, 1036
   Speech to a Special Session of Congress, *4:* **1013–32**
   Treaty of Versailles, *4:* 1030
   Wilson, Woodrow, *4:* 1030–31
Hardscrabble (Grant), *3:* 646, 667
Harken Energy, *5:* 1602
Harpers Ferry, Virginia, *2:* 526, 528, 529, 559; *3:* 648
Harriet Lane Home for Invalid Children (Baltimore), *2:* 538
Harriet Lane (naval ships), *2:* 537
Harris, Katherine, *5:* 1611, 1612
Harrison, Anna, *2:* **341–45,** 341 (ill.)
   American Revolution baby, *2:* 342
   marriage and family, *2:* 343
Harrison, Benjamin, *2:* 328, 344–45; *3:* 3: **811–26,** 811 (ill.), 815 (ill.), 817 (ill.), 820 (ill.)
   administration, *3:* 821
   "centennial president," *3:* 822, 825, 827
   comparisons with grandfather, *3:* 822
   early years, *3:* 812–16
   election of 1888, *3:* 788, 812, 818, 819; *5:* 1608, 1613
   election of 1892, *3:* 782, 812, 821, 830
   foreign policy, *3:* 819–20

foreign relations, *3:* 811–12

legal career, *3:* 816, 828

marriage and family, *3:* 814, 821, 822, 828, 829

Message to the Senate Supporting the Annexation of Hawaii, *3:* 831–35

military career, *3:* 816, 829

nicknames, *3:* 822

political career, *3:* 816–22, 829

presidency, *3:* 819–22

Harrison, Benjamin (William Henry's father), *2:* 327; *3:* 813

Harrison, Caroline, *3:* 789, 821, **827–30,** 827 (ill.)

active first lady, *3:* 829

art lover, *3:* 827

marriage and family, *3:* 828–29

White House improvements, *3:* 827–28

Harrison, Jane Irwin, *2:* 344

Harrison, John, *3:* 813

Harrison, John Scott, *2:* 344

Harrison, Mary (Mary Scott Lord Dimmick), *3:* 822, 825 (ill.)

Harrison, Thomas, *3:* 813

Harrison, William Henry, *1:* 157; *2:* **323–40,** 325 (ill.), 328 (ill.), 330 (ill.), 348 (ill.); *3:* 812, 822

administration, *2:* 337

Battle of Tippecanoe, *2:* 333

early years, *2:* 327–28

election of 1836, *1:* 301

election of 1840, *1:* 229, 306; *2:* 336

Inaugural Address, *2:* 325, 326, **347–54**

marriage and family, *2:* 328, 341, 343

military life, *2:* 328–31, 342–43

political career, *2:* 331–36, 343, 344

Tyler, John, *2:* 338, 353

Harvey, George, *4:* 965

Hauptmann, Bruno Richard, *4:* 1065

Hawaii annexation, *3:* 789, 820–21, 831–32, 834, 853; *4:* 981

Message to Congress Opposing (Cleveland), *3:* 790, **803–8**

Message to the Senate Supporting (Benjamin Harrison), *3:* 808, 820–21, **831–35**

Hawaiian Islands, *3:* 808

Monroe Doctrine, *1:* 214; *2:* 369

Hawthorne, Nathaniel, *2:* 488

Hay, John, *2:* 590

Hayes, Lucy, *3:* **699–703,** 699 (ill.), 701 (ill.)

active and giving, *3:* 702–3

"Lemonade Lucy," *3:* 702

"Mother Lucy," *3:* 686, 701

Hayes, Rutherford B., *3:* **679–98,** 681 (ill.), 688 (ill.), 696 (ill.), 701 (ill.); *5:* 1618

administration, *3:* 695

civil service reform, *3:* 689, 694–95, 753

early years, *3:* 682–83

effectiveness as president, *3:* 709–10

election of 1876, *3:* 681, 689–94, 691, 693, 706, 718–20; *5:* 1608, 1613

financial policy, *3:* 695, 697

inaugural address, *3:* 694

legal career, *3:* 683–86

marriage and family, *3:* 685, 686, 700

military career, *3:* 686–87, 701

political career, *3:* 686–87

presidency, *3:* 694–96

retirements, *3:* 687, 697, 702–3

Speech on the End of Reconstruction, *3:* **705–10**

tainted election, *3:* 689–94, 718–20

Head Start, *5:* 1328, 1338, 1343–44

Health insurance

failed Clinton health plan, *5:* 1559–60

failed New Deal legislation, *4:* 1141

Great Society legislation, *5:* 1328

Hearst, George, *3:* 854

Hearst, William Randolph, *3:* 850, 854–55, 855 (ill.); *4:* 1026

Hearts and Hammers, *5:* 1602

Hellcats of the Navy, *5:* 1473

Hemings, Madison, *1:* 104–5

Hemings, Sally, *1:* 104–5

Hendricks, Thomas A., *3:* 781 (ill.)

election of 1876, *3:* 693

election of 1884, *3:* 782

Henry, Lou. *See* Hoover, Lou

Henry, Patrick, *1:* 97, 98, 99, 99 (ill.), 169

Hepburn Act, *3:* 895, 916; *4:* 980

Hermitage (Jackson), *1:* 261, 276, 281, 283

Herndon, Ellen Lewis. *See* Arthur, Ellen

Herron, Helen. *See* Taft, Helen

Herut (Freedom) Party, *5:* 1446

"He's Going to Marry Yum-Yum" (song), *3:* 798

Hessians, *1:* 10

High-altitude aerial surveillance, of Soviet Union by United States, *4:* 1245, 1250–51

"High crimes and misdemeanors," *5:* 1548, 1572

Higher Education Act, *5:* 1328

Highland (Monroe), *1:* 214

Highways. *See also* Infrastructure

Eisenhower, Dwight D., *4:* 1239, 1248

Highway Beautification Act of 1965 (Lady Bird Johnson), *5:* 1344

Hill, Anita, *5:* 1521

Hinckley, John, Jr., *5:* 1479

Hindenburg, Paul von, *4:* 1102

Hiram College, *3:* 715–16, 730

Hiroshima, *4:* 1101, 1184, 1198, 1222

"His Accidency." *See* Tyler, John

"His Obstinacy." *See* Cleveland, Grover

Hispaniola, *3:* 656–57

Hiss, Alger, *4:* 1206; *5:* 1363

The Historic Guide to the White House, 5: 1303

The History of the Standard Oil Company (Tarbell), *3:* 924

History of Woman Suffrage (Anthony and Stanton), *3:* 785, 787

Hitler, Adolf, *4:* 1003, 1102, 1147, 1149; *5:* 1275

Hobart, Garret A., *3:* 848, 858, 888

Hoes, Hannah. *See* Van Buren, Hannah

Holden, William, *5:* 1495

Holmes, Oliver Wendell, Jr., *3:* 891, 892–93, 893 (ill.), 936 (ill.)

Holt, Joseph, *2:* 526 (ill.)

Home loans (mortgages), New Deal legislation, *4:* 1140

Home Owners' Loan Corporation (HOLC), *4:* 1140

Homestead Act, *2:* 568, 573, 605, 620–21

Homosexuals in the military, *5:* 1558

Hooker, Joseph, *2:* 569

Hoover Commission, *4:* 1106, 1121

Hoover Dam, *4:* 1105–6, 1122

Hoover, Herbert, *4:* 1085–1107, 1087 (ill.), 1093 (ill.), 1105 (ill.)

administration, *4:* 1097

early years, *4:* 1088

economic policy, *4:* 1098–99, 1103, 1106–7, 1120–21

election of 1928, *4:* 1095, 1096–97, 1117

election of 1932, *4:* 1104–5, 1121, 1134

foreign policy, *4:* 1099–1102

Great Depression, *4:* 1023, 1120–21

marriage and family, *4:* 1089, 1091, 1110

mining career, *4:* 1088–89, 1110

public service career, *4:* 1092–96, 1121

retirement, *4:* 1105–6, 1114

Roosevelt, Franklin D., *4:* 1121

"Rugged Individualism" campaign speech, *4:* 1115–22

World War I relief efforts, *4:* 1091–92, 1110–11

World War II, *4:* 1105

Hoover, Lou, *4:* 1109–14, 1109 (ill.), 1113 (ill.)

active and involved first lady, *4:* 1111–12

marriage and family, *4:* 1110

subtle acts of charity, *4:* 1112, 1113

work with Girl Scouts, *4:* 1111, 1114

world travelers, *4:* 1110–11

"Hooverizing," *4:* 1092

Hoovervilles, *4:* 1103, 1103 (ill.), 1135

Hopkins, Harry L., *4:* 1137, 1143

"Hotshot." *See* Carter, Jimmy

"House divided" speech (Lincoln), *2:* 559; *5:* 1618

House, Edward, *4:* 993

House of Burgesses (Virginia), *1:* 9, 97

House of Representatives. *See also* Congress; Senate

Adams, John Quincy, *1:* 220, 234–35

Ford, Gerald R., *5:* 1404–5

House Committee on Un-American Activities, *4:* 1143, 1206; *5:* 1363, 1372, 1474

House Intelligence Committee, *5:* 1556

House Judiciary Committee, *5:* 1380, 1407, 1576

House Ways and Means Committee, *2:* 462, 609

impeachment hearings against Bill Clinton, *5:* 1575–76

impeachment hearings against Richard Nixon, *5:* 1377, 1380, 1407

impeachment of Andrew Johnson, *2:* 616

Ways and Means Committee, *2:* 609

Housing, New Deal legislation, *4:* 1140

Houston, Samuel, *2:* 369, 385, 468 (ill.)

Howard, John E., election of 1816, *1:* 193

Howe, William, *1:* 10, 12–13, 14

Huerta, Victoriano, *4:* 969

Hughes, Charles Evans, *4:* 974, 1024, 1025, 1026–27, 1027 (ill.), 1094
  election of 1916, *4:* 966
  League of Nations, *4:* 1026
Hughes, Sarah, *5:* 1321, 1323 (ill.)
Hull, William, *1:* 297, *2:* 331
Human rights
  Adams, John Quincy, *1:* 246
  Carter, Jimmy, *5:* 1444, 1452–53, 1461–62, 1467
  Clinton, Hillary Rodham, *5:* 1585
  Humphrey, Hubert H., *5:* 1336–37
  King, Martin Luther, Jr., *5:* 1293
  Roosevelt, Eleanor, *4:* 1165
"Human Rights and Foreign Policy" Speech (Carter), *5:* **1461–68**
Humphrey, Hubert H., *5:* 1336–37, 1337 (ill.)
  election of 1960, *5:* 1337
  election of 1964, *5:* 1326
  election of 1968, *5:* 1335, 1337, 1366, 1367
The Hundred Days (New Deal legislation), *4:* 1137, 1138–41, 1172
Hungary, Communist era, *4:* 1252
"Hush money" (Watergate), *5:* 1378
Hussein, Saddam, *5:* 1523, 1523 (ill.), 1524, 1525, 1537

I

"I Have a Dream" speech (King), *5:* 1291, 1293
"I Like Ike," *4:* 1245 (ill.), 1261 (ill.)
Ickes, Harold, *4:* 1137, 1139
"If You Ask Me" (Eleanor Roosevelt), *4:* 1164
Illinois
  Lincoln, Abraham, *2:* 555, 556, 557
  Stevenson, Adlai E., *4:* 1247
Immigrants
  Asian Americans, *5:* 1338
  Chinese Americans, *3:* 696, 761, 762
  German Americans, *4:* 999
  Irish Americans, *1:* 67
  Japanese Americans, *4:* 1101
  Latino Americans, *5:* 1338
  Mexican Americans, *5:* 1319, 1328
Immigration Reform Act, *5:* 1329, 1338
Impeachment and impeachment hearings

Clinton, Bill, *2:* 617; *5:* 1547, 1548
  Johnson, Andrew, *2:* 616–17
  Nixon, Richard, *5:* 1377, 1380–81
Imperialism, *3:* 790–91, 803, 804, 851; *4:* 972
Inaugural addresses. *See under* Harrison, William Henry; Kennedy, John F.; Lincoln, Abraham; McKinley, William; Pierce, Franklin; Polk, James K.; Reagan, Ronald; Van Buren, Martin
Inaugural ball, first, *1:* 156, 165
Inauguration Day
  calendar change, *4:* 1145
  longest speech, *2:* 337, 347
Income tax
  first corporate, *3:* 933
  graduated, *4:* 968
  Populists' view, *3:* 823
Independent counsel, *5:* 1572
Independent Party, *5:* 1527
Independent Prosecutor Act, *5:* 1576
Independent Treasury System, *1:* 141, 302; *2:* 404–5
Indian Appropriation Act, *3:* 656
"Indian Lands" ("Indian territory"), *1:* 258, 274–75, 306; *2:* 431–32; *3:* 770
Indian Removal Act, *3:* 770
Indiana
  Harrison, Benjamin, *3:* 816, 817
  Harrison, William Harrison, *2:* 329, 331, 334
Indiana Territory, *2:* 330
Indians. *See* Native Americans
Individualism, Hoover's **"Rugged Individualism" speech,** *4:* **1115–22**
Indochina, *5:* 1287, 1302, 1331
Industrial Revolution, *3:* 892
Industrialization, *2:* 525; *3:* 834, 870, 909, 918
  "American System" (Clay), *1:* 228, 230–31
  post–Civil War, *3:* 870
  vs. conservation, *3:* 896
Industry, standardization program (Hoover), *4:* 1092
"Infamy" speech (Franklin D. Roosevelt), *4:* 1181, 1182
Inflation
  Carter, Jimmy, *5:* 1445
  Ford, Gerald R., *5:* 1414–15
Infrastructure
  Adams, John Quincy, *1:* 230–31, 235
  Eisenhower, Dwight D., *4:* 1239, 1248
  New Deal projects, *4:* 1138–39

Ingersoll, Jared, election of 1812, *1:* 155
"Inner city," *5:* 1329
"Innocent until proven guilty," *1:* 65
Integration (desegregation)
   Eisenhower, Dwight D., *4:* 1249
   Kennedys, John F. and Robert F., *5:* 1288–89
   Marshall, Thurgood, *5:* 1332
   Truman, Harry S., *4:* 1229–32
Internal Security Act (McCarran Act), *4:* 1207
International Congress for Women Workers, *4:* 1161
International Development Advisory Board, *5:* 1412
International expansionism, World War I era, *4:* 972
International law, *4:* 1026–27
International peace agreements, *4:* 1046
International politics
   Kissinger, Henry, *5:* 1371
   "new world order," *5:* 1537, 1538, 1543
International trade
   Fillmore, Millard, *2:* 479–84
   GATT (General Agreement on Tariffs and Trade), *5:* 1560
Internationalism, *3:* 852
Interstate commerce, *3:* 911; *4:* 1026
Interstate Commerce Commission, *3:* 784, 895, 901, 916, 941; *4:* 980, 1062
Interstate highways, *4:* 1239, 1248
Inventions, *2:* 525; *4:* 1057
   Bell, Alexander Graham, *3:* 724–25
   Jefferson, Thomas, *1:* 101
Investments, *4:* 1082
Iran, *5:* 1448
   Iran-Contra arms sales scandal, *5:* 1488–89, 1518–19
   Iran hostage crisis, *5:* 1449, 1450–51, 1452 (ill.), 1478, 1501–2
   Iraqi invasion of Kuwait, *5:* 1523
   Perot, H. Ross, *5:* 1526
Iraq
   Address to Congress on the Crisis in Kuwait (Bush) *5:* **1537–44**
   economic sanctions, *5:* 1563
   invasion of Kuwait, *5:* 1512, 1523–25, 1537, 1607
   "no fly" zone, *5:* 1524
Iron Curtain, *4:* 1156, 1248, 1254
Islamic fundamentalists, Iran hostage crisis, *5:* 1450

Israel
   Bush, George, *5:* 1525
   Camp David Accords, *5:* 1446–47, 1466
   Carter, Jimmy, *5:* 1445
   Ford, Gerald R., *5:* 1417
   Iraqi missile attack during Gulf War, *5:* 1523
   Kissinger, Henry, *5:* 1371
   Israeli-Palestinian peace negotiations, *5:* 1563, 1568, 1578–79
It Takes a Village: And Other Lessons Children Teach Us (Hillary Rodham Clinton), *5:* 1585
Italy, *3:* 820
   World War II, *4:* 1147

J

Jackson, Andrew, *1:* 233 (ill.), **255–78,** 257 (ill.), 265 (ill.), 269 (ill.), 273 (ill.), 275 (ill.)
   Adams, John Quincy, *1:* 219–20, 226–27, 236; *2:* 519
   bank charter veto, *1:* 269, 285–86, 289
   Calhoun, John C., *1:* 267–68, 269–72, 299
   election of 1824, *1:* 39, 227, 282, 298; *5:* 1612
   election of 1828, *1:* 266, 267, 282, 298
   election of 1832, *1:* 267, 272, 298; *2:* 401
   frontier youth, *1:* 259–61
   Jacksonian Democrats, *2:* 399, 412
   "King Andrew," *1:* 272–76, 275 (ill.), 286
   marriage, *1:* 261–62, 266–67, 279–80, 281
   military exploits, *1:* 196, 264–65, 281–82, 299
   nullification, *1:* 268–69, 299
   political career, *1:* 257, 262, 265–66
   Polk, James K., *2:* 397
   presidency, *1:* 266–73
   retirement, *1:* 276
   Van Buren, Martin, *1:* 297–301, 309, 315
   Veto Message Regarding the Bank of the United States, *1:* **285–90**
   vetoes, *2:* 349
   war hero, *1:* 263–64
Jackson, Elizabeth Hutchinson, *1:* 261
Jackson, Rachel, *1:* 261–62, **279–83,** 279 (ill.)

adoptive family, *1:* 281, 282
death, *1:* 266–67
frontier girl, *1:* 280–81
slandered, *1:* 279–80
Jacksonian Democrats, *1:* 272,
297–98, 300–301, 309; *2:* 399,
519, 603–4
Japan
attack on Pearl Harbor, *4:* 1150,
1185
cherry trees for Nellie Taft, *3:* 947
MacArthur, Douglas, *4:* 1209
Manchurian invasion, *4:* 1100,
1102, 1147, 1181
Perry opens trade, *2:* 468, 473,
499, 501
Russo-Japanese War, *3:* 895–96,
903; *4:* 970
World War I, *4:* 978
World War II, *4:* 1150, 1152,
1153, 1184, 1185, 1197–98,
1199, 1199 (ill.), 1221–22,
1226–27
Japanese internment camps (World
War II), *4:* 1101
Jaworski, Leon, *5:* 1379
Jay, John, *1:* 20, 23, 27, 27 (ill.), 152
election of 1789, *1:* 19
election of 1800, *1:* 109
Jay's Treaty, *1:* 26, 27, 28
Jay Cooke & Company, *3:* 658–59
Jay's Treaty, *1:* 26, 27, 28, 224, 240
"The Jazz Age," *4:* 1049
The Jazz Singer, *4:* 1063
Jefferson, Martha, *1:* 97, 103, 104,
121–24, 122
courtship duet, *1:* 122
marriage and family, *1:* 123–24
Jefferson, Peter, *1:* 94
Jefferson, Thomas, *1:* 20, 22 (ill.),
71 (ill.), **91–120,** 93 (ill.), 133
(ill.); *5:* 1618
Adams, John, *1:* 108–9, 110, 119
Alien and Sedition Acts, *1:* 70
anti-Federalists, *1:* 60
Committee of Five, *1:* 126
constructionist, *1:* 136, 137
death and epitaph, *1:* 119
Declaration of Independence, *1:*
98, 126–28, 147
early life, *1:* 94–95
election of 1796, *1:* 61; *5:* 1612
election of 1800, *1:* 109–10; *5:*
1612
election of 1804, *1:* 109
Hamilton, Alexander, *1:* 106–7
Hemings, Sally, *1:* 104–5
Madison, James, *1:* 109
marriage and family, *1:* 97, 103,
121–24
Monroe, James, *1:* 183

**Opinion on the Constitutional-
ity of a National Bank,** *1:*
135–42
presidency, *1:* 110–18
retirement, *1:* 118–19
Virginia's new government, *1:*
99–106
Washington, George, *1:* 107
writer and politician, *1:* 95–98,
123, 126
Jennings, Lizzie, *3:* 750
Jim Crow laws, *3:* 871; *4:* 1204
John F. Kennedy Center for the Performing Arts, *5:* 1313
Johns Hopkins University, *3:* 829
Johnson, Andrew, *2:* **599–621,** 601
(ill.), 614 (ill.), 618 (ill.)
administration, *2:* 610
early years, *2:* 602–3, 624
effectiveness as president, *2:* 602
election of 1864, *2:* 562, 606–7
**Final Annual Message to Con-
gress,** *2:* 619, **629–36**
foreign policy, *2:* 610–11
impeachment, *2:* 616–17; *3:* 639
marriage and family, *2:* 603, 624,
625
negative political rallies, *2:*
614–15
political career, *2:* 603–7, 624
presidency, *2:* 607–19, 625
succeeds Lincoln, *2:* 610, 635
Johnson, Eliza, *2:* **623–27,** 623 (ill.)
ill first lady, *2:* 625
marriage and family, *2:* 624
Johnson, Herschel V., election of
1860, *2:* 562
Johnson, Hiram W., election of
1912, *4:* 966
Johnson, Joshua, *1:* 224, 240
Johnson, Lady Bird, *5:* 1308 (ill.),
1323 (ill.), 1324 (ill.), **1341–47,**
1341 (ill.), 1345 (ill.)
campaign of 1964, *5:* 1344
Head Start, *5:* 1343–44
highway beautification project, *5:*
1344
marriage and family, *5:* 1342
"Mrs. Johnson at Work," *5:* 1346
Johnson, Louisa Catherine. *See*
Adams, Louisa
Johnson, Lyndon B., *5:* 1308 (ill.),
1315–40, 1317 (ill.), 1323 (ill.),
1325 (ill.), 1329 (ill.)
administration, *5:* 1327
civil rights, *5:* 1274, 1280,
1325–26, 1327
domestic program: The Great Society, *5:* 1326–30
early years, *5:* 1318–19
education policy, *5:* 1328

election of 1960, *5:* 1281–82,
1322–23
election of 1964, *5:* 1326
election of 1968, *5:* 1335
foreign policy: Southeast Asia, *5:*
1330–34
"Great Society" Speech, *5:*
1349–56
Gulf of Tonkin incident report, *5:*
1330–31
Kennedy, John F., *5:* 1274,
1322–23
Kennedy, John F. (assassination),
5: 1294, 1317
marriage and family, *5:* 1321,
1342, 1346
military service, *5:* 1321
political career, *5:* 1319–22,
1342–43
presidency, *5:* 1323–35, 1343
retirement, *5:* 1338, 1346
Roosevelt, Franklin D., *5:*
1320–21
social unrest, *5:* 1334–35
Vietnam War, *5:* 1318, 1330–31,
1333–34, 1338, 1374
Johnson, Richard M.
election of 1836, *1:* 301
election of 1840, *2:* 336
Johnson, Sam Ealy, *5:* 1318
Johnson, Samuel Ealy, Sr., *5:* 1318
Johnston, Henry Elliott, *2:* 538
Joint Committee on Reconstruction, *2:* 613
Jolson, Al, *4:* 1074 (ill.)
Jones, Paula, *5:* 1573
Jonkman, Bartel J., *5:* 1403
Joseph (Native American chief), *3:*
770
Journal of the Federal Convention
(Madison), *1:* 150
Journalism. *See also* "Yellow journal-
ism"
exposé, *3:* 917
Judiciary, *1:* 83
under Articles of Confederation,
1: 38
circuit court system, *3:* 931
Judiciary Act, *1:* 20, 111
Jumel, Eliza Brown, *1:* 116
The Jungle (Sinclair), *3:* 895, 924
"Just Say No!" antidrug campaign,
5: 1493, 1497, 1497 (ill.)

K

Kalakaua, king of Hawaii, *3:* 831
Kansas, *2:* 501, 514, 524, 528
admitted as free state, *2:* 525

free state, *2:* 547
Kansas-Nebraska Act, *2:* 499–500,
514, 524, 528, 557, 560; *3:* 751
Kansas Territory, *2:* 525
Kearny, Stephen, *2:* 407, 408
"Keep the ball rolling" (campaign
slogan), *2:* 334 (ill.)
Kefauver, C. Estes, election of 1956,
4: 1244
Kelley, Florence, *4:* 1142
Kellogg-Briand Pact, *4:* 1061, 1063
Kellogg, Frank B., *4:* 1061, 1062–63,
1063 (ill.)
Kelly, Grace, *5:* 1302
Kemble, Fanny, *3:* 668
Kemp, Jack, election of 1996, *5:*
1555
Kennebac Journal, *3:* 756
Kennedy Center for the Performing
Arts, *5:* 1313
Kennedy, Edward, *5:* 1305 (ill.),
1306 (ill.)
Kennedy, Jacqueline, *5:*
1299–1306, 1299 (ill.), 1306
(ill.), 1308 (ill.), 1323 (ill.)
assassination of husband, *5:*
1304–5
Coolidge, Grace, *4:* 1075–76
editorial career, *5:* 1305
the "Jackie look," *5:* 1303
the "Kennedy style," *5:*
1299–1300
marriage and family, *5:* 1279–80,
1301–2
marriage to Onassis, *5:* 1305
writer and photographer, *5:*
1300–1301
Kennedy, John F., *4:* 994 (ill.); *5:*
1271–97, 1273 (ill.), 1277 (ill.),
1281 (ill.), 1285 (ill.), 1308
(ill.), 1552 (ill.)
administration, *5:* 1283
assassination, *5:* 1273, 1291–94,
1295, 1304, 1312, 1323
back injury, *5:* 1274–75, 1276,
1279, 1302
"Camelot" (Kennedy style), *5:*
1287–90
civil rights, *5:* 1290–91, 1312
Clinton, Bill, *5:* 1549
domestic policy, *5:* 1290–91,
1295–96
early years, *5:* 1274–75
election of 1960, *5:* 1281–82,
1282, 1337, 1613
foreign affairs, *5:* 1282–87, 1295
funeral, *5:* 1294–95, 1304
Inaugural Address, *5:* **1307–13,**
1308 (ill.)
on Jefferson, *1:* 93
Johnson, Lyndon B., *5:* 1322–23

Kennedy-Nixon debates, *5:* 1282, 1365

Khrushchev, Nikita, *5:* 1284–85, 1286, 1290

marriage and family, *5:* 1279–80, 1301–2

memorable phrases, *5:* 1307–8

military service, *5:* 1276–78

New Frontier program, *5:* 1273, 1290

political career, *5:* 1278–80

presidency, *5:* 1282–91, 1302–3

Profiles in Courage, 2: 617; *3:* 939

PT-109, *5:* 1276–78, 1277

Roosevelt, Eleanor, *4:* 1165

Ross, Edmund, *2:* 617

state funeral, *5:* 1295

Vietnam, *5:* 1312, 1333–34

Kennedy, John F., Jr., *5:* 1302, 1305, 1305 (ill.), 1306 (ill.)

Kennedy, Joseph, *5:* 1274

Kennedy, Joseph, Jr., *5:* 1278

Kennedy, Robert F., *5:* 1280, 1288–89, 1289 (ill.), 1305 (ill.), 1334, 1335, 1337

assassination, *5:* 1289, 1305, 1367

attorney general, *5:* 1288

Kennedy Schlossberg, Caroline, *5:* 1302, 1305, 1305 (ill.), 1306 (ill.)

"The Kennedy style," *5:* 1282, 1287–90, 1299–1300

Kent State University protest demonstration (1970), *5:* 1373, 1374 (ill.), 1396

Kentucky

Clay, Henry, *1:* 228, 229

Maysville Road bill, *1:* 273, 299

remains in Union, *2:* 563

Kentucky Resolution, *1:* 70, 73, 109, 154

Keokuk, *2:* 434

Kern, John W., election of 1908, *3:* 933

Kettle (San Juan) Hill charge, *3:* 888; *4:* 970

Key, Francis Scott, *1:* 157, 158–59, 159 (ill.)

A Key to Uncle Tom's Cabin, 2: 471

Keynes, John Maynard, *5:* 1326

Khan, Agha Muhammad Yahya, *5:* 1371

Khmer Rouge, *5:* 1417

Khomeini, Ayatollah Ruhollah, *5:* 1450–51

Khrushchev, Nikita, *4:* 1245, 1251, 1252–53, 1253 (ill.); *5:* 1285 (ill.), 1290, 1372

Kennedy, John F., *5:* 1284–85, 1286

Nixon, Richard, *5:* 1364

"Kid Glove." *See* Harrison, Benjamin

Kim Il Sung, *4:* 1210

"A kinder, gentler nation" (George Bush), *5:* 1519

"King Andrew." *See* Jackson, Andrew

King, Leslie Lynch, Jr. *See* Ford, Gerald R.

King, Martin Luther, Jr., *5:* 1289, 1291, 1292–93, 1293 (ill.), 1325 (ill.), 1334–35, 1367, 1582

King, Rufus

election of 1804, *1:* 109

election of 1808, *1:* 155

election of 1816, *1:* 193

King, William Rufus, election of 1852, *2:* 493, 495

Kissinger, Henry, *5:* 1369, 1370–71, 1371 (ill.), 1408

"Kitchen debate," *5:* 1364

Kitt, Eartha, *5:* 1344

Kleindienst, Richard, *5:* 1378

Kling, Florence. *See* Harding, Florence

Know Nothing (American) Party, *2:* 469, 484

Knox, Frank, *4:* 1146, 1152

election of 1936, *4:* 1134

Knox, Henry, *1:* 20, 22 (ill.), 52

Knox, John, *2:* 396

Knox, Philander C., *3:* 935; *4:* 1022

Knute Rockne: All American (film), *5:* 1473, 1476

Korbel, Josef, *5:* 1562

Korea and Korean War, *4:* 1209, 1210

Carter, Jimmy, *5:* 1439

Eisenhower, Dwight D., *4:* 1244

Korean War, *4:* 1207–10, 1244

MacArthur, Douglas, *4:* 1209

Marshall, George C., *4:* 1201

Kortright, Elizabeth. *See* Monroe, Elizabeth

Kortright, Lawrence, *1:* 205

Kosovo, Serbia, *5:* 1564

Ku Klux Klan, *3:* 656

Ku Klux Klan Act, *3:* 656

Kuwait, Iraqi invasion, *5:* 1512, 1523–25, 1537, 1607

L

La Follette, Robert M., *3:* 937

election of 1924, *4:* 1056, 1060

Labor, *1:* 307; *4:* 969

Kennedy, John F., *5:* 1290

Perkins, Frances, *4:* 1143
Taft, Robert A., *3:* 939
Truman, Harry S., *4:* 1203
Laborer(s), Populism, *3:* 823
"Lady Bird." *See* Johnson, Lady Bird
Lafayette, Major General, *1:* 33 (ill.),
    186–87, 187 (ill.)
Lafayette, Marquise de, *1:* 205,
    206–7
Lake Okeechobee, *2:* 432
Lame duck presidents, *2:* 635; *4:*
    1145
Lance, Bert, *5:* 1444
Land acquisition. *See also* Expan-
    sionism; specific acquisition,
    e.g., Louisiana Purchase
Harrison, William Henry, *2:* 330
Land-rights issues, Native Ameri-
    cans, *1:* 231–32
Landon, Alfred M., election of
    1936, *4:* 1134, 1140
Lane, Harriet, *2:* 521, 535 (ill.),
    535–38
    art lover, *2:* 537
    English style White House, *2:* 536
    loses sons to rheumatic fever, *2:*
    538
Lane, Joseph, election of 1860, *2:*
    562
Langdon, John, *1:* 155
Laos, *5:* 1287, 1331, 1373, 1375,
    1396
Latin America, *2:* 525–26
    Hughes, Charles Evans, *4:* 1027
    Kennedy, John F., *5:* 1284
    Monroe Doctrine, *1:* 200, 209
    Rockefeller, Nelson, *5:* 1412
    Roosevelt Corollary to Monroe
      Doctrine, *3:* 891–94, 903
    Roosevelt, Franklin D., *4:* 1145
    Taft, William Howard, *3:* 956
Latino Americans, *5:* 1338
Laulewasika, *2:* 332
Lawrence, Abbot, *2:* 464
Lazio, Rick, *5:* 1586
Le Duc Tho, *5:* 1370–71
League of Nations, *4:* 976, 977, 981,
    1003, 1005, 1007, 1010–11,
    1020, 1022, 1026, 1041, 1046
    Fourteen Points speech (Wil-
      son), *4:* 976, **997–1004**
    Reparations Commission, *4:* 978,
      984, 1027
League of Women Voters, *4:* 1112,
    1161
Lebanon, *5:* 1447, 1483
Lecompton, Kansas, *2:* 501
Lee, Alice Hathaway. *See* Roosevelt,
    Alice Lee
Lee, Francis Lightfoot, *3:* 648

Lee, Henry "Light-Horse Harry," *1:*
    4, 14; *3:* 648
Lee, Mary Anna, *2:* 507
Lee, Richard Henry, *1:* 97, 98,
    100–101, 101 (ill.), 125–26; *2:*
    328; *3:* 648
Lee, Robert E., *2:* 529, 568, 569–70,
    596; *3:* 648–49, 649 (ill.), 650,
    671–78, 673 (ill.)
    Confederate surrender, *3:* 671–78
Legislative branch, *1:* 82–83
LeMay, Curtis E., election of 1968,
    5: 1366
"Lemonade Lucy." *See* Hayes, Lucy
Lend-Lease program, *4:* 1147
Leon County, Florida, election of
    2000, *5:* 1610
"Letter from Birmingham Jail"
    (Martin Luther King Jr.), *5:*
    1293
"A Letter to the Duchess of Suther-
    land and Ladies of England in
    Reply to Their 'Christian Ad-
    dress' on the Subject of Slavery
    in the Southern States (Julia
    Tyler), *2:* 382
Letters from the Federal Farmer
    (Richard Henry Lee), *1:* 101
Levies. *See* Tax(es)
Lewinsky, Monica, *5:* 1574, 1576
Lewis and Clark expedition, *1:*
    112–13, 114–15
Lewis, Meriwether, *1:* 112, 114–15
Liberalism, Hoover's view, *4:* 1117
Liberia, *1:* 198; *2:* 498
Liberty Party, *2:* 404
Library of Congress, *1:* 118; *3:* 687
Libya, *5:* 1483
Lieberman, Joseph, *5:* 1575
    election of 2000, *5:* 1609
"Light-Horse Harry." *See* Lee, Henry
    "Light-Horse Harry"
Liliuokalani, queen of Hawaii, *3:*
    789, 803, 811, 820, 831–32
Lily (newspaper), *3:* 786
Lincoln, Abraham, *2:* 472, **549–74,**
    551 (ill.), 558 (ill.), 567 (ill.),
    582 (ill.); *5:* 1618
    administration, *2:* 563
    assassination, *2:* 570, 571, 578,
      596, 607
    circuit court lawyer, *2:* 556
    Civil War, *2:* 546–47, 562–70,
      573, 581–82
    "Cooper Union" speech, *2:* 559
    early years, *2:* 552–54
    effectiveness as president, *2:* 571
    election of 1860, *2:* 527, 530, 562
    election of 1864, *2:* 562, 606–7
    Emancipation Proclamation, *2:*
      456, 567–68, **581–86,** 582 (ill.)

Gettysburg Address, *2: 587–91*
Grant, Ulysses S., *3:* 650
Homestead Act, *2:* 568, 573
"house divided" speech, *2:* 559, 560
inaugural of 1861, *2:* 563
Lincoln-Douglas debates, *2:* 559, 560–61
marriage and family, *2:* 555, 566, 576, 577, 578
Mexican War, *2:* 425, 556
"Peoria speech," *2:* 558
political career, *2:* 551, 554–62, 577
presidency, *2:* 562–71, 577–78
Reconstruction, *2:* 571–72
Second Inaugural Address, *2:* 593–97, 607
Seward, William H., *2:* 612–13
slavery issue, *2:* 455–56, 555, 557, 558
Lincoln, Mary, *2:* 575–80, 575 (ill.)
loss of relatives, *2:* 577–79
marriage and family, *2:* 576–77
Southern belle, *2:* 576–77
Lincoln, Robert Todd, *2:* 579 (ill.), 579–80
Lincoln, Tad, *2:* 578, 579
Lincoln, Willie, *2:* 566, 577
Lind, John, *1:* 133
Lindbergh, Charles A., *4:* 1049, 1064–65, 1065 (ill.), 1066
Lindbergh, Charles Augustus (son), *4:* 1065
Lindenwald (Van Buren), *1:* 309
Liquor, bootleg, *4:* 1059
Literacy, *5:* 1531–32, 1533–34, 1621, 1624
Literature Club of Cincinnati, *3:* 685
Lithuania, democratization, *5:* 1485
"Little Ben." *See* Harrison, Benjamin
Little Big Horn, Battle of, *3:* 770
"The Little Magician." *See* Van Buren, Martin
Little Rock, Arkansas, *4:* 1249
Livingston, Robert R., *1:* 133 (ill.), 189
Committee of Five, *1:* 126
Lloyd, James, *1:* 225
Lloyd George, David, *4:* 975 (ill.), 1011
Lobbyists, *4:* 968
Lochner v. New York, 3: 892
Locke, John, *1:* 99, 102–3, 103 (ill.)
Lodge, Henry Cabot, Jr., *5:* 1279
election of 1960, *5:* 1282
Lodge, Henry Cabot, Sr., *4:* 978, 980–81, 981 (ill.); *5:* 1279
Logan, John A., *3:* 781 (ill.)
election of 1884, *3:* 782

London Naval Conference (1930), *4:* 1100
Louis XIV, *4:* 1149
Louis XVI (king of France), *1:* 22, 188, 191
Louis XVIII (king of France), *1:* 195
Louisiana, *2:* 562
election of 1876, *3:* 692
postwar governments, *3:* 694
Louisiana Purchase, *1:* 112–13, 113 (ill.), 154, 189
Lowden, Frank O., *4:* 1020
Loyalists, *1:* 60
Luckett, Edith, *5:* 1494
Lumber industry, *3:* 899
Lusitania, 3: 901; *4:* 974, 974 (ill.)
Luzon Mountains, *3:* 945

M

MacArthur, Arthur, *4:* 1208
MacArthur, Douglas, *4:* 1104, 1201, 1208–9, 1209 (ill.), 1210
Machine voting recounts, election of 2000, *5:* 1614, 1616–17
Macomb, Alexander, *1:* 304–5
Maddox, Lester G., election of 1976, *5:* 1442
Madison, Dolley, *1:* 163–68, 163 (ill.), 311, 312; *2:* 377, 417
advisor to first ladies and hostesses, *1:* 167, 311, 312; *2:* 55, 95
Dolley turban, *1:* 165
grande dame, *1:* 167
"Lady Presidentess," *1:* 165–67
marriage, *1:* 164–65
modest beginnings, *1:* 163–64
Morse telegraph, *2:* 77
War of 1812, *1:* 166
Madison, James, *1:* 143–61, 145 (ill.)
Bill of Rights proposal (Madison), *1:* 169–78
early life, *1:* 146–47
election of 1808, *1:* 155
election of 1812, *1:* 155
Father of the Constitution, *1:* 150–54
Federalist Papers, 1: 152
Hamilton, Alexander, *1:* 152–53
inauguration ball and address, *1:* 156
Jefferson, Thomas, *1:* 153
marriage, *1:* 154, 164–67
Monroe, James, *1:* 192
presidency, *1:* 155–60
retirement, *1:* 160
War of 1812, *1:* 156–59

Maine, *2:* 369
  Blaine, James G., *3:* 756–57
Maine, 3: 849, 850, 851 (ill.), 855,
  887
Majority rule, *1:* 103
Malcanang Palace, *3:* 946
**"The Man with the Muck Rake"
  speech** (Theodore Roosevelt),
  3: 917–24
Manchuria, Japan invasion, *4:*
  1100, 1102, 1147, 1181
Mangum, Willie Person
  election of 1836, *1:* 301
  election of 1840, *2:* 336
Manhattan Project, *4:* 1223
"Manifest Destiny," *2:* 410, 412,
  420; *3:* 795, 853. *See also* Ex-
  pansionism
Mann-Elkins Act, *3:* 941
Manning, Helen Taft, *3:* 948
Manual voting recounts, election of
  2000, *5:* 1614, 1616–17
Manufacturing code program
  (Hoover), *4:* 1092
Mao Tse-tung (Mao Ze-dong), *4:*
  1210; *5:* 1278, 1372
Marbury v. Madison, 1: 64–65, 73, 111
Marbury, William, *1:* 111
Marcy, William, *2:* 500 (ill.)
Marion Star, 4: 1017, 1018
Marshall, George C., *4:* 1101,
  1200–1201, 1201 (ill.), 1202
  Eisenhower, Dwight D., *4:*
  1240–41, 1242
Marshall, John, *1:* 64–65, 65 (ill.),
  66, 111, 117, 193
Marshall Plan (European Recovery
  Plan), *4:* 1201, 1202; *5:* 1363
Marshall, Thomas R., *3:* 901
  election of 1912, *4:* 966
  election of 1916, *4:* 966
Marshall, Thurgood, *5:* 1332–33,
  1333 (ill.), 1334
Marx, Karl, *5:* 1482–83
Maryland, remains in Union, *2:* 563
Mason, George, *1:* 151, 151 (ill.),
  170
Mason, John Y., *2:* 497
Masons, *2:* 462
Massachusetts
  Adams, John, *1:* 56–59
  Adams, John Quincy, *1:* 223, 224
  Coolidge, Calvin, *4:* 1054
  Lodge, Henry Cabot, *4:* 980
Massachusetts militia (Minutemen),
  1: 10, 12
Maysville Road bill, *1:* 273, 299
McAdoo, William Gibbs, *4:* 1021,
  1095
McCardle, Eliza. *See* Johnson, Eliza

McCarran Act (Internal Security
  Act), *4:* 1207
McCarthy, Eugene, *5:* 1289, 1335,
  1337, 1367
McCarthy, Joseph R., *4:* 1206–7,
  1245
  Eisenhower, Dwight D., *4:* 1245
  Kennedy, Robert F., *5:* 1288
  Marshall, George C., *4:* 1201
McCarthy, Timothy, *5:* 1479 (ill.)
McClellan, George B., *2:* 569; *3:*
  648–49
  election of 1864, *2:* 562
McDowell, Ephraim, *2:* 396
McElroy, Mary, *3:* 765–68
McGovern, George S., *4:* 994 (ill.);
  5: 1334
  election of 1972, *5:* 1366, 1372
McIntosh (Fillmore), Caroline
  Carmichael, *2:* 472, 472 (ill.)
McKee, Mary Harrison, *3:* 830
McKenna, Joseph, *3:* 936 (ill.)
McKinley, Ida, *3:* 858, **863–67,** 863
  (ill.)
  assassination of husband, *3:*
  866–67
  losses cause frail health, *3:* 865
  marriage and family, *3:* 865
  protected in public, *3:* 866
  vibrant youth, *3:* 863–64
McKinley Tariff Act, *3:* 789, 819,
  846, 870–71
McKinley, William, *3:* 822–23,
  837–62, 839 (ill.), 847 (ill.),
  859 (ill.), 861 (ill.), 865 (ill.)
  administration, *3:* 850
  annexation of Hawaii, *3:* 834
  assassination, *3:* 858–59, 859
  (ill.), 866–67
  bimetallism, *3:* 845–46
  early years, *3:* 841–43
  economic policy, *3:* 849, 870
  election of 1892, *3:* 846
  election of 1896, *3:* 807, 848–49
  election of 1900, *3:* 848, 858
  First Inaugural Address, *3:*
  869–75
  marriage and family, *3:* 844–45,
  865
  military service, *3:* 844
  political career, *3:* 789, 844,
  845–49, 865
  presidency, *3:* 849–58, 866
  tariffs, *3:* 846, 870–71
McLean, John, *1:* 211 (ill.)
McNairy, John, *1:* 261
McNary, Charles L., election of
  1940, *4:* 1134
McNary-Haugen Bill, *4:* 1066–67,
  1068
McReynolds, James C., *3:* 936 (ill.)

Meade, George, *2:* 569
Means, Abigail Kent, *2:* 507
Meat-packing industry, *3:* 895
Media coverage, *4:* 968. *See also*
    Journalism; Radio; Television;
    Yellow Journalism
  Clinton, Hillary Rodham, *5:*
    1583–85
  Ford, Gerald R., *5:* 1414, 1415
  news agencies call election 2000,
    5: 1608, 1609
Medicaid, *5:* 1328
Medicare, *5:* 1328, 1561
Meiji, emperor of Japan, *3:* 660, 668
Mellon, Andrew W., *4:* 1022–23,
    1023 (ill.), 1024, 1098
Mellon National Bank, *4:* 1022,
    1023
Memoirs, Year of Decisions (Truman),
    4: 1211
Mencken, H. L., on Coolidge,
    Calvin, *4:* 1068–69
Mercenaries, *1:* 10
Merchant marine, *4:* 1061
Meredith, James, *5:* 1291
Merit system, *3:* 784
Merry Mount (Adams), *1:* 223
**Message to Congress Opposing
    the Annexation of Hawaii**
    (Cleveland), *3:* 803–8
**Message to the Senate Supporting
    the Annexation of Hawaii**
    (Benjamin Harrison), *3:*
    831–35
Metal detector, *3:* 722, 725
Methodist Woman's Home Mission-
    ary Society, *3:* 703
Mexican Americans, *5:* 1319, 1328
Mexican War, *1:* 229; *2:* 371, 391,
    406 (ill.), 406–10, 424, 520, 612
  Adams, John Quincy, *1:* 235
  Calhoun, John C., *1:* 271
  Frémont, John C., *2:* 408, 410
  Grant, Ulysses S., *2:* 425; *3:* 640
  Kearny, Stephen, *2:* 407, 408
  Lee, Robert E., *3:* 648
  Lincoln, Abraham, *2:* 425, 556
  Perry, Matthew C., *2:* 498
  Pierce, Franklin, *2:* 490–93
  Polk, James K., *2:* 406, 410
  Scott, Winfield, *1:* 305; *2:* 407
  Stockton, Robert, *2:* 407
  Taylor, Zachary, *2:* 425, 432–36
  Van Buren, Martin, *2:* 425
Mexico
  Clinton, Bill, *5:* 1565
  Grant, Ulysses S., *3:* 660
  leased oil lands seized, *4:* 1061
  North American Free Trade
    Agreement (NAFTA), *5:* 1525,
    1560

Pershing, John J. "Black Jack," *4:*
    971
  Polk, James K., *2:* 404
  Revolution of 1920, *3:* 937
  Rockefeller, Nelson, *5:* 1412
  Wilson, Woodrow, *4:* 969–72
  Zimmerman note, *4:* 1006
Miami tribe, *2:* 332
Michigan
  Ford, Gerald, *5:* 1403–4
  Michigan Territory, *2:* 440
Michner, H. T., *3:* 818
Middle class, *4:* 1057
Middle East, *5:* 1370, 1371, 1525
Midnight appointments, *1:* 71, 73
Military, "Don't ask, don't tell" pol-
    icy, *5:* 1558
Military draft, World War II, *4:* 1152
Military leaders, as presidential can-
    didates, *2:* 468 (ill.)
Military spending. *See* Defense
    spending
Militia
  Massachusetts, *1:* 10
  Tennessee, *1:* 262
  Virginia (American Revolution),
    1: 6
Militia Act of 1796, *2:* 563
Miller, William E., election of 1964,
    5: 1326
Millie's Book (Barbara Bush), *5:* 1533
Milligan, Lambdin, *3:* 816
Milosevic, Slobodan, *5:* 1564
Milton, John, *1:* 88
Minimum wage, failed New Deal
    legislation, *4:* 1141
Minnesota, free state, *2:* 547
Minutemen (Massachusetts militia),
    1: 10, 12
"Misdemeanors," *5:* 1572
"Missile gap," *4:* 1248, 1250–51
Missile reduction (Bush-Gorbachev,
    1991), *5:* 1522, 1523
Mississippi, *2:* 562
  Davis, Jefferson, *2:* 564
  Meredith, James, *5:* 1291
Mississippi River, *1:* 113–14
  flood of 1927, *4:* 1060, 1093–96
Mississippi River Commission, *3:*
    817–18
Missouri
  remains in Union, *2:* 563
  statehood debate, *1:* 228
Missouri
  Japanese surrender, *4:* 1199 (ill.)
  Truman, Harry S., *4:* 1191, 1194
Missouri Compromise of 1820, *1:*
    197, 198–99, 202–3; *2:* 411,
    451, 524, 557
Missouri River, *1:* 112
Mitchell, John, *5:* 1378, 1380

Model Cities Act, *5:* 1328

Mondale, Walter, *5:* 1443–44
  election of 1976, *5:* 1442
  election of 1980, *5:* 1477, 1518
  election of 1984, *5:* 1477, 1486,
    1518, 1562

Money supply. *See also* Currency
  supply
  "free silver," *3:* 789, 845
  gold standard, *1:* 274; *3:* 695,
    717, 789, 791, 845, 848
  greenbacks, *3:* 652–55
  hard money, *3:* 717
  Populists' view, *3:* 823

Monopolies, *1:* 286. *See also* Trusts

Monroe Doctrine, *1:* 181, 197,
    199–200, 201 (ill.), 202,
    209–15, 211 (ill.); *3:* 696
  Adams, John Quincy, *1:* 220
  Cleveland, Grover, *3:* 791
  Johnson, Andrew, *2:* 611
  Polk, James K., *2:* 404
  Roosevelt Corollary, *3:* 891–94

Monroe, Elizabeth, *1:* 205 (ill.),
    205–8
  reserved social style as first lady,
    1: 207–8
  saves Madame Lafayette, *1:* 206–7

Monroe, James, *1:* 169–70,
    179–203, 181 (ill.), 211 (ill.)
  Adams, John Quincy, *1:* 226
  diplomatic career, *1:* 188–92, 214
  early years, *1:* 182–83
  election of 1816, *1:* 193
  election of 1820, *1:* 193; *5:* 1612
  Jefferson, Thomas, *1:* 183
  Madison, James, *1:* 192
  marriage and family, *1:* 185, 205,
    206
  Monroe Doctrine, *1:* **209–15**
  Northwest travels, *1:* 183–84
  political career, *1:* 192–93
  presidency, *1:* 193, 196–201
  slavery policy, *1:* 198–99
  Washington, George, *1:* 188–89

Monrovia, Liberia, *1:* 198

Monterrey, Battle of, *2:* 433–34, 436

Montgomery Improvement Association, *5:* 1292

Monticello (Jefferson), *1:* 97,
    100–101, 104, 122, 123, 123
    (ill.), 124

Montpelier (Madison), *1:* 146, 153
    (ill.), 167

Moore, Sara Jane, *5:* 1414

Moravians, *2:* 416

Morgan, Edwin D., *3:* 751

Morgan, John Pierpont (J. P.), *3:*
    791, 792–93, 793 (ill.), 934–35

Morgan v. Virginia, *5:* 1332

Moro tribe (Philippines), *4:* 970

Morrow, Anne, *4:* 1065

Morse, Samuel, *2:* 399, 462

Morse telegraph, *1:* 167; *2:* 77

Mortgages, Great Depression, *4:*
    1098–99

Morton, Levi P., election of 1888, *3:*
    819

Moseley, George, *4:* 1240

Mount Vernon (Washington), *1:* 6,
    8–9, 16, 33 (ill.)

Mount Wallaston (Adams), *1:* 223

Moynihan, Daniel Patrick, *5:* 1312,
    1586

*Mr. Buchanan's Administration on the
  Eve of the Rebellion* (Buchanan),
    2: 531

"Mr. Polk's War." *See* Mexican War

"Mr. Republican." *See* Taft, Robert
  A.

"Mrs. Bush's Story Time," *5:* 1533

"Mrs. Roosevelt's Column" (Eleanor
  Roosevelt), *4:* 1164

Muckrakers, *3:* 896, 924

"Mudslinging," *3:* 919

Muir, John, *3:* 898 (ill.)

Mulattoes, *1:* 199

Mulligan Letters, *3:* 756

Mullins, Priscilla, *1:* 221

Munich Pact of 1938, *5:* 1275

Municipal building code program
  (Hoover), *4:* 1092

Murphy, "Happy," *5:* 1412–13

Muskie, Edmund S., *5:* 1562
  election of 1968, *5:* 1366

"My Day" (Eleanor Roosevelt), *4:*
    1164

My Memoir (Edith Wilson), *4:* 994

My Turn (Nancy Reagan), *5:* 1497

N

NAFTA (North American Free Trade
  Agreement), *5:* 1525, 1560

Nagasaki, *4:* 1101, 1184, 1199, 1226

Nancy (Nancy Reagan), *5:* 1497

Nancy Reagan Afterschool Program,
    5: 1499

Nancy Reagan Foundation, *5:* 1498

Napoleon I (Napoleon Bonaparte,
  emperor of France), *1:* 111–12,
    189, 194–95; *4:* 1149

"Napoleon of the stump." *See* Polk,
  James K.

Napoleonic wars, *1:* 274, 298–99

*Narrative of the Life of Frederick Dou-
  glass, An American Slave* (Douglass), *2:* 597

NASA. *See* National Aeronautics and
  Space Agency (NASA)

Nasser, Gamal Abdel, *5:* 1446, 1447

Nast, Thomas, *3:* 690

National Aeronautics and Space Agency (NASA), *4:* 1250; *5:* 1290, 1322

National American Women Suffrage Association, *3:* 787

National Association for the Advancement of Colored People (NAACP), *4:* 1164; *5:* 1332

National bank. *See also* Bank of the United States
    charter, *1:* 289
    Federalists' view, *1:* 21, 24–25, 135–37
    Federalists vs. anti-Federalists, *1:* 105–6, 135–37
    First Bank of the United States, *1:* 21, 25, 140–41, 285
    Second Bank of the United States, *1:* 141, 159, 269, 273, 276, 285–86, 289, 300; *2:* 367

National Bank, Constitutionality of (Jefferson), *1:* 135–42

National Civil Service Reform League, *3:* 760

National Consumers' League, *4:* 1142

National Cultural Center, *5:* 1312–13

National debt, *1:* 21–22
    Hayes, Rutherford B., *3:* 695
    Jackson, Andrew, *1:* 273–74
    Reagan, Ronald, *5:* 1481–82, 1490

National Defense Education Act, *4:* 1250

National Democratic Party, *2:* 372

National Endowment for the Arts, *5:* 1329, 1425

National First Ladies' Library, *3:* 863

National Foundation for the Arts and Humanities, *5:* 1329

National Gallery of Art, *4:* 1023

National health insurance
    failed Clinton health plan, *5:* 1559–60
    failed New Deal legislation, *4:* 1141

National Industrial Recovery Act (NIRA), *4:* 1027, 1139, 1172

National Labor Relations Act, *4:* 1141

National Labor Relations Board (NLRB), *4:* 1141

National League of Families of American Prisoners and Missing in Action in Southeast Asia, *5:* 1496

National Liberation Front. *See* Vietcong (Vietnamese communists)

National monuments, *3:* 899

National park(s), *3:* 899

National Progressive Republican League, *3:* 937

National Public Radio, *5:* 1330

National Recovery Administration (NRA), *4:* 1139

National Republican Party, *1:* 272, 300, 301

National Security Council, *5:* 1370, 1417

National Socialist Party (Nazis), *4:* 1102
    Lindbergh, Charles A., *4:* 1065

National Union Convention, *2:* 614

National Union Party, Republican Party, *1:* 62

National Women Suffrage Association, *3:* 787

National Youth Administration, *4:* 1139, 1164; *5:* 1321

Native Americans. *See also* specific tribe or nation, e.g. Seminole nation
    Adams, John Quincy, *1:* 231–32
    Arthur, Chester A., *3:* 769–74
    Battle of Toledo, *1:* 26
    Black Hawk, *2:* 434–35
    Cass, Lewis, *2:* 440
    Cleveland, Grover, *3:* 784–85
    Coolidge, Calvin, *4:* 1066
    Curtis, Charles, *4:* 1096, 1097
    Grant, Ulysses S., *3:* 656
    Harrison, William Henry, *2:* 330
    Indian Appropriation Act, *3:* 656
    Jackson, Andrew, *1:* 258, 274–75
    Jefferson, Thomas, *3:* 769–70, 771
    Lane, Harriet, *2:* 537
    Monroe, James, *1:* 199
    Polk, James K., *2:* 421
    Taylor, Zachary, *2:* 431–32
    Tecumseh and the Prophet, *2:* 332–33, 434
    U.S. citizenship, *3:* 774
    Van Buren, Martin, *1:* 306

NATO. *See* North Atlantic Treaty Organization (NATO)

Natural resources, *3:* 896–99

Naturalization Act, *1:* 67, 68, 108

Naval disarmament conferences, *4:* 1027, 1046, 1100

Naval Lyceum, *2:* 498

Navy
    Arthur, Chester A., *3:* 761, 762
    Perry, Matthew C., *2:* 498–99
    Roosevelt, Theodore, *3:* 886, 887

Nazis (National Socialist Party), *4:* 1065, 1102, 1195, 1223

Nessen, Ron, *5:* 1425

Neutrality

Washington, George, *1:* 23
World War I, *4:* 973, 998
Nevada, *2:* 568
New Deal, *4:* 984, 1135, 1138–41,
    1151, 1154, 1167, 1172. *See
    also* e.g., Social Security Act; in-
    dividual acts
    Johnson, Lyndon B., *5:* 1321
    Roosevelt, Eleanor, *4:* 1163–64
    Roosevelt, Franklin D., *4:* 1167,
        1172, 1179
New Democrats, *5:* 1554
New Freedom agenda, *4:* 959, 967,
    974, 984
New Frontier program, *5:* 1273,
    1290
New Hampshire, *1:* 169
    Pierce, Franklin, *2:* 489, 490–91
New Jersey
    Cleveland, Grover, *3:* 142
    Wilson, Woodrow, *4:* 965
New Jersey Plan, *1:* 150
New Mexico, *2:* 503
    free state, *2:* 439–40, 452, 466
New Nationalism, *4:* 967
New Orleans, Battle of, *1:* 263–64,
    265 (ill.)
New Orleans, Louisiana, *1:* 111–12,
    189, 263
"New South," *5:* 1515
"New world order," *5:* 1537, 1538,
    1543
New York
    Arthur, Chester A., *3:* 749, 762,
        766
    Cleveland, Grover, *3:* 779–82, 783
    Conkling, Roscoe, *3:* 752–53
    Fillmore, Millard, *2:* 460–62
    Perkins, Frances, *4:* 1137,
        1142–43
    Roosevelt, Franklin D., *4:*
        1131–33
    Roosevelt, Theodore, *3:* 883, 884,
        885, 888
    Van Buren, Martin, *1:* 294, 297,
        315
New York Customs House, *3:* 695,
    752, 753
New York Evening Journal, 3: 854
New York Journal, 3: 850
New York Public Library, *3:* 691
New York State Industrial Commis-
    sion, *4:* 1142
New York Stock Exchange, *4:* 1098
New York Times, 5: 1396
New York World, 3: 852–53
News conference, *4:* 968
News reporting, *3:* 923
Newsweek, 5: 1575
Ngo Dinh Diem, *5:* 1287

Nicaragua, *3:* 936–37, 950; *4:* 1061,
    1100
    Marxist revolution (1979), *5:*
        1482
Nicolay, John, *2:* 590
Nineteenth Amendment, *3:* 787
Ninety-ninth Pursuit Squadron, *4:*
    1232
Nixon, Julie, *5:* 1388 (ill.)
Nixon, Pat, *5:* 1301,**1385–90,** 1385
    (ill.), 1388 (ill.)
    marriage and family, *5:* 1387
    political life, *5:* 1387–89
    role as first lady, *5:* 1389
    shy of public spotlight, *5:* 1385,
        1388, 1389
Nixon, Richard, *5:* 1281 (ill.),
    1357–84, 1359 (ill.), 1369 (ill.),
    1379 (ill.), 1388 (ill.)
    administration, *5:* 1368
    audiotapes, *5:* 1360, 1376, 1379
        (ill.), 1379–80, 1432
    Bush, George, *5:* 1516
    "Checkers" speech, *5:* 1364
    early years, *5:* 1360
    economic policy, *5:* 1368–69
    Eisenhower, Dwight D., *5:* 1364
    election of 1952, *4:* 1243, 1244;
        5: 1364
    election of 1956, *4:* 1244
    election of 1960, *5:* 1281–82,
        1365
    election of 1968, *5:* 1366–67
    election of 1972, *5:* 1366, 1372
    Environmental Protection
        Agency, *5:* 1367
    Ford, Gerald R., *5:* 1404, 1406,
        1407
    foreign relations, *5:* 1369–73
    Hiss case, *5:* 1363
    House Committee on Un-Ameri-
        can Activities, *4:* 1206
    impeachment process, *5:* 1377,
        1380–81, 1428
    Kennedy-Nixon debates, *5:* 1282
    Khrushchev, Nikita, *5:* 1364, 1372
    marriage and family, *5:* 1361, 1387
    military service, *5:* 1361, 1387
    Pardon of Richard Nixon (Ford),
        5: 1381, 1408–11, **1427–33**
    People's Republic of China, *5:*
        1273 (ill.), 1369, 1372–73
    political career, *5:* 1361–67,
        1387–89
    presidency, *5:* 1364–81, 1389
    public opinion, *5:* 1428
    resignation and retirement, *5:*
        1381–82, 1389, 1408
    "Silent Majority" Speech, *5:*
        1391–97

vice presidential good will tour,
5: 1364
Watergate scandal, *5:* 1359, 1360,
1375–82, 1427, 1432
Wilson, Woodrow, *5:* 1392
Nixon, Tricia, *5:* 1388 (ill.)
Nobel Peace Prize
Gorbachev, Mikhail, *5:* 1484
Kellogg, Frank B., *4:* 1063
King, Martin Luther, Jr., *5:* 1293
Kissinger, Henry, *5:* 1370–71
Le Duc Tho, *5:* 1370–71
Marshall, George C., *4:* 1201
Roosevelt, Theodore, *3:* 879, 896,
903
Wilson, Woodrow, *4:* 976
Nonconsecutive terms, *3:* 782
Noriega, Manuel, *5:* 1522, 1607
Normandy Beach, *4:* 1241
Norris, George W., *4:* 1140–41
Norris-LaGuardia Anti-Injunction
Act, *4:* 1107
North. *See* Regionalism
North American Free Trade Agree-
ment (NAFTA), *5:* 1525, 1560
North Atlantic Treaty Organization
(NATO), *3:* 941; *4:* 1149, 1207,
1243, 1260; *5:* 1563
North Carolina, *1:* 178
joins Confederacy, *2:* 563
North Korea, *4:* 1209, 1210
Clinton, Bill, *5:* 1564, 1565
Eisenhower, Dwight D., *4:* 1244
Marshall, George C., *4:* 1201
North Vietnam, *5:* 1287, 1330,
1331–34, 1373, 1396
Eisenhower, Dwight D., *4:*
1245–48
Johnson, Lyndon B., *5:* 1334
largest ever aerial bombing, *5:*
1375, 1396
Perot, H. Ross, *5:* 1526
Northern Ireland, Great Britain, *5:*
1568
Northern Pacific Railroad, *3:* 793
Northern Securities Company, *3:*
890, 915
Northwest, *1:* 183
Northwest frontier, *2:* 328
Northwest Ordinance of 1787, *1:*
184
Northwest Territory, *2:* 329–30
Notes on the State of Virginia (Jeffer-
son), *1:* 93, 102–3
Nuclear Test Ban Treaty, *5:* 1286
Nuclear weapons
Cuban missile crisis, *5:* 1286
development, *4:* 1223, 1226
Eisenhower, Dwight D., *4:* 1245
Gorbachev, Mikhail, *5:* 1484
Gore, Al, *5:* 1556

Kennedy, John F., *5:* 1308–9
Khrushchev, Nikita, *4:* 1253
North Korea, *5:* 1565
Reagan, Ronald, *5:* 1484
Stimson, Henry L., *4:* 1101
Truman, Harry S., *4:* 1196,
1197–98, 1221–22, 1226–27
Nuclear Weapons and Foreign Policy
(Kissinger), *5:* 1370
Nueces River, *2:* 406, 433
Nullification, *1:* 235–36, 268–69,
299
Calhoun's theory, *1:* 267–68,
270–71
Madison's view, *1:* 160
Nuremberg trials, *3:* 939

O

Oberon (Wieland), *1:* 220
O'Connor, Sandra Day, *5:* 1483,
1486–87, 1487 (ill.)
Office of Economic Opportunity
(OEO), *5:* 1328
Office of Inter-American Affairs, *5:*
1412
Office of Management and Budget,
3: 941
**Official Terms of Confederate Sur-
render**, *3:* 674
Ohio
Garfield, James A., *3:* 714, 716
Grant, Ulysses S., *3:* 641
Harding, Warren G., *4:* 1017,
1019
Harrison, William Henry, *2:* 329,
330–31
Hayes, Rutherford B., *3:* 685,
686–87, 701–2
McKinley, William, *3:* 846, 865
Taft family, *3:* 938
Taft, William Howard, *3:* 928–30
Oil deposits, federal, *4:* 1030
Oil price hike, Carter era, *5:* 1445
"O.K.," *1:* 306
Old-age pension, New Deal legisla-
tion, *4:* 1141
"Old Hickory." *See* Jackson, Andrew
"Old Kinderhook." *See* Van Buren,
Martin
"Old Man Eloquent." *See* Adams,
John Quincy
"Old Rough and Ready." *See* Taylor,
Zachary
"Old soldiers never die; they just
fade away" (MacArthur), *4:* 1209
Old Tippecanoe. *See* Harrison,
William Henry

Old Whitey (Taylor's horse), *2:* 436, 444 (ill.)

Olympic Games (1980), boycott, *5:* 1467

On the Wings of Eagles (Perot), *5:* 1526

Onassis, Aristotle Socrates, *5:* 1305

Onassis, Jacqueline Kennedy. *See* Kennedy, Jacqueline

O'Neill, Tip, *5:* 1488 (ill.)

"The only thing we have to fear is fear itself" (Franklin D. Roosevelt), *4:* 1135, 1168

"The Open Door" (Grace Coolidge), *4:* 1075

Open Door Policy, *3:* 851

Operation Desert Shield, *5:* 1523

Operation Desert Storm, *5:* 1523–23

Opinion on the Constitutionality of a National Bank (Jefferson), *1:* 135–42

Opposing parties, presidency and vice presidency, *1:* 61

Orchestra Association (Cincinnati), *3:* 944

Oregon, free state, *2:* 547

Oregon Territory, *1:* 113, 197; *2:* 403, 404, 405, 424, 440, 451, 520

Oregon Trail, *2:* 408

Orlando, Vittorio, *4:* 1011

Osceola, *1:* 305

Osgood, Samuel, *1:* 20

Ostend Manifesto, *2:* 497, 521–22

Oswald, Lee Harvey, *5:* 1294, 1294 (ill.), 1324

Our American Cousin, *2:* 571, 578

Oval Office, *2:* 477

P

Pacific Rim nations, *5:* 1560

Pahlavi, Mohammad Reza, Shah of Iran, *5:* 1448–49, 1449 (ill.), 1450, 1467

Paine, Thomas, *1:* 188, 190–91, 191 (ill.)

Palestine and Palestinians, *5:* 1446, 1447

Palestinian-Israeli peace negotiations, *5:* 1563, 1568, 1578–79

Palm Beach County, Florida, election of 2000, *5:* 1609, 1616

Palo Alto, Battle of, *2:* 433

Panama, *3:* 903; *5:* 1445
  Noriega, Manuel, *5:* 1522, 1607

Panama Canal, *2:* 442, 443; *3:* 696, 894, 931; *5:* 1466

Pan-American Conference, *3:* 757

Pan-American Exposition, McKinley assassination, *3:* 866–67

Panic of 1837, *1:* 276, 289, 293, 302

Panic of 1873, *3:* 658–59, 695

Panic of 1893, *3:* 790, 793

Paper money. *See* Currency; Gold standard

Pardon of Richard Nixon (Ford), *5:* 1381, 1408–11, **1427–33**

Paris Summit (1960), cancellation, *4:* 1251

Parker, Alton B., *3:* 894
  election of 1904, *3:* 895

Parks, Rosa, *5:* 1292

Partisanship, *3:* 748; *5:* 1521, 1599

Party system, modern, *1:* 300

Patronage system, *3:* 663, 713, 721, 722, 748, 751, 781, 885

Patterson, Martha Johnson, *2:* 625–26, 626 (ill.)

Paul, François Joseph, *1:* 16

Payne-Aldrich Act, *3:* 932

Payne, Dolley. *See* Madison, Dolley

Peace agreements, *4:* 1046; *5:* 1282

Peace Corps, *4:* 1165; *5:* 1312, 1337

Peace movement (Vietnam War), *5:* 1334

"Peace through strength" (Reagan), *5:* 1482

Peanuts, *5:* 1441 (ill.)

Pearl Harbor, Oahu, Hawaii, *4:* 1150, 1151 (ill.), 1181, 1182, 1185, 1200, 1222, 1240

Pendleton Civil Service Reform Act, *3:* 723, 726, 760, 761–62, 784

Pendleton, George H., *3:* 760
  election of 1864, *2:* 562

Pennsylvania
  Buchanan, James, *2:* 518
  Stevens, Thaddeus, *2:* 608

Pennsylvania Fiscal Agency, *3:* 657

Pennsylvania Gazette, *1:* 17

Pension (old-age), New Deal legislation, *4:* 1141

"Pentagon Papers," *5:* 1375–78, 1396–97

People's Party. *See* Populist Party (People's Party)

People's Republic of China, *4:* 1210; *5:* 1563. *See also* China
  Bush, George, *5:* 1516
  Carter, Jimmy, *5:* 1445
  Clinton, Bill, *5:* 1558–59
  Kissinger, Henry, *5:* 1371
  Korean War, *4:* 1209
  Nixon, Richard, *5:* 1273 (ill.), 1369, 1372–73

"Peoria speech" (Lincoln), *2:* 558

Perestroika ("restructuring"), *5:* 1482, 1484

"The Period of No Decision," *3:* 834

Perkins, Frances, *4:* 1137, 1142–43, 1143 (ill.)

Perot, H. Ross, *5:* 1526–27, 1527 (ill.)
  election of 1992, *5:* 1525, 1527, 1555
  election of 1996, *5:* 1527, 1555, 1558, 1561

Perry, Matthew C., *2:* 468, 473, 498–99, 499 (ill.), 501

Perry, Oliver Hazard, *1:* 157

Pershing, John J. "Black Jack," *4:* 970–71, 971 (ill.), 972, 976, 1200

Persian Gulf crisis. *See* Gulf War

The Personal Memoirs of U. S. Grant (Grant), *3:* 661, 669, 672

Peru, *5:* 1467

"Pet banks," *1:* 289

Philadelphia, Pennsylvania, *1:* 78, 132, 164

Philippines, *3:* 851, 852, 858; *4:* 1100
  Eisenhower, Dwight D., *4:* 1240
  MacArthur, Douglas, *4:* 1208–9, 1240
  Pershing, John J. "Black Jack," *4:* 970–71
  Spanish American War, *3:* 887
  Taft, William Howard, *3:* 931, 944–45

Physical disability, New Deal legislation, *4:* 1141

Pierce, Barbara. *See* Bush, Barbara

Pierce, Benjamin (father of Franklin), *2:* 488, 489

Pierce, Benjamin (son of Franklin), *2:* 488, 494, 506

Pierce, Franklin, *2:* 468 (ill.), **485–503,** 487 (ill.), 492 (ill.), 494 (ill.), 496 (ill.), 500 (ill.)
  administration, *2:* 497
  Compromise of 1850, *2:* 495–97
  early years, *2:* 488
  election of 1852, *2:* 483, 493–94, 495, 521
  Inaugural Address, *2:* 494, **509–14**
  marriage and family, *2:* 489–90, 494, 505, 506
  military career, *2:* 490–93
  political career, *2:* 489, 493–94
  presidency, *2:* 495–501
  retirement, *2:* 501–2

Pierce, Jane, *2:* **505–7,** 505 (ill.)
  reclusive first lady, *2:* 507
  tragic loss of sons, *2:* 506

Pike, Zebulon, *1:* 114

Pilgrim's Progress (Bunyan), *3:* 918

Pinchot, Gifford, *3:* 896–97, 899 (ill.)

Pinckney, Charles C., *1:* 66, 115
  election of 1800, *1:* 109
  election of 1804, *1:* 109
  election of 1808, *1:* 155, 165

Pinckney, Thomas, election of 1796, *1:* 61

Pittsburgh, Pennsylvania, *4:* 1022

Plains Indian Wars, *3:* 769, 770

Platform, political. *See* Political platform

Platt, Thomas Collier, *3:* 758, 888

Plymouth Notch, Vermont, *4:* 1054, 1055–56, 1074, 1075

Pocahontas, *4:* 991

Podgorny, Nikolai, *5:* 1369 (ill.)

Poland
  Communist era, *4:* 1252
  democratization, *5:* 1482, 1522
  war relief, *4:* 1092
  World War II, *4:* 1147

Polio (Roosevelt, Franklin D.), *4:* 1162

Polish Relief Commission, *4:* 1105

Political appointees, *3:* 721. *See also* Patronage system

Political cartoons
  1856 presidential campaign, *2:* 469 (ill.)
  Polk and Webster, *2:* 407 (ill.)

Political machine, *3:* 751–53

Political parties, Washington's view, *1:* 46–47

Political patronage. *See* Patronage system

Political platform, lacking in Harrison/Tyler campaign, *2:* 364–65

Politics, international. *See* International politics

Polk, James K., *2:* 354, **393–413,** 395 (ill.), 400 (ill.), 402 (ill.), 407 (ill.)
  annexation of Texas, *2:* 372, 386, 419, 420
  Calhoun, John C., *1:* 271
  early years, *2:* 395–97
  election of 1844, *2:* 372, 401, 403–4
  gallstone surgery, *2:* 396
  Inaugural Address, *2:* 404, **419–25**
  Jackson, Andrew, *2:* 397
  marriage, *2:* 397, 416, 417
  political career, *2:* 397–404, 416
  presidency, *2:* 404–11, 417
  retirement, *2:* 411
  slavery issue, *2:* 410–11
  Taylor, Zachary, *2:* 436

Polk Place, *2:* 411, 415, 417–18

Polk, Sarah, *1:* 167; *2:* 381, 411, **415–18,** 415 (ill.)
  marriage, *2:* 416

popular first lady, *2:* 417
private political involvement, *2:* 415, 416–17
Poor Richard's Almanack, 1: 17
Pope, John, *3:* 649
Popular vote, *1:* 19, 61, 109, 155, 193, 227. *See also* election results under specific president
Populism, *3:* 821, 823, 886
Populist Party (People's Party), *3:* 824, 848
Postmaster General. *See also* administration of specific president
first, *1:* 20
Postwar South. *See* Reconstruction
Potawatomi, *2:* 435
Potsdam conference, *4:* 1196, 1198 (ill.), 1221, 1222
Potsdam Declaration, *4:* 1197
Pottawatomie Creek, *2:* 528
Poverty
King, Martin Luther, Jr., *5:* 1293
"War on Poverty," *5:* 1326, 1343
Powell, Colin, *5:* 1544
Powers, Abigail. *See* Fillmore, Abigail
Powers, Francis Gary, *4:* 1251
Prendergast, Tom, political machine, *4:* 1191, 1193
Presbyterians, *2:* 396
President(s)
dark horse, *2:* 403, 493; *3:* 688, 721–22
father-son, *1:* 71, 219; *5:* 1528, 1597
first press conference, *4:* 959
lame duck, *2:* 635; *4:* 1145
married in office, *2:* 380
physically challenged, *4:* 1132–33
served nonconsecutive terms, *3:* 777
Supreme Court chief justice, *3:* 940
youngest, *3:* 889
Presidential candidates, military leaders as, *2:* 468 (ill.)
Presidential election(s). *See* election by year under each president
closest results in presidential history, *5:* 1615
federal supervision, *3:* 697
first, *1:* 18–19
Presidential elector(s), selection, *5:* 1613
Presidential Nomination Acceptance Speech (George W. Bush), *5:* 1625–32
"Presidential Polonaise" (Sousa), *2:* 381
Presidential powers
commander in chief, *4:* 997
limitations, *2:* 347–49
Lincoln, Abraham, *2:* 551, 566
McKinley, William, *3:* 860
Roosevelt, Franklin D., *4:* 1154, 1173
Presidential primaries, *5:* 1631
Presidential succession, *2:* 357–58, 366–67
Presidential veto
Hayes, Rutherford B., *3:* 695, 696
Jackson, Andrew, *1:* 276
Johnson, Andrew, *2:* 619
President's Commission on Mental Health, *5:* 1457
President's Commission on the Status of Women, *4:* 1165
President's Committee on Equality of Treatment and Opportunity in the Armed Services, *4:* 1229, 1230
The President's Daughter (Britton), *4:* 1015
President's (Presidential) Palace, *1:* 70, 79, 121. *See also* White House
President's Science Advisory Committee, *4:* 1250
President/vice president
born in same county, *2:* 339
different parties, *2:* 607
youngest-ever combined ticket, *5:* 1555
Press
Clinton, Hillary Rodham, *5:* 1583–85
Ford, Gerald R., *5:* 1414, 1415
news agencies call election 2000, *5:* 1608, 1609
Press conference(s)
with first lady, *4:* 1035
first presidential, *4:* 959
Preston, Thomas J., Jr., *3:* 801
The Princeton, 2: 380
Princeton University, *3:* 794, 800; *4:* 963, 964–65, 995
Privateers, *1:* 205
"Proclamation 4311, Granting a Pardon to Richard Nixon" (Ford), *5:* 1408–9, 1427
Profiles in Courage (John F. Kennedy), *2:* 617; *5:* 1279, 1302
Progressive "Bull Moose" Party, *3:* 900, 937
Progressive Party, *4:* 1204
Progressivism, *3:* 886, 927; *4:* 968
Prohibition, *4:* 1058–60, 1115
Harding, Florence, *4:* 1036
Harding, Warren G., *4:* 1020
repeal, *4:* 1102

The Prophet (Tenskwatawa), *2:* 330, 331 (ill.), 332, 333
Prophet's Town, *2:* 332
Protective tariffs, *2:* 608. *See also* Tariff(s)
Protectorate, *3:* 832
Protest movement (Vietnam War, 1968), *5:* 1334, 1355, 1367, 1391–92, 1396–97, 1475–76
"Silent Majority" Speech (Nixon), *5:* **1391–97**
Prussia, *1:* 195
Adams, John Quincy, *1:* 224–25, 241
PT-109, *5:* 1277
Public Credit Act, *3:* 652
Public utilities, New Deal legislation, *4:* 1140–41
Public Works Administration (PWA), *4:* 1139
Puerto Rico, *3:* 850
Pulitzer, Joseph, *3:* 850, 852–53, 853 (ill.)
Pulitzer Prize
Kennedy, John F., *5:* 1279, 1302
Lindbergh, Charles, *4:* 1065
Pure Food and Drug Act, *3:* 895, 915, 924; *4:* 980
Puritan(s), *1:* 56–57; *4:* 1016

Q

"Quads," *4:* 964–65
Quakers (Society of Friends), *1:* 163–64; *3:* 786; *4:* 1088; *5:* 1360
Quasi-War, *1:* 66, 70
Quayle, Dan
election of 1988, *5:* 1519
election of 1992, *5:* 1555
Quezon, Manuel, *4:* 1208
Quota system, immigration, *5:* 1329

R

Rabin, Yitzhak, *5:* 1565 (ill.), 1568
Race relations
Grant, Ulysses S., *3:* 655–56, 659
Harding, Warren G., *4:* 1045
Kennedy, John F., *5:* 1290–91
Race riots (1968), *5:* 1334
Racial segregation. *See* Segregation
Wallace, George, *5:* 1367
Racial segregation. *See also* Segregation

King, Martin Luther, Jr., *5:* 1292–93
Marshall, Thurgood, *5:* 1332
Radical Republicans, *2:* 566, 601, 609, 610, 613; *3:* 752
Grant, Ulysses S., *3:* 656
impeachment of Andrew Johnson, *2:* 616, 619
Stevens, Thaddeus, *2:* 608–9, 609 (ill.), 610, 614 (ill.)
Radio, *4:* 1040, 1045, 1051, 1092
Roosevelt, Franklin D., *4:* 1137, 1150, 1175, 1182
Railroad(s), *2:* 473, 525, 564; *3:* 770, 784. *See also* Infrastructure
Morgan, J. P., *3:* 792–93
overexpansion, *3:* 790
rate reform, *3:* 895; *4:* 1026
transcontinental, *2:* 497–99
World War I, *4:* 976
Railroad Pension Act, *4:* 1172
"Railsplitter." *See* Lincoln, Abraham
Rainbow Battalion, *4:* 1208
Raleigh Tavern (Williamsburg), *1:* 9
Rand, Ayn, *5:* 1566
Randolph, Edmund Jennings, *1:* 20, 22 (ill.); *2:* 361, 362–63, 363 (ill.)
Randolph, Lucretia. *See* Garfield, Lucretia
Randolph, Patsy Jefferson, *1:* 124
Randolph, Peyton, *2:* 362
Rationing, World War II, *4:* 1152
Ray, James Earl, *5:* 1293
Reading and family literacy, *5:* 1531–32, 1533–34, 1623-24
Reagan, Nancy, *5:* 1381 (ill.), **1493–99**, 1493 (ill.), 1497 (ill.), 1498 (ill.)
acting career, *5:* 1494
California's first lady, *5:* 1496
Foster Grandparents Program, *5:* 1496
"Just Say No!" to drugs, *5:* 1497
marriage and family, *5:* 1495
role as first lady, *5:* 1496–98
tough times and retirement, *5:* 1498–99
"The Reagan Revolution," *5:* 1507
Reagan, Ronald, *5:* 1366, 1381 (ill.), **1469–92**, 1471 (ill.), 1476 (ill.), 1479 (ill.), 1485 (ill.), 1488 (ill.), 1490 (ill.), 1498 (ill.)
acting career, *5:* 1473–74, 1495
administration, *5:* 1480
Alzheimer's disease, *5:* 1489, 1493–94, 1499
assassination attempt, *5:* 1479, 1479 (ill.), 1493, 1518
Carter, Jimmy, *5:* 1502

Cheney, Dick, *5:* 1606, 1607
defense spending, *5:* 1481–82
early years, *5:* 1472–73
economic policy (Reaganomics), *5:* 1478, 1479–81, 1506–7
election of 1976, *5:* 1417, 1442, 1477
election of 1980, *5:* 1417, 1452, 1477, 1478, 1517
election of 1984, *5:* 1477, 1486, 1518
First Inaugural Speech, *5:* **1501–8**
foreign policy, *5:* 1482–83
Gorbachev, Mikhail, *5:* 1482, 1484–85, 1485 (ill.), 1522
governor of California, *5:* 1474–76, 1496
"The Great Communicator," *5:* 1483–86, 1502
Iran-Contra arms sales, *5:* 1488–89
Iran hostage crisis, *5:* 1449, 1450–51, 1452 (ill.), 1478, 1501–2
marriage and family, *5:* 1473, 1495
medical problems, *5:* 1498, 1499
political career, *5:* 1474–78, 1496
presidency, *5:* 1479–89
retirement, *5:* 1493, 1499
spokesman for General Electric, *5:* 1474
Truman, Harry S., *5:* 1507
Reaganomics, *5:* 1479–81
Recession of 1990, *5:* 1521
Reciprocal trade agreements, *3:* 858, 871
Roosevelt, Franklin D., *4:* 1140, 1145
Reciprocal Trade Agreements Act, *4:* 1140
Recollection of the Confederate Surrender (Grant), *3:* **671–78**
Reconstruction, *2:* 472, 571–72, 596, 635; *3:* 689–92, 735
End of Reconstruction speech (Hayes), *3:* **705–10**
Garfield, James A., *3:* 718
Grant, Ulysses S., *3:* 640–41, 655–56, 659
Hayes, Rutherford B., *3:* 689, 692
Johnson, Andrew, *2:* 611–14; *3:* 639
Stevens, Thaddeus, *2:* 609
Reconstruction Act of 1867, *2:* 609, 615, 618
Reconstruction Finance Corporation (RFC), *4:* 1103, 1138
Recounts, election of 2000, *5:* 1614, 1616–17

Recovery measures (New Deal), *4:* 1139
Red Cross, *4:* 1260
"The Red Fox of Kinderhook." *See* Van Buren, Martin
Red River, *1:* 113
Reform
  government, *3:* 886, 917
  labor, *1:* 307; *4:* 1094–95
  social, *4:* 1094–95
Reform measures (New Deal), *4:* 1139–41
Reform Party, *5:* 1527
Regionalism, *2:* 399, 452; *3:* 682
  Washington's view, *1:* 51; *2:* 452, 540
Rehnquist, William, *5:* 1483
Reid, Whitelaw, election of 1892, *3:* 782
Relief agencies. *See also* Disaster relief; War relief
  Great Depression, *4:* 1136–37
Relief measures (New Deal), *4:* 1138–39
"Remarks on Taking the Oath of Office as President" excerpt (Ford), *5:* 1408–9
"Remember the *Maine!,*" *3:* 849, 851 (ill.), 855
"Rendez-vous with destiny" speech (Franklin D. Roosevelt), *4:* 1182
Reno, Janet, *5:* 1570–71, 1571 (ill.), 1576
Republic of Germany, *4:* 1003, 1006. *See also* Germany
Republic of Hawaii, *3:* 807. *See also* Hawaii annexation
Republic of South Africa, *5:* 1522
Republic of Texas, *2:* 385, 386, 420. *See also* Texas
Republican government, *1:* 82
Republican National Committee, *5:* 1516
Republican Party, *2:* 484, 501
  campaign of 1912, *3:* 937
  conservatives, *5:* 1419, 1474, 1476–77, 1483, 1507, 1511, 1521, 1525
  formation, *2:* 501, 514, 522, 609
  Harrison, Benjamin, *3:* 817–18
  Lincoln, Abraham, *2:* 558, 607
  National Union Party, *1:* 62
  Taft, Robert A., *3:* 938
Republicans, radical. *See* Radical Republicans
"Return to normalcy" (Harding), *4:* 1016, 1024
Revenue acts, *4:* 1057

"Revolution Against the Constitution" speech (Garfield), *3:* 735–43

Revolutionary War. *See* American Revolution

Rhode Island, *1:* 178

Richards, Ann, *5:* 1603, 1623

Richardson, Eliot, *5:* 1378

Richardson, William A., *3:* 658

Rickover, Hyman, *5:* 1439

Riders (legislative), *3:* 736

Ridgway, Matthew B., *4:* 1210

Righteous and Harmonious Fists, *3:* 858; *4:* 1089

The Rights of Man (Paine), *1:* 190

Rio Grande, *2:* 391, 406, 410, 424, 433

River of Doubt (Roosevelt River), *3:* 900

Roads. *See* Infrastructure

"Roaring Twenties," *4:* 979, 1016, 1045, 1049, 1115

Robards, Lewis, *1:* 261, 279

Robards, Rachel Donelson. *See* Jackson, Rachel

Robb, Charles, *5:* 1346

Robbins, Anne Frances. *See* Reagan, Nancy

Robeson, George, *3:* 652

Robinson, Joseph T., election of 1928, *4:* 1096

Rochambeau, Jean-Baptiste, *1:* 16

Rockefeller, John D., *3:* 934; *5:* 1408, 1414, 1416

Rockefeller, Nelson, *5:* 1366, 1370, 1412–13, 1413 (ill.), 1417

Rocky Mountains, *2:* 408

Rodham, Hillary. *See* Clinton, Hillary Rodham

Roe v. Wade, 5: 1477

Rolfe, John, *4:* 991

Roman Catholicism, *4:* 1094, 1096; *5:* 1280

Ronald and Nancy Reagan Research Institute, *5:* 1489, 1494, 1499

Roosevelt, Alice Lee, *3:* 882, 883, 884 (ill.), 906

Roosevelt, Anna ("Bamie"), *3:* 884

Roosevelt, Corinne, *3:* 906

Roosevelt, Edith, *3:* **905–8,** 905 (ill.)
active household manager, *3:* 906–7
charming first lady, *3:* 905, 907
marriage and family, *3:* 906
Republican spokesperson, *3:* 908

Roosevelt, Eleanor, *4:* 1113 (ill.), 1146 (ill.), **1159–65,** 1159 (ill.), 1163 (ill.), 1179 (ill.)
columnist, *4:* 1164
husband stricken with polio, *4:* 1162

most politically active first lady, *4:* 1159, 1162–65
social causes, *4:* 1161, 1162–64
Truman, Harry S., *4:* 1196

Roosevelt, Franklin D., *4:* **1123–57,** 1125 (ill.), 1131 (ill.), 1144 (ill.), 1146 (ill.), 1153 (ill.)
administration, *4:* 1136
assassination attempt, *4:* 1135
commander in chief, *4:* 1155–56
death while in office, *4:* 1154, 1165, 1196
declares war on Japan, *4:* 1152 (ill.)
early years, *4:* 1126–27
Eisenhower, Dwight D., *4:* 1241
election of 1920, *4:* 1021
election of 1932, *4:* 1104–5, 1106, 1121, 1134
election of 1936, *4:* 1134, 1140–41
election of 1940, *4:* 1134, 1150, 1153–54, 1173
election of 1944, *4:* 1134
fireside chats, *4:* 1179 (ill.), 1179–80
First Fireside Chat, *4:* **1175–80**
First Inaugural Address, *4:* **1167–73**
foreign policy, *4:* 1145–54, 1156
Great Depression, *4:* 1125, 1162
Hoover, Herbert, *4:* 1121
marriage and family, *4:* 1127–28, 1160–61
memorable phrases, *4:* 1182
New Deal, *4:* 1125, 1135–45, 1163–64
one hundred days, *4:* 1135–37
Perkins, Frances, *4:* 1143
physically challenged, *4:* 1126, 1130–31, 1132–33, 1162
political career, *4:* 1128–33, 1161–62
presidency, *4:* 1135–54
progressive legislation, *4:* 1137–45
Smith, Alfred E., *4:* 1095
superstitious nature, *4:* 1150
Supreme Court, *4:* 1027
War Message to the American People, *4:* **1181–85**
World War II, *4:* 1125–26, 1148–49, 1153, 1155–56
Yalta Conference, *4:* 1149, 1154, 1156, 1195

Roosevelt, Sara, *4:* 1179 (ill.)

Roosevelt, Theodore, *3:* **877–904,** 879 (ill.), 885 (ill.), 887 (ill.), 889 (ill.), 898 (ill.), 932 (ill.)
administration, *3:* 897

African safari, *3:* 899, 908
assassination attempt, *3:* 900
Brazilian expedition, *3:* 900, 908
conservation, *3:* 896–99
early years, *3:* 880–81
effectiveness as president, *3:* 901
election of 1900, *3:* 848, 858, 874
election of 1904, *3:* 894–95
election of 1912, *4:* 966; *5:* 1558
First Annual Address to Congress, *3:* 890–91, **909–16**
foreign policy, *3:* 891–94, 895–96, 903
governor and reformer, *3:* 888
"The Man with the Muck Rake" speech, *3:* **917–24**
marriage and family, *3:* 882, 883–84, 906–7
military service, *3:* 851, 887–88
Nobel Peace Prize, *3:* 879, 896, 903
political career, *3:* 882–86, 888–89
post-presidential life, *3:* 899–900, 907–8
presidency, *3:* 889–99, 907
Roosevelt Corollary to Monroe Doctrine, *3:* 891–94, 903
"trustbuster," *3:* 860, 874, 890–91, 910, 911; *4:* 1062
Root, Elihu, *4:* 1100
"Rose of Long Island." *See* Tyler, Julia
Ross, Edmund Gibson, *2:* 617, 617 (ill.), 619; *5:* 1279
Rough Riders, *3:* 887 (ill.), 888
Ruby, Jack, *5:* 1294, 1294 (ill.), 1325
Ruckelshaus, William, *5:* 1379
Rudolph, Lucretia. *See* Garfield, Lucretia
"Rugged Individualism" campaign speech (Hoover), *4:* **1115–22**
Rumsfeld, Donald H., *5:* 1414
Rural areas, 1920s, *4:* 1115
Rush, Richard, election of 1828, *1:* 267
Rusk, Dean, *5:* 1286
Russia, *1:* 195. *See* Union of Soviet Socialist Republics (USSR)
Adams, John Quincy, *1:* 223, 225–26, 241
Roosevelt, Franklin D., *4:* 1145
Russo-Japanese War, *3:* 895–96, 903; *4:* 970
World War I, *4:* 973
Russia (Republic, 1991), *5:* 1485, 1522, 1565
Ruth, Babe, *4:* 1049, 1063
Rutledge, Ann, *2:* 555
Rwanda, *5:* 1563
Ryan, Nolan, *5:* 1603
Ryan, Thelma. *See* Nixon, Pat

S

Sac. *See* Sauk tribe
Sacajawea, *1:* 115, 115 (ill.)
Sadat, Anwar, *4:* 1146–47, 1148 (ill.); *5:* 1445
"Safety fund system," *1:* 302
Sagamore Hill (Theodore Roosevelt), *3:* 884
Saigon evacuation, *5:* 1415
St. Albans (school), *2:* 538
Saint Helena, *1:* 195
St. Lawrence Seaway, *4:* 1061
St. Louis Post-Dispatch, 3: 852
SALT. *See* Strategic Arms Limitation Treaty (SALT)
San Francisco Examiner, 3: 854
San Francisco general strike (1934), *4:* 1143
San Jacinto, Battle of, *2:* 385
San Juan (Kettle) Hill charge, *3:* 888; *4:* 970
Sanborn Contracts scandal, *3:* 658
Sanderson, James, *2:* 381
Sandinistas (El Salvador), *5:* 1483
Sanford, Edward T., *3:* 936 (ill.)
Santa Anna, Antonio López de, *2:* 406, 436
Santo Domingo, *3:* 654
Saratoga, Battle of, *1:* 13
Sartoris, Algernon, *3:* 668
Satellite, first, *4:* 1248
Satellite nations (European), democratization, *5:* 1482
"Saturday Night Massacre," *5:* 1379
Saudi Arabia, *5:* 1523, 1537
Sauk tribe, *1:* 305; *2:* 332, 431, 434, 554
Sawyer, Charles, *4:* 1210
Saxton, Ida. *See* McKinley, Ida
Scalia, Antonin, *5:* 1483
Schenck, Charles, *3:* 893
Schlesinger, James, *5:* 1414
Schlossberg, Caroline Kennedy, *5:* 1302, 1305, 1305 (ill.), 1306 (ill.)
Schwarzkopf, Norman, *5:* 1544
Science and technology
Bell, Alexander Graham, *3:* 724–25
during Cold War, *4:* 1248, 1250, 1269
U.S. nuclear-powered submarine, *5:* 1439
Scopes, John T., *3:* 857
Scott, Caroline Lavinia. *See* Harrison, Caroline
Scott, Dred, *2:* 523–24
Scott, Winfield, *1:* 304–5, 305 (ill.), 306; *2:* 436, 468, 468 (ill.), 491, 494 (ill.)

election of 1852, *2:* 483, 494, 495

Screen Actors Guild, *5:* 1474, 1495

SDI (Strategic Defense Initiative) ("Star Wars"), *5:* 1482

Seaton, Josephine, *2:* 417

Secession

formal declaration, *2:* 517

threat by Southern states, *2:* 440–41

Second Continental Congress, *1:* 12. *See also* Continental Congress

Second Inaugural Address (Lincoln), *2:* **593–97**

Second Manassas, Battle of (Second Battle of Bull Run), *2:* 566

Second National Bank, *1:* 141, 159, 269, 276, 285, 300; *2:* 399–401

"Second Reply to Congressman Robert Y. Hayne of South Carolina" (Webster), *2:* 370

The Second World War (Churchill), *4:* 1149

Secretary of State. *See also* administration of specific president

first, *1:* 20

Secretary of the Navy. *See also* administration of specific president

first, *1:* 20

Secretary of the Treasury. *See also* administration of specific president

first, *1:* 20, 24

Secretary of War. *See also* administration of specific president

first, *1:* 20

Securities and Exchange Commission (SEC), *4:* 1140

Sedition Act, *1:* 67, 68, 69, 73, 108

Segregation, *2:* 596; *4:* 1045, 1204, 1249; *5:* 1343

Kennedy, John F., *5:* 1288–89

Kennedy, Robert F., *5:* 1288–89

Marshall, Thurgood, *5:* 1332

Truman, Harry S., *4:* 1229–32

Segregation in the Military: Executive Order Banning (Truman), *4:* **1229–32**

Select Committee to Investigate Presidential Campaign Practices), *5:* 1376–77, 1377 (ill.), 1378

Selective Service Administration, *4:* 1152

Seminole nation, *1:* 196, 264, 305, 306; *2:* 332, 431

Seminole War, *1:* 275

"Semper Fidelis" (Sousa), *3:* 799

Senate. *See also* Congress; House of Representatives

impeachment hearings against Bill Clinton, *5:* 1576, 1577

impeachment hearings against Richard Nixon, *5:* 1377, 1378

impeachment of Andrew Johnson, *2:* 616–17

Johnson, Andrew, *2:* 620

Message Supporting the Annexation of Hawaii (Benjamin Harrison), *3:* **831–35**

treaty ratification, *2:* 369; *4:* 978, 1003

Watergate hearings, *5:* 1376–77, 1377 (ill.), 1378

Sensationalism, *3:* 854, 910, 917, 924

Serbia (Kosovo region), *5:* 1564

Serbians, World War I, *4:* 972–73

Sergeant, John, election of 1832, *1:* 267

Seven Days' Battles, *2:* 566; *3:* 649

"Seventh-inning stretch," *3:* 935

Sewall, Arthur, election of 1896, *3:* 848

Seward, William H., *2:* 464, 559, 571, 612–13, 613 (ill.), 635

Alaska, *2:* 611

radical Republican, *2:* 566

"Seward's Folly," *2:* 611, 613

Sex discrimination. *See* Women's rights

Sexual harassment charges, Clinton, Bill, *5:* 1573, 1574

Sexual orientation, and military service, *5:* 1558

Seymour, Horatio, *2:* 619; *3:* 652

election of 1868, *3:* 651

Shadwell, *1:* 94, 95

Shah of Iran, *5:* 1448–49, 1449 (ill.), 1450, 1467

The Shame of Cities (Steffens), *3:* 924

Shanghai Communique of 1972, *5:* 1371

Shaw, *4:* 1151 (ill.)

Shawnee, *2:* 332

Sheridan, Philip H., *2:* 570

Sherman Antitrust Act, *3:* 819, 915, 933, 935

Sherman, James S.

election of 1908, *3:* 932, 933

election of 1912, *4:* 966

Sherman, John, *3:* 721, 754

Sherman, Roger, *1:* 133 (ill.)

Committee of Five, *1:* 126

Sherman, William Tecumseh, *2:* 570; *3:* 816

Sherwood Forest (Tyler), *2:* 373, 381

Shiloh, Battle of, *2:* 566; *3:* 644, 647, 650

Shriver, R. Sargent, election of 1972, *5:* 1366

"Shuttle" diplomacy, *5:* 1370, 1371

"Silent Cal." *See* Coolidge, Calvin

"Silent majority," *5:* 1373

"Silent Majority" Speech (Nixon), *5:* **1391–97**

Silver, *1:* 274; *3:* 789, 791, 823, 825, 848, 856

Sinclair, Upton, *3:* 895, 896, 924

Singleton, Angelica. *See* Van Buren, Angelica Singleton

Sioux, *4:* 970

Sirica, John, *5:* 1376, 1379

Sit-ins (1960s), *5:* 1355

Skelton, Martha Wayles. *See* Jefferson, Martha

Skull and Bones Society (Yale), *5:* 1513, 1599

Slave(s)
    freed, *2:* 596; *3:* 655–56
    fugitive. *See* Fugitive Slave Act

Slave states and territories, *1:* 197, 271, 308; *2:* 467 (ill.)

Slave trade
    abolished in capital, *2:* 466
    Amistad case, *1:* 245–46
    Antelope case, *1:* 246
    illegal, *2:* 369
    international, *2:* 440

Slavery issue, *1:* 197, 308; *2:* 451–52, 556–57
    Adams, John Quincy, *1:* 220, 234–35
    Buchanan, James, *2:* 523–25, 531, 539–41, 546–47
    Douglas, Stephen, *2:* 560–61
    Fillmore, Millard, *2:* 464–67
    Garfield, James A., *3:* 716
    Johnson, Andrew, *2:* 606
    Lincoln, Abraham, *2:* 455–56, 555, 557, 558, 561, 581–82, 606
    Pierce, Franklin, *2:* 487, 493, 495–97, 509
    Polk, James K., *2:* 410–11
    Republican Party, *3:* 685, 751
    Seward, William H., *2:* 612–13
    Stevens, Thaddeus, *2:* 608–9
    Taylor, Zachary, *2:* 439–41, 451–57
    Tyler, Julia, *2:* 382
    women's movement, *3:* 786–87

"Slavocracy," *1:* 234

Slidell, John, *2:* 406

Slogans, campaign. *See* Campaign slogans

Smallpox, *1:* 5

Smith, Abigail. *See* Adams, Abigail

Smith, Alfred E., *4:* 1094–95, 1095 (ill.), 1142
    election of 1928, *4:* 1096, 1117

Smith, Margaret. *See* Taylor, Margaret

Smith, Rosalynn. *See* Carter, Rosalynn

Smith v. Allwright, *5:* 1332

Smith, William, election of 1836, *1:* 301

Smithson, James, *1:* 221

Smithsonian Institution, *1:* 221; *2:* 538

"Smoke-filled room," *4:* 1021

Social legislation. *See also* Great Society; New Deal
    end of progressivism, *5:* 1490

Social reform, *4:* 1094, 1142

Social Security Act, *4:* 1141, 1143

Social Security System, *4:* 1137, 1270; *5:* 1561

Social unrest (1960s), *5:* 1318

Social values, conservative Republican, *5:* 1476–77

Socialism, *4:* 1116
    elections of 1932 and 1936, *4:* 1144–45

Society of Friends (Quakers). *See* Quakers (Society of Friends)

"Solid South," *3:* 662

Somalia, *5:* 1561–62, 1563

"Son of Liberty." *See* Lee, Richard Henry

Soulé, Pierre, *2:* 497

"Sound money," *3:* 695

Soup kitchens, *4:* 1099 (ill.)

Sousa, John Philip, *2:* 381; *3:* 799

Souter, David, *5:* 1521

South. *See also* Civil War; Regionalism; Secession
    Johnson, Lady Bird, *5:* 1343
    post–Civil War. *See* Reconstruction
    Reconstruction, *2:* 570–71, 609

South Africa, *5:* 1522

South America, Monroe Doctrine, *1:* 210

South Carolina
    announces secession, *2:* 530, 562
    election of 1876, *3:* 692
    nullification issue, *1:* 258, 268–69, 270–71
    postwar governments, *3:* 694
    secession threat, *2:* 363, 370; *3:* 869–70

South East Asia Treaty Organization (SEATO), *4:* 1248

South Korea, *4:* 1209, 1210
    Eisenhower, Dwight D., *4:* 1244
    Marshall, George C., *4:* 1201

South Mountain, Battle of, *3:* 686

South Vietnam, *5:* 1287, 1330, 1331–34, 1373, 1396, 1415

Eisenhower, Dwight D., *4:* 1245–48
Kennedy, John F., *5:* 1287
Southeast Asia
Eisenhower, Dwight D., *4:* 1245–48
Johnson, Lyndon B., *5:* 1318, 1330–34, 1335
Kennedy, John F., *5:* 1287
Southern Baptist Convention, *5:* 1453–54
Southern Christian Leadership Conference, *5:* 1292–93
Southern Democrats
Dixiecrats (States' Rights Democratic Party), *4:* 1204, 1231; *5:* 1336–37
post–Civil War, *3:* 692, 783
Southern Lebanon, *5:* 1447
Souvestre, Marie, *4:* 1160
Soviet Union. *See* Union of Soviet Socialist Republics (USSR)
Spain, *1:* 196
Amistad case, *1:* 234, 245
Monroe Doctrine, *1:* 209, 210
Ostend Manifesto, *2:* 497, 521–22
Spanish American War, *3:* 849–51, 886–88; *4:* 970
Spanish Florida, *1:* 196, 264
Treaty of San Lorenzo, *1:* 46
Virginius incident, *3:* 655, 659–60
Spanish American War, *3:* 791, 822, 849–51, 874; *4:* 981
news coverage, *3:* 854–55
Pershing, John J. "Black Jack," *4:* 970
Roosevelt, Theodore, *3:* 851, 887–88
Sparkman, John J., election of 1952, *4:* 1244
Speakeasies, *4:* 1059
Specie Resumption Act, *3:* 659
Spectrum 7, *5:* 1602
Speech education, *3:* 724–25
Speech on Government and Business (Coolidge), *4:* 1077–83
Speech on the End of Reconstruction (Hayes), *3:* 705–10
Speech to a Special Session of Congress (Harding), *4:* 1013–32
Spiegel Grove (Hayes), *3:* 697, 702
"Spin doctoring," *4:* 1021
The Spirit of St. Louis (airplane), *4:* 1064, 1066
The Spirit of St. Louis (book) (Lindbergh), *4:* 1065
Spoils system. *See* Patronage system
Sputnik, *4:* 1248, 1252–53; *5:* 1322
"Square Deal," *3:* 891

Stalin, Joseph, *4:* 1148, 1153, 1153 (ill.), 1196, 1198 (ill.), 1221; *5:* 1484
Stalwarts, *3:* 721, 722, 752, 753, 756, 758, 759
Arthur, Chester A., *3:* 753, 767
Conkling, Roscoe, *3:* 752
election of 1880, *3:* 752, 754–55, 757
Stamp Act of 1765, *1:* 57
Standard Oil Company, *3:* 924, 934; *4:* 1062
Standardization program (Hoover), *4:* 1092
Stanton, Edwin M., *2:* 552, 610, 616, 619; *3:* 651
Stanton, Elizabeth Cady, *3:* 785, 786
Star Route case, *3:* 722, 760
Stark, Lloyd, *4:* 1194
Starr, Kenneth, *5:* 1574, 1576
Starr Report, *5:* 1575
"Stars and Stripes Forever" (Sousa), *3:* 799
"The Star-Spangled Banner" (Key), *1:* 157, 159
The State (Wilson), *4:* 964
State(s)
under Articles of Confederation, *1:* 38, 43
free. *See* Free states
responsible for infrastructure, *1:* 274
slave. *See* Slave states and territories
State banks, *1:* 274, 289, 300
State Department, *3:* 935
State of the Union Address, *5:* 1355. *See also* Annual Address to Congress
Clinton, Bill, *5:* **1587–93**
States' rights, *1:* 20, 154; *5:* 1471. *See also* Anti-Federalists; Federal government; Federalists
Pierce, Franklin, *2:* 489, 493, 509–10
Tyler, John, *2:* 361, 363–64, 365–68
States' Rights Democratic Party (Dixiecrats), *4:* 1204, 1231; *5:* 1336–37
States' rights vs. federal government, *1:* 286, 299
Steam warships, *2:* 498
Steamboats, *2:* 525
Steffens, Lincoln, *3:* 924
Stephens, Alexander H., *2:* 556
Sterne, Lawrence, *1:* 124
Stettinius, Edward R., *4:* 1246
Stevens, Thaddeus, *2:* 608–9, 609 (ill.), 610, 614 (ill.)
Stevenson, Adlai E. (grandfather)

election of 1892, *3:* 782; *4:* 1246
election of 1900, *3:* 848
Stevenson, Adlai E. (grandson), *4:* 1246–47, 1247 (ill.)
   election of 1952, *4:* 1243, 1244, 1247; *5:* 1364
   election of 1956, *4:* 1244, 1247; *5:* 1280
Stewart, Alexander T., *3:* 652
Stewart, Potter, *5:* 1487
Stillman, Isaiah, *2:* 435
Stillman's Run, *2:* 435
Stimson Doctrine, *4:* 1102
Stimson, Henry L., *4:* 1100–1101, 1101 (ill.), 1102, 1152, 1196
Stock market crash of 1929, *3:* 663; *4:* 1082, 1098–99
Stock market crash of 1987, *5:* 1481, 1566–67
Stockdale, James B., election of 1992, *5:* 1555
Stockton, Richard, election of 1820, *1:* 193
Stockton, Robert, *2:* 407
"Stonewalling," *5:* 1380
Story, Joseph, *2:* 417
Stowe, Harriet Beecher, *2:* 467, 470–71, 471 (ill.), 513
Strassmann, Fritz, *4:* 1223
Strategic Arms Limitation Treaty (SALT), *5:* 1371, 1372
Strategic Arms Limitation Treaty II (SALT II), *5:* 1445
Strategic arms reduction (Bush-Gorbachev, 1991), *5:* 1522, 1523
Strategic Defense Initiative (SDI) ("Star Wars"), *5:* 1482
Strike(s)
   Boston police strike (1919), *4:* 1054
   Great Depression, *4:* 1144–45
   San Francisco general strike (1934), *4:* 1143
   steel mill strike (1952), *4:* 1210–11
Stuart, Jeb, *2:* 529
Submarine warfare
   German, *4:* 973, 998, 1150
   U.S. nuclear-power, *5:* 1439
Substance-abuse awareness
   Ford, Betty, *5:* 1425
   Reagan, Nancy, *5:* 1497, 1498–99
Suburbs, vs. cities, *5:* 1329
Succession, presidential, *2:* 366–67
Suez Canal, *4:* 1248
Suffrage movement. *See* Women's rights
Sullivan, John, *1:* 14
A Summary of the Rights of British America (Jefferson), *1:* 97–98
Sunday Morning Massacre, *5:* 1414

Supply-side economics, *5:* 1481
Supreme Court, *1:* 20; *3:* 940; *4:* 1144 (ill.)
   Amistad case, *1:* 245–46
   Brown v. Board of Education of Topeka, *2:* 561; *4:* 1249, 1254; *5:* 1292, 1332
   Bush, George, *5:* 1521
   Dred Scott case, *2:* 524–25, 558, 560, 561
   election of 2000, *5:* 1597, 1598, 1613, 1616–17
   electoral votes, *5:* 1613
   Holmes, Oliver Wendell, *3:* 891, 892–93
   Hughes, Charles Evans, *4:* 1026, 1027
   Jackson, Andrew, *1:* 274
   Lochner v. New York, *3:* 892
   Marshall, John, *1:* 64–65, 111
   Marshall, Thurgood, *5:* 1332–33
   Morgan v. Virginia, *5:* 1332
   National Industrial Recovery Act, *4:* 1027
   Nixon, Richard, *5:* 1367–68, 1380, 1382
   O'Connor, Sandra Day, *5:* 1483, 1486–87
   Reagan, Ronald, *5:* 1483, 1490
   Rehnquist, William, *5:* 1483
   Roosevelt, Franklin D., *4:* 1027, 1139, 1144, 1144 (ill.), 1172–73
   Scalia, Antonin, *5:* 1483
   Schenck case, *3:* 893
   Shelley v. Kramer, *5:* 1332
   Smith v. Allwright, *5:* 1332
   Souter, David, *5:* 1521
   Standard Oil antitrust case, *3:* 934
   Sweatt v. Painter, *5:* 1332
   Taft, William Howard, *3:* 940, 947
   Thomas, Clarence, *5:* 1521
Sutherland, George, *3:* 936 (ill.)
Sweatt v. Painter, *5:* 1332
Symmes, Anna. *See* Harrison, Anna
Symmes, John Cleve, *2:* 342
Syria, *5:* 1371

T

Table tennis diplomacy, *5:* 1372
Tabula rasa, *1:* 102
Taft, Alphonso, *3:* 929, 938
Taft, Bob, *3:* 938
Taft, Charles Phelps, *3:* 948
Taft family, *3:* 938–39

Taft-Hartley Act, *3:* 939; *4:* 1203; *5:* 1363
Taft, Helen, *3:* 930, **943–48,** 943 (ill.), 945 (ill.)
  active role as first lady, *3:* 946–47
  life in Manila, *3:* 944–45
  social activism, *3:* 947
  stroke causes setback, *3:* 946
  Washington's cherry blossoms, *3:* 947
Taft, Robert A., *3:* 938–39, 939 (ill.), 940–41, 948; *5:* 1279
Taft, Robert A., Jr., *3:* 938
Taft, William Howard, *3:* **925–42,** 927 (ill.), 932 (ill.), 936 (ill.), 945 (ill.)
  administration, *3:* 934
  "Dollar Diplomacy," *3:* 936, 949–50
  early years, *3:* 928–30
  election of 1908, *3:* 899–900, 933
  election of 1912, *3:* 937–40; *4:* 966, 1019
  Final Annual Message to Congress, *3:* **949–56**
  foreign policy, *3:* 931, 935–37, 949–50, 955–56
  legal career, *3:* 929–30, 940
  marriage and family, *3:* 930
  political career, *3:* 930–32, 944–46
  presidency, *3:* 932–40, 946–47
  Supreme Court chief justice, *3:* 940, 947
  trustbusting, *3:* 923
Taiwan, *4:* 1210
Talleyrand-Périgord, Charles-Maurice de, *1:* 66, 67 (ill.)
Tallmadge Amendment, *1:* 198
Tallmadge, James, *1:* 198
Tammany Hall, *3:* 690
Tank Corps, *4:* 1238–39
Tapes, Watergate, *5:* 1360, 1376, 1379–80, 1379 (ill.), 1407, 1432
Tarbell, Ida, *3:* 924
Tariff(s), *3:* 869. *See also* Tax(es)
  Cleveland, Grover, *3:* 788
  Fillmore, Millard, *2:* 462
  first, *1:* 20–21
  McKinley, William, *3:* 825, 846, 848–49, 869–71, 875
  Polk, James K., *2:* 405
  Taft, William Howard, *3:* 932–33
  Tariff of Abominations, *1:* 232, 235
  Tyler, John, *2:* 368
  Wilson, Woodrow, *4:* 959, 968
Tax(es). *See also* Tariff(s)
  British, *1:* 9, 57–58

Federalists vs. anti-Federalists, *1:* 106
  first, *1:* 20–21
Tax-cut bill
  Johnson, Lyndon B., *5:* 1326
  Reagan, Ronald, *5:* 1487
Tax reform, *4:* 1023
Taxe(s)
  Federalists' view, *1:* 21
  vs. federal deficit, *5:* 1568
Taylor, Claudia Alta. *See* Johnson, Lady Bird
Taylor, Margaret, *2:* **447–49,** 447 (ill.)
  marriage and family, *2:* 447–48
  military wife, *2:* 447–48
  private first lady, *2:* 449
Taylor, Sarah Knox, *2:* 448, 564
Taylor, Zachary, *1:* 167; *2:* **427–45,** 429 (ill.), 433 (ill.), 438 (ill.), 463 (ill.)
  administration, *2:* 443
  Annual Address to Congress, *2:* **451–56**
  Compromise of 1850, *2:* 442, 465
  early years, *2:* 429–30
  election of 1848, *1:* 229, 309; *2:* 439, 520
  inauguration of, *2:* 442 (ill.)
  marriage and family, *2:* 431, 447, 448, 564
  Mexican War, *2:* 425, 432–36
  military career, *2:* 430–36, 447, 448
  Old Whitey (horse), *2:* 436, 444 (ill.)
  political career, *2:* 436–39, 456
  presidency, *2:* 439–42
  slavery issue, *2:* 439–41
  untimely death, *2:* 442, 443
Teapot Dome Scandal, *4:* 1028 (ill.), 1029–30, 1055
Technology, *2:* 525
  communications, *4:* 1040, 1045
Tecumseh, *2:* 330, 330 (ill.), 332–33, 431, 434
Telegraph, *2:* 399, 525; *3:* 724
Telephone, *3:* 724–25; *4:* 1098
Television, *4:* 1147; *5:* 1323
  "Checkers" speech (Nixon), *5:* 1364
  Gulf War, *5:* 1544
  Iran-Contra hearings, *5:* 1489
  Kennedy-Nixon debates, *5:* 1282, 1365
  news agencies call election 2000, *5:* 1608, 1609
  Reagan-Carter debates, *5:* 1478
  Watergate hearings, *5:* 1376, 1406
Temperance movement

Anthony, Susan B., *3:* 786
Hayes, Lucy and Rutherford B., *3:* 700–701
Tennessee
Jackson, Andrew, *1:* 262–63
Johnson, Andrew, *2:* 603, 605, 606, 620, 627
joins Confederacy, *2:* 563
Polk, James K., *2:* 396, 399, 401
Tennessee Coal and Iron Company, *3:* 935
Tennessee Valley Authority (TVA), *4:* 1140–41
Tenskwatawa (The Prophet), *2:* 330, 331 (ill.), 332, 333
Tenure of Office Act, *2:* 616, 618–19
Territories(s)
Indiana. *See* Indiana Territory
Northwest. *See* Northwest Territory
Oregon. *See* Oregon Territory
slave, *1:* 271; *2:* 467 (ill.)
Terrorism, *5:* 1451, 1483
Texas
annexation, *1:* 308; *2:* 359, 369, 371, 372, 385–92, 419–20, 424, 451
Bush, George, *5:* 1515
Bush, George W., *5:* 1600–1603
Johnson, Lyndon B., *5:* 1318–19, 1321
Kennedy, John F., *5:* 1291–94
slave state, *1:* 271
Texas Book Festival, *5:* 1624
Texas Rangers (baseball team), *5:* 1602, 1623
Thames, Battle of the, *1:* 157; *2:* 331, 333
Theory of Nullification, *1:* 235–36. *See also* Nullification
"There you go again" (Reagan), *5:* 1478
Thirteenth Amendment, *2:* 514, 568, 570, 596, 611, 612; *3:* 677
This Country of Ours (Benjamin Harrison), *3:* 812
This Is My Story (Eleanor Roosevelt), *4:* 1164
Thomas Amendment, *1:* 198–99
Thomas, Clarence, *5:* 1521
Thomas, George H., *2:* 570
Thomas, Jesse B., *1:* 198
Thompson, Jacob, *2:* 526 (ill.)
"Thoughts on Government" (John Adams), *1:* 59, **81–89**
Three Mile Island nuclear reactor accident, *5:* 1448
Through the Brazilian Wilderness (Theodore Roosevelt), *3:* 900
Thurman, Allen G., election of 1888, *3:* 819

Thurmond, J. Strom, election of 1948, *4:* 1205, 1231; *5:* 1337
Tiffany, Charles Lewis, *3:* 761, 767
Tilden, Samuel J., *3:* 689, 690–91, 691 (ill.)
election of 1876, *3:* 693, 719; *5:* 1556
The Times of My Life (Betty Ford), *5:* 1422
Tippecanoe, Battle of, *1:* 306; *2:* 330 (ill.), 330–31
"Tippecanoe and Tyler Too!," *1:* 306; *2:* 325, 336–37, 364, 376
Todd, Dolley Payne. *See* Madison, Dolley
Todd, Mary. *See* Lincoln, Mary
Tomlinson, Charles, *1:* 133
Tompkins, Daniel D., *1:* 211 (ill.)
election of 1816, *1:* 193
election of 1820, *1:* 193
Tonkin (gulf) incident, *5:* 1330–31
Topeka, Kansas, *2:* 501
Toucey, Isaac, *2:* 526 (ill.)
Tower, John, *5:* 1607
"Town meeting" political debate, *5:* 1525
Tracy, Spencer, *5:* 1495
Trade
Buchanan, James, *2:* 525–26
Coolidge, Calvin, *4:* 1061
Fillmore, Millard, *2:* 479–84
McKinley, William, *3:* 858
Taft, William Howard, *3:* 936, 949–50
The Trail of Tears, *1:* 305, 306, 307 (ill.)
Transcontinental railroad, *2:* 497–99
Treaty(ies). *See also* North Atlantic Treaty Organization (NATO); South East Asia Treaty Organization (SEATO); Strategic Arms Limitation Treaty (SALT)
Algiers Treaty, *1:* 26, 29
Clayton-Bulwer Treaty, *2:* 442
Greenville Treaty, *2:* 332; *3:* 769
Jay's Treaty, *1:* 26, 27, 28, 224, 240
Nuclear Test Ban Treaty, *5:* 1286
Senate treaty ratification, *2:* 369; *4:* 978, 1003
treaty negotiation, *1:* 28
Treaty of Fort Wayne, *2:* 330
Treaty of Ghent, *1:* 226, 264
Treaty of Guadelupe Hildago, *2:* 410, 451
Treaty of Paris, *1:* 16
Treaty of Portsmouth, *3:* 895–96
Treaty of San Lorenzo, *1:* 26, 46

Treaty of Versailles, *4:* 977, 978, 981, 984, 993, 1003, 1010, 1011, 1025, 1026, 1030, 1039

Treaty of Washington, *3:* 655

Webster-Ashburton Treaty of 1842, *2:* 368–69, 371

Treaty negotiation, *1:* 28

Treaty of Fort Wayne, *2:* 330

Treaty of Ghent, *1:* 226, 264

Treaty of Guadelupe Hildago, *2:* 410, 451

Treaty of Paris, *1:* 16

Treaty of Portsmouth, *3:* 895–96

Treaty of San Lorenzo, *1:* 26, 46

Treaty of Versailles, *4:* 977, 978, 981, 984, 993, 1003, 1010, 1011, 1025, 1026, 1039

Treaty of Washington, *3:* 655

Trenton, Battle of, *1:* 11, 13

Triangle Shirtwaist Company fire, *4:* 1094, 1142

Tripp, Linda, *5:* 1574, 1576

Tristam Shandy (Sterne), *1:* 124

Truman-Austin Bill, *4:* 1194

Truman, Bess, *4:* 1195 (ill.), **1215–19,** 1215 (ill.), 1218 (ill.)
  behind-the-scenes role, *4:* 1215
  childhood sweethearts, *4:* 1216
  marriage and family, *4:* 1217

Truman Committee, *4:* 1194

Truman Doctrine, *4:* 1202

Truman, Harry S., *4:* 1105 (ill.), **1187–1213,** 1189 (ill.), 1195 (ill.), 1198 (ill.), 1203 (ill.), 1218 (ill.), 1243 (ill.)
  Address to the Nation About the Bombing of Japan, *4:* **1221–27**
  administration, *4:* 1197
  assassination attempt, *4:* 1207
  atomic bomb, *4:* 1196, 1197–99
  atomic bomb development, *4:* 1101, 1227
  atomic bomb use, *4:* 1184, 1221–22, 1226
  "The buck stops here," *5:* 1428
  civil rights, *4:* 1204, 1229–32
  Cold War, *4:* 1199–1202
  "Dewey Defeats Truman," *4:* 1204 (ill.), 1205–6
  domestic policy, *4:* 1202–5
  early years, *4:* 1190–91
  election of 1944, *4:* 1134, 1194–95
  election of 1948, *4:* 1190, 1205–6, 1231
  Executive Order Banning Segregation in the Military, *4:* **1229–32**
  Fair Deal, *4:* 1206
  foreign affairs, *4:* 1196–1202

MacArthur, Douglas, *4:* 1201, 1209

marriage and family, *4:* 1191, 1216–17

military service, *4:* 1191, 1217

political career, *4:* 1191–94, 1217–18

presidency, *4:* 1196–1211, 1218

Reagan, Ronald, *5:* 1507

retirement, *4:* 1211, 1218

S. stands for, *4:* 1190

senator, *4:* 1193–94

steel mill strike (1952), *4:* 1210–11

Tyler, John, *2:* 391

World War II, *4:* 1195–99

Truman, Margaret, *4:* 1218

Trustbusting
  Roosevelt, Theodore, *3:* 860, 874, 890–91, 910, 911; *4:* 1062
  Taft, William Howard, *3:* 903, 915, 923, 933–35

Trusts, *3:* 849, 909, 911

Turban (Dolley Madison), *1:* 165

Turkey
  Cold War, *4:* 1199–1202
  World War I, *4:* 1004, 1005

Tuskegee Airmen, *4:* 1232

Twain, Mark (Samuel Clemens), *3:* 661, 669

Tweed Ring, *3:* 690

Tweed, William "Boss," *3:* 690

Twelfth Amendment, *1:* 73, 115; *5:* 1612

Twentieth Amendment, *4:* 1145

Twenty-third Amendment, *5:* 1613

Two Treatises of Government (Locke), *1:* 102

Tyler, John, *2:* **355–74,** 357 (ill.), 372 (ill.)
  administration, *2:* 368
  anti-Jacksonian, *2:* 364
  Calhoun, John C., *1:* 271; *2:* 369
  early years, *2:* 360–61
  election of 1836, *1:* 301
  election of 1840, *1:* 306–7; *2:* 336, 364–65
  election of 1844, *2:* 372
  "His Accidency," *2:* 365–68
  marriage and family, *2:* 361, 368, 373, 376
  political career, *2:* 361–64, 376
  Randolph, Edmund Jennings, *2:* 363, 376
  succeeds William Henry Harrison, *1:* 229; *2:* 338, 353
  Webster, Daniel, *2:* 369

Tyler, Julia, *2:* **379–83,** 379 (ill.)
  Civil War, *2:* 382
  Confederate support, *2:* 382
  letter to the English ladies, *2:* 382

marriage and family, *2:* 380, 381
the Rose of Long Island, *2:* 380
Tyler, Letitia, *1:* 167; *2:* 364,
    375–83, 375 (ill.)
    marriage and family, *2:* 376
    one public appearance, *2:* 375,
        377
Tyler, Priscilla Cooper, *2:* 376–77

U

U-2 aerial surveillance incident, *4:*
    1250–51; *5:* 1285
U-boats, *4:* 973
UN. *See* United Nations (UN)
Un-American Activities Committee
    (HUAC). *See* House Committee
    on Un-American Activities
Uncle Tom's Cabin, 2: 467, 470–71,
    513
"Unconditional Surrender." *See*
    Grant, Ulysses S.
Underground Railroad, *2:* 495–96,
    528
Underwood Tariff Act, *4:* 959, 968
Unemployment
    Great Depression, *4:* 1098, 1102,
        1103, 1103 (ill.), 1104, 1135
    World War II, *4:* 1152
Unemployment insurance, New
    Deal legislation, *4:* 1141
"Unindicted co-conspirator" (Wa-
    tergate), *5:* 1380
Union Army, *2:* 547, 568–70, 594;
    3: 645, 671
    Battle of Gettysburg, *2:* 588
Union(s) (labor)
    Perkins, Frances, *4:* 1143
    Taft-Hartley Act, *3:* 939, 941; *4:*
        1203; *5:* 1363
    Taft, Robert A., *3:* 939, 941
Union of Soviet Socialist Republics
    (USSR). *See also* Russia
    break-up of Soviet Union, *5:*
        1485, 1522–23
    Cold War, *4:* 1199–1202, 1245,
        1248, 1251, 1264; *5:* 1283–86
    collective farms, *5:* 1484
    Cuban missile crisis, *4:* 1253; *5:*
        1273, 1286
    détente, *5:* 1372–73, 1482
    Gorbachev, Mikhail, *5:* 1484–85,
        1522
    invasion of Afghanistan, *5:* 1467
    Khrushchev, Nikita, *4:* 1252; *5:*
        1372
    nuclear weapons development, *4:*
        1226
    space race, *4:* 1248, 1252–53

Sputnik, 4: 1248, 1252–53; *5:* 1322
Strategic Arms Limitation Treaty
    (SALT), *5:* 1371
Strategic Arms Limitation Treaty
    II (SALT II), *5:* 1445
U-2 aerial surveillance incident,
    4: 1250–51
World War II, *4:* 1147, 1148–49,
    1242
Union Pacific Railroad, *3:* 657
Union Steel Company, *4:* 1022
United Nations (UN), *4:* 977, 982,
    1004, 1046
    Bush, George, *5:* 1515–16, 1523
    Clinton, Hillary Rodham, *5:* 1585
    Gulf War, *5:* 1523–25, 1537,
        1543–44
    Korean War, *4:* 1209, 1210
    military response to aggression
        (assertive militarism), *5:*
        1543–44, 1561, 1564
    Roosevelt, Eleanor, *4:* 1165
    Stevenson, Adlai E., *4:* 1247
    Truman, Harry S., *4:* 1196
    U.N. Declaration of Human
        Rights, *4:* 1165
United Service Organization (USO),
    4: 1260
United States, *1:* 150–54. *See also
    under* U.S.
    Alliance for Progress, *5:* 1284
    Atlantic Charter, *4:* 1148
    atomic weapons, *4:* 1221–23,
        1226–27
    Cold War, *4:* 1199–1202, 1206–7,
        1248, 1251, 1264; *5:* 1283–86
    Cuba (Bay of Pigs invasion), *5:*
        1283–84
    Cuba (Cuban missile crisis), *4:*
        1253; *5:* 1273, 1286
    détente, *5:* 1482
    Gulf War, *5:* 1512, 1523–25, 1524
        (ill.), 1537–38, 1543–44
    Iran hostage crisis, *5:* 1449,
        1450–51, 1452 (ill.)
    League of Nations, *4:* 977
    Marshall Plan, *4:* 1202
    modern identity, *3:* 874–75
    Monroe Doctrine, *1:* 209–10,
        213–14
    North American Free Trade
        Agreement (NAFTA), *5:* 1525
    People's Republic of China, *5:*
        1371
    slave states and territories, *2:* 467
        (ill.)
    space race, *4:* 1248, 1252–53
    Strategic Arms Limitation Treaty
        (SALT), *5:* 1371
    Strategic Arms Limitation Treaty
        II (SALT II), *5:* 1445

U-2 aerial surveillance incident, *4:* 1250–51
United Nations, *4:* 977
Vietnam War, *5:* 1330–35, 1338, 1391–92, 1396–97
Watergate scandal, *5:* 1359, 1375–82
World War I, *4:* 973–76, 1005, 1092
World War II, *4:* 1147, 1150–52, 1221–23, 1226–27, 1240–42
United States Bank, *1:* 228
United States v. Susan B. Anthony, 3: 787
University of Virginia, *1:* 214
Upper Creek nation, *1:* 263
Urban areas, 1920s, *4:* 1115
Urban laborers, Populism, *3:* 823
U.S. citizenship, Native Americans, *4:* 1066
U.S. Civil Service Commission. *See* Civil Service Commission
U.S. Congress. *See* Congress
U.S. Constitution. *See* Bill of Rights; Constitution; specific amendments, e.g., Twenty-third Amendment
U.S. Forest Service. *See* Forest Service
U.S. House of Representatives. *See* House of Representatives
U.S. Housing Authority, *4:* 1140
U.S. Navy. *See* Navy
U.S. Senate. *See* Senate
U.S. Steel Corporation, *3:* 793, 934, 935
U.S. Supreme Court. *See* Supreme Court
U.S.S. *K–1, 5:* 1439
U.S.S. *Maddox, 5:* 1331
U.S.S. *Maine, 3:* 849, 850, 851 (ill.), 855, 887
U.S.S. *Mayaguez, 5:* 1417
U.S.S. *Missouri, 4:* 1199, 1199 (ill.), 1226
U.S.S. *Pomfret, 5:* 1439
U.S.S. *Seawolf, 5:* 1439
U.S.S. *Shaw, 4:* 1151 (ill.)
USSR. *See* Union of Soviet Socialist Republics (USSR)
Utilities
  federal regulation, *3:* 899
  New Deal legislation, *4:* 1140–41

V

Valley Forge, *1:* 11 (ill.), 15
  Washington, Martha, *1:* 33

Van Buren, Angelica Singleton, *1:* 167; *2:* 377
  hostess for her father-in-law, *1:* 311, 312
Van Buren, Hannah, *1:* 311–13, 311 (ill.),
  marriage and family, *1:* 312
Van Buren, Martin, *1:* 266, 273 (ill.), 277, **291–310,** 293 (ill.), 303 (ill.), 308 (ill.); *3:* 690
  Adams, John Quincy, *1:* 246
  Calhoun, John C., *1:* 300
  early years, *1:* 294–95
  election of 1832, *1:* 267
  election of 1836, *1:* 301; *5:* 1612–13
  election of 1840, *2:* 336
  election of 1844, *2:* 401, 402
  election of 1848, *1:* 308–9; *2:* 439
  Inaugural Address, *1:* 315–21
  Jackson, Andrew, *1:* 297–98, 300–301, 309, 315
  legal career, *1:* 295–96, 312
  marriage and family, *1:* 296–97, 312
  Mexican War, *2:* 425
  political career, *1:* 297–301
  presidency, *1:* 302–8
  retirement, *1:* 309
Van Devanter, Willis, *3:* 936 (ill.)
Van Ness, Marcia, *2:* 417
V-E Day (Victory-in-Europe Day), *4:* 1196
Venezuela, *3:* 791
Veracruz, Battle of, *4:* 969
Vermont
  Coolidge, Calvin, *4:* 1051–52, 1055–56
Veterans
  Vietnam War, *5:* 1338
  World War I, *4:* 1104, 1113
Veto Message Regarding the Bank of the United States (Jackson), *1:* 285–90
Veto, presidential. *See* Presidential veto
Vice president
  becomes president after death of predecessor, *2:* 358, 364, 465, 607; *3:* 758, 890; *4:* 1056, 1196; *5:* 1323
  first, *1:* 60–62
  John Adams' view, *1:* 60
  resignation of predecessor, *5:* 1408–9
Vicksburg, Battle of, *2:* 568; *3:* 640, 644, 650, 667
Vicksburg, Mississippi, *2:* 565
Victoria, queen of England, *2:* 536; *3:* 660, 668

Victory-in-Europe Day (V-E Day), *4:* 1196
Vietcong (Vietnamese communists), *5:* 1287, 1334
Vietnam and Vietnam War
  Eisenhower, Dwight D., *4:* 1245–48
  Ford, Gerald R., *5:* 1412–14, 1415
  Gore, Al, *5:* 1556
  Gulf of Tonkin incident, *5:* 1330–31
  Johnson, Lyndon B., *5:* 1318, 1330–31, 1333–34, 1338, 1374
  Kennedy, John F., *5:* 1287, 1312, 1333–34
  Kissinger, Henry, *5:* 1370–71
  Nixon, Richard, *5:* 1372–75, 1391–92, 1396–97
  Perot, H. Ross, *5:* 1526
  "Silent Majority" Speech (Nixon), *5:* **1391–97**
Vietnam Era Reconciliation Program, *5:* 1412–14
Vietnam veterans, *5:* 1338
Vietnam Veterans War Memorial, *5:* 1397
Vietnam War protest movement, *5:* 1334, 1366, 1373, 1374 (ill.), 1391–92, 1396–97, 1475–76
Vietnamization, *5:* 1375, 1392, 1396
Villa, Francisco "Pancho," *4:* 971, 972
Vincent, Lynne. *See* Cheney, Lynne
Virginia
  Harrison, William Henry, *2:* 327–28
  Henry, Patrick, *1:* 97, 99
  Jefferson, Thomas, *1:* 94–95, 97–98, 119
  joins Confederacy, *2:* 563
  Lee, Richard Henry, *1:* 97
  Lee, Robert E., *3:* 677
  Madison, James, *1:* 146, 147, 148, 150
  Marshall, John, *1:* 64–65
  Monroe, James, *1:* 182–83, 189
  Tyler, John, *2:* 373, 382
  Washington, George, *1:* 4–6, 8–9, 16
Virginia conventions (1774, 1775), *1:* 97, 98, 147, 151, 152
Virginia Declaration of Rights, *1:* 151
"Virginia Dynasty," *1:* 182
Virginia militia, *1:* 9
Virginia Plan, *1:* 150
Virginia Resolution, *1:* 70, 109, 154
Virginius incident, *3:* 655, 659–60
Volcker, Paul A., *5:* 1566

Volusia County, Florida, election of 2000, *5:* 1610
"Voodoo Economics," *5:* 1517
Voter fraud, election of 1876 (Hayes-Tilden), *3:* 692–93, 705
Voters' intent, election of 2000, *5:* 1614, 1615
Voting practices reform, *5:* 1598
Voting rights
  African American, *3:* 705, 871; *5:* 1288
  Florida law on recounts, *5:* 1610–11
  League of Women Voters, *4:* 1112
  women. *See* Women's rights
Voting Rights Act of 1965, *5:* 1289, 1322, 1328
"Voyage of Understanding" (Harding), *4:* 1030

W

"W." *See* Bush, George W.
Waco compound fire (Texas), *5:* 1570–71
Waging Peace (Eisenhower), *4:* 1255
Walker Tariff Act, *2:* 405
Wallace, Elizabeth Virginia. *See* Truman, Bess
Wallace, George C., *5:* 1291
  assassination attempt, *5:* 1366
  election of 1968, *5:* 1366, 1367
Wallace, Henry A., *4:* 1137, 1194, 1204
  election of 1940, *4:* 1134
War. *See also* American Revolution; Civil War; French and Indian War; Gulf War; Korean War; Mexican War; Quasi-War; Spanish American War; Vietnam and Vietnam War; War of 1812; World War I; World War II
  declaration by Congress, *4:* 997
  preparedness, *4:* 982
  presidential authority, *2:* 571–72
"War Democrats," *2:* 606
"War Hawks," *1:* 270
War Manpower Commission, *5:* 1336
War Message to Congress (Wilson), *4:* **997–1004**
War Message to the American People (Franklin D. Roosevelt), *4:* **1181–85**
War of 1812, *1:* 118, 146, 156–59, 157 (ill.), 166–67, 192–93, 304; *2:* 361, 440
  Harrison, William Henry, *2:* 331

Jackson, Andrew, *1:* 263
Taylor, Zachary, *2:* 431
Tecumseh, *2:* 333
"War on Poverty," *5:* 1326, 1343
War Powers Act (1973), *5:* 1411
"War to end all wars" (Wilson), *4:* 976
Ward, William T., *3:* 817 (ill.)
Warren, Betty Bloomer. *See* Ford, Betty
Warren, Earl
election of 1948, *4:* 1205
Warren Commission, *5:* 1295, 1324
Washburne, Elihu B., *3:* 652
Washington, Booker T., *3:* 894
Washington Conference (naval forces reduction), *4:* 1027
Washington, D.C., *1:* 21, 70–71, 79; *3:* 947
cherry blossom trees, *3:* 947
Wilson, Ellen, *4:* 989–90
Washington, George, *1:* 1–30, 3 (ill.), 11 (ill.), 22 (ill.), 33 (ill.)
administration, *1:* 20, 22 (ill.), 62
American Revolution, *1:* 9–16, 11 (ill.)
Articles of Confederation, *1:* 37–44
Constitution, *1:* 16–19
early years, *1:* 4–6
election of 1789, *1:* 19
election of 1792, *1:* 19
election of 1820, *5:* 1612
Farewell Address of 1796, *1:* 45–52
French and Indian War, *1:* 7–8
Lafayette, Major General, *1:* 186–87, 187 (ill.)
life at Mount Vernon, *1:* 8–9
marriage and family life, *1:* 8–9, 28, 32
Monroe, James, *1:* 188
presidency, *1:* 19–28, 52
retirement, *1:* 27–28
warning against regionalism, *1:* 51; *2:* 452, 540
Washington, Lawrence, *1:* 5
Washington, Martha, *1:* 8, 31–35, 31 (ill.), 33 (ill.)
early years, *1:* 32
role as first lady, *1:* 34
Valley Forge, *1:* 33
Washington Monument, *2:* 442; *3:* 702, 761
Washington Post, 5: 1405
Water Quality Act, *5:* 1330
Watergate babies, *5:* 1411–12
Watergate scandal, *5:* 1359, 1375–82, 1427, 1428, 1432, 1516

audiotapes, *5:* 1360
Ford's Pardon of Richard Nixon, *5:* 1427–33
hearings, *5:* 1376–77, 1377 (ill.), 1378
Wayles, Martha. *See* Jefferson, Martha
Wayne, Anthony, *1:* 14, 26; *2:* 328, 332
Ways and Means Committee, *2:* 462, 609
Weaver, James B., *3:* 824, 824 (ill.)
election of 1892, *3:* 782, 789–90, 821
Weaver, Robert C., *5:* 1290
Webb, Lucy. *See* Hayes, Lucy
Webster-Ashburton Treaty of 1842, *2:* 368–69, 371
Webster, Daniel, *1:* 286; *2:* 370–71, 371 (ill.), 407 (ill.), 468 (ill.); *5:* 1279
election of 1836, *1:* 301
election of 1840, *2:* 336
Harrison, William Henry, *2:* 337, 365
Tyler, John, *2:* 369
Weed, Thurlow, *2:* 461, 464, 597
Welch, Laura. *See* Bush, Laura
Welfare system
California, *5:* 1476
Clinton reform package, *5:* 1560
West Germany, *5:* 1285, 1485
West Point, *3:* 642–43
West Potomac Park, *3:* 947
West Virginia, *2:* 568
Western expansion. *See* Expansionism
Wheatland (Buchanan), *2:* 521, 531, 538
Wheeler, Burton K., election of 1924, *4:* 1060
Wheeler, William A., *3:* 688 (ill.)
election of 1876, *3:* 693
Whig candidate, *2:* 437 (ill.)
Whig Party, *1:* 229, 234, 301; *2:* 338–39, 370
campaign banners, *2:* 463 (ill.)
election of 1836, *2:* 335–36, 401
Fillmore, Millard, *2:* 443, 462, 463, 484
Harrison, William Henry, *2:* 326, 336–37, 353–54
Taylor, Zachary, *2:* 429, 436, 438, 441
Tyler, John, *2:* 338–39, 363, 365–68
"Whip Inflation Now" (WIN) program, *5:* 1415
Whiskey Rebellion, *1:* 23
Whiskey Ring, *3:* 658
Whiskey tax, *1:* 21–22

White Cloud, *2:* 435
White, Frank, *5:* 1553
White House (Dent family), *3:* 666
White House (Washington, D.C.), *1:* 70, 79, 166 (ill.), 242, 267, 269 (ill.); *2:* 476–77, 536; *3:* 702, 761, 768, 827–28, 829, 907, 946; *4:* 1035, 1112–13, 1207, 1218; *5:* 1299, 1303
    alcohol, temperance, and Prohibition, *3:* 702; *4:* 1036
    anniversary party, *3:* 946–47
    "Camelot," *5:* 1287–90, 1299
    celebrity dinners, *4:* 1074, 1074 (ill.)
    china collection, *3:* 827
    electrification, *3:* 828, 829
    "Elegant Arthur," *3:* 761, 767, 768
    Harrison, Caroline, *3:* 827–28
    Kennedy, Jacqueline, *5:* 1303
    land donation, *1:* 21
    library, *2:* 476–77
    Lincoln room, *4:* 1112–13; *5:* 1304–5
    Lincoln's assassination, *2:* 626
    Monroe room, *4:* 1112–13
    séance, *2:* 577
    War of 1812, *1:* 166–67
    weddings, *2:* 377; *3:* 660, 668, 788, 798–99, 799 (ill.), 907; *4:* 989; *5:* 1346
White, Hugh Lawson
    election of 1836, *1:* 301
    election of 1840, *2:* 336
"Whitewashing," *3:* 919
Whitewater scandal, *5:* 1569–72, 1574, 1576
Why England Slept (John F. Kennedy), *5:* 1275
Wickersham, George W., *3:* 934
Wieland, Christoph Martin, *1:* 221
Wilde, Oscar, *5:* 1301
Wilderness Campaign (1864), *2:* 569 (ill.), 569–70; *3:* 646 (ill.)
Wildlife refuges, *3:* 899
Wilhelm II, Kaiser of Germany, *4:* 1149
Wilkins, Roy, *5:* 1325 (ill.)
Wilkinson, James, *1:* 116, 304
Williams, James D. "Blue Jeans," *3:* 817
Willkie, Wendell L., election of 1940, *4:* 1134, 1150
Wilmot, David, *2:* 410, 556
Wilmot Proviso, *2:* 410, 556
Wilson, Edith, *4:* 979, **991–95,** 991 (ill.), 994 (ill.)
    active in business and with foundations, *4:* 992, 994–95
    "chief of staff," *4:* 993–94

    courtship and marriage, *4:* 993
Wilson, Ellen, *4:* 963–64, **987–90,** 987 (ill.)
    expert landscape painter, *4:* 987, 989
    marriage and family, *4:* 988
    White House weddings, *4:* 989
Wilson, Henry, *3:* 658
    election of 1872, *3:* 651
Wilson, Woodrow, *4:* **957–85,** 959 (ill.), 965 (ill.), 975 (ill.), 977 (ill.), 983 (ill.)
    administration, *4:* 967
    Bryan, William Jennings, *4:* 989
    early years, *4:* 960–63
    election of 1912, *3:* 937–38; *4:* 965–68, 966
    election of 1916, *4:* 966, 974
    election of 1920, *4:* 979, 1039
    foreign policy, *3:* 941, 956; *4:* 960, 969–78, 982–84, 993
    Fourteen Points (Wilson), *4:* **997–1004**
    health problems, *4:* 960, 993–94
    League of Nations, *4:* 976, 977, 1003, 1005, 1007, 1010–11, 1020
    Lodge, Henry Cabot, *4:* 978, 980–81, 981 (ill.)
    marriage and family, *4:* 988, 989, 993
    Nixon, Richard, *5:* 1392
    Nobel Peace Prize, *4:* 976
    political career, *4:* 965
    presidency, *4:* 968–79, 993
    president of Princeton University, *4:* 964–65, 988, 989
    Princeton University, *3:* 801
    retirement, *4:* 979, 994
    tariff reform, *4:* 959, 968, 989
    teaching career, *4:* 963–65, 988
    Treaty of Versailles, *4:* 977, 978, 981, 984, 993, 1003, 1010, 1011, 1025, 1026, 1039
    War Message to Congress, *4:* **997–1004**
    wife Edith as political confidante, *4:* 993–94
    World War I, *4:* 969, 997–99, 1002–4, 1005–6, 1010
Winnebago, *2:* 332, 435
Wirt, William, *1:* 211 (ill.)
Wisconsin Heights, Battle of, *2:* 435
"Wizard." *See* Marshall, George C.
Woman, first to hold Cabinet post, *4:* 1143
"Women Doers" luncheon incident, *5:* 1345–46
Women's Conference on Law Enforcement, *4:* 1111–12

Women's rights, *3:* 785; *5:* 1397, 1425
  Adams, Abigail, *1:* 75
  Anthony, Susan B., *3:* 785
  Cleveland, Libbie, *3:* 785, 799
  Harding, Florence, *4:* 1033, 1035
  O'Connor, Sandra Day, *5:* 1425
  Stanton, Elizabeth Cady, *3:* 785
Women's suffrage, *3:* 702; *4:* 1020, 1033, 1075, 1112
Wood, Leonard, *4:* 1020
Woodrow Wilson School of Public and International Affairs (Princeton University), *4:* 995
Works Progress Administration, *4:* 1138
Works Projects Administration, *4:* 1107, 1138
Workshops, *3:* 883
The World Crisis (Churchill), *4:* 1149
World War I, *3:* 955–56; *4:* 960, 969, 972–76, 997–99, 1005–6, 1010, 1091, 1100
  business and war effort, *4:* 1116–17
  Churchill, Winston, *4:* 1148
  debt payments, *4:* 1102
  freedom of speech cases, *3:* 893
  Hoover, Lou, *4:* 1110
  MacArthur, Douglas, *4:* 1208
  Marshall, George C., *4:* 1200
  peace talks, *4:* 976–78
  Pershing, John J. "Black Jack," *4:* 971
  postwar prosperity, *4:* 1078
  Roosevelt, Theodore, *3:* 900–901
  Taft, Robert A., *3:* 938
  war relief, *4:* 1087, 1091–92
World War II, *4:* 1003, 1147–54
  American neutrality, *4:* 1147, 1181
  armaments embargo, *4:* 1147
  atomic weapon development, *4:* 1221–22, 1226–27
  Churchill, Winston, *4:* 1147, 1148–49, 1149 (ill.)
  Eisenhower, Dwight D., *4:* 1240–42
  Japanese surrender, *4:* 1199 (ill.)
  Kennedy, John F., *5:* 1276–78
  MacArthur, Douglas, *4:* 1208–9
  Marshall, George C., *4:* 1200
  military preparedness, *4:* 1194
  Roosevelt, Franklin D., *4:* 1148–49, 1181–85
  Stimson, Henry L., *4:* 1101
  Taft, Robert A., *3:* 938

Truman, Harry S., *4:* 1195–99, 1221–22, 1226–27
Wounded Knee Massacre, *3:* 774; *4:* 970
Wright, Fielding L., election of 1948, *4:* 1205
Writ of mandamus, *1:* 65
Wye River Accord (1998), *5:* 1568
Wyman, Jane, *5:* 1473, 1495
Wyoming
  Cheney, Dick, *5:* 1606
Wythe, George, *1:* 82, 83, 83 (ill.)

X

XYZ Affair, *1:* 66, 108

Y

Yalta Conference, *4:* 1149, 1154, 1156, 1195
Yarborough, Ralph W., *5:* 1515
Years of Trial and Hope, 1946–1952 (Truman), *4:* 1211
"Yellow journalism," *3:* 850, 854, 886, 910, 917, 924
Yellowstone National Park, *3:* 656, 899
Yeltsin, Boris, *5:* 1485, 1522
Yom Kippur War, *5:* 1446
Young, Andrew, *5:* 1444
"Young Hickory." *See* Polk, James K.
"Young Hickory from the Granite State." *See* Pierce, Franklin
Young Men's Christian Association (YMCA), *3:* 792
Young, Whitney, *5:* 1325 (ill.)
Youngstown Sheet and Tube Co. v. Sawyer, *4:* 1211
Yugoslavia (former), *5:* 1562–63

Z

Zangara, Giuseppe, *4:* 1135
Zapata Off-Shore Company, *5:* 1515
Zapata Petroleum Company, *5:* 1515
Zelaya, José Santos, *3:* 936
Zimmerman, Alfred, *4:* 1006
Zionism, *5:* 1446